A Bluestocking
in Charleston

A Bluestocking in Charleston

THE LIFE AND CAREER OF LAURA BRAGG

LOUISE ANDERSON ALLEN

UNIVERSITY OF SOUTH CAROLINA PRESS

UNIVERSITY OF SOUTH CAROLINA *BICENTENNIAL*

© 2001 University of South Carolina

Published in Columbia, South Carolina, by the
University of South Carolina Press

Manufactured in the United States of America

05 04 03 02 01   5 4 3 2 1

Library of Congress Cataloging-in-Publication Data
Allen, Louise Anderson, 1949–
    A bluestocking in Charleston : the life and career of Laura Bragg /
Louise Anderson Allen.
        p. cm.
    Includes bibliographical references and index.
    ISBN 1-57003-370-6 (cloth : alk. paper)
    1. Bragg, Laura M. (Laura Mary), 1881–1978. 2. Women museum
directors—South Carolina—Charleston—Biography. 3. Women museum
directors—Massachusetts—Pittsfield—Biography. 4. Charleston Museum
(Charleston, S.C.) 5. Berkshire Museum. 6. Charleston (S.C.)—Biography.
7. Women—South Carolina—Charleston—Biography.
I. Title.
AM3.6.B73 A75   2001
069'.2'092—dc21   00-011817

Contents

Illustrations

Abbreviations

AAA	Archives of American Art
AAM	American Association of Museums
ARC	Avery Research Center for African American History and Culture
BM	Berkshire Museum
CAM	Citadel Archives and Museum
CCPL	South Carolina Room, Charleston County Public Library
CCSD	Records and Archives, Charleston County School District
CLS	Charleston Library Society
CMLA	Charleston Museum Library/Archive
COC	Special Collections, College of Charleston Library
CRB-M	Columbia University Rare Book and Manuscript Library
CUA-C	Columbia University Archives and Columbiana Library
MBU-T	Boston University School of Theology
SCA	College Archives, Simmons College
SCHS	South Carolina Historical Society
SCL	South Caroliniana Library, University of South Carolina
SIA	Smithsonian Institution Archives
SP	Sears Papers, Special Collections Library, Duke University
VMA	Valentine Museum Archives
Bulletin	*Bulletin of the Charleston Museum*

Preface

We stare backwards into time,
and continue to find
new plots, new patterns.

Margaret Drabble, *A Natural Curiosity*

A good biography tells a story that moves dramatically from beginning to end. In this moving from the start of a life to the end, a subject's uniqueness and the patterns shared with others become apparent. Puzzling out the narrative of Laura Bragg's life began for me as a part of my doctoral studies. Just over the span of the first few months of research the patterns and some of the plots of her life story were apparent to me. And over the past four years I have come to know Bragg better than I know my husband of more than twenty-nine years or my dearest friends. As I conducted the research into Bragg's life, I recognized some of her dimensions and patterns in my own. Writing this biography also presented me with new possibilities and new directions for myself.

In many ways, I am as visible in this biography as Bragg is. My selection of documents and statements and my choice of a quote or an incident are as revealing about me, as her biographer, as they are about her. The reconstruction, selection, and inclusion of events and the analysis all expand our knowledge about Bragg through my lens. That is why writing biography is also an autobiographical process. What Bragg and I share is a close relationship with our fathers and a belief that education can transform the world. What we did not share when I first wrote about Bragg was the choice of a professional life over a personal life. Now we do, as I am teaching in North Carolina while my husband and home are still in Charleston. What I wished I shared with her initially was a greater willingness to question traditional boundaries and hierarchies and the ability to break out of the societal restrictions that bind women. Now I am testing those boundaries. Bragg was an innovator, an explorer, and she was an anomaly in the South. I have yet to be any of those, but now I hope to become all of them.

I have chosen to use Bragg's last name throughout this document to signify her dominance in all of her relationships except for two specific ones. With her father she was always his student, and it was this relationship that molded all the others in her life. She met Paul Rea, the director of the Charleston Museum and her supervisor, as an equal, just as a New Woman would. All of the women who shared emotional relationships with her are identified with their first names, with occasional use of last names for clarity. I also chose to signify the importance of the Charleston Museum throughout her life by capitalizing the word *Museum* to refer to just that specific museum, even though she worked with several over the course of her life.

This biography represents my understanding of the truth of Bragg's life. As unique as her life was, it was also similar to the lives of other Progressive Era women. I hope those patterns and plots are apparent to feminist biographers and historians alike. If so, I will have succeeded in setting Bragg within the context of her times, offering a story of a New Woman who lived her life by her brains, autonomously, and answerable to no man.

Acknowledgments

Like many manuscripts, this one has evolved over time. However, the one true constant in my analysis of Bragg's life has been the guidance and support of James Sears, and it is to him that I owe the largest intellectual portion of this book. He first introduced me to Laura Bragg when he served as my dissertation adviser, and it was his consistent encouragement as well as his belief in my abilities that convinced me that I should write her biography. Jim has been my professional mentor, and now he is my colleague and friend; in each role he has proven to be an unerring guide for my writing and for my intellectual growth. He has continually challenged me by his own example to reach deep inside myself for the discipline to engage in educational research. Our seemingly endless dialogue about education and southern women has enriched me, as well as honed my analysis of Bragg's life. I cannot begin to express my gratitude for his friendship, his wisdom, his good humor, and his generosity.

My friendship with Katherine Reynolds also began with the dissertation process when she sharpened the manuscript in its earlier stages. Now, as collaborators, we have shared many conversations about southern women and Progressive Era education that have shaped my understanding of Bragg as a northern New Woman in the New South. I also thank Julie Neurer and Sally Ridgeway for their warmth, encouragement, and confidence in me; they offered sound advice and support throughout the beginning stages of writing this biography.

I was fortunate to be named the first Avery Postdoctoral Fellow of the Avery Research Center for African American History and Culture at the College of Charleston. I wish to thank Marvin Dulaney for awarding me this fellowship, which provided me with time and the resources to understand the societal conditions of Charleston's black community and how and why Bragg's actions as a museum administrator were so important and so atypical during the Jim Crow period. I also benefitted from a Scholar in the Community grant from the South Carolina Humanities Council, which supported my continued research in documenting Bragg's actions as an educator, mentor, and visionary at the Charleston Museum. This four-part lecture series along with the other ten papers I have presented provided me with a rich source of material about Bragg, social progressivism, and Charleston's cultural history during the first three decades of the twentieth century.

Like all researchers, I am indebted to an army of archivists and reference librarians. These angels on earth provided me with countless bits and parcels of information that were necessary to complete as much as possible the puzzle of Laura Bragg's life. I encountered courtesy and helpfulness in every institution that I visited or contacted by telephone or mail. I must particularly thank Sharon Bennett and Mary Giles, archivists at the Charleston Museum in the Library/Archive, who gave me months of wonderful company and most especially for their "Christmas in July" present. Sarah Foss joined the museum's staff later and was invaluable in helping me with the lecture series, slides, and images for this manuscript. Tim Decker, Marion Grant, and Kathy Beebe at the Berkshire Museum and Teresa Roane of the Valentine Museum gave me wonderful assistance in retrieving archival documents during the days I conducted research at both museums.

I am more than grateful to the reference librarians at the Mount Pleasant Library—Sheila Amos, Mary Sizemore, and Victoria West—who cheerfully performed so many large, small, and essential tasks as they aided me in confirming dates, places, and people in this story that spanned almost ninety-seven years; they were (and are) invaluable to my research. The other archivists and librarians who willingly treated my requests as their own search for knowledge include Claire Goodwin at Simmons College; Jane Yates at The Citadel Archives and Museum; Nancy Merrill at the Exeter, New Hampshire, Historical Society; Madelyn Williamson, the town historian of Epping, New Hampshire; Judy Kennedy of the Exeter, New Hampshire, Library; Bill Cox at the Smithsonian Archives; Joanne Rogers of the Orr's Island Library in Maine; Jane Brown at the Waring Historical Library; Stephen Pentek of Boston University School of Theology Library; Dale Patterson of The United Methodist Church Archives at Drew University; and Brenda Hearing of the Carnegie Archives of Columbia University.

I owe a great debt of gratitude to Gene Waddell, who provided me with encouragement, copies of his taped interview with Bragg, and a copy of his personal diary; his assistance has extended throughout the research and into bringing the manuscript to publication. I am particularly grateful to those people who knew Bragg well during the last thirty years of her life and who willingly allowed me to interview them. There are four to whom I owe special thanks: Margaretta Pringle Childs, Mary Martin Hendricks, Miriam Pope Herbert, and Mary Hollings. These ladies graciously opened their homes to me and answered questions on more than one occasion.

I have been blessed with a number of friends and colleagues who have contributed to the completion of Bragg's biography. Joan and Bill Kennerty gave me my first and important lead to contacts in Charleston and Pittsfield. Judi Fitzgerald proofed and edited the first version of the manuscript, and Dan Marshall performed the same task with the last version. Sara Davis, Mark Meyer, Bobbi Pappineau, Lorraine Powers, Beverly Varnado, and Martha Waters offered moral support, wisdom, guidance, and patience throughout the years that I explored Bragg's life. Colleagues and fellow researchers Bernie Powers, Sidney Bland, and Barbara Bellows offered advice, introduced me to resources, and provided me with data that have broadened this study of Bragg's life. Harlan Greene was especially helpful with the John Bennett Papers. David Percy of the South Carolina Historical Society provided me with support for the Bragg research. I am thankful that Alex Moore with the University of South Carolina Press has been such a knowledgeable and supportive acquisitions editor. His choices of reviewers, Susan Williams and Marcia Synnott, helped to strengthen the manuscript in its later stages.

It is to my family that I owe the greatest debt, and I offer them my heartfelt thanks. As my first role models, my mother and my late father gave me many gifts, among them a respect and tolerance for others and the ability to persevere in all endeavors. They attempted to make me a southern lady and at the same time, from an early age, encouraged me to be a lifelong learner. John, my husband of twenty-nine years, has provided me with the time, space, patience, and financial and emotional support I needed throughout this process. And my beloved Astro always gave me constant companionship and unconditional love.

A Bluestocking
in Charleston

Prologue

> Where are the women and children in History? Why do they
> seldom appear? Have they had nothing to do with shaping the
> events of this world? Are men the only actors in the great
> drama?
>
> Father Abram J. Ryan, "Southern Women and Children"
> *Banner of the South,* 4 April 1868

FATHER ABRAM J. RYAN OFFERED THIS PLEA in 1868. While more is
certainly known today about the history of women, both specifically and
generally, than was known in 1868 or even in 1968, there is still much that
is unknown. Most of the research that has been published about southern
women in the years since Anne Firor Scott's seminal work, *The Southern
Lady,* first appeared in 1970 has centered primarily on suffragists, social
workers, and those who were active in voluntary associations engaged in
reform, such as the Women's Christian Temperance Union and the Federation of Women's Clubs. At the dawn of the twenty-first century Father
Ryan's questions remain largely unanswered by southern historians about
those twentieth-century women in the South who were not involved in
the fields listed above.

In her afterword to the 1995 twenty-fifth edition of *The Southern Lady,*
Scott acknowledges that "there is a good deal to be learned about the
behavior of women in the Progressive Era in the South."[1] One recent publication (1997) about a southern woman writer of the Progressive Era, *A
Devil and a Good Woman, Too: The Lives of Julia Peterkin,* by Susan Millar
Williams, offers information, as does the recent research into Ellen Glas-
gow and Eudora Welty. Glenda Gilmore's 1996 book, *Gender and Jim Crow,*
is one of only a few that recovers the place of black women in the South's
political history during the Progressive Era. Fewer authors have focused on
New Women who were not suffragists, authors, or clubwomen, such as
Laura Bragg.

Born in Massachusetts in 1881 and deaf by the age of six, Bragg spent
two of her childhood years in Mississippi while her father was a professor
of math at a freedmen's college. At the age of eight she was made aware of
the painful conditions of being black and uneducated in the South. She
also saw how whites and blacks lived in separate but combined worlds.
After being tutored at home, she attended high school in New Hampshire
and Massachusetts and received a degree in library science from Simmons
College with its first graduating class in 1906. Her first professional position was as a social service librarian on Orr's Island, Maine, for two years.

The climate drove her away, and she next worked as a teaching assistant in the 115th Street branch of the New York Public Library. Bragg was induced by Director Paul Rea to Charleston and the Charleston Museum with the idea of saving a collection and an uneducated populace. When Bragg first arrived in 1909, society in the city as well as across much of the South was dominated by men even more so than in other regions of the country. She was an assertive woman who showed initiative and success in her role as a museum administrator. As the curator of books and public instruction, she developed the first educational programs in a southern museum and designed the installations in the new Charleston Museum building, while Director Rea taught at the College of Charleston and the Medical College of South Carolina.

Unmarried, Bragg devoted all of her time and energy to her profession. She promoted the Museum nationally through her membership in the American Association of Museums, on the state level in her work with the state teachers' association, and locally through her community involvement with the Charleston Chamber of Commerce.[2] Not thinking of her primary place as "in the home," as many of her southern counterparts did, she acted as if she were the equal of any man. She exemplified the New England version of the New Woman in the South.

Though she briefly flirted with suffragist work, she used her profession as a museum administrator to practice social reform and opened doors by presenting new possibilities to both the ordinary citizen and the social elite. Bragg was not the typical New Woman in the South as documented by recent literature. She was exotic, different, and a maverick.

In Charleston, Bragg was described as a woman ahead of her time. One Charlestonian, even though she did not much care for "Miss Bragg," called her "a fresh drink of water in the cultural desert of Charleston."[3] In Pittsfield, Massachusetts, where Bragg was the director of the Berkshire Museum in 1931, she was called "a flame, a vibrant woman" and was seen as a "mover and a shaker" because she captured the attention of the community and the New York art world with her modern art exhibits.[4]

In 1920 Bragg was the first woman to be named director of the oldest museum in the United States, the Charleston Museum. It was she who opened that museum to blacks in 1921, not even four years after the trustees had instituted a policy denying admission to black adults. She was also a founder of the Charleston Free Library, a goal she sought and achieved after almost twenty years of activity. She taught a course in museum administration at Columbia University, mentoring women in the profession. She conducted a survey of southern museums for the American Association of Museums in 1924. She directed the reorganization of three museums—in Charleston, Richmond, and Pittsfield—and also helped to establish museums in North Carolina, Tennessee, Virginia, Kentucky, Arkansas, Alabama, Georgia, Florida, and Texas.

Her national recognition as the director of the Charleston Museum led Laurence Vail Coleman, executive secretary of the American Association of Museums, to recommend her to Zenas Marshall Crane, a wealthy northern industrialist. Crane was so impressed with Bragg and her achievements at the Charleston Museum that he lured her away to Pittsfield to be the director of his family's museum. He accomplished this by doubling her salary and by promising her carte blanche in transforming his rich man's attic of a museum into an educational institution.

As in Charleston, Bragg made the Berkshire Museum attractive to both the common man and the culturally elite. She mounted several extraordinary modern art exhibits that caused a stir not only in the backwater of Pittsfield but also in the larger art world of New York, where she was well connected. Bragg had a keen eye with modern sensibilities. She recognized the genius of Alfred Maurer and first exhibited his work in a one-man show. Her exhibition of Shaker antiques in 1932 was hailed as visionary, since few people outside the Shaker community knew of their beauty. She nurtured young artists by encouraging them and providing museum work during the hardest years of the Depression. She was the first museum director in the country to exhibit and purchase Alexander Calder's steel sculptures and the first to use two additional Calder mobiles as architectural installations.[5]

As in Charleston, she saw the Berkshire Museum not only as a democratic institution but also as an educational institution whose purpose was to provide a place of discovery and learning. Bragg's stated belief was that if people could not come to the museum, she would send the museum to them. This goal was achieved by her invention of traveling school exhibits, "Bragg boxes," which were sent out to urban schools and then to those in remote areas of both South Carolina and Massachusetts. These exhibits were miniature stage sets that displayed scenes of other countries, cultures, or nature, accompanied by teachers' stories and relevant objects for students to touch and handle. As other museums in Birmingham, Atlanta, Richmond, Reading, Kalamazoo, and San Antonio and the school system of Wake County, North Carolina, learned of the success of these traveling exhibits, they incorporated them as part of their educational outreach programs. Reported on in *The New York Times,* the exhibits were also adopted by the American Museum of Natural History for the New York City exhibits. Adopted by museums in different sections of the country, Bragg boxes had become nationally recognized educational tools.[6]

Bragg's fame as a museum educator was so widespread that she spoke to the National Progressive Education Association meeting in 1932 about museums as educational institutions. Her concept of museums has extended even beyond her years as a museum administrator, for today the American Association of Museums has adopted museum principles similar to hers calling for every exhibit in a museum to educate, with that being the central role for a museum in the twenty-first century. Through the vigor of her actions and personality Bragg changed the course of events not only in Charleston, Richmond, and Pittsfield, but also in other museums and indirectly in the lives of people who have visited museums or used educational outreach programs, such as traveling school exhibits.

A Feminist Biography

Jacqueline Dowd Hall has written that "feminist biographers are often engaged in acts of trying to restore to their rightful place foremothers who have been ignored, misunderstood, or forgotten."[7] Not only a foremother who has been forgotten, Bragg is also a heroine—someone who by the very force of her character changes the course of history and is thus a fitting subject of a biography. But heroines and heroes alike have public and private lives that also shape their personalities while they are transforming history. Leon Edel believes that a biographer writes a life story by weaving the life mask with life myth into a rich tapestry.[8] By intermingling the public face, the life mask, with the private face, the life myth, a biographer can expose the underlying construction of a person's life. This biography attempts to weave a tapestry of Bragg's life, revealing the wonderful legacy this Progressive Era feminist left behind not only in the world of museum education but also in the lives she touched and influenced. It is my hope that this biography will offer insights into how a New Woman came south and responded to an almost unheard of opportunity for a woman, to be a professional in a male-dominated profession in what still remains a patriarchal society.

It is expected that this biography of Laura Bragg, a northern New Woman, will also assist and inform the work of historians in the revision of historical attitudes toward the New Woman in the South. According to Estelle Freedman, recent studies have been guilty of excessive generalization—the tendency to write about "the" American woman, when in actuality race, class, region, and ethnicity have significantly divided American women in the twentieth century. If scholars study the lives of individual women who lived during the Progressive Era, whether in the South or the North, perhaps they will begin to discover patterns of responses to both opportunities and discrimination. Historians then can generalize successfully about the New Woman after extensive research has been completed. They can begin to certify whether "women were active participants or struggling victims in American history."[9] This biography makes clear that Laura Bragg was a dauntless and fearless participant in creating her share of American history throughout her professional career.

Learning to Be
a Social Reformer

What we call the beginning is often the end
And to make an end is to make a beginning.

T. S. Eliot, "Little Gidding"

HAROLD "HAL" NORVELL SAID THAT Laura Bragg could only be who she was in Charleston and that is why she returned to the Holy City in 1939, after she retired from her controversial directorship at the Berkshire Museum in Pittsfield, Massachusetts. "One of the reasons she chose Charleston was that it was a provincial backwater. She was a larger fish in a smaller pond. . . . Charleston was a framework for her . . . personality . . . a perfect frame where she was set up like a jewel in a casing or in a picture frame. . . . She could make change happen here. . . . [and] it was an environment where she could exercise a great deal of influence." It was in Charleston that she found her niche, her own little space in history. It was the place where she could be a reformer or a missionary, as she called herself. And it was in the Holy City that she met like-minded artists, writers, and others who responded to her teaching and welcomed this "autocratic, elegant, brilliant New Englander" as a rightful member of Charleston's aristocratic society.[1]

Born in Whitinsville or Northbridge, Massachusetts, on 9 October 1881, Laura May Bragg was the eldest of three children. Her siblings were Ernest, born three years later, and Barbara, who was five years younger than Bragg. At six, just after Barbara's birth, Bragg contracted scarlet fever, which left her with progressively increasing deafness. Her father refused to consider this a handicap and sought a cure or a treatment by consulting with Alexander Graham Bell's school, which was located in a building rented by Boston University. While there was no cure, Bragg did learn to read lips quite successfully. Her father refused to allow her hearing loss to impede her childhood, so the rest of the family followed his lead, treating her as if she could hear. Smart, quickly perceptive, insatiably curious, and with a remarkable memory, she responded to her father's teaching and found wonder in his world of books.[2]

Her father, the Reverend Lyman Bragg, claimed lineage descending in direct line from William LaGrande, *grand porteur* of William the Conqueror, down through the Porters, Pickins, Lymans, and Gaylors of colonial times. One of his favorite quotations was "Kind hearts are more than coronets, and simple faith, more than Norman blood." Bragg was proud of her ancestry and often spoke with pride of her forefathers who arrived in America in 1630 on the *Mary* and the *John*. In an interview in *The News and Courier* she spoke of an ancestress who "was an unwilling participant in the famous Deerfield massacre and other antecedents [who] were part of the warp and woof of that part of North America."[3]

Lyman Bragg was educated first at Morrisville Academy and then at Montpelier Seminary. He attended Middlebury College and graduated in 1875, intending to become a physician. He gave his first religious testimony at a camp meeting when he was seventeen, and while he believed he lacked the qualities to be a minister, he was ultimately convinced to attend Boston University School of Theology and finished there in 1878 with a master's degree. While he became a Methodist minister just as his father was, he did not follow his father's footsteps down quite the same path. Daniel Pitkin Bragg, Lyman Bragg's father, was a blacksmith when he joined the Methodist Church. When Lyman was seven, Daniel left his business and became a local supply pastor for churches in the St. Albans District of Vermont for the New England Conference of the Methodist Church. This meant that he could perform pastoral duties, which he did for thirty-five years, but he was not considered a professional clergyman who could claim a pension. Lyman Bragg was first a supply pastor and then was fully ordained in 1880 as a Methodist minister. He was a member of the New England Conference serving fourteen different pastorates in both Massachusetts and New Hampshire during his twenty-nine-year career. Laura Bragg's mother was the former Sarah Julia Klotz, who was originally from Hackettstown, New Jersey. She attended a music conservatory, and Bragg recalled that her mother was an excellent clergyman's wife.[4]

Laura Bragg was born on the cusp of the Progressive Era in 1881, and most of her professional life (from 1906 to 1939) occurred during the forty-year span of its influence, from 1890 to 1930. Thus, the Progressive Era provided the foundation and philosophy of Bragg's life and her desire to do the "work of the people."[5]

Historians generally agree that the Progressive movement in the United States lasted from around 1890 through 1920, while most southern historians concede that the effects of the movement lingered into the 1930s. In the South, Progressive reform movements, led by women, intensified after World War I with the passage of the Nineteenth Amendment. In the North the movement ended at about the time the South was beginning to deal with the conditions existing among the rural population.[6]

The Progressive Era and its subsequent reforms grew out of and were in response to the First and Second Industrial Revolutions that occurred in the nineteenth century. In need of work and searching for a better life, a wave of immigrants, first from the northwestern parts of Europe and then from southern and eastern Europe, swept across the country. These different cultural groups and nationalities with their languages and customs tended to settle in the cities near the factories that employed them. Usually living in substandard quarters, immigrants endured the societal conditions underscored by the gap between the rich and the poor. By the turn of the century most American cities contained enormous concentrations of both wealth and poverty. It was at this point that the Progressive movement developed.[7]

The Progressive movement was paternalistic in design and execution, and its reformers believed solutions to the societal conditions of abuse and injustice lay with the expansion of state intervention. Although the movement was initially conceived in the growing middle-class white urban environment of the North, reformers reshaped public life across the nation as well as in that region. Paradoxically, while these reformers embraced uplift and progress, they also believed in a hierarchy of race and culture; while they avidly embraced democracy, they also endorsed coercion and control to achieve their goals. For them, reform could only come through governmental restraints and social control of the cultural, social, and political institutions of the country.[8]

Many American women shaped this movement with a profusion of new voluntary associations, institutions, and social activities. The collective power of these New Women reached its height during this era in their push for social reform as well as suffrage. Progressives (whether male or female) were "the solid middle-class [who] voted Republican. . . . and the heroines were the new college educated women." These women were a political and social force in America, believing themselves to be the political, social, and economic equals of men.[9]

Coined by American magazine writers in the 1890s, the term "New Women" was first used by Henry James in his novels. The phrase referred to American women of affluence and sensitivity who, according to Carroll Smith-Rosenberg, were a "specific sociological and educational cohort of women born between the late 1850s and 1900, [and] represented the new demographic trends of later marriages for middle-class women . . . college educated and professionally trained at a time when relatively few men were. The New Women rarely married, and by the early twentieth century many had won a place within the new professions. . . . In short, the New Women rejected conventional female roles and asserted their right to a career, to a public voice, to visible power and they laid claim to the rights and privileges customarily accorded middle-class men."[10]

Identifying two successive generations of New Women, Smith-Rosenberg characterized the first wave of New Women as those with roots deep in small-town America. They attended women's colleges in the 1870s and 1880s and advanced professionally between the 1880s and World War I. Outspoken feminists such as M. Carey Thomas of Bryn Mawr, Jane Addams of Hull House, and Florence Kelly of the National Consumers' League addressed industrial, racial, and sexual justice in their work. As evidenced by her music studies and her age, Bragg's mother was a member of this generation.[11]

Laura Bragg belonged to the second generation of New Women, who were often taught by members of the first generation. This second wave flourished during the years immediately before and after World War I, moving into the creative and artistic fields. As politically active as members of the first generation of New Woman, feminists such as Gertrude Stein, Isadora Duncan, and Edna St. Vincent Millay emphasized self-fulfillment and the flamboyant presentation of the self, with less emphasis on social issues. Seeking absolute equality with men, they also wanted to be as successful in their careers, as politically active, and as sexually free as their male counterparts.[12]

It is not surprising that members of Bragg's family, as products of the era, were reform-minded, given their education and northern middle-class heritage. Bragg's mother was a member of the Women's Christian Temperance Union. Her paternal grandmother, Laura Church Bragg, for whom she was named, read voraciously and at the age of sixty-one graduated from the Chautauqua Literary and Scientific Circle. And her father joined the American Association of Colored Youth while the family was living in Holly Springs, Mississippi.[13]

After having served seven different pastorates around Massachusetts, Reverend Bragg's health failed in 1890. He then left the pulpit and joined another form of Methodist ministry when he became a math professor at Rust University, a black freedmen's school in Mississippi. Founded by the Freedman's Aid Society of the Methodist Episcopal Church in 1866, the institution was the first attempt at higher education for blacks in the state, though it offered primarily elementary and secondary instruction.[14]

The Freedman's Aid Society and other philanthropic societies such as the American Missionary Society, the American Baptist Home Society, and the Presbyterian Board of Missions established and sustained institutions for black education during this period of reconstruction and the rise of the New South. Lyman Bragg's Methodist group and the other societies believed that it was their responsibility to lend a helping hand to blacks through classical education, which was seen as a means to liberate and achieve racial equality for black men. They also offered constant criticism of the mob violence, disenfranchisement, and poor educational opportunities that were the plight of blacks throughout the South at this time.[15]

Southern whites dominated blacks by defining and enforcing the circumscribed world within which both races lived. Racial fears and white violence were standard in communities across the region. And southern whites were especially cognizant of how northern missionaries and their families, such as the Braggs, behaved with their black students and the black community at large. White southerners resented these societies, calling their educators "meddling Yankees, strangers, alien and antagonistic" because they feared that blacks would learn too much in school. So the white administrators (Rust College appointed its first black president in 1920) encouraged their professors to behave circumspectly within the white community so as not to draw attention to themselves or to the school. Usually ostracized by the whites, the missionaries interacted with that community on a surface level.[16]

There was another barrier that Bragg and his family had to deal with as northern white Methodists in the South. Having split along regional lines in 1846, the Methodist Episcopal Church was particularly disliked in the South after the war. When the northern branch of the church returned to the area, it was granted the protection of federal troops to regain control of Methodist property. Northern church leaders stated publicly that they would displace southern white Methodists, and they were pledged to converting and educating freedmen as well as promoting loyalty to the federal government among southerners. Reverend Bragg remained at Rust until 1892, when the secretary of the Freedman's Society reported, "The North is literally absorbing the South. . . . this absorption must go on until the end shall be not fraternity, but identity. There shall be no more South, it will be all North and all Christian."[17]

While church leaders may have viewed their work as successful, blacks in Mississippi were facing mounting violence as the 1892 elections approached, with four people dying, several wounded, and seven reported missing after racial clashes across the state. Rust is located in Marshall County, Mississippi, and Booker T. Washington noted on his tour there that the area was known as an educational center for blacks. It was also one of the safest places to be black in Mississippi, as only three lynchings were recorded in the county during the forty years following the Civil War. That was not the case in nearby counties, where there were twenty-seven lynchings, proving that mobs were active in every region of the state. Thus safety may have been more a matter of luck and geography than goodwill among men in Marshall County.[18]

Across the South in the year's span of time from 1891 through 1892, 150 blacks were lynched; 7 were burned alive, 1 was flayed alive, and 1 was disjointed. These statistics were used by a Methodist leader of the northern branch as a call to condemn lynching. The denomination was the first to do so and was joined by the Congregationalists and northern Presbyterians in 1892. That same year Bragg took his family home to New England where he became a member of the New Hampshire Conference of the Methodist Episcopal Church. He never taught math or returned to the South again.[19]

Though the family continued to average a move every two years during the rest of her childhood and youth, by all accounts Laura Bragg's family life was happy, and her memories were pleasant ones. Christmastime was filled with gaiety, for her father would dress in a big fur coat and play Santa. All of the family would fix the tree, and her parents would see that the children had fun, traditionally giving the same "black diamond" necklace every Christmas to some family member. She loved snow and snowshoeing, which took her deep into the forest where she could observe the winter birds, whose names she would learn from the books in her father's library.[20]

Her father served as minister to the Methodist church in Epping, New Hampshire, for six years until his retirement in 1919. There he continued his civic and reform duties by promoting "the welfare of the town, the churches, and the fraternities." He also wrote for the local newspaper; using the name "Alpha," he covered births, deaths, social and church news, and other items of interest. He shared these articles with Bragg. In her letter of 10 December 1918 to him she wrote that his "Alpha account of Grandma made very nice reading," and she asked him to send her more "Alphas."[21]

Bragg gained her love of learning in his library, for her father possessed a library whose contents ranged from theology and philosophy to science and literature. Throughout many of the letters Bragg wrote to her father, one or more of these subjects was a major topic. Often she was either recommending a book to him or responding to one of his recommendations with her own comments. In 1914 she wrote, "I have been much absorbed in Kent's book.... The book has been very helpful to me and I cannot be too glad you sent it to me. I shall send for the first volume soon as I want to know how Kent treats Genesis." Books were very much a part of her father's world and thus, naturally, a part of her own life. Bragg owned five thousand books when she died. Indeed, one of the ladies who attended her Wednesday morning cultural classes in the 1950s said that Miss Bragg would rather buy a book than food.[22]

Her letters addressed her father as "Dadda dearest," and she would close them by asking that he tell her mother hello. Her father was her confidant, and in an interview conducted when she was ninety-two, Bragg said that her father was the most wonderful man she had ever known. To him she wrote about her life's work: "Then I am ambitious and have strained every nerve to prepare myself for the botany work of the summer. I intend to be the botanist of this part of the country. . . . I intend to make a name for myself if I live long enough." Bragg was his intellectual companion and his apt student, and from this relationship she learned how to be both teacher and student. She wrote to him about one of their favorite subjects, astronomy: "Last night I went star-gazing. . . . Mira in Cetus was unusually bright in the south while to the southeast blazed Sirius, with Procyn low in the east. When you stop to realize all the first magnitude stars which the dome above such a horizon must include and combine with them the wonderful combination which Saturn and Mars are now making you simply are silent with the wonder of it." On another occasion she wrote: "Dadda, I am glad you called my attention to the Smithsonian Report for 1895. . . . Then astronomy has been most fascinating to me through its relation to mythology." And in 1914 she wrote to him, "I want you to teach me more about practical gardening this summer."[23]

Her mother was well aware of the closeness and affinity between father and daughter, and she wrote Bragg that she was sure her daughter "would doubtless have had an existence as you are your Father's child even if I had never been born." Bragg's resemblance to him was marked, not only in facial features but also in physique. She had his long face with large, broad nose and a tall, thin body. So distinct was the resemblance that one of her mother's friends commented: "Your Laura and I had a wonderful visit together. What a remarkable person and personage she is! I was astonished and overcome to find her so like her father. I think I never saw so marked a resemblance between father and daughter before." Her relationship with her mother was not as close, in part because she considered herself different from her mother. Bragg recalled that her mother "was one of those people that could make you laugh or cry just as she chose." Given those feelings, it is not surprising that Bragg thought her mother's life was undesirable. "Mother's life seems so barren—just that of a household drudge too tired for the world of books in which I am so glad you can find your salvation," she wrote her father.[24]

Bragg's closeness to her father mirrors other early feminists' strong relationships with their fathers. Also similar to Bragg, many of these feminists emotionally and physically rejected their mothers and the conventional roles they filled in their marriages. Her father's imprint upon her identity marked her sense of self, her work, her love relationships, and her understanding of sexual differences. As the first man in Bragg's life, her father strongly influenced her psychological development. Many fathers of early feminists rejected conventionality for their daughters and encouraged their intellectual growth. Bragg's father had done this in response to her deafness.[25]

Some historians and social scientists have identified the early-life patterns of nineteenth-century feminists and lesbians, who tended to be either only children or the first-born with the father playing the role of teacher and mentor and the mother passive and uninvolved. Through the closeness with the father, the daughter developed what were viewed as masculine interests and attributes. As the oldest child in her family, Bragg spent the first years of her life receiving all of her parents' attention. Once Barbara was born, Laura was still the center of her father's world. Barbara once told a Charlestonian that she had grown up waiting on her sister as had the rest of the family. Whether that was sibling rivalry or not, Bragg was her father's favorite, and all in the family knew it.[26]

Bragg was able to construct a sense of herself with an ego strength that typically only boys had the opportunity to develop, allowing her to become a more independent being. With private tutors, her father's training, and a well-developed mind, Bragg's high school career in Amesbury, Massachusetts, and Lisbon, New Hampshire, left her well prepared for college (in both towns her father served the Methodist churches as minister). Wellesley College was her first choice because her brother's girlfriends attended college there, so she waited a year for a place in Wellesley's dormitory to become available. On 9 October 1902 Simmons College held its opening ceremony, and since she met Simmons College's standards of admission and there was room for her in the dormitory, she decided to attend that institution.[27]

Attending Simmons in Boston was an agreeable experience for Bragg. Boston's population had more than doubled in thirty years, with almost six hundred thousand people calling it home in 1902. Most of them were immigrants from Ireland, Canada, Russia, and Italy, and most of the working class were Roman Catholics. The city boasted the nation's first subway system, which had opened in 1897. After Bragg arrived there, she felt that nothing could draw her away from Boston. She explored the world of culture at the Boston Library and the Boston Museum of Fine Arts, which built a new building near the college campus, and she studied botany, her first love, at the Natural History Museum. Her penchant for being first could have begun there, as she was a member of Simmons College's first class. Bragg's four years at Simmons provided her with the means to a professional career, which was the exact intent of its founder.[28]

Simmons College was first envisioned as an institution in the 1870 will of John Simmons, a Boston merchant, who had written, "It is my will to found and endow an institution to be called the Simmons Female College, for the purpose of teaching medicine, music, drawing, designing, telegraphy, and other branches of art, science, and industry best calculated to enable the scholars to acquire an independent livelihood."[29] Most formal training for females at that time consisted of little more than music, etiquette lessons, and practice for getting in and out of carriages, though there were more than a few women's colleges that offered different types of education.

Due to a fire, financial reversals, and disputes within the Simmons family, the college did not begin operation until more than thirty years after his death. Initially there were no classrooms or campus, so the opening ceremony was held in the assembly hall of the leased college dormitory, with 125 students (from California and Georgia but mostly from the New England states) of the 146 who had been accepted in attendance. The president, the dean, and the trustees were also there. The simple ceremony, including speeches given by President Lefavour (who made "no marked impression" on Bragg) and Miss Arnold ("who was most charming"), a few prayers, and a reception afterward, marked the beginning of Bragg's college life and her road to independence.[30]

During the first year at Simmons, Bragg's library training classes were held in another house leased by the college, down the street from Simmons Hall (which also housed the dormitory, the dining hall, and the reception rooms, parlors, and offices of the college). She lived in a small suite or bachelor apartment, which cost her father and mother, who were then living in Bristol, New Hampshire, about three hundred dollars that year for room and board. Meals were provided in the basement dining room. Students sat at long tables accommodating nine to eleven students, with a faculty member at the head of each table. Until the faculty person at the head had begun to eat, the girls at a table were not allowed to touch their food. One faculty member was well known for being more interested in conversation than in food, and people at other tables sometimes ate dessert long before that professor had even begun to eat the first course.[31]

Bragg had been a serious child, and in Boston she was even more so because she was preparing for her professional career. Still, there were opportunities for fun. All of the girls who lived in Simmons Hall were given latchkeys to the front door. They were allowed to stay out until ten o'clock any night they had no studying to do. While the latchkey system worked well for a while, faculty members, some of whom also lived in the dormitory, discovered that the ten o'clock rule was not being observed. Their solution was to have a new lock put on the front door, which was locked promptly at ten o'clock. Unable to get back into the dorm, girls had to rely on their friends who lived on the first floor (Bragg lived on the top, or fourth, floor of the building) to open the front door for them.[32]

Other events that provided distraction from the serious work of studying included an apartment fire that threatened Simmons Hall one winter night. The girls were aroused from sleep and told to gather their belongings and prepare to leave for rooms at a nearby hotel. The flight became unnecessary, as Boston's fire department contained the blaze and the girls returned to the dormitory. Many Massachusetts Institute of Technology students roomed near Simmons Hall, and they staged impromptu concerts for the girls in the dormitory. Whenever weather permitted, the students would wait on the outside steps for the postman, hoping for at least a letter and maybe a check too.[33]

In the spring of the first year the girls were given a picnic by the dean, Miss Arnold, and her secretary, Miss Cunningham, in the "splendid" woods at Milton. At the end of the year the college president honored the students with a reception, and they were allowed to hold a dance (no men were invited) with the "express condition that it was not to set a precedent."[34]

The dean in Bragg's day was Sarah Louise Arnold, who was the graduate of a normal school and had taught for a time in public schools, serving as a supervisor of grammar schools in both Minneapolis and Boston. Perfectly at ease delivering her talks from a platform, she was a fluent speaker with a seemingly inexhaustible vocabulary and constantly used metaphors in her speech. She was frequently invited by women's clubs to describe the new kind of educational opportunity offered by Simmons College. She was "dear" to Bragg, and the feeling must have been mutual, for Miss Arnold gave her "a half dozen silver teaspoons on my graduation. I was going to Orr's Island to do social settlement and library work and she said I would need them."[35]

The Simmons College library course was another part of the school's great experiment, for in 1902 the only other library training available was offered at summer school at Amherst and at another small school in Pittsfield. Most large libraries trained their employees themselves, while the smaller ones were staffed by those who had no formal training. The library school was directed by Mary E. Robbins, who determined the curricula of Bragg's first-year courses, which included handwriting, cataloging, shorthand and typing, English, French, German, physics, hygiene, and physical training. With the twenty-three other girls enrolled in the library course, Bragg studied both technical work and general collegiate courses that would prove beneficial in work as a librarian. The first-semester courses were the same as those of the secretarial course offered by the college. She sat through lectures, with the opportunity of practice work following, and served an apprenticeship in a library. The Boston Public Library placed its books at the service of the college. She heard specialists speak about the various phases of library work from time to time, and she made visits to bookstores, binderies, and libraries.[36]

Bragg worked during her first semester at Simmons "for the Albany library man," though she worried that her course load might interfere with working. Another major concern for her then, and throughout her life, was earning enough money, and until her father's death she turned to him for financial support. "I have earned not twenty dollars this term. I must make up next. I will write you when I need the rest of the money. . . . Next year I hope to be earning. I am happy now but it will be perfect bliss if ever I earn a good salary. When I think of a time when my debts are all paid and I am earning enough to help others, my breath fairly stops with the joy of it."[37]

Feeling shaky about her first examinations, she told her father that she was sure she would pass all her courses except German: "Our translation has been all at sight and I can't hear it." Bragg's fears about her grades were unfounded, for she made A's in four of the courses and B's in the others. The A in English was "more than I ever expected to do in my whole life," she wrote her role model father. However, her hearing impairment was also proving to be a problem in the big churches of Boston: "Tonight I sat in the front row and didn't get a single thought, only a few disconnected words." During January of her freshman year her mother and sister were coming to visit, and she had spent all day wondering "to what churches I can take mother and Barbara when they come down." Writing about four different churches, she outlined for her father just what each offered the worshiper.[38]

Bragg was almost twenty-one when she entered Simmons. In addition to the year-long wait for admittance to Wellesley, her late entrance could also possibly be attributed to her illnesses as a child or to the two years the family spent in Mississippi. Even though she was probably older than the other girls in her class, this must have been an eye-opening year for a girl who had lived most of her life in small towns either in New Hampshire or Massachusetts as the daughter of the town's Methodist minister. How bound her world before college must have seemed in comparison to what she was experiencing in Boston. And it was at Simmons that she remembered becoming aware of homosexuality, when a teacher asked her about the amount of time she was spending with a friend, Lucy. The teacher told her to be careful.[39]

Bragg continued to live in the Simmons Hall dormitory during her second year at college, but she moved down a floor; and her parents had moved to Hudson, New Hampshire. Other changes included the library course becoming a library school. Simmons was a female college, and not surprising for the time, it had an all male advisory council, with an ex officio member who was the lone female to advise the female library students. The goal of the school was to train students to become assistants for large libraries or to assume charges of small libraries. All of the students' responsibilities remained the same: class lectures with guest speakers from time to time and visits to other sites where students were encouraged to investigate the various phases of library work. For the first time the study of current events was included in the curriculum. Bragg's courses included English; French; German; library courses of classification, cataloging, and reference work; and a history course.[40]

While some of the Simmons classes had been held at Massachusetts Institute of Technology the first year, that institution was now overcrowded and needed the space for its own students, so it became necessary for Simmons to find classroom space. The college rented the top three floors of a five-story building, with elevators, called Boylston Chambers. There was space for a chemistry laboratory, a small biology laboratory, a lecture room, and a combined library and reading room. Having an elevator to reach a nine o'clock class on the fifth floor was wonderful, although Bragg wrote that it was not so wonderful when the elevator was on the fifth floor and someone was on the first, with only a moment to spare before that same class started.[41]

Student life settled into more of a routine, and since there were now freshmen to deal with, the sophomores made the decision that there would be no hazing. The sophomores taught the freshmen how to conduct a class meeting, and daily themes in English were the bane of the sophomores' existence, though they cherished the patience and solicitude of their English professor. The year ended with the sophomores giving the freshmen a picnic at Miss Cunningham's woods in Milton.[42]

In 1903 the trustees had finally decided where to locate the school's campus in Boston and began a building program on what had been a dumping ground for the city on The Fenway, just "down the vast undeveloped marsh stretching away from Isabella Stewart Gardner's palace toward the Back Bay district and the Charles River." The broad and open campus between the college and the dormitory was bounded by the river, and there were shaded walkways with lots of trees, a favorite place for the college girls, including Bragg, to walk. While Mrs. Gardner "might be the terror of her in-laws and proper Bostonians, she was kind to the young," for occasionally she would open the palace to Simmons girls, letting them have the run of it.[43]

During the first semester of her junior year Bragg had to have surgery, which meant that she would be away from classes for a period of time. The day before she was to go into the hospital, Bragg visited "dear" Miss Arnold at Simmons College to tell her why she could not come back "perhaps for many weeks." Arnold was visibly upset by Bragg's news, and with tears in her eyes she muttered to Bragg, "you poor child, you poor child," while stroking her hand. Miss Arnold called her a good scholar and told Bragg that she would be able to make up the missed work.[44]

In a letter written to "My dear, dear Father" the day after seeing Miss Arnold, Bragg described her hospital room, her roommates, and the mottoes on the wall above her bed. This letter speaks to her fear that she "may not get well" (a recurring fear until well past middle age) but does not indicate what her medical problems were. We also have evidence of the strong connection and deep, abiding love this daughter had for her father: "Indeed nothing does [worry me] except that I have not been a good and loving daughter. . . . How I love you. . . . I am afraid to show it as much as I feel, but these last years, it has grown so strong it hurts sometimes."[45]

Her mother was in Boston for the surgery, writing Reverend Bragg that Laura should come home rather than go to his sister Julia's place in Dorchester to recuperate. But Julia won out, and Bragg remained in Boston with her after the surgery. A month later Bragg wrote her father in Hudson, New Hampshire, where the family was now living, telling him how she was doing: "an off-day, . . . just feeling uncomfortable, headachy and tired." While she did not feel well, she had enjoyed visitors: "Five of the college girls came to see me yesterday and Annie Marfield came today and brought me roses."[46]

While Bragg convalesced, Simmons was becoming a college with a campus and college life. If she had been able to return to Simmons for the first semester of her junior year in 1904, she would have found the library school to have a more focused mission, as it "trains its students for the duties which are involved in the administration of a library." Her absence also saved her from the long journey from the Simmons Hall dormitory, which was still in use, to the college building on The Fenway while the other new buildings were under construction. Two new dormitories (North Hall and South Hall) were built, and the first Simmons junior prom was held on 15 December 1905—the first college party that included men.[47]

Miss Arnold had told her not to worry about college, and when Bragg returned to Simmons in January she began the process of making up an entire semester's work. She took her history examination, and then in June 1905 she passed all of her first-semester courses with credit: English, economics, German, library reference, and practices. During the semester she also took the same classes (biology, business methods, English, library economy, practice, and reference) as the rest of the girls. And she took those exams as scheduled, passing all with credit.[48]

While Bragg had returned to classes for the next semester, there was not space for her to room in the dormitory, so she remained in Dorchester, away from Simmons and town. Board cost her six dollars for two weeks. Additionally, she also had to budget for streetcar fares for getting to and from the college for classes. Living with Aunt Julia was not easy for Bragg—the house was kept bitterly cold to save on gas (Bragg was told to go to bed at 9:15 P.M.), and Aunt Julia gave Bragg more advice than she had had altogether "in the five years previous." But the biggest issue was money, for Aunt Julia changed her charge for board from one minute to the next. Once it would be three dollars per week, and then it would be three dollars and fifty cents per week. Julia was so upsetting to Bragg that she asked her father to handle all money dealings.[49]

Living with Aunt Julia may not have been wonderful, but everything about Simmons was. Her work was going well, and college life was "just delightful." She was studying and had attended an event hosted by Miss Arnold in Simmons Hall for some of the faculty: "it was a festive occasion with a fine dinner and reception and dancing after. I met lots of girls and had a blissful time." While renewing old friendships and making new ones was grand, for her the best part of the evening and what pleased her the most was that dear Miss Arnold called Bragg a brilliant student.[50]

Bragg found the new dormitory "fine" and had time to use the "couches, steamer chairs, morris chairs, pillows and steamer rugs. I go there every day, wrap up in a rug on a couch, rest and study." She did not much mind the going back and forth on the streetcars between Dorchester and downtown Boston, which took about forty-five minutes, once she had reduced it to a system. But Aunt Julia's home remained depressing to Bragg, so much so that when she returned to Simmons for the fall semester she lived on campus again among her friends.[51]

In late summer of 1905 before her senior year, Bragg cared for her father's mother during a long illness. Living in her grandmother's house, cooking and cleaning, she found that "housework has taken a great deal of time . . . after you left so I succeeded in getting all downstairs swept, dusted, and not a little washed. You would not know the dining room, it is so picked up. Then this morning I cleaned Grandma's room . . . I can put my hand in most places now without my teeth going on edge." She wrote to her father and requested that he ask her mother for recipes for some light meals that "I can make for Grandma." In later years Bragg did not keep house, and when a national survey, conducted by Procter and Gamble, asked to photograph her in the act of cooking, she replied that she seldom cooked. Bragg was not a homemaker then or later in her life.[52]

In her fourth year at Simmons, Bragg attended art lectures given by John Cotton Dana on Japanese prints. She called them an inspiration that "in me at least gave birth to an ever-growing interest in Japanese art." Bragg's courses included the history of libraries, library economy, practice, reference, business methods, accounting, and English. She took biology as an elective, "which is fine," she reported to her father. "As yet it is all micro-scopic investigation without much idea of what you are doing. We are studying ferns. . . . This biology takes seven hours a week of class work beside study." Her study of ferns was to continue for many years, both at Orr's Island where she had her first position and in South Carolina. One of her few published papers was in the *American Fern Journal,* July–September 1914 issue. It was called "Preliminary List of the Ferns of the Coast Region of South Carolina North of Charleston" and dealt with the classification of ferns in South Carolina.[53]

One of the responsibilities of each Simmons student was to serve an apprenticeship each semester at a library or a museum. In the last semester of her senior year Bragg was fortunate to work with Charles Johnson, who was the curator of the Museum of the Boston Society of Natural History. Studying with him, she learned to make bird surveys and to press flowers and ferns. He also trained her for museum work, a common practice at the time, since there were no facilities for training museum workers.[54]

Bragg was "wholesomely happy [at Simmons]. . . . Each day seems too short for all the joy I can pile into it . . . just luxuriate in college and the life here . . . the dormitory life is nice this year." Her friend Miss Robbins, the director of the Library Science School, had advised her not to take a heavy load of courses, calling Bragg too ambitious. "She, as well as nearly everyone, is particularly pleased to have me looking so well and she says she is going to take care of me and not let me overwork. . . . She came to tea with me the other afternoon. . . . We are such good friends that I know she will help me next summer to some position."[55]

Hearing in the big churches of Boston continued to be a problem for Bragg, but in her classes at Simmons she could hear pretty well, and in one course she could hear every word. In November of the fall semester a friend took her to see her own ear specialist. This friend had also suffered with scarlet fever as a child, which had left her with perforated eardrums. This specialist, Dr. Shaw, had made them grow again. How hopeful Bragg must have been when she heard this story, and yet the doctor was painfully honest when he told Bragg, "you will never hear any better than you do now." He did offer a suggestion: "the only thing which would help at all is a more equable climate and that would hardly do sufficient good to be worth trying."[56]

College life was a source of pleasure for Bragg. Friends dropped by her rooms; she visited art galleries; she walked about the campus with other friends; and she enjoyed the festive occasions on which Dean Arnold included her, such as dinners at which the dean entertained the "illustrious faculty." Bragg gloried in being at Simmons. And she shared her joy in her letters to her father with her words and descriptions. She was also thankful for him: "I cannot tell you how grateful I am but you shall know someday."[57]

During her senior year (1905–1906) all of her classmates' plans focused on graduation. They held their senior prom in December in the new dormitory. They were entertained at a reception by the sophomores, and the juniors entertained them at Miss Arnold's home. There were monthly socials at Simmons Hall to which the "1902" girls were invited. And for Bragg personally there was great news that potentially could change those graduation plans. In early January 1906 her friend Miss Robbins had indeed helped her find a position, one that would give Bragg what she had always wanted—"to get with a college library."[58]

Miss Robbins offered her a chance to catalog the library at Purdue University at a salary of fifty dollars per month, a position which would involve leaving Simmons just after midyear examinations in order to begin by 10 February. Knowing that it would mean not graduating with her class was hard, but she felt that "the practical comes before the sentimental." Calling it a fine chance, she was flattered that Miss Robbins had come to her, "rather than to anyone else. There are others who would be only too glad of it." The chance to earn a salary and to work until her debts were paid were the reasons she chose to accept the offer before she wrote to her father for his advice. For her, the money was the impetus that compelled her to try the "West," even though "it is dreadful to think of being so far away from home but it might be the same in June."[59]

However, that opportunity failed to materialize after all. She graduated from college during the commencement exercises on 13 June 1906, receiving a bachelor of science degree in library science. What was an experiment in providing an education for women, combining both cultural and vocational training, had become a full-fledged institution of higher learning. But most males still considered higher education for women an object of scorn. Reporting the commencement exercises under the headline "Maidens Given Collegiate Degree," a reporter for one of the Boston papers also carefully pointed out that the women "had learned the proper way to decorate a room, and the most approved style of ventilation and plumbing, and every one of them can tell a bread pan from an ice cream freezer."[60]

The prophecy of the class of 1906 began with a citation about Bragg, calling her a well-known American writer with a list of works too long for publication. Her most notable work was a reminiscent history of the first class of Simmons College, which she penned her senior year. She was renowned for her rapidity as the chief reviewer of American books. The prophetess recalled "the appalling number of books she absorbed during the English course." And if more information were desired about Bragg, the reader of the class history was directed to consult Miss Helen Norris, a classmate from Boston.[61]

The emergence of women's colleges was one of the first success stories of the early women's movement, offering middle-class women an opportunity for an independent role outside the patriarchal family. By the time Bragg graduated from Simmons College in 1906, more than forty thousand women were enrolled in institutions of higher learning—such as Mt. Holyoke (founded in 1837), Vassar (founded in 1865), and Radcliffe (founded in 1879)—and represented over a third of all college students. "Between 1890 and 1920, the number of professional degrees granted to women increased 226 percent at three times the rate of increase for men." As a result of her college education, Bragg began a professional career, something unheard of only fifty years earlier for middle-class women.[62]

A product of the Progressive Era and a second-generation New Woman, Bragg believed that women were the political, social, and economic equals of men. Choosing to live her life autonomously, Bragg did not see her world as divided into the two spheres then still commonly accepted by society as proper for women: the public (professional) and the private (domestic). And her first step into the public world was one she had prepared for at Simmons.

But the college prophecy could not have envisioned that Bragg's next adventure would be on Orr's Island, an isolated island just off the coast of Maine. While she may not have been offered the position at Purdue, she was given another opportunity just before graduation to be a librarian at a social service library begun by a group of Bostonians as a welfare project. Orr's Island was quaint and poor, with island men earning their livelihoods from the sea. Fishing boats and dories lined the coves and inlets of the island, and there were lobster pots and nets at every house. Gray-shingled saltboxes, handed down from one generation to the next, were scattered about the island. Summer visitors, known as highlanders, lived back in the hills, up the twisting island roads.[63]

Only one other librarian, Mrs. Cook, had worked at the Orr's Island

Library before Bragg, who expected to be on the island for only one year. She signed the library register on 6 July 1906, indicating that she had taken over the duties on that date. She never made another entry in the book. If her days were as filled as the one she described as typical to her father in her 30 July 1906 letter, it is no wonder, for she simply had not a moment to spare.[64]

On the day described she arose at 4:30 A.M. to read a book that she later used to teach the island boys how to make tepees; had breakfast at 7:30 A.M.; corrected a report for her supervisor, Miss Thuring; and then rode her bicycle down to the library where people flocked in to check out and return books. Then she taught the boys and read to them, all the while helping people find books in the library. By then it was only noon, when she had her lunch and baby-sat a child who had brought nothing to eat. Several of the children brought in a collection of butterflies, which Bragg preserved, and then she helped them make butterfly nets and sent them on their way to catch more. At 4:00 in the afternoon there was a trustee meeting, and the day ended with some girls bringing her a snake to kill. In the meantime the boys had returned with more butterflies, which she chloroformed. When one of the boys tried to take the snake out of the jar, it got away, causing some exciting moments until it was recaptured. At 6:00 P.M. there were still nine children in the library with her sitting around the fire, watching the flames, and talking until they were sure the snake was dead.[65]

Bragg was finally able to end her day at the library at 6:30 P.M. She bicycled back to the home where she was boarding, had her supper before the open fire, and began writing to her "dear Father" at 9:00 P.M. her account of her day. Later that week she spent time on the beach learning about the shorebirds and other coastal animals and plants, and she went sailing on another afternoon.

She had inherited a love of botany from her father, and on Orr's Island she spent hours studying flowers and gathering specimens to mount—not inking in the classifications until her father came. Not only did she want him to verify her work, but she knew that he would like to do that. In a later letter she reminded him, "I am saving lots of plants for you to identify. Please bring your Gray's Botany." It was with these specimens that the Orr's Island Museum began. During her time on the island she also had the opportunity to study biology and botany at Tufts College Biological Laboratory, just across the bay from Orr's Island.[66]

It would seem that Bragg's father was the only male figure in her life. In college she was surrounded by girlfriends and interacted with two female faculty members, Miss Robbins and Miss Arnold, who had taken a special interest in her. And if she dated any young man during those years at Simmons, she never wrote about it to her father, who was her confidant.

While living on Orr's Island she came into contact with a Mr. Prince, whom she definitely disliked. His manner was so unnerving to Bragg that she wrote her father about him on two separate occasions. Mr. Prince was the wealthiest man on the island and was also quite active in the island's Methodist church. And while she found him to be cordial and solicitous, she still found him distasteful. She had heard that "the young men simply laugh if you speak of Mr. Prince in connection with a good life or religion."[67]

Much later in life Bragg said she was engaged four times, once to a boy named George Pike, who sent Bragg the announcement of his wedding to another woman while she was living on Orr's Island. Bragg also recalled that her mother said to her one day, "Laura, do you really love this boy [George]? If you do, why do you hate for him to touch you?" Bragg replied, "Have they got to keep touching you?"[68]

Bragg made new friends on the island and was also joined by old ones. Her friend and the dean of the Library Science School at Simmons College, Mary Robbins, came to Orr's Island for that first summer to help Bragg get started with her work. She was also joined by Charles Johnson, of the Boston Museum of Natural History, and his wife, who spent a month's vacation there helping Bragg mount specimens collected on the beaches or brought in by the fishermen, who provided the island's main source of income. Her sister, Barbara, also spent several months with her and was there for Thanksgiving Day in 1906, and she traveled home with Bragg to Greenland, New Hampshire, for a family Christmas that year.[69]

When Bragg first agreed to go to Orr's Island she thought it would be only for a year. During that year she trained a local girl to serve as the librarian. But by February 1907 she had decided to stay, and she believed that "the parents were with her now." Bragg taught not only the children but also the adults—how to give haircuts and how to cut out dress patterns—and she helped the mothers care for infants. She had learned the "rudiments of settlement work in Boston during her college years." (Simmons College had opened the country's second school for social workers during her junior year.)[70]

During her first months on the island she had had some problems with the young men, who were hostile to the library; she wrote to her father: "I have had one or two experiences with the boys but seem to have gained them [now] instead of lost them." Bragg won them over, and by winter they had begun to help her keep the library open on winter evenings. On one Saturday evening in late November 1906 she held a "little entertainment" at the library with forty-two islanders in attendance. On another winter evening a Washington birthday party was held, with the local ladies dressed in colonial costume.[71]

When she had lived with Aunt Julia while in college, Bragg had pleaded with her father to handle her finances. Now, living so far away from home, this arrangement proved to be cumbersome and time-consuming. Reverend Bragg would pay her bills whenever she sent him notice in one of her letters. He was quite willing to continue in the role of provider and purse-string holder, but the system was not working, as she wrote him: "This way of handling my money is driving me distracted." She was in charge of the library money, had to keep out cash, and had to file accounts with her supervisor, Miss Thuring, in addition to worrying about paying for her own expenses and then asking him to send checks out for her.[72] It was too much for Bragg to think about then and a sign that financial planning would always prove to be a problem for her.

She spent some time in the summer of 1907 back in Boston and met her future sister-in-law, Adel. Barbara came back to Orr's Island for part of the summer, and they lived on the Back Shore in a cottage owned by a highlander. Bragg had "a room with a separate entrance and a private veranda. I have arranged it all very prettily." But within six months she was to have moved again because there was too much responsibility in keeping house, or so she told her father.[73]

Being home or coming home began to be frequent phrases in Bragg's letters from July 1907 until she left the following summer. She finally decided in January 1908 that she could not remain on the island. Bragg was so homesick that she asked her mother to spend a week with her in April 1908. Interestingly, Mrs. Bragg wrote Reverend Bragg that his daughter "just wanted me," and Bragg's postscript to this note read, "I am happy as can be to have my mother all to myself." She was thin and worn, and her mother believed that she needed a complete change for a time.[74]

After her mother's visit Bragg wrote in her next letter home to her father, "I will not come back here under any circumstances. I simply cannot stand the climate." She had to wear several sets of clothing just to bear the winter winds whenever she went out. The long winter season and the cold were more than she could stand even with her beloved dog, Imp, as her companion. She had decided that she had to move closer to home and somewhere warmer.[75]

Leaving Orr's Island in the summer of 1908, Bragg lived with her mother's sister, Anna, while working at a temporary position at the New York City Public Library during the time when a number of branches were being opened. She served as a teacher's assistant in 1908, beginning work in November for fifty-five dollars a month. She described her position to her father as "really fine," and she believed the chance of promotion to be good and felt that the experience was just what she needed.[76]

Having just begun in this position, Bragg did not go home for

Christmas that year. Instead she went to New Jersey to be with her mother's family in Hackettstown. The town was filled with aunts, uncles, and cousins all visiting back and forth during the days she spent with them. She attended her mother's church, where "everyone was as nice to me as possible for Mother's sake and all asked about her." She wistfully wrote her father, "I cannot half wish that you and Mother lived there, say on a farm like Uncle Nathan's." She was tired of the moving, year after year, as the family followed her father from church to church.[77]

Though Bragg may have been tired of her family's nomadic life, she was contemplating returning south to do missionary work, similar to her father's work in Mississippi. Within a month of writing her father so wistfully about a "farm like Uncle Nathan's," Bragg had spoken to Paul Rea, the director of the Charleston Museum, about taking the position as its librarian. She wrote her father, "I am going to accept Charleston if I get the appointment." Hearing that the salary was to be only six hundred dollars a year, she still felt that "Charleston is best." She assured her father that even if the Charleston job did not materialize she had the appointment with the New York Public Library, so she knew she would be all right either way. By February she must have known that she had not received the Charleston post. The Museum's first librarian was Elizabeth Van Hoevenberg, who began working there in March 1909. On 23 February 1909 she wrote her father, "I know you and Mother will be happy to learn that I have given up the Charleston scheme and shall stick it out in New York awhile longer."[78]

Within five months Van Hoevenberg resigned, and Rea knew when he left the Museum for the summer that he needed a new librarian. Bragg met Dr. Rea in Portland, Maine, where he described Charleston, the Museum, and its connection with the college. He won her over by making his offer seem like missionary work. Bragg said later that what caught her attention and intrigued her was the opportunity to work with Rea as his assistant in bringing to life the oldest museum in the western hemisphere. Being the daughter of a minister and a social missionary, Bragg must have seen that the greater attraction would be to reform and educate southerners just as her father had done when she was a child in Mississippi.[79]

Bragg traveled to Charleston for the month of July. With Rea's help she worked out the arrangements for having her boxes sent from Boston by the Clyde Line. She looked over her work for the winter, "the work I so love," and pronounced it "all that I could desire." A part of the work was "to undertake through the Natural History Society a systematic study of the flora of the Carolina coast region," and she asked her father to send her a list of ferns when he had time.[80]

She called the search for a place to live a "dreadful hunting," as she was such a homebody "that I am not happy until I have a corner I can call my own." The only drawback she could see about her new life in Charleston was "the preponderance of the insect world," which she told her father she was learning how to control. Her father must have written her about attending a Methodist church, for she wrote him in reply, "I think it cannot cause you displeasure if I attend an Episcopalian church instead. Professor Rea wishes me to attend St. Michael's where he goes. The people with whom he wishes me to be thrown in are chiefly Episcopalians, as are most people in Charleston."[81]

Most Charlestonians in 1909 were not, in fact, Episcopalians. More than 50 percent of the total population was African American (who were not likely to be Anglicans), and most white people attended a variety of churches other than Episcopalian: Presbyterian, Methodist, Baptist, fundamentalist, and Catholic, as well as Jewish synagogues. But Episcopalians occupied the uppermost social class and were in control of the social power structure of the city. While the Methodists tended to occupy a different social class, most of the people who attended churches of this denomination would not be helpful, financially or socially, for the work Bragg would be doing at the Charleston Museum.[82]

Bragg returned to New York City and her position at the library for one final month in August 1909. Her time in Charleston had been strenuous, but she was well and strong and ready for her new life to begin. Her friends at the library made a fuss over her leaving and gave a farewell party in her honor. She made a final visit to the Metropolitan Museum of Art, which "has a wonderful collection but I do not find so many pictures which I love as I do at Boston." While she thought it was nice to be back in New York City for this short time, Bragg was on the road to a life of independence.[83] She was poised to enter a new world of professional museum work that would not only transform her own life, but also those of the Charleston Museum and other museums in the South.

Creating a Museum

It is the use of material in a museum that is more important
than its mere preservation.

Laura M. Bragg, *Bulletin of The Charleston Museum,*
January 1917 and January 1919

IN *GONE WITH THE WIND*, RHETT tells Scarlett that he is returning to
Charleston, where there was a little bit of charm and grace left in the
world. But in 1907 novelist Henry James saw the city as a place of ruins
and widows, "of gardens and absolutely of no men—or of so few that, save
for the general sweetness, the War might still have been raging and all the
manhood at the front." Should either man have sailed into Charleston harbor with Laura Bragg in September 1909, he would have found the Holy
City little changed, for while it possessed some grace and charm, there was
little else of appeal.[1]

Bragg recalled arriving in the Charleston harbor on a Clyde steamer,
the *Arapahoe,* and seeing the town in the autumn light. Landing just after
lunch on 4 September, she found the city bathed in sunlight, the crape
myrtle in bloom, and the city's air a "melange of the odors of heavy salt,
pluff mud," and the above-water-level sewer drains. These smells "befouled
the air," as the primary means of human waste disposal in the city were
some twelve thousand privies whose contents leached into the soil.
Charleston's streets were a patchwork of mostly dirt roadways, and only
about a third were paved in granite, brick, or asphalt. Some of the streets
in the oldest section of the city were of gravel, oyster shells, cinders, or cobblestones. Certainly it was a city in which time had stood still, a city almost
untouched by modernization. A travel writer visiting the city declared,
"Charleston is perhaps the only city in America that has slammed its front
door in Progress' face and resisted the modern with fiery determination."[2]

In recalling the large mansions built along the seawall of Charleston's
High Battery, Bragg remarked in an interview, "There wasn't a gallon of
white paint in the city. There was a shabbiness about it that was simply
charming." Salt air did not respect either paint or plaster, and Charlestonians were said to be "too poor to paint and too proud to whitewash." Fortunately, the homes were built of heart pine and cypress and had survived
the Civil War, the hurricanes, and the Great Fire of the century just past.
What Bragg saw, however, was an adventure and an opportunity for new
experiences. "The obvious ignorance was divine. They needed her. Like

young Alexander the Great before her, [she] saw worlds to conquer," a local reporter wrote after an interview with Bragg when she was seventy-four.[3]

Charleston was one of the last places in the South where business still began after ten in the morning in the business district along Broad Street and dinner was served in the middle of the afternoon. Families with names such as Middleton, Pinckney, Rutledge, and Heyward dominated the economic and political institutions just as they had for past generations, since "economic stagnation froze the city's social structure." The Civil War, Reconstruction, and financial disasters had not diminished their control over local affairs. While the advent of progressivism had shaken the system, this group of white men formed political alliances with the few newcomers who also "recognized family name, gentlemanly behavior, and a South-of-Broad address as minimum requirements for playing the game."[4]

With much of the planter aristocracy still in power and overtly thwarting economic growth, the city had gained a reputation as an antiindustrial area. The gracious and charming southern gentlemen literally scared off new people with money and ideas, thus saving the city and its citizens from anything that might have challenged the prevailing social and racial mores of the ruling class. While other cities of the New South were infused with new money, new ideas, and new people, Charleston proudly embraced its "genteel poverty," and society became more inflexible, inward-looking, and provincial. There were few new jobs; most women still stood mute on the pedestal; and blacks, kept functionally illiterate by white supremacists, provided cheap and plentiful labor.[5]

Typical evenings for the white elite were spent at home reading in family circles or strolling along High Battery. While life was quiet, orderly, and peaceful in the beautiful but unpainted homes South of Broad and along High Battery, that was not the case in the working-class neighborhoods along the Cooper River.[6] Not only was the city divided politically, socially, and racially, but those divisions were also reflected across the state.

Charleston and the lowcountry had been controlled by the planter aristocracy since the time of British colonialism. It was more dependent upon farming than the upcountry, which steadily became more urbanized and more industrialized. The lowcountry landed gentry were seen as morally permissive by the upcountry's fundamentalist farmers and mill workers, who were quite different from them in their view of the world as one of moral absolutes.[7]

The "colored problem" was a never-ending source of public discussion and political conflict in the state. Blacks comprised 58 percent of the state's population in 1900. The dominant white patriarchal political and social class structure manipulated and repressed the black man in the name of maintaining social order. Leaders such as "Pitchfork Ben" Tillman, elected governor in 1890, and Coleman Blease, elected to the office in 1910, fanned the flames of racial hatred and provoked bitter animosity from the business, financial, and professional men (southern Progressives), whom they scorned as gentlemen. While their terms as governor were not consecutive, Blease was a self-professed heir to Tillman's politics, appealing to the racial, religious, and class prejudices of many South Carolinians. Both men were obstructionists who feared Progressive reforms, understanding that should the common man become educated, he could begin to question their politics, tactics, and motives. Blease was especially astute in recognizing and cultivating the political power of mill villagers, using his 1912 campaign to appeal to working-class whites' prejudices and their belief that all white men were equal.[8]

Charleston was also engaged in a similar political battle, which included four groups whose leaders were struggling for control of City Hall in the early decades of the twentieth century. The most important of the four, Progressive capitalists, simply ignored blacks and the "colored problem." Affluent by Charleston standards, they were typically Presbyterians and Methodists, with a few Episcopalians. Called the "Broad Street Ring," they were conservative managers of the city's money. They sought new industries for the city, welcomed federal projects with federal money, and enjoyed good relations with the more progressive governors of the state. These men tended to ignore prostitution, gambling, and liquor sales even though all were illegal. Another group was made up of reactionaries who opposed any new industries and looked askance at federal projects. Usually Episcopalian, they saw only the South and considered the rest of the nation as foreign territory. Columbia and the state government received no respect from them. While they inherited land and beautiful old houses, their families had lost their real wealth in the Civil War.[9]

The third group, Protestant populists, were members of the various fundamentalist and Pentecostal sects, and they favored enforcement of laws against gambling and prostitution. Not only were they antiblack, anti-Catholic, and anti-aristocrat, they were isolationists. The fourth group was the newest to the city. Called Catholic populists, these leaders favored industrial development, were urban in orientation, and tolerated the vices of drinking, prostitution, and gambling. They comprised about 15 percent of the city's population and were of either Italian or Irish ancestry. They were bitterly anti-British and antiaristocrat.[10] Overall, however, none of the four political groups saw blacks as any more than second-class citizens.

The General Assembly of South Carolina had enacted a series of laws segregating the races between 1896 and 1906, but Charleston City Council waited until 1912 to pass its own Jim Crow laws separating blacks and whites on trolley cars. This action was opposed by Mayor John Patrick

Grace, who had appointed the first blacks as city commissioners. These ordinances were then extended to theaters, drinking fountains, parks, hospitals, and anywhere else the two races could meet and intermingle. During the Jim Crow era, which lasted until the mid 1960s, the two races coexisted generally peacefully under the formula arrived at by Charleston's Progressive Era leaders: "Humanity but not equality, economic but not political opportunity."[11]

Emancipation, Appomattox, Reconstruction, and the turn of the century had not altered to any great degree black participation in Charleston's social, political, and economic structures. Their roles were virtually unchanged from antebellum times, based upon the myth of a mutually beneficial relationship with reciprocal responsibilities. Whites still held a sense of noblesse oblige "for the dependent helpless race," while "blacks were expected to remain content with their lowly lot in life." There was no pretense of equality, and their shared sense of reciprocity was dependent upon both groups knowing and accepting their prescribed roles.[12]

Until 1920 blacks formed the majority population of the city. Many of them lived in squalid conditions in the dependencies, servants' quarters, and carriage houses that were located in the alleyways or backyards of the aristocracy's mansions. (This housing pattern was still in existence well into 1940 when sociologists Karl Taeuber and Alma Taeuber conducted a study that found Charleston to be the least racially segregated of 109 American cities.)[13] With such close proximity between the races, personal and familiar contact was nurtured. Many white homes still employed black women as domestic live-ins, thus continuing a paternalistic relationship that had existed before the Civil War.

The only real contact, then, that blacks had with whites was as house servants. By design, custom, and later by law, the white world of Charleston had no opportunity to mix either socially or in the business world with members of the black population, nor was any contact sought. White Charlestonians and other South Carolinians chose to preserve their superiority without relinquishing the noblesse oblige and the gentility and graciousness that defined their lives.[14]

The color line assigned blacks and whites different positions, rights, privileges, and arenas of action. It also defined and limited the access and approach that each group had with and toward the other. This imaginary and arbitrary line developed from a collective understanding that blacks, by virtue of the color of their skin, did not deserve or qualify for equal status with whites, and they had no right to expect to be accepted socially. Whites dominated and subordinated blacks, thus excluding blacks from power within the political and commercial institutions of the city.[15] That was the way it was—until Bragg arrived at the Museum.

Just as the city and its social institutions had suffered from the war and its aftermath, so had the Charleston Museum. The Museum was a part of the College of Charleston, and the president had hired Dr. Paul Rea in 1903 to teach biology and premedical courses, as well as to be the curator of the museum housed on the college's campus in a classroom. Rea surely must have been both brilliant and possessed with great energy, as he was also a professor of embryology and physiology at the Medical College of South Carolina, whose campus was only several blocks away. Rea had just recently persuaded city council to fund the museum and to purchase the Thompson Auditorium, which held seating for eight thousand people.[16]

This building, located in Cannon Park, was near the campus of the Medical College at the corner of Rutledge Avenue and Calhoun Street and was not a far walk from the college. Rea knew that, with thirty-five thousand feet of floor space, there was more than enough room available not only to install exhibits, but also to provide office space, a library, lecture rooms, laboratories, and preparation rooms. The exterior of the building was in the beaux arts style, which belied the empty hulk inside. It had been hastily constructed in ninety days for a 1899 reunion of Confederate veterans.[17]

It was Bragg's responsibility to take charge of the Natural History Society and to install the old museum in Thompson Auditorium. Her other tasks included a large part of the educational activity in addition to the care of the library. According to Rea, by publication time of the October 1909 *Bulletin of The Charleston Museum,* "The appearance of the book stacks has been greatly improved by the binding of many periodicals."[18]

Bragg's address for the first two years she lived in Charleston was 126 Wentworth Street, at the Schirmer residence. Bragg had never enjoyed life more. She had bought herself a "green and yellow hammock," and with her opera glasses she thoroughly enjoyed her evenings stargazing. However, she admitted to her father that she was lonely, "as I have as yet met so few people whom I care to know. Our class of people are not back as yet." People of Bragg's class were either still in the mountains or at their beach homes on Sullivan's Island, fleeing the summer heat.[19]

Bragg's love of botany found a home in the Museum's Natural History Society. Bragg was elected president in November 1909, and she and the other members undertook as their first project a survey of the city's trees. They were to identity species and varieties and were urged to "make as much progress as possible . . . while leaves are still to be found on the trees."[20] The society also took field excursions to barrier islands and to plantations in the surrounding countryside, with Bragg teaching the locals about their own geography and history on the trips.

By the time of her twenty-eighth birthday on 9 October, she had friends who invited her to go to the Market. In a 24 October letter she provided her father with a vivid description that captured the scene: "It is a classic (Greek) building, beautifully proportioned. Under it and far behind down to the river extends a passage enclosed by great arches—all white. Some stalls had fat old Negro women in charge, bandana handkerchiefs on their heads . . . the vultures . . . keep the place exceedingly clean. The lower end of the market is closed now owing to the growth of grocery stores up town, but in former days each morning saw the ladies of the town, accompanied by a Negro servant with a basket, choosing their family dinners. It must have been worth seeing. It is now, even."[21]

Bragg stayed in Charleston through the holiday season and was ill for most of January 1910. The next month she wrote her father, thanking him for his share in her presents: "You have always done so much for me and been so good to me." In the twenty-five years of correspondence between Bragg and her father that has survived, there are two recurring themes, both appearing in this letter. The first is money and her management of it. "The financial part always troubles me when I let myself think of it," she wrote. And she complained that living was high: "there is nothing cheap in Charleston." The second theme concerns books: "I have just finished the biology volume" (her father had purchased the same science library as Rea had for the Museum's library); and "I have read none of Sir Oliver Lodge's works. . . . Some of the other books you have been reading I would greatly like to read also, but they do not seem to come my way."[22]

Bragg accomplished a great deal during her first full year at the Museum. While there was no money to acquire new books, the Museum had a large library of old books, 385 of them bound and another 800 prepared for binding. The activities developed by Bragg for the Natural History Society had created enough interest that some books were now lent outside the building.[23]

It was not unusual for libraries and museums to operate as single institutions, which had been the custom before the turn of the century. And it continued to be common practice for small museums, such as the Charleston Museum, to provide library services in cities without libraries, as Charleston was until 1931. The use of libraries at this time opened educational opportunities for some with a freer atmosphere than existed in the public schools of the day. Rea's director's report reflected this attitude by acknowledging "that there can be no doubt that the value of the library to the public would be greatly increased by placing a part at least on a circulating basis, and the location of the Museum is ideal for this purpose." The Museum's *Bulletin* further reported that the library was a valuable accessory in constructing the exhibit labels, and it was a place "where tired sightseers may find interesting reading."[24]

Bragg's work in the Department of Public Instruction was chiefly with the Natural History Society, which had been divided into junior and senior sections due to the large increase in membership. She had also "provided lectures and demonstrations for classes from the training school . . . at Memminger Normal School, Ashley Hall, Bennett School and Miss Nathan's kindergarten [as well as] . . . to the Charleston Advertising Club, Stokes' Business College, and a number of business men."[25]

Bragg was happy in her work and in learning new subjects. She was sure that she was in the right place: "at last I am sure. How I love it!" Her work now largely determined her reading: "I have dipped rather deeply this winter into biological literature and so have read many of the works." Her father remained the center of her world. In letters to him she wrote that she was looking forward to seeing him and sharing with him all that she had learned: "You will be so surprised to find me so learned next summer. What fun next summer will be." She missed him and thought of him as she tramped through the woods: "I don't know of anyone else whom I find quite so congenial as my own Dad."[26]

In the summer of 1910 Bragg returned home to Newfields, New Hampshire, where her family was living. She spent two days in Boston on museum matters, visiting a typewriter office, a bookshop, and finally the Boston Museum of Natural History, where she worked in the library and studied birds and mollusks. Writing Rea, she reported that she had "put in some hours studying trees on streets and in Boston Common . . . I have seen so many birds. I spent the afternoon in the woods with them."[27]

That letter to Rea was the beginning of her summer correspondence with him. For the ten years that he served as director and she as his assistant, Bragg wrote him about her vacation activities. He read about her visits to other museums and how what she had learned would help her when she returned to the Charleston Museum in the fall. Rarely did she not go home to New England and her father for the summer. But no matter, she wrote to Rea during every vacation until he left the Museum for a new directorship at the Cleveland Museum in 1920. Rea often responded to her letters, answering her questions and posing his own.

During her trips to other museums Bragg was learning how to make museums come alive instead of existing merely as mausoleums for the collection of inanimate objects. Museums, as Bragg came to understand them from her visits north, should seek to educate the public through their well-thought-out installations of exhibits. Bragg's new installations at the Charleston Museum, with illustrative labels, transformed what had been a scientific, natural history museum for the academic elite into a public institution.[28]

This shift in emphasis from an exhibitionist to an educational function brought with it social implications. Under Bragg's leadership the Charleston Museum would reach into the community, finding new patrons in the different social classes.[29] While this understanding was relatively new even to the museums in the Northeast, it was almost unheard of in the South, due to the poverty, isolation, and racism that predominated in the region. What few museums there were in the South were cemeteries for relics.

As a self-proclaimed social missionary and reformer, Bragg came to understand that museums (and the Charleston Museum in particular) were powerful instruments for self-improvement. She learned through development of traveling school exhibits that if the public would not, or could not, come to the Museum, then she could make patrons aware of what the Museum had to offer them. The traveling exhibits led Bragg to an even greater discovery: that the Museum was "an engine of social change, [and] an opportunity to do good for ordinary people on a massive scale."[30]

This was a radical change from the past for museums, because their role had experienced a dramatic shift in emphasis. At the beginning of the nineteenth century the major objectives for museums were to educate, inform, and inspire the general public. Fundamentally understood to be educational institutions, museums were open to those who did not have the benefit of an extended education. Through objects and pictures museums could teach those who were not skilled in teaching themselves.[31]

Then around 1860 specialized societies restricted public access to museums, and education was abandoned as a museum function. Rather, the emphasis at museums was placed on entertainment. At the same time that museums lost their social purpose, women also abandoned their interests in establishing museums. They returned to that work at the beginning of the Progressive Era when museums once again became "necessary institutions in social education" and art was seen as a civilizing influence. During this time of reform wealthy women returned to the field and established art museums (Gertrude Vanderbilt began the Whitney Museum, and Abby Rockefeller, Mary Quinn Sullivan, and Lizzie Bliss founded the Museum of Modern Art, both in New York City) as one aspect of their philanthropic work.[32]

During the post–Civil War period the museum movement's primary motivation was a need to instill literacy in the American public. As social institutions, museums assumed the task of uniting society at a common place where the social classes could meet on a level foundation. They offered a tolerance for equality, which could be achieved through learning. It has been noted by museum historians that "those who run American museums have never fully agreed on what museums should teach, to whom or for what ends, but from the outset museums have undertaken to teach someone something."[33]

Working in the early decades of the twentieth century, John Cotton Dana, director of the Newark Free Public Library and Museum, and Henry Watson Kent, the supervisor of museum instruction at New York's Metropolitan Museum of Art, were both trained as librarians, as was Bragg. Both saw museums as powerful instruments for self-improvement and in their work tried to reach all parts of their communities. Seeing museums as places of active interpretation, they believed that it was the duty of the institutions to develop the interest of the citizens.[34]

Since the early emphasis of America's museums was educational and because women had long served as teachers, many gravitated toward museum education. Though Bragg's first position at the Charleston Museum was as librarian, she also taught science classes at the Museum and at a local private girls' school. In addition she created the traveling school exhibits that were the major focus of her educational program, which was considered a part of her responsibilities. Bragg understood that the exhibits would arouse interest first in the children, who would come back with their parents.

By March 1911 Bragg's work had taken off in so many different directions that she was appointed curator of books and public instruction, but with no increase in pay. Rea recognized the need for a librarian's assistant, so Bragg's sister, Barbara, was offered a temporary position from March until June. Barbara remained at the Museum for more than two years as her sister's assistant, then returned home at the age of twenty-six to live with her parents for at least the next three years. Bragg also supported her sister with a monthly allowance after she left the Museum. Barbara later became a secretary for the Portsmouth Naval Station.[35]

The Museum had finally moved to its new building, the Thompson Auditorium, with the assistance of the young members in the junior section of the Natural History Society. These youngsters had carried collections of local shells and local birds' nests and eggs, groups of minerals, and the smaller mammals as well as the entire Manigault bone collection through the streets of Charleston. By having these children move the museum collection, Bragg hoped to create an interest for learning in them and for the museum's activities. In fact, many of them became interested in museum work, including E. I. R. "Ned" Jennings, a "little boy with a cleft palate that couldn't talk plain." Soon after Ned showed up at the Museum, she enlisted his help in raising ten thousand silk cocoons, which were part of the 1911 silk culture exhibit. Bragg cited this exhibit as the beginning of the Museum's educational program, as she gave twenty-eight lectures on the topic and twelve hundred schoolchildren visited it during school hours.[36]

Bragg also befriended two young girls during those early years at the Museum, Anita Pollitzer and Josephine Pinckney. Anita Pollitzer attended the first Natural History Society meeting in October 1909, forming a friendship with Bragg that lasted until Anita's death in 1975. Josephine Pinckney's father was president of the trustees, but it was her brother Charles Cotesworth Pinckney who introduced Bragg to her. They also were lifelong friends as well as next-door neighbors on Chalmers Street, where Bragg bought a house in 1927.[37]

In the same year that Bragg arrived in the city, another northerner came south and founded Ashley Hall, a fashionable private school for the daughters of the city's white elite. Mary Vardrine McBee, the headmistress, wrote Bragg in the summer of 1911 asking her to teach zoology and botany for an hour a day at the school. Bragg sent the letter on to Rea at Wood's Hole, Massachusetts, where he was conducting research. She wrote, "Tell me what you think of it and what you want me to do. Personally I have no desire to teach for Miss McBee." But Bragg was agreeable to the plan if it would be advantageous to the Museum and "forward our cooperative schemes." Miss McBee had asked that Bragg tell her what terms were fair. So Bragg wrote Rea that it was important to charge between $200 and $300. Bragg believed that the headmistress's intention was to "get the Museum to teach the classes for love. Cheap!!"[38]

Though "loath to bother with it," Rea was attracted to the money the proposition would bring into the Museum. In his reply to Miss McBee, Rea set forth the Museum's conditions under which Bragg would teach the Ashley Hall girls, which were the same terms that Bragg had suggested. Miss McBee agreed to a charge of $250 and was willing to have the girls travel to the Museum for classes, but since the school's catalog had already been issued, she was unable to print a statement in it about the Museum's cooperation.[39]

Bragg was glad that Rea had absolutely approved of her terms, calling the offer a "clever piece of sharp dealing on her [Miss McBee's] part." Because Charleston was such a small town, Bragg had somehow learned of several incidents at the private school, "that kindergarten deal and one or two other matters," that caused her to lose respect for Miss McBee. Bragg wrote Rea: "Except in a matter of pure business in future [I] will have absolutely no relations with her. I should not have accepted even her public invitations if I had understood her . . . as I do now." Both women were strong-willed and highly educated. Bragg and Miss McBee remained only business associates throughout her time at the Museum.[40]

While Rea and Bragg failed in their attempt to meet and plan her work for Ashley Hall during their summer vacation, she did spend some time developing a lesson plan. However, after all the letters back and forth and all the planning, Bragg did not teach a full load to the Ashley Hall girls that fall. Miss McBee paid the Museum $100 for their trouble, though Rea had said that he considered $150 a fair compromise over the "peculiar situation." Therefore, Miss McBee got out cheaply after all.[41]

Finances continued to be an issue in Bragg's personal life. Rea had advanced Bragg money before he left on his vacation. In his 7 July letter he asked her to endorse her paycheck over to him and return the check. And not a month later she asked him for an advance on her next paycheck. With a fairly stern tone in his reply, he admonished her to plan ahead and ask for the advance before he had settled the previous month's accounts. But he still covered her request with his personal check. Until both men left her life, Bragg relied on Rea and her father to ease her way whenever her fiscal mismanagement became a problem.[42]

Bragg spent the first week of her vacation that summer in New York, where she devoted that time to museum visiting. She also spent time in Boston, again studying installation principles at the museums there. The September 1911 letters to Rea provide the evidence of what she was learning in the northern museums and how she then applied that knowledge to her work in Charleston. She believed that Dr. Lucas, of the American Museum, had the best theories and that the institution was "already showing the mark of his hand." She found another director's explanation, regarding museum principles as best illustrated by practical examples, good and enlightening. Given her future preservation efforts, it is noteworthy that in 1911 she asked Rea to recommend some museums for her to visit in Salem, and he also suggested that she visit some of the historic houses and rooms in the area. He thought that since the Peabody Museum was similar to the Charleston Museum, it would "provide a good example of what can be accomplished on a small amount of money."[43]

Bragg had planned to visit the mountains of North and South Carolina to study the flora of the region after returning from vacation in late August. However, a severe hurricane struck Charleston on 28 August. Two people were killed, and property losses exceeded $1 million.[44]

Bragg returned to Charleston on the same Clyde steamer, the *Arapahoe,* that had brought her to the city in 1909. While the trip down the coast was "slow and squally, it was not particularly rough. Charleston truly presented a pitiful appearance but already begins to look more normal," she wrote Rea on 2 September, just days after the hurricane had hit the city. Rea was still camping with his family in New Hampshire, and she suggested, "Confidentially, my opinion is that the best thing you can do is to keep away and let people forget there is a museum until their own roofs are covered."[45]

The museum building suffered comparatively little damage, though it sprang a leak in its tin roof and several windows were blown in, with water damaging the case that held the elk exhibit. Fortunately, one of the museum's workers had braved the storm to come to the building and had covered everything with tarpaulins. Miraculously, no damage was done by water to the other exhibits. The roof, however, required extensive repairs.[46]

Astutely, Bragg was quick to point out to Rea that the "loss is really not so terrific and in another month no one will feel so poor as at present. Just lie low until things quiet down. Then you may find money as easy as ever."[47] Bragg, a northerner, had experienced the effects of her first hurricane, and yet she intuitively understood the cause and effects of hurricanes and money. And the museum was always to need money—for the building, for books, for the installation of exhibits, and for many other reasons.

The Museum's Natural History Society had grown to nearly one hundred members and now carried on a large part of the educational work of the public instruction department. Bragg was so busy that in her letter to her father written just before Christmas Day in 1911 she did not mention the holiday or even missing her father or her home: "I must get to the museum and prepare four nature study lessons suitable for first grade children. I have to give a lecture this afternoon before a teachers' association. My work is launching out so fast that I can hardly keep up with it. Now I am deep in report statistics. Every week is so full of the extra things, meetings, lectures, etc." Although the Natural History Society consumed most of her time that fall, she was also invited to give monthly talks on nature work to the Association of First Grade Teachers. Her theme was how to adapt lessons written by northern publishers to southern conditions.[48]

In the first few months of 1912 Bragg's work overwhelmed her, and she became so unwell that her physician believed she would break down completely unless she took a three- or four-month vacation. She continued to be so ill that in March 1912 she seriously considered resigning her position at the Museum. She wrote Rea that Dr. Maybank had allowed her to work at home a few hours each day, which she had devoted to the schoolwork, but she wanted to return to the museum, "to try it once more."[49]

Returning to the Museum after six months of part-time work, she began preparation for what she thought would be her life's work. Bragg wrote her father that she was "carrying much work which required much preparation. I have had to study very hard. . . Then I am ambitious and have strained every nerve to prepare myself for the botany work of the summer." Bragg's ambitions were driving her. Her intent was to be known as the botanist of the coastal regions. Her father heard of her drive and her goals—she told him that she intended to make a name for herself, if she lived long enough. She knew the only way to make that name was to publish, and she knew the next step was to travel through South Carolina, where she would "have the valley and mountain flora both available." Her plans for tramping through the mountains included taking Barbara, her sister, and a friend whom she had met during her first year in Charleston.[50]

Whether or not this or any of her illnesses was psychosomatic, Bragg was driven—and fearless it would seem. She pushed on with her life's work that summer of 1912, which took her far away from her father. She seemed sad when she wrote him: "I wish I were coming home. Sometimes I get very discouraged and feel that I just must come home and stay with you and mother and I may suddenly decide to do so even yet. But I feel I just must do this botany work if I am to accomplish my life work."[51]

Bragg let Rea know that she planned to spend two weeks "lost to civilization. I really cannot tell where I shall be as my tramping trip may lead me anywhere. I expect to go to Caesar's Head, sometime but shall leave destinations to be decided from day to day." After being gone for a month she wrote Rea again, "I have had a very successful two weeks at Caesar's Head. Do not know that I have made many important records but I have at least done what has not been done before for *South Carolina*." She also wrote her father at the same time: "full of new experiences and of infinite value in my botanical work. I intend to make a name for myself in this line . . . I confess I am so lonely up here that I can scarcely make myself stay. There are friends east, west, north and south wanting me but I feel that the botany places me here, so I am trying to stand it. I did not know before that I was so dependent."[52]

Bragg continued to tramp the woods for ferns and other botanical specimens throughout most of the decade. She went to Summerville, where she found plants and habitats that she had never seen before, and she spent weeks at the Heyward plantation, Wappoola, on the Cooper River. She wrote Rea that she hoped to do for the Cooper River plant life what had been done for other regional locales by earlier botanists. So sure of her work and its appeal, she wrote a New York publishing company proposing a field book on southern flora.[53]

Barbara had accompanied her sister on this tramp. Barbara's paycheck was forwarded by Rea's secretary, Amy Woods, who let Barbara know that she understood how it felt to live in Charleston: "I did not dare to breath[e] the fact that I am a suffragist while I was in Charleston. It is bad enough to have to admit to being a Yankee." Admitting that one was a Yankee stirred negative emotions for many southerners who were still carrying on the cause of the Civil War and who also recalled Radical Reconstruction as the worst period in the state's history. Also in 1912 Barbara, Amy, and Bragg all found Charleston to be a place where equality for women was not openly discussed. By this time southern women had embraced volunteerism and many Charleston women belonged to clubs, such as the Civic Club (which Bragg had joined in 1910, soon after coming to the city). However, few southern women had moved into the public sphere by embracing suffrage.[54]

The Museum had expanded the services it provided to the public schools. Bragg's report in the December 1912 Museum *Bulletin* outlined the twelve types of assistance given to both public and private schools of the county. These included a lecturer and lecture room, a guide to the general collections of the museum, a reading room, field trips, copies of the Charleston nature study course (written by Bragg), and twenty-five school exhibits, each packed in an attractive portable wooden case. The subjects included animal exhibits, such as a "southern fox squirrel, brown rat, lion cub, . . . beach specimens showing the types of the animal and plant life of the Isle of Palms; picture exhibits; and the iron and steel exhibit."[55]

This iron and steel exhibit, containing maps of iron ore deposits along with photographs and specimens that illustrated the mining, transportation, and manufacturing of iron and steel, was first demonstrated by Rea at the State Rural School Improvement meeting in December 1907. Charleston teachers were instructed to apply to the director for its use. With Rea often absent from the Museum and not available to work with the schools, it is not surprising that few teachers used the exhibit. In the following year it was used only once at Memminger (which was then both a high school and a normal school for training teachers). In his 1909 letter to Museum members, before Bragg was hired, Rea had called for more circulating school exhibits to be made available. (This one exhibit about the steel and iron industry continued to be used at the high school level through 1913.)[56]

Once she was hired, Bragg took Rea's one unimaginative exhibit of loose items and improved upon it in several innovative ways. In addition to increasing the number of exhibits, she added a story for teachers to read to the students, and she sent the exhibits out on a circulating basis, rather than waiting for requests. But Bragg's invention of the portable suitcase for the school exhibits was inspired. It meant that more of the exhibits could be shipped and with greater ease. The exhibits were in green wooden boxes with handles and hinged doors. When opened they displayed staged scenes that helped children understand wildlife within their habitats or the people, customs, and backgrounds of other cultures and countries.[57]

Predictably, these traveling exhibits became a frequent instructional tool in the first-grade classes of the local schools. In 1913 A. B. Rhett, superintendent of Charleston public schools, wrote to Bragg, in reply to her request for information, that the exhibits were used along with her nature study course by 1,750 students in twenty-eight classes in the "White Schools with a rather constant amount of regularity"; however, in "the Colored Schools not so much use was made of them on the whole." At least one black student, Grace Dobbins, clearly recalled the exhibits more than eighty years after seeing them at Simonton, an overcrowded black school: "The exhibits came on a weekly basis. The opened suitcase would sit on the teacher's desk while she read us the story. . . . If there was an animal inside [of the exhibit], we would touch it."[58]

The astonishing fact is that boxes went to all schools, both black and white, in the city. Providing the same educational services to both black and white children during this era was both fearless and brazen. Just as her father had been a missionary in Mississippi, Bragg was a self-professed social reformer who was intent upon providing educational opportunities to all. But her actions flew in the face of social conventions of the time. Not only was she offering an innovative teaching technique in a poorly organized school system, she was also offering a sense of parity, regardless of skin color.

William Link identified South Carolina as one of three southern states (the others were Alabama and Mississippi) whose educational officials were weakest in modernizing the system in the early 1900s. Even South Carolina's education superintendent in 1900 understood this, writing in his annual report, "It is a misnomer to say that we have a system of public schools. In the actual working of the great majority of the schools in the state, there is no system, no orderly organization. . . . Each District has as poor schools as its people will tolerate—and in some Districts anything will be tolerated." And by 1911 county and state supervision had just begun for white schools, while the custom of state supervisors was to shut their eyes to the miserable conditions in the black schools.[59]

In South Carolina support for public education was almost nonexistent for whites and even scarcer for blacks. The state government had been under pressure since 1877 to reduce educational expenses, especially in black schools. Education was distrusted by whites for several reasons: "it was begun by the Radical Reconstruction government; it implied racial equality; and it might 'spoil' good Negro field hands and improve [their] political potential." By 1895 the systematic financial starvation of the black schools was apparent in the superintendent's annual reports. For example, the state had raised expenditures per white student to $3.11 at the same time that it reduced expenditures for blacks to $1.05 per student. By 1915 "the ratio of expenditures for the schooling of white and black children was about twelve dollars to one." And by 1920, though well over half of the state's students were black, only 11 percent of the state's education money was spent on them—$26.08 for each white student and $3.04 for each black student.[60]

With access to a quality education denied by whites, most blacks understood that they would be laborers, domestics, or custodians—all jobs not far removed from the antebellum plantation days of slavery. Fearing the possible consequences of an educated black citizenry, whites had enacted laws and supported customs that denied blacks an education. Once slaves were freed, and for nearly a half-century after Reconstruction, whites still feared educated blacks. So white supremacists, in South Carolina and across the South, continued to prevent access to equal educational opportunities, understanding that knowledge would have provided an escape from the servitude under which many blacks still lived. Schooling was the key to the maintenance of the white race's dominance over blacks. As with all other institutions of power, blacks were not permitted active participation in the educational system once the state's 1895 constitution was ratified. While education offered the poor white masses deliverance from apathy and ignorance, whites wanted to ensure that blacks did not share equally in the educational system. It should be noted that South Carolina did not entirely neglect black schooling, but educational inequality was institutionalized long before World War I.[61]

Unwilling to alleviate the imbalance between the races by spending more money on the black schools, the all-white Charleston city school board forced black students to attend school part-time or in double sessions. (This practice continued until the 1950s.) The city finally built a vocational school (Colored Industrial School, later called Burke) for blacks in 1910, but there were only eight grades. It became a high school in 1924 but did not grant state diplomas until 1929. Whenever local taxes were increased during Mayor John Grace's first term (1911–1915), white schools were remodeled and upgraded while little was done to improve the black schools.[62]

With this imbalanced financial support from both state and local governments came vast inequalities in schooling between the races. Black schools were overcrowded and underfinanced. Black students attended school for a shorter term, left school at an earlier age, and usually attended classes in primitive one-room buildings. Typically, each black teacher taught sixty students a year, while a white counterpart taught fewer than forty. Salaries were also inequitable, with white teachers receiving more than double the pay of black educators. Also, by law only white teachers could teach in city schools, and black teachers were forced out into county schools. This changed when the Charleston chapter of the National Association for the Advancement of Colored People (NAACP) formed in 1917.[63]

The membership gathered nearly five thousand signatures on a petition asking for the employment of black teachers in the city's black schools, which was presented to the South Carolina General Assembly in 1919. Paradoxically, Mayor Grace supported their cause, pointing out that "blacks paid their taxes and contributed to the wealth of the community." The petition was successful, as state legislators outlawed white teachers in the city's black schools. This decision did not affect the museum's provision of educational services to black schools. A decade later Bragg wrote to the chairman of the trustees of the Eastman Art Gallery in Laurel, Mississippi: "At that time with white teachers in the colored schools naturally no discrimination was made. Exhibits went to all alike. Later colored teachers replaced white. Naturally we continued to send the exhibits as we had done before."[64]

The result of blatant discrimination was an astounding illiteracy rate for black South Carolinians. From 1880 through 1930 the illiteracy rate for blacks across the country declined from 17 percent to about 4 percent. At the same time the state's average also declined from 55 percent to about 15 percent. But that rate for 1880 in South Carolina included more than 78 percent black illiterates, which declined to almost 27 percent by 1930. Without money, education, or training blacks could not expect to participate in the city's social and political institutions. State funding to black schools slowly increased over time (though not at the same rate as funding for white schools). However, agencies other than the public school system contributed to the decline in the number of illiterates. These included northern philanthropic organizations, such as the Rosenwald Fund and the General Education Board, and private black schools, such as Charleston's Avery Institute, which was operated by the American Missionary Board. Because the exhibit boxes were provided to both black and white students, they offered black students at Avery and other black schools a cultural parity that existed nowhere else in the city.[65]

Bragg's third year at the Museum proved pivotal. She had survived an illness—probably a nervous breakdown—and had accomplished what no one else had in her botanical work for the state. Additionally, she had greatly expanded the work of the Museum's public instruction department from one circulating exhibit to twenty-five. Bragg expressed her hope for the new year in the Museum *Bulletin:* "to reach the large numbers who are just coming to realize the advantages which accrue to them through cooperation with the Museum."[66]

At age thirty-one Bragg was fast becoming a mentor to some of the young boys who had assisted in the move from the college. One of "her boys" (as she called them), Ned Hyer, who was also a member of the Natural History Society, approached her about the Museum's support in attending taxidermy school. She wrote Rea: "it might be worth our while to develop this boy. He seems to me fitted for just such work if he can acquire the artistic knowledge as well as the mechanical."[67] This experience proved to be indicative of her ability to draw the best, not only from herself, but also from others. Bragg had found her sense of self, and she had enough confidence in her ability to assess people and also in her relationship with Rea to write him this letter, knowing that he would trust her judgment.

Bragg continued to push herself at the Museum throughout the winter and into the spring of 1913. By the time of her vacation, when she reached New York City on her way home to Epping, she became seriously ill with what she described as throbbing pains all over and was also unable to walk. Her mother came down from New Hampshire to sit by her hospital bed, and her physician was concerned enough over her condition to write Rea, who was on his vacation: "Her illness has been so serious that she should not return to her work for some weeks, and I am writing to ask if she may be released from her duties for about two months. . . . At present she is sitting up in a wheelchair for a few hours each day, but has not been allowed to walk." Rea agreed to Doctor Littell's request but pointed out that after 15 October, "it will be a difficult matter to carry the work without her presence and if she is able to work only a part of the time I should prefer to have her in Charleston then."[68]

Possibly due to her childhood illnesses, Bragg always got a lot of attention when she was sick. One of her good friends from Charleston, Hester Gaillard, a stenographer, had learned of her illness and traveled north to be with her in the hospital. Her other friends in Charleston were so concerned that one of them, Isabelle "Belle" Bowen Heyward, who was later to become her companion for more than ten years, sent a series of notes to St. John's Infirmary, one of which said: "I miss my companion of last year! I am thinking of you constantly. My love to you always I. B. H."[69]

Bragg left the hospital in New York and went home to her father and family in Epping for her recuperation. Her sister, Barbara, helped her walk a few steps in the yard every day, and she continued to gain strength and weight. But Barbara warned Rea, "I doubt if she is able to do anything very strenuous for a number of weeks especially anything that requires physical exertion." Bragg returned to Charleston and the Museum in late September, just as Rea had asked, working two to four hours a day and "planning the winter's work with her accustomed enthusiasm."[70]

Bragg was living next door to Hester, in the Pringle house at 24 Church Street, when Hester became ill that October. Now it was Bragg's turn to nurse her friend. "I think that all the people I love best are unhappy this year, and I have my own troubles as well," she wrote her father. Yet Bragg was also concerned about her father, who no longer had an assigned congregation and thought he was at the end of his usefulness as a minister. She was so concerned about her father's spirits that she asked him not to "ever think again some of the things you have just written me." There is an intimation in this letter to her father that Bragg may have contemplated suicide at some point because she writes of "longing for the release that the Lord has for each person when their time comes." And she seems to have resolved that the reason she was on earth was "for the good that I can do, not for the happiness I can get. I have missed what seems to me the greatest thing in life and am only just learning not to be bitter over it. I have not your great faith but I have something which helps me and I hope I may fight as good a fight as you have done." Bragg had just celebrated her thirty-second birthday when she wrote this letter to her father. Seemingly each year her physical health would deteriorate after many months of hard work and then would rebound after several months of mental rest.[71]

There are indications throughout the family letters that each family member may have suffered from some degree of depression. Bragg's mother wrote her that Reverend Bragg would have had a happier, more successful life if she had not married him and that she was tormented by her realization that she had failed him and his children—referring to them as his, not theirs. She also wrote Bragg that she [Laura] would have had a better heritage if she had had a different mother. Both her brother, Ernest, and sister, Barbara, seemed to share the family's mental illness. For example, Bragg wrote several letters to her father about Barbara's mental state, calling her "unbalanced," with a mental attitude. Ernest once wrote to Bragg: "If you have come to that place where life . . . means little, where the days seem like an endless grinding routine . . . , then you and I are in the same boat on a river whose current flows out of a hereditary past."[72]

Bragg had moved into a room in Hester Gaillard's house next door at 22 Church Street in the fall of 1913, and Hester took her to see the Edison talking pictures that had come to Charleston. She found them to be remarkable and was enthralled to see the actors "talking and singing as if alive." Her thoughts centered on her work and on helping Hester grow fit and happy again. Bragg was thankful that her family had pulled her through her last illness. She was strong, both physically and mentally, it would now seem. She wrote her father: "It is indeed good to be well. Everyone has been so kind."[73]

Her relationship with Hester and then the one with Belle were known as romantic friendships, also called "Boston marriages" by feminist historians. Commonplace in New England during the nineteenth and early twentieth centuries, one of the partners was more active and public while the other was more retiring. Late in life Bragg named Belle a lesbian and recalled that "lots of women were lesbians when I came to Charleston. It was all very innocent. I had at least five friends who were. . . . There was just a shortage of men and it was as though the women were married."[74] Whether their relationships were in the North or in the South, these women were loving companions and partners to each other.

Lillian Faderman's study determined that one of the most outstanding facts about women who live by their brains, such as Bragg, was friendship, "profound friendships that extended through every phase and aspect of a woman's life." These relationships were with long-term partners who shared duties and with whom their emotional, physical, and financial resources were pooled. Romantic friendships offered women an alternative to being married without replicating their mothers' domestic roles. Their battle to be autonomous was twofold: the struggle to stay single and to separate from the family sphere.[75]

Many ambitious women who were driven to succeed would not submerge their "egos as required by heterosexual marriages." Thus their long-term partners were other women, and to all intents they were married, as they pooled their resources in these relationships. Such arrangements offered a woman "companionship, nurturance, a communion of kindred spirits, romance (and undoubtedly, in some but not all relationships, sex)— all the advantages of having a significant other in one's life and none of the burdens that were concomitant with heterosexuality." Bragg thought she had found in her relationship with Hester a mate who offered her a nurturing home where she could be safe and secure. Hester, after all, had rushed to New York City to sit by her bedside as she lay ill. Now, living with her, Bragg surely believed that kind of support would continue as she worked at the Museum.[76]

Rea had heeded her suggestion about "her boy" Ned Hyer, sending him to study taxidermy in New York. Ned started the new year of 1914 with a letter to Bragg. Fortunately, Ned received a reply, though she asked that he excuse her typewritten letter as she said she was too busy to write. As time passed and her responsibilities increased at the Museum, she would lament to her father and later to friends that she never had time to write personal letters though she loved to receive them. "This was written so far nearly a week ago. Writing seems a hopeless piece of work with me." What was hopeless was finding time for personal letters. But she was writing— all of the Museum's publications.[77]

Bragg asked Ned to tell her in his next letter about all the interesting work he was doing, and she gently reminded him of her expectations. When she traveled north that summer she expected that he would have a lot of work to show her. And when he returned home Ned gave a lecture and exhibition at the Museum with the local paper headlining the report "A Brilliant Sculptor, Mr Edward Hyer Does Brilliant Work in Modeling Animal Forms." For her, mentoring meant both responsibilities on her part and results on the part of the protégé.[78]

Bragg was attending an Episcopal church, but it was not Rea's St. Michael's. Her friends, including Hester, attended St. Luke's, where the minister had spent some time talking with Bragg about the faith of the Methodist and Episcopal churches. When her father sent her religious books, she would share them with the rector. The minister wanted her to be confirmed in 1914, but she was unsure. Bragg's constant search for knowledge and understanding had led to an examination of her own faith. This type of examination has been recognized as an important part of achieving intellectual independence. Consequently, Bragg did not believe there was conclusive evidence of Christ's birth to determine the divine nature of Jesus. She wrote her father, "If Mr. Wood will confirm me with this belief, I wish to be, but I cannot go further."[79]

Bragg was so pleased with her work at the Museum and her life in Charleston that she wrote in the Simmons College alumnae newsletter in May 1914: "Charleston is the best place on earth. Boston is dead slow compared with it. . . . I would like to know who else in our class has anything so fascinating as I have . . . to take a launch trip nearly every week to some fascinating place . . . of teaching something about all the birds and plants we see . . . learning oceans of new things yourself. . . . The collecting . . . takes me to the loveliest old places, old plantation houses that you would love to see, and among some of the quaintest and most delightful old-time people."[80] It would seem that Charleston had supplanted Boston in Bragg's mind. Could her happiness have resulted from the fact that she was now involved with activities she loved—teaching and learning—that she had a partner, and that she was now involved with some of those quaint and delightful old-time people?

As much as she was working at the Museum, it seemed to Bragg that her friend Hester was working even harder as a stenographer. Bragg told her father in a letter that Hester was "unhappy over business trouble." Bragg knew that she could only help Hester "by keeping busy with my own interests and just being ready for her when she comes from work. It is terrible to have her work so—she is never home until ten at night." Hester's brother died soon after Bragg moved in with her, and Bragg was distressed for her friend: "my heart bleeds for her. I wish I could bear some of the burdens. They are heavy."[81] Now their roles were reversed, with Bragg as the supporter and Hester as the center of attention.

Life was good, but Bragg was still ready to go home for the summer, writing, "I'll be so glad to get home, Dadda. I'm tired." She was also anxious to visit the family's summer cottage at Hedding and the Methodist camp meeting grounds at Epping. She had decided that she would rest first and then visit museums later. The staff at the Museum had been concerned that Rea would take the directorship at Brooklyn and she would go with him. Both refused the offer and decided to stay in Charleston "to accomplish good results" and "the big thing we have dreamed of," she reminded Rea that summer of 1914.[82]

Bragg's summer vacation was full. She visited the Children's Museum, the Art Museum, and the Gray Herbarium in Boston, and she studied installation procedures at the National Museum and visited the Zoological Gardens in Washington. She found this time an inspiration, "both for my work and my intellectual life. The beautiful pictures I saw gave me great pleasure. Then the Morgan collection opened my eyes to a realization of the life of the Middle Ages in Europe and made history clearer. The Rodin statues at the Metropolitan delighted me."[83]

Vacation at her father's camp at Hedding was relaxing, even to "my dignity," which throughout her life remained cool, controlling, and aloof. Here she spent time out-of-doors, analyzing plants continuously and visiting with her paternal grandmother, whom she admired. After her death Bragg wrote her father: "To be her granddaughter is a good inheritance." On this particular visit she and her father enjoyed his new telescope, making observations of the heavens: "Jupiter looked about the size of the moon when full. And its satellites could be distinctly seen." While Bragg's vacations with her family were consumed with activities with her father, a niece who visited the Bragg household during those summers recalled the family as "rather austere and not close." Bragg, the fair-haired child, gloried in the attention of her father, and the rest of the world drifted around them and their activities.[84]

Ned's success in taxidermy school placed Bragg in an advantageous position with Rea. He began to defer even more to her judgment and treated her as his equal during this period. After one of their conferences Rea wrote a supportive response to her many requests, and he asked her opinion about various subjects. The letters written by both of them during this time are friendly, collegial, and even playful. The respect that Rea gave her in agreeing with her about exhibits and the purchasing of items for the Museum indicated a comradeship that had grown over time.[85]

By the end of 1914 the Museum's Department of Public Instruction under Bragg's leadership had created sixty-three traveling school exhibits.

Her work at the Museum continued to include teaching nature study courses for first-, second-, and third-grade public school teachers. The natural history exhibits were regularly used in the elementary grades, while the industrial exhibits were in use in the sixth and seventh grades. There were even some public schools where the principals used the exhibits in all the grades, and fourteen private schools in the city borrowed them.[86]

What Bragg had discovered about the exhibits was their drawing power. Bragg's intent was to reach more students and teachers. She accomplished this by sending the exhibits to the schools rather than waiting for requests, since this ultimately "thus indirectly through the interest aroused . . . attracts more children to the Museum," as she wrote in the Museum *Bulletin*. The popularity of the exhibits stretched from as far north as Georgetown to as far south as Beaufort, and soon a regular schedule was put into operation to handle the teachers' requests for the traveling school exhibits. With Bragg's lectures on a variety of subjects to entice them, eighteen teachers brought their classes to the Museum in 1915 to study special subjects.[87]

The Museum's work with the public schools had so impressed the Board of Public School Commissioners that they passed a special resolution on 26 January 1914 asking for further extension of the Museum's work with the city schools and seeking formal affiliation with the Museum.[88] Clearly, Bragg's work was being recognized as educational and useful by and for the powers within the school system.

A product of northern progressivism, Bragg saw herself first as a social missionary who recognized the ignorance and apathy of the population that resulted from political and social forces that controlled the city and state. The librarian/curator had become an accidental educator with her traveling school exhibits. She saw them as means of achieving education of the masses through the Museum's extension service. She was practicing social progressivism with its own brand of education. In time Bragg became a cultural missionary, reshaping the cultural and social landscape of Charleston through the Museum and her educational programs.

The South's slowness to adopt Progressive educational reform provided middle-and upper-class women with a theater for their activities. Thinking that the apathy and ignorance of a rural population were obstacles to social reform, they believed the best technique of dealing with this was through mass education. Both in the North and in the South, Progressives had ties to business, manufacturing, and the professions; they usually came from the same social class; and they were centered in cities and towns. There were two other concerns that made the southern brand of progressivism unique: the extreme poverty of the region and the rural disbursement of the population. It is important to understand that while southern men who were reformers could be aggressive in their actions, southern women, or even northern women such as Bragg, who called themselves Progressives had to confront the narrow viewpoints that defined their lives. Such views served as an impediment to entering public life and also caused southern women to tread cautiously around racial issues.[89] At the time neither issue seemed to present a major problem for Bragg, however.

As a result of these barriers, reforming education across the South took a different route than in the urban North. In the South education was distinctive because the basic unit of administration remained the local school district, which controlled all facets of education with little adherence to research, standards, or systematic management. For example, in Kentucky there were eight thousand school districts, all located in rural towns. In Charleston, South Carolina, there were twenty-two school districts with 104 elementary schools, and most of those were in the rural part of the county. Progressives saw towns and their services as modernizing influences that would extend Progressive values into the rural populations. For southern reformers there was an additional goal to reduce local control over schools by increasing state and county supervision. This was best accomplished by the consolidated school. Bragg understood the importance of creating a desire for this organizational structure in such a rural state and county. Writing the state superintendent of education in 1928, she claimed, "These exhibits are particularly important for the smaller isolated schools where the teacher has few helps. In Charleston County they have proved an important factor in creating the desire for consolidated schools and better equipment."[90]

An educational historian, Lawrence Cremin, has written in his *Transformation of the School: Progressivism in American Education, 1876–1957* that Progressive reformers, such as John Dewey, sought to "democratize intellectual culture to the point where it could be made available to all." Bragg's goals meshed with those of Dewey, who was one of the most important figures in Progressive educational reform. Dewey believed that the end of education was growth, which was part of a democratic society. He looked to the schools as means of preserving and promoting democracy within the new social order for which Progressives were working. School was a "form of community life in which all those agencies are concentrated that will be most effective in bringing the child to share in the inherited resources of the race, and to use his own powers for social ends." Serving as an agent of socialization, the school and its teachers prepared the student for life by providing instruction in responsible political behavior and training in vocational skills.[91]

What Bragg saw and experienced in her dealings with the community was a poor school system. She also knew that many of the teachers were graduates of the state's normal schools, with little pedagogical training. Because the professionalization of education came later to the South than to the North, educational reform presented women without college degrees in education an avenue to practice their reform activities unhampered by those who were more highly trained. Due to the rural nature of the South, Progressives had to "engage in extension activity or be doomed to insignificance." Such activity provided reform-minded women with an extensive sphere of activity and influence.[92]

Bragg was such a woman. She was a college graduate with a degree in library science, and she was one of fewer than fifty thousand women in the country with college diplomas in 1909 when she arrived in Charleston. In South Carolina she could do social missionary work by practicing educational reform through the Museum and its extension activity of the traveling school exhibits. Her educational program was the first of its kind in the South. The work with the traveling school exhibits offered both students and teachers a window on the world beyond the city, town, or crossroads in which they lived. Not only were teachers and students seeing the world, but the world outside of Charleston was also finally coming to the city.[93]

Women across the country were demanding the right to vote, and some were calling for even more radical reforms, claiming that women were the equal of men and deserved to be treated comparably. But Bragg had not given much thought to suffrage and equality. Brought up by a father who nurtured her intellect and encouraged her ambitions, Bragg understood the idea of equality and said in an interview late in life that she expected that it would come in time. This radical upbringing was influenced by her father's association with Dr. Anna Shaw, who had been at Boston University when he was in seminary. Shaw later became the leader of the National American Woman Suffrage Association.[94]

In the summer of 1914 Bragg met a friend of her family in Boston. Abbie Holmes Christensen, a northern suffragist and educator, was married to a plantation owner in Beaufort, South Carolina, where she had founded a school for blacks called the Shanklin School. It was her conversation about equal suffrage that impressed Bragg, who wrote Abbie before Christmas: "I now see the truth of the need for equal suffrage." Abbie replied, "Thank heavens, suffrage workers have multiplied in these later years, and the cause advances, tho slowly." Then in February 1915 Bragg heard Lila Meade Valentine, a suffragist leader from Richmond, whose speech "fairly converted the city. Such enthusiasm, wonderful fascinating personality," as Bragg noted on the reverse of the program she saved.[95]

Founded in response to Valentine's speech, the Equal Suffrage League of Charleston was established in 1915, and its first president was Susan Pringle Frost, a local realtor and a true daughter of the Old South. Her roots went back to the founding of the state in 1670, but her family's wealth had disappeared in the Civil War. Educated as a secretary at St. Mary's College in Raleigh, North Carolina, she had returned to her home in 1891 and worked, unpaid, in a Broad Street law office until the South Carolina Interstate and West Indian Exposition of 1901. She then became the personal secretary to the exposition's director, and it was this experience that gave Sue Frost a wider vision of the world.[96]

An active clubwoman, Frost was a southern New Woman who joined with other Progressive Charleston women such as the Poppenheim sisters to alter the cityscape in various areas: the arts, politics, education, and finally preservation. Thus while Bragg, the northern New Woman, was not alone in her efforts to change the city, she was very different from these southern New Women of Charleston. Sue Frost, Louisa Poppenheim, and Christine Poppenheim had all left the state to attend college (the Poppenheims were graduates of Vassar). But they had returned home to where their families had power and position as well as some wealth, or at least the memory of it. Bragg had none of those when she moved to Charleston, and though she sought her family's shelter and comfort at times, she never returned home to live with them. Bragg was a woman who lived by her brains, making her own way and her own mark in the world.

Because Bragg was so different from the women in South Carolina, she serves as an example of New Women who were not of the southern variety. Southern women historians, such as Hall, assert that there has been a New Englandization of America's history and that the southern New Woman would not be described in the same way. Scott agrees with Hall, contending that the southern version of the New Woman still maintained the charm and graciousness that had been part of the southern ideal, both in her public and in her private life. The southern New Woman had not lost her femininity nor abandoned her responsibility for having children, as some could say about the New England New Woman. For while "the Southern girl may like to earn a little money. . . . the ideal in the back of her head is a nice house in the home town and a decorative position in society." That was not, nor had it ever been, Bragg's ideal. With her reformer zeal as a cultural missionary and with her deafness as a handicap, Bragg was a different type of New Woman in the South.[97]

In the South the involvement of New Women in the suffrage movement had greatly enlarged the political life of southern women and had encouraged their involvement in other social and political reforms. Through organizations and clubs they established libraries, expanded schools, investigated labor conditions, secured the passage of child labor

laws, organized settlement houses, and even worked for interracial cooperation. Many of those activities were engaged in by Frost and the Poppenheim sisters. Even with all their activity in the public sphere, Scott found
that southern women understood that to secure a hearing before the men
in power it was necessary to maintain the demure demeanor that southern
men expected of southern ladies, if only for the sake of appearance.[98]

The image of the southern lady as gracious, charming, deferential, and
submissive to men had survived intact and remained relatively unchanged
since the Civil War. The acceptable calling for the proper southern lady was
to be a man's wife and to pass her time engaged in church, club, or social
work. Elite white women still lived a fairly sheltered life, and if they
worked outside the home, social mores dictated that they should not be
alone on city streets after sunset. Sue Frost's family was incensed that she
opened a real estate office on Broad Street, where office buildings contained no rest-room facilities for women.[99] By the time Frost opened her
office, Bragg had wandered the streets of Boston as a college student, lived
alone on an isolated Maine island, and moved to a southern town where
she knew no one. If Sue Frost, a daughter of the Old South, was an embar-
rassment, how did the social and power elite view Bragg?

Bragg knew the two other Frost sisters, Rebecca (Rebe) and Mary,
who were schoolteachers through her educational program. She had first
met Rebe, who came to the Museum, before becoming friendly with
Mary and Sue. Bragg enjoyed visiting in their Logan Street home on Fri-
day nights. These three, along with Bragg and other Charleston women,
were all part of the same social group. When Sue bought a house on the
Isle of Palms, called The Ranch, Bragg was invited out with a group of
friends for dances at the Pavilion, where they would sleep over before
returning to the city.[100]

Bragg did join the Suffrage League, probably because of her devotion
to another suffragist, Anita Pollitzer, who later became a leader of the
National Woman's Party. Interviewed in 1974 about South Carolina's suffrage efforts, Bragg recalled that she just naturally joined because her
friends were in the league. Tellingly, she confessed that she was not much
of a joiner: "I'm more apt to create something than join something created
by somebody else." Bragg also remembered that league meetings were "just
a group of ladies . . . [whose] activity was mostly through oral talk . . . eternal talk." Bragg did not agree with Sue "because she was violent for . . . suffrage." The Charleston league eventually split over "whether to be militant
with Alice Paul [whom Sue Frost supported], or to be evolutionary with
Carrie Chapman Catt." Bragg and Sue then drifted apart, though after
World War I they shared an interest in preservation efforts.[101]

Bragg's personal life also changed in February 1915. Even though she assured her father that she had remained friends with Hester Gaillard, Bragg moved into Belle Heyward's home at 7 Gibbes Street. Belle was the other friend who had written Bragg during her illness in the summer of 1913. Just as Hester and she had enjoyed a romantic friendship, Belle was also dear to Bragg. One Charlestonian, Francis Brenner, whose mother was a close friend of both women, recalled, "I don't think Aunt Belle had anybody else as close as Aunt Laura."[102]

There were several reasons why Bragg chose to leave Hester and join Belle's household. Hester's dairy had gone into bankruptcy, and her troubles created an atmosphere in her home that was in marked contrast to that of the Heyward house. In Hester's house she had one room, while at 7 Gibbes Street, Bragg had more space with two rooms, "making the whole of the third floor. I have a sitting room of my own at last." Brenner was sure the rooms were fixed for "Aunt Laura." He recalled that though "she was not a demanding woman, she was very sharp, [and] knew how to get anything she wanted out of anybody . . . it did not make any difference who they were . . . she could maneuver around [anyone]."[103]

Unlike Hester, Belle did not have to work, and Bragg wrote: "People are always laughing at things here. It is the happiest household I have ever lived in." Bragg's letters to "Dadda dearest" were filled with Belle and all that she did for her: "Belle has made me one of the family and I am more comfortably situated than I have ever before been. . . . Belle has nursed me as devotedly as a professional could [she had been sick in bed again for a week] and as lovingly as a very dear friend, which she is."[104]

Belle Heyward offered Bragg residence in a house filled with silver from both the Heywards and the Bowens, which was indicative of the family's past wealth. "In Charleston birth is looked upon not as a beginning but as a continuation," and Belle's family lineage reached back into colonial times and those of the planter aristocracy. They were "the descendants of King's officers, Lords Proprietors [the English owners of the South Carolina colony], a Signer of the Declaration of Independence and Confederate officers." Bragg's association with Belle introduced her to a new world of social contacts that would ultimately benefit her both professionally and personally.[105]

For Bragg, 1915 proved to be a pivotal year professionally as well as personally. The Museum became incorporated, with a board of trustees, that year. Rea considered the incorporation "a long and difficult piece of work but one absolutely necessary for the permanent growth of the Museum." Bragg's salary remained the same at $840 a year, as it had been for two years. Rea, on the other hand, received a 50 percent raise, from $1,200 to $1,800.[106]

With incorporation, the Museum became a municipal institution. The emphasis was now on an educational function, which brought with it social implications. Initially founded by the planter aristocracy in 1773, the Museum's patrons had been the educated upper class of the city. While Charleston had been slow at first to embrace Jim Crow, the Museum's 1915 charter of incorporation left little doubt as to the white politicians' intent where the "colored problem" was concerned. The Museum and its use were now specifically granted for the white citizens of Charleston, and if the trustees failed to adhere to the stipulations, management of the Museum was to revert to the college.[107] As with many other covenants, this clause was never enforced, due to the prevailing political climate.

After incorporation the Charleston Museum had to reach into the community to find new patrons, first in the different social classes and finally among the black citizens. In May 1915 the local paper brought Bragg and her Department of Public Instruction to the public consciousness, reporting that she was the "director of a university" at the Museum where four thousand students participated in the educational programs she had designed. The work was "offered to all boys and girls from the first grade ... through the college preparatory or high schools in the white and negro schools." By this time the city school board commissioners required that each teacher in the primary grades use Bragg's southern nature study curriculum, which had been matched to the traveling school exhibits. She was also teaching summer school for teachers at the Museum, and her course topics included home geography, nature study, and local history. Bragg had arranged for the teachers in attendance to earn college or normal school credits for the course.[108]

As usual, Bragg spent the summer in New Hampshire with her family at their cottage at Hedding, studying museums and botany. In New York she visited the Children's Museum and libraries. She took two botanical trips and studied the American aborigines at the American Museum in preparation for an installation being planned by the Museum. On her way back to Charleston she stopped in Philadelphia, Washington, and Richmond, "searching diligently for new ideas."[109]

During her trip north Bragg also prepared a speech on the biological side of the "woman question," which she had been asked to present to the Thursday Club in Charleston. "Several clubs in the city are studying the problem of woman's place in the world, not only politically, but historically, socially, etc.," Bragg wrote Rea in a letter that was pointed and straightforward. She had read what was currently known about sexuality, and she believed that there was a benefit to having the "woman problem" discussed scientifically.[110] Her comments to Rea were based on her scientific, analytical, and dispassionate reading. That she was invited to give the lecture to other women is indicative of the respect others had for her intellect and also for her social position within the community. It is possibly also indicative of the female community's awareness that she had found her own answer to the "woman question."

As always, Bragg had read and continued to read widely on many subjects as well as on the question of sex. She was aware of the different theories of "the evolution of sex, biologically and socially. . . . The writers on sex seem to make an issue of the fundamental character of secondary sexual characters. The writers on the women's side are trying to prove an original equality of the sexes." But for her the burden of proof had to rest on the biological aspect of the question. Bragg's intent in her 24 August 1915 letter to Rea was to propose that the Natural History Society might study sex and its relation to heredity and eugenics. In her opinion, the intersection of the topics ought to make two interesting lectures, "treating of such evolution in the plant and animal world as high as man, and a second dealing with man alone." She believed that the topics were of great interest in Charleston because of the influence of Mrs. Robert Thomas, president of both the Century and Thursday Clubs and a force in the Suffrage League. Bragg called Thomas "an extreme [woman] advocating everything which favors woman's emancipation."[111]

Rea's brief response (less than one-half page) to the topic of the speech was that Bragg seemed to have her thoughts well organized. The remaining one and a half pages of his letter were devoted to what he needed to do and what he needed her to help him do. Claiming that he would have a difficult time in the fall, Rea did not think that he would have time to give the lectures himself and needed Bragg to prepare something. It was reported in the local paper that Bragg did give one lecture to the Natural History Society in October, which was called "The Evolution of Sex." She focused on the equality of the sexes and explained the theories and their biological bases.[112]

Bragg acknowledged sexuality more as a matter of science than of personal relevance—her partnership with Belle notwithstanding. Of her own sexuality, she said, "I am deeply tender, but I have never been much interested in sex." Bragg's paradoxical views allowed her to identify Belle as a lesbian (a woman who loved women) but not herself; she saw herself not as a woman at all, but as a *person*—a dominant, controlling person. Her unconscious denial of her own sexuality then and later in life contradicts her pattern of relationships. Bragg was supported by and nurtured, and loved and lived with women exclusively.[113]

Such equivocation was not atypical of women of Bragg's era who were involved on some level with other women. Noted educator M. Carey Thomas, president of Bryn Mawr College, spent her entire life loving women yet felt compelled to express negative attitudes about homosexuality later in life. Mary Woolley, president of Mount Holyoke College, lived with her partner Jeanette Marks in a committed relationship, what they called a "marriage," for more than fifty years. But in 1908, in an unpublished essay about the painfulness of romantic college friendships, Marks described love between women as "unpleasant," an abnormal condition, a sickness. Marks published an article on a similar topic in 1911, warning about the dangers of romantic friendships, and in 1926 considered writing "a book on homosexuality in literature, in which an emphasis would be on insanity and suicide associated with same-sex love." In a time and society characterized by repression of women's sexuality, Bragg may have simply chosen to ignore an examination of her own self and sexuality.[114]

The "woman problem" or "question" did involve romantic friendships, such as the one she enjoyed with Belle, but that was not part of "The Evolution of Sex." These types of relationships had been acceptable as long as they did not threaten the male hegemony. Eventually this climate would change in Charleston, just as it had in the rest of the country. Men came to see the New Woman as a threat because she challenged existing gender relations and the distribution of power. Drawing comfort and inspiration from other women, pioneering new roles, and insisting upon a rightful place within the genteel world, the New Woman came to be seen as physiologically unnatural because she rejected motherhood and men. Because of New Women's openness about sexual issues and morals as well as rejection of gender distinctions, middle-class men saw them as the ultimate symbols of social disorder and as unnatural. At around the turn of the century many Americans' fears about love between women began to surface as there was a sudden explosion of medical publications on perversions and sexual disorders—although not yet in Charleston.[115]

Bragg's birthday in October 1915 was made special by Belle: "My birthday was a most festive day. The family had presents on the breakfast table for me, . . . and a box of bookplates from Belle. . . . The bookplates are supposed to be most appropriate as suggesting the midnight candle I burn and my great wisdom. I insist the owl looks like Belle sagely advising me to go to sleep. Belle gave a little party for me in the evening and it was all very sweet. She does everything to make me happy that she can." Bragg was a member of Belle's family now. Instead of being the supporter, Bragg was the center of the household, as she had been as a child. Aristocratic Belle was Bragg's supporter, protector, and partner who provided Bragg with a warm, loving, and emotionally supportive home.[116]

In the fall of 1915 Bragg's main focus was her work with the Natural History Society and with the school extension program. There were now sixty-four different school exhibits, and she gave a speech to the State

Teachers' Association about the Museum's Department of Public Instruction. School Superintendent Rhett suggested to Bragg that she also speak to the meeting of the Association of Elementary Schools in Florence. There she gave teachers a description of the nature study exhibits—which included birds, animals, and plants—and the commercial exhibits—which included grains, fabric materials, minerals, and building stones.[117]

Her professional and personal life had settled into more of a routine by the following year. The days were full, and there were long lapses in time between letters to her "dear Dadda." Her rooms at Belle's had received some improvements, with new bookcases and two low tables that were built for her by the Museum's carpenters. With the bookcases she could display her books again, marked with the bookplates given by Belle for both her birthday and Valentine's Day.[118]

At the Museum, Bragg devised a plan for the history of man exhibit, illustrating the "development of civilization from the most primitive peoples through the Egyptians and Assyrians to modern times" and using large casts of Egyptian and Assyrian sculpture. She had the old exhibits cleaned and studied how to catalog them. The way she displayed them illustrated the Museum principle that exhibits should be made "to conform to the fundamental theory that it is the use rather than the mere preservation of the material [that] is important." Her time outside of her museum work was consumed by Belle, whose mother had died. Belle felt her mother's death "terribly."[119]

Bragg now included supplementary information from *National Geographic* or government bulletins in the school exhibits. Other items that would provide additional explanations about the subject were also part of the exhibit. Besides the nature scenes, there were now small stage sets of other countries, along with the industrial exhibits. As a member of the National Association of Audubon Societies, Bragg noticed their offer in 1916 to provide copies of Educational Bulletin No. 42 and wrote to them, "I could use [this bulletin] . . . most advantageously with our traveling exhibit of the Orchard Oriole." No doubt these additions were improvements, because by 1916 there were seventy-four traveling exhibits in continual use in the nine schools of the city and by the 146 teachers.[120]

The Charleston Museum employed a delivery wagon first and then a truck to take groups of exhibits to the city schools on a rotating circuit. Those used during the previous week would then be transferred to the next school on the list, continuing around the circuit. As each exhibit completed "the circuit of public schools it is returned to the museum for cleaning and repair and then is sent out on a circuit to the private schools in the city. Once the second circuit is complete, the exhibit is sent out to the county schools and to a few distant places in the State." The expense of distributing the exhibits among the county schools and schools around the state was borne by the schools, while city schools were not charged for their use—since much of the Museum's money came from the city budget. Using reform language, as well as offering a foreshadowing of the future issue of funding, a 1916 Museum document stated, "This work is of a missionary nature and is done with a view ultimately of securing state funds for the circulation of these exhibits throughout South Carolina."[121]

In the early summer of 1916 Bragg wrote her father that Belle would be traveling north with her for a family visit to the cottage at Hedding Campground. They planned to be there for about six weeks until late in August. Then Bragg would work in Boston for nine days, with Belle in tow. This visit was a milestone, as it signified to Bragg's New England family Belle's importance in her life. Once the two women returned to Charleston, Bragg wrote her father in September, "You were all so sweet to Belle. It is going to make home nearer this winter, having her familiar with you all."[122]

Charleston had suffered another hurricane during their absence. Though the storm was not as severe as the one of 1911, the books in the Museum's library were damaged because of a leaky roof. While the city recovered, Bragg worked in New York City, in the Metropolitan Museum's Egyptian department, where she purchased for herself a wonderful vase from a predynastic cemetery dating to about 4000 B.C. As planned, she also spent nine days working at the art museum in Boston.[123]

Upon Bragg's return to Charleston, she found that the rector at St. Luke's, Mr. Wood, had decided that he would confirm her, in spite of her religious beliefs and doubts. Bragg and her father had had wonderful talks about religion that summer at Hedding, and in her mind she had rationalized that "Confirmation does not mean nor depend on conversion. It is more a declaration of intention on my part and a symbol of the seal of God on his child on the part of the church." She was confirmed at St. Luke's Episcopal Church on Sunday, 4 October 1916. Bragg's compulsion to join the Episcopal Church could be attributed to Wood's powers of persuasion and/or to her desire to be with the people of "our class."[124]

Bragg made her first trip outside of the city school system to demonstrate the traveling school exhibits in October 1916. She took twenty of the exhibits to community fairs at Edisto Island and at Rockville, both small fishing villages on the coast below Charleston. It was the first time most of the teachers and students had seen the boxes, though some of the teachers had attended lectures and classes at the Museum and knew Bragg. Her presentations were so successful that the rural school board members in both places agreed to pay the postage costs in order to have the exhibits on a regular schedule.[125]

While Bragg's personal and professional worlds were married in contentment, the larger world had been in turmoil since the assassination of Archduke Ferdinand in 1914. Reelected in 1916 on the slogan "He kept us out of war," President Wilson addressed a special session of Congress to declare a state of hostility against Germany in April 1917.

With its deepwater port, Charleston felt the impact of World War I greatly. An expanded Naval Shipyard, first opened in 1901, brought boom times. A new torpedo basin was built; other harbor improvements followed, including a new lighthouse; and the main harbor channel was widened. The number of military men increased to ten thousand, and civilian employment increased by another five thousand. While former mayor John P. Grace had opposed U.S. support of England against Germany in editorials of his *Charleston American,* he and the city supported hostilities once war was declared. The only inconvenience some Charlestonians faced was the closing of the brothels by federal authorities to safeguard the health of its military personnel.[126]

"Bragg's boys," including Ned Jennings, went to war. Jennings had attended Porter Military Academy (the city's elite private school for males) before leaving Charleston in 1916 to patrol the Mexican border as the youngest soldier in the Charleston Light Dragoons. Ned had returned from that assignment to enroll in the College of Charleston, only to have war declared. Unable to fight because of his cleft palate, he volunteered as a medical corpsman serving in Europe. In 1918, while working for hours under heavy fire in a field hospital, a severe gas attack blinded him temporarily, and he was hospitalized in England.[127]

Calling the war era "stirring times" in a letter to her father, Bragg was glad that it was her lot in life to "live just here during them," but she was sorry that she was too deaf to be a nurse. The war also affected the staff at the Museum. Rea was involved with war savings bond work across the state and away from the Museum. "Bragg's boys" were departing, Bragg wrote her father, "one by one, some to officers' training camps, others to assignments in the Navy. Ned Hyer joined the Dragoons here. Burnham [Chamberlain] has gone to Fort Oglethorpe and Rhett [Chamberlain] is feeling pretty sad because the government made him take his discharge from the Dragoons and stick to his electrical engineering." Ned Hyer stayed overseas longer than the others, in the Army of Occupation, and during this time he sent her books, cards, and pictures from Versailles, France. Bragg displayed them all in the Main Hall at the Museum.[128]

During a city parade to welcome home a war hero, Bragg noted the

62   A Bluestocking in Charleston

irony of Confederate veterans carrying United States flags. In a letter to her
father she wrote: "That was a marvellous thing to me who knows how
they love and treasure their Confederate flag. On foot among the woman's
organizations was the Daughters of the Confederacy. Some of its members
were old women, one over 70." What struck Bragg was the "bigness" of the
people; the juxtaposition of "America," "The Star-Spangled Banner," and
"Dixie" (Bragg called this song "rattling good music," though the words
made no sense to her), all being played at once; and the absolute loyalty of
the southerners, "as if the last fight had not been under another flag."[129]

Bragg spent Christmas reading about Renaissance art, American
archaeology, the art of reproducing pictures, and etching. She had learned
to conserve her energy by resting and going to bed early rather than going
out, thinking, or sewing in the evening. She had been well, not having had
a cold the entire winter. And Belle was making the home at 7 Gibbes even
nicer for her: "Belle is putting a new bathroom in our house. She has to
sacrifice a part of the upstairs veranda but the added comfort will be
tremendous to me, especially as here-to-fore the bathroom I used was on
the first floor."[130]

The house at 7 Gibbes had become hers and Belle's, and Belle was her
partner who supported her, cared for her, and made a home for her. When
Rea offered to help Bragg obtain the better-paying directorship of the St.
Johnsbury Fairbanks Museum in St. Johnsbury, Vermont, she refused his
offer. She did not want to leave Charleston. It was home now, and she was
uncertain as to whether she could live for a long period of time in New
England again.[131] The work she loved was in Charleston, and her heart was
there with Belle.

During her exploring with the Natural History Society members, she
had the opportunity to meet Anne King Gregorie, whose family owned
Oakland Plantation outside the city on Porcher's Bluff, beyond Mount
Pleasant. Gregorie had conducted an extensive study of the Sewee Indian
tribe, which used to roam the coastal areas of the state near Charleston and
Mount Pleasant. Having heard of Bragg's interest in both the American
Indian and botany, Gregorie invited her to visit the plantation that summer. Visiting Oakland in June 1917, Bragg discovered a world of sea and
marsh that would from then on attract her.[132]

Bragg and Gregorie became close enough for Bragg to admit that she
was unhappy. "Don't let misunderstandings grow serious my dear," she
wrote. "They cause too much heartache. I so wish everyone could be
happy—the more because I am not." And for a while Gregorie was enam-
ored of Bragg, "a wonderful personality—a big mind in a fragile body. . . .
She is an able woman, cursed with more brains than any woman I know—

or man either. Her brains are a blessing to others, however. She is doing a great work. I esteem it a privilege that she is my friend."[133]

Belle had a vacation home on Sullivan's Island where she entertained company continuously. Just off the coast of Charleston, the island was the summer home for many of the people Bragg considered to be of her class. After leaving Oakland Plantation, Bragg spent the rest of the summer there, telling her father, "the surf rolled in over as beautiful a beach as there could be. I even went in bathing which I had vowed I would never do again." In all the years she had lived in Charleston only one summer up to that point—in 1912—had been spent away from her family. She did not go home for the summer in 1917 because at that time her life in Charleston was full, and she had no desire to leave. She was busy with Belle and busy at the Museum, putting in new Polynesian and African exhibits.[134]

The Museum crossed another milestone in 1917, one that would take it further away from its municipal charter and eventually allow Bragg to completely defy the Jim Crow color line. That year the Museum's trustees affirmed an executive committee decision to allow classes of black students admittance to the Museum when accompanied by a teacher. Within that same policy, however, the trustees decreed that black adults were to be denied admission, even black maids accompanying white children under the age of five.[135]

It is possible that this policy of admitting black students was a result of the efforts of Benjamin F. Cox, the principal of Charleston's Avery Normal Institute. He wrote Paul Rea, the Museum's director, within days of enactment of the trustees' new policy, acknowledging the new "privileges to be received at the Museum." Located within three blocks of the Museum, Avery was a private school for blacks founded by the American Missionary Association in 1865.[136]

Once the Museum moved from the College into the old Thompson Auditorium in 1911, many of Avery's students walked by the Museum on their way to and from school each day. Some recalled being fascinated with the turnstile, the whale skeleton suspended from the ceiling, and the many other wonders it contained. One of the Avery students, who became a bricklayer, remembered Bragg when he saw her later in her life. She recalled that he spoke warmly of the Museum and of the times when his classes visited there. These stories offer evidence that blacks eventually felt welcome at the Museum and saw Bragg as a "liberal-minded woman from Massachusetts who had developed a reputation for encouraging the African-American community to visit the Museum."[137]

Grace Dobbins, who transferred from the city's public school system to Avery, remembered her class walking from Avery to the Museum. She recalled that there was always a guide who was "cordial. . . . [indicating that the] Museum was pleased to have us." Dobbins also recalled that when the black students were at the Museum, there were no white classes in attendance. But then the policy was not to have two white classes at the same time either. "We never care to have classes from two white schools at the same time as the attention of the staff would then have to be divided," Bragg wrote another progressive museum administrator in Mississippi.[138]

Avery's curriculum was in marked contrast to that of the black public schools. The private-school students were expected to follow a course of study "along New England classical lines, which included French, Latin, English, the sciences, and mathematics." The school was a cultural center for the black community as well, with a strong music department and a library open to the public. In contrast, public school officials believed that it "was important to give the colored pupils training along industrial lines . . . [as this is] the education which the Negro needed most." First adopted by Charleston's white board of school commissioners in 1910, Booker T. Washington's plan of industrial education had been denounced four years earlier by Charleston's growing black middle class, many of whom had attended Avery. Still, the city's white male school board members felt that they knew what was best.[139]

In Rea's absence during the war years (1917–1918), Bragg was fully in charge of the Museum and as usual overworked. She had labored throughout the summer months without going home to New England for a vacation and fell ill. This time she was so sick that she was confined to her home at 7 Gibbes Street for more than four months, not returning to work at the Museum until April 1918 and only then to work part-time. Even though she had anticipated returning to work full-time by September, she was still unable to work for more than three or four hours a day well into 1919. For more than a year Bragg's health, physically and probably mentally, prevented her from working full days.[140]

During this illness she wrote to her father in early February that she could not remember the past Christmas season: "You see my ambition for my work has been too great and I have not been well since the last week in August. Each week grew harder but I could find no place to stop." Even though she continued to work, it was not until early December that she could push herself no longer. Her drive for success had caused her to have a breakdown. Upon entering Baker Sanatorium (Bragg called it the "best and nicest" hospital in Charleston), "Dr. Maybank performed a minor surgical procedure, a dilation and curettage, cleaning the lining of the uterus." Bragg was also suffering from another physical ailment—she had strained her back lifting heavy trays of minerals the previous spring. But in Dr. Maybank's opinion, what caused her breakdown was "the result of years of brain activity in excess of bodily strength." He warned her that if she kept on overworking, as she had been doing, she would be a total wreck.[141]

Maybank's assessment of "brain activity in excess of bodily strength" was typical of the diagnoses offered by the medical establishment during the late 1800s and early 1900s to females who sought education and then professional careers. Typically, Victorian male physicians reflected the growing fear of learned women and the effects of their studying on their physical health and their ability and desire to marry and have children. Bragg had worked diligently at the Museum installing exhibits and developing the traveling school exhibits during the fall and winter months. In previous years even Bragg's vacations had involved work, since each time she traveled home for the summer she spent weeks studying at other museums and libraries in Boston, Washington, and New York. While Bragg may have believed that her ambition was to make a name for herself as a botanist, she was doing all the work of a progressive museum director while receiving no recognition or compensation for her efforts. One of Bragg's museum colleagues recognized Bragg's symptoms and wrote after her promotion, "I have no doubt you are already much improved physically as a result. That's psychological, isn't it?"[142]

As bad as Bragg felt, her father's health was of concern to her, as he had fallen on a patch of ice in the winter of 1918, straining the muscles in his hip. Bragg was anxious that she had no money to help her father and family: "I ought to be able to help you and it hurts that I can't. Truly if I had had health I could have had money too but I can't work any harder than this position requires." The family was looking for a farm to buy, and Bragg wrote to her father: "Wish it could have been that old brick house on the road between Newfields and Exeter. That is the loveliest situation I know and so near our good Newfields friends." Eventually her parents moved into a house on a farm much like the one her Uncle Nathan had and that she had wished for at Christmas in 1908.[143]

Bragg spent almost two months with her family in Epping during the summer of 1918. "In spite of the anxieties I have been happier than for many years and home has been a real home. I get so that I think of Charleston as home but this summer I have come to feel that it is also home where you and mother are," she wrote her father after she returned to Charleston. On her way back south she had visited Salem, the museums in Cambridge, and the Peabody Museum at Harvard, and she had spent "a grand afternoon with Professor McCurdy at Yale. He taught me an enormous amount. I saw types of all the paleolithic European cultures." Bragg, as museum administrator, was back at work even before she left the Northeast. Although she anticipated returning to work after her vacation in Epping, she was still unable to work for more than three or four hours a day. Bragg was among the 18,500 Charlestonians who fell ill to the influenza epidemic; three weeks after an armistice was announced she entered Baker Sanatorium for treatment.[144]

She was depressed about the effects of this last illness, telling her father: "I confess sometimes I cannot help but think that the world would have been richer if influenza had taken me as it has so many stronger ones." She wrote him that Dr. Maybank had warned her that the influenza had possibly affected her heart. Both the flu and concern over damage to her heart had again restricted what she could and could not do at the Museum. She remained ill for much of 1918, limiting her time at the Museum, and at home Belle had "implicit directions which leave very little opportunity to overdo." Bragg spent more than $270 on hospital stays, medicines, and medical attention in 1918, but she was pleased that "at present I owe practically nothing. . . . Influenza was not good for me."[145]

The Bragg family in Epping had a wonderful Christmas in 1918 with Barbara there. As part of that New Hampshire Christmas, Bragg and Belle had remembered all the family members with joint presents. And in Charleston, Belle had given Bragg personalized notepaper similar to the kind she had given her father, "only feminized." Bragg had a wonderful holiday also, even though she was not feeling well, and she listed her gifts in a letter to her father. One of the Chamberlain twins, Rhett, had given her a large print of a Parisian scene, while the other one, Burnham, and his wife had given her white silk stockings; both Hyer and Jennings had given her books; and Helen von Kolnitz, one of "her girls," had given her Joyce Kilmer's *Main Street,* a book of poetry published just before the author's death on the French battlefield.[146]

The gift of Kilmer's work was in honor of Bragg's (and Helen's) newfound focus. While she was at home convalescing for much of 1918 and into 1919 (she was still only working three hours a day at the Museum), Bragg had become interested in poetry. She subscribed to *Poetry, A Magazine of Verse,* giving her brother, Ernest, a subscription to the magazine. She had two anthologies of modern poetry that she "prized greatly," and she was thankful that her father sent her clippings of poems. She quoted Henry Wadsworth Longfellow in her letters to her father, and she thought Edgar Guest to be "cheery and helpful but scarcely a poet—rather a versifier, don't you think." She even tried her hand at writing poetry, sending a piece about her time at Oakland Plantation the previous summer to Anne King Gregorie.[147]

Bragg recalled that at that time there was only one book in the Charleston Library Society, a subscription library, on any poetry written since Alfred, Lord Tennyson. Bragg persuaded her friends to read some modern poets: Amy Lowell, Carl Sandburg, and Vachel Lindsay. Bragg was in contact with Harriet Monroe, the editor of *Poetry,* who encouraged her "to educate up the rest of Charleston" with contemporary poetry. Bragg urged the new poetry on Helen von Kolnitz, who had written verse since her school days at Ashley Hall (and who was later to become poet laureate of South Carolina), and on Josephine Pinckney, who wrote both poetry and prose.[148]

Bragg did not go north for the summer of 1919. Still weak, in July she went instead to Caesar's Head in Greenville County, where she intended to write: "The strong features here are the food and the air. I eat like an anaconda. . . . I am trying to get stronger. . . . As yet I can walk only a very short distance and I may find I can do little more all summer. . . . I am very happy in spite of my weakness. I have so many people to love me and the Museum is so good about my sickness." She had to make a choice between going home for the summer or being able to return to the Museum and full-time work. She chose work and her ambitions.[149]

However few hours Bragg was able to work through the fall of 1919, she was able to increase the circulation of the traveling school exhibits to all the white schools in the county, with the parcel-post cost assumed by the county school commissioners. Seven of the city public schools (both black and white) received the exhibits, as did ten of the private schools. Additionally, the Museum was shipping the exhibits to more distant places across the state, including to Greenville Woman's College for use as a demonstration of grammar-school teaching methods.[150]

Bragg and her would-be poets held informal meetings during the fall at 7 Gibbes Street. Both Helen von Kolnitz and Josephine Pinckney brought their writings to Bragg for her critical eye to review. They were joined by another, Elizabeth Miles, who also wanted to write and discuss poetry. Bragg's 1906 class prophecy came true—she did become a reviewer, of poetry. While recuperating, Bragg was still able to participate in the whirl of teas and receptions of the Charleston social season, and she also enjoyed evening soirees at the painter Alice Huger Smith's studio in the Pink House on Chalmers Street. There she met DuBose Heyward, an insurance broker and one of Belle's distant cousins. Heyward told Bragg about spending Wednesday evenings with John Bennett, author of *Master Skylark,* and Hervey Allen, when they also discussed poetry. Bragg invited Bennett and his wife, Susan ("Susie") Smythe, and Heyward and Allen to her home at 7 Gibbes to hear "her girls" read their poetry.[151]

Bennett, Heyward, and Allen were creative and complex men. John Bennett, an Ohio news reporter, had come to Charleston in 1898 for health reasons. Tactful, modest, "warm-hearted and generous," he was soon married to Smythe and into Charleston aristocracy. Writing occasionally, Bennett wanted to be an illustrator and enjoyed drawing cartoons and painting scenery for local theatrical productions. He was fascinated with the folklore of Charleston blacks and collected stories from fishermen, domestics, and stable boys. He later wrote prose and poetry such as *The Treasure of Peyre Gaillard, Madame Margot,* and *The Pigtail of Ah Lee Ben Loo,* which won the Newbery Medal for the best children's book in 1928.[152]

Heyward was the only native Charlestonian among the three. Only four years Bragg's junior, he bristled at being thought of as one of "her boys," as she tended to call any man who associated with her and was younger. Thin and frail with a dark complexion and a patrician manner, he completed just one year of high school. His father was killed in a rice mill machinery accident, and Heyward pursued odds jobs ranging from peddling newspapers on street corners to working the Charleston wharves, where he oversaw the black stevedores.[153]

Following his service in World War I, Heyward retreated for solace to the North Carolina mountains. Failing to persuade either Bragg or Pinckney to wed, Heyward married Dorothy Kuhns, whom he met at the MacDowell writers' colony in New Hampshire. Dorothy encouraged him to focus on fiction and drama rather than poetry. In 1925 his first novel, *Porgo* (later retitled *Porgy*), set on the Charleston waterfront and employing the Gullah dialect, was published. Heyward was the first southerner to treat blacks seriously in literature. This novel dovetailed with the emerging white interest in the Harlem Renaissance, resulting in the stage production of the now-classic *Porgy and Bess,* which was set to George Gershwin's music.[154]

Critical in Heyward's development as a poet and writer were the Legare Street gatherings at Bennett's home, which "found the two younger men [Allen and Heyward] in lively and sometimes heated discussion in Bennett's parlor, with the senior member of the trio criticizing and suggesting as he listened to a poem or a story still hot from the creative fire. . . . his critical powers . . . given the name 'fanging' indicating half in jest the severity of his observations." Of importance, too, was Bragg, whose criticism Bennett called "not criticism, I know, but rhapsody" and to whom Heyward later wrote, "what a real help your criticism of my stuff was."[155]

Just returning from the battlefields of the Meuse-Argonne and a French hospital, Ohioan Hervey Allen toured Charleston on his way to Florida to visit his aunt. Entranced by the Holy City, Lieutenant Allen filled an unexpected teaching vacancy for the spring term of 1919 at Porter Military Academy based on his "looks" and strong character references, including one from the headmaster of the prestigious St. Albans School.[156]

One of Allen's students that first year was John Bennett, Jr., the writer's son. Invited to the Bennett home for dinner, the thirty-year-old bachelor Allen impressed the elder Bennett with his encyclopedic mind, hearty laugh, and the ability to tell stories with delightful detail and poetic dialect.

Towering well over six feet, with enormous hands and yet writing in fine script, Allen was an evangelical experimenter who first published verse from his military experiences in Mexico and France, notably "Ballads of the Border" and the bitter "Blindman."[157]

While teaching English and history at Porter, Allen began his research on Edgar Allan Poe, published as *Israfel*. He admired Poe for his macabre nature as well as short-story experimentalism. Allen worked late into the night on the second floor of the rectory at Porter, having convinced the headmaster that he should not live in the student dormitory since "one of the reasons for not being married is to keep my peace of mind, and as I figure it, I might as well be married to two or three women as to live in the barracks with the 'shrimps' beating tom toms and blowing horns. ... A little quiet time for study is all I ask of life just now."[158]

Carrying his briefcase stuffed with his writing in progress, research notes, and one or two partly read books, he walked into his classroom wearing English gabardine breeches and high leather boots. A walking cane betrayed his limp acquired from a pole vaulting injury suffered at the United States Naval Academy and aggravated by falling shrapnel in the war. A respected teacher, Allen occasionally whizzed chalk over the head of a drowsy student, leaped onto an unoccupied desktop in dramatizing a lecture, or stressed English usage with catchy phrases such as "A preposition is a bad word to end a sentence with."[159]

At Bragg's early reading sessions Belle served refreshments and saw to everyone's comfort, while Bragg served as host and reviewer. The meetings were so successful that they became biweekly affairs at which the group spoke about poetry, mostly their own, and some serious books—for example, *Convention and Revolt in English Poetry*, which had just been published. These gatherings continued at 7 Gibbes throughout the winter and into the early summer of 1920. Then the group took a holiday from their meetings, with Bragg going home to Epping, Allen off to summer school at Harvard, and Heyward to his mountain home in Hendersonville.[160]

Belle's role as Bragg's partner continued to become more accepted by each of them, as well as by Bragg's parents. Belle had chosen Reverend Bragg's birthday present in 1919, supposedly because she had a knack for choosing gifts. Tellingly, Belle was named the executor of Laura Bragg's will that same year. Sarah Bragg wrote Belle, "I feel that you, dear friend, have a larger share in her success because you have given her such a delightful home and such a generous, helpful friendship." And Belle's feelings toward Bragg were written in these words when Bragg was in Epping during the summer of 1920: "Believe that I miss you very, very much and am thinking of you constantly always, your loving Belle."[161]

Bragg recovered from another bout with the flu just after the turn of the new year in 1920. Rea cautioned her not to overdo, and Belle became frightened over her health. By mid February she felt well enough to write the *Bulletin of The Charleston Museum* and then dictate it over the phone to Rea. And she wrote her father that she was finally beginning to feel like working again. Though she was at the Museum only a few hours daily, she had given two lectures and was scheduled to give four more. She called these talks "such fun, particularly as I have had to make no special preparation for them." The history courses she took in college as well as her own personal reading in the years since had provided her with the necessary knowledge.[162]

The poetry group was not the only important beginning in Bragg's life that fall of 1919 and into the winter and spring of 1920. At about the same time that Bragg was recovering from her latest illness, Rea had come under attack from certain members of the city council, who questioned what work he actually did at the Museum. With teaching positions at both the College of Charleston and the Medical College of South Carolina, he was not working at the Museum often. Yet his salary for the Museum's directorship alone was almost $3,000, while Bragg, the curator of public instruction, and Rea's secretary both earned the same amount—$960, which was less than a third of Rea's salary. In March 1920 the Investigation Committee of the Ways and Means Committee of city council recommended "that Professor Rea do more practical work himself which would permit of dispensing with the services of one curator, or, if this is not practical then reduce the salary of the Director to a basis more commensurate with the actual duties he performs."[163] Rea resigned soon after this report was given to the Museum's board of trustees. Accepting the directorship of the Cleveland Museum, he supported Bragg as his successor.

Bragg went home to Epping, and Rea remained in Charleston to work out the plans for handing the Museum over to her. In an executive committee meeting Dr. Charles Kollock, a board member, proposed that Bragg be named Rea's successor, with Ned Hyer as assistant director. Rea wrote Bragg that he "expressed the great satisfaction that I feel in this program as an assurance of the further successful development of the Museum."[164]

Rea's support of Bragg as his successor is evident in his letter to her: "I am very glad you are planning to be back on the first of September so that we can work the situation out together as far as possible before I leave. . . . I hope you are getting a good rest and that you will come back full of energy for the big task that I know you will enjoy so much this fall." Bragg was elected the first full-time director of the Charleston Museum on 6 August 1920 at a salary of $2,200, still less than Rea, who had worked part-time. Her "boy" Ned Hyer was elected assistant director at a similar salary.[165]

Rea was pleased, and with his heartiest congratulations he wished her "the fullest measure of success and as much joy in the work as I have had. It is a great satisfaction to me the work will continue under your intimate knowledge of its history and traditions and your sympathy with my ambitions for it."[166] Bragg's election in 1920 to this post assured her a place in history. She was the first woman to be named director of a public scientific and natural history museum at that time, and hers was the oldest museum in the country.

Lyman Daniel Bragg,
Laura Bragg's father
(South Carolina
Historical Society)

Sarah Julia Klotz Bragg,
her mother (South
Carolina Historical
Society)

Barbara Bragg, her sister (South Carolina Historical Society)

Ernest Bragg, her brother (South Carolina Historical Society)

Laura Bragg, 1906 Simmons College yearbook (College Archives, Simmons College)

Simmons College, main college building, ca. 1904 (College Archives, Simmons College)

Library A in main college building, ca. 1906 (College Archives, Simmons College)

President Henry Lefavour and Dean Sarah Arnold of Simmons
(College Archives, Simmons College)

Mary Robbins, assistant professor of library science (College Archives,
Simmons College)

Class of 1906, Simmons College yearbook (College Archives, Simmons College)

Orr's Island Library, Maine

The Charleston Museum, ca. 1920 (Courtesy of The Charleston Museum, Charleston, S.C.)

First-floor exhibits of the Charleston Museum (Courtesy of The Charleston Museum, Charleston, S.C.)

Laura Bragg, ca. 1920s (Courtesy of The Charleston Museum,
Charleston, S.C.)

Isabelle ("Belle") Bowen Heyward, ca. 1901–1902 (S.C. Interstate and West Indian Exposition file, South Carolina Room, Charleston County Public Library, Charleston, S.C.)

E. I. R. ("Ned") Jennings, 1928 (*The Charlotte Observer,* Charlotte, N.C.)

Helen McCormack, from 1925 College of Charleston Yearbook (Special Collections, College of Charleston Library)

Daniel Cannon Room, once known as the Thomas Pinckney Memorial Room. The woodwork, from the Cannon house on Queen Street, was donated by the Pinckney family as a memorial to Captain Pinckney in 1920. (Courtesy of The Charleston Museum, Charleston, S.C.)

Thomas Pinckney Memorial Room, once known as the Colonial Room, 1929 (Courtesy of The Charleston Museum, Charleston, S.C.)

Recognition for the
Charleston Museum and Laura Bragg

Museums equalize the opportunities between the rich and the
poor.

Laura Bragg, *Bulletin of the Charleston Museum,*
January–February 1921

WITH BLACKS BECOMING POLITICALLY ACTIVE AND southern women
demanding equality, Charleston was beginning to stir out of a self-imposed
slumber. However, it was still a conservative and provincial backwater in
comparison to the rest of the country. Thus, the 1920s in the Holy City
probably roared a little differently than in other places. "Doin' the
Charleston" meant more than dancing; it meant having a good time. Blind
tigers, or Charleston's bars, generally ignored the state and federal prohibi-
tion laws. And Charlestonians and the city's officials passionately opposed
"their enforcement and both the citizens and the city itself were noted as
being wringing, sopping, dripping wet." One could always find a drink or
a good time in Charleston. Bragg thought the 1920s in Charleston were
the greatest and most exciting years of her life.[1]

Not only did the Museum have a new leader, but the city had another
mayor. John P. Grace, a Catholic Populist, who both favored industrial
development and tolerated the city's vices of drinking, prostitution, and
gambling, was reelected in 1919 to the post he had first won in 1911.
Grace's ideas on progressivism included "reform . . . serving the masses; justice for all people . . . and [a government that] would contribute toward
progress." Due to his influence, between 1919 and 1923 the city constructed a new High School of Charleston; increased teachers' salaries; and
ended tuition charges at both the high school and the College of
Charleston.[2]

During the four years of Grace's second term, Charleston went from
an economic boom to a bust. The wartime economy extended into 1921,
and federal money flowed into the city. There was a high demand for farm
goods, even though the boll weevil had destroyed 90 percent of the Sea
Island cotton crop in 1919. This eventually led to a depressed cotton industry and many bank closings. Wartime prosperity ended just as quickly as it
began, with a postwar depression that lasted several years. Some four thousand Charlestonians fled the city's pessimistic economy. By the end of his

term in 1923 Grace had increased taxes to provide additional city services. These amenities added more than $3 million to Charleston's municipal debt, which put the city at risk of bankruptcy.[3]

Standard Oil Company opened a new refinery along the banks of the Cooper River on the site of the former Navy Yard, and a new asbestos plant, employing one thousand mostly white workers, opened in the Neck, an area about six miles from the city in the northern area of the county. Since few blacks were hired by either company, segregated mill villages developed in the surrounding areas of the Neck. The city, though, remained racially mixed, with blacks and whites residing side by side or down the alley from each other. Many blacks still resided in the servants' quarters of fine homes south of Broad. Regardless of location, however, their housing, unlike that of whites, was usually "devoid of the minimum of sanitary conveniences, and their lanes and alleys were open sewers."[4]

With this industrial development and prosperity the city's future looked bright, for the white citizens at least. Charleston had a population of almost one hundred thousand, and those citizens operated nearly thirty-five hundred cars. With the automobile came traffic problems, for the city's streets remained unpaved and were too narrow to accommodate opposing traffic. Bragg soon had her own car, with the Museum paying half the cost as part of her salary.[5]

When Bragg became director of the Charleston Museum in 1920, her professional career and promotion were not representative of a nationwide trend for women. In the decade between 1920 and 1930 the rate of employment for American women rose only from 23 percent to 24 percent. During this period women joined other professions in the male sphere, though their jobs were primarily in the service sector. While the vast majority of professional women were elementary-school teachers, librarians, and nurses, others were becoming doctors, lawyers, architects, and judges, though the rate of employment for women in these professions actually declined by 1930.[6]

During the first half of the twentieth century men with advanced degrees almost exclusively filled the curatorial and directorial positions in museums, just as the majority of college and upper-level teaching positions were filled by men. It was unusual for women to have advanced degrees in the early twentieth century. Those who did were more often than not unmarried and thought to be nonconformist in their decisions in not following the traditional female role. Most women in museum work played the role of supporter to their male counterparts, as Bragg did with Rea initially. Since men were the heads of households and the heads of institutions, they made the rules and set the tone.[7]

Over time some outstanding women who were seen as independent, brilliant, and determined did earn appointments as directors and curators, but they were perceived as lonely in their leadership positions. Standing out from the norm, these pioneers paved the way and helped to establish women's professional credibility in the museum field through their dedication and competence. Museums were seen as appropriate arenas for development of the talents and skills of these exceptional and autonomous women of the early twentieth century. As one of those pioneers, Bragg came to be respected in her field for her expertise and her forceful personality.[8]

Participating in a profession and becoming director of the first museum in the nation during this period surely marks Bragg as an exceptional woman. Her confidence, professional knowledge, and self-awareness put her in conflict with the dominant male structure, especially in the South. When professional women, such as Bragg, behaved appropriately, according to their professional status, they were criticized for being less than womanly. However, if they chose to behave otherwise, they lost the prestige, respect, and influence afforded their position. Those who followed unique career paths, such as Bragg, endured struggles both professionally and socially.[9]

Bragg formally began her duties as director of the Museum on 1 October 1920, and "her boys" joined her on the staff in official positions. The twins, Burnham and Rhett Chamberlain, were curators; and Ned Hyer was her assistant director. "Her girl" Helen von Kolnitz assumed Bragg's former position as curator of public instruction. Bragg notified the Simmons College newsletter of her promotion: "I am not directly in library work, but I will find my library training of service." It proved to be so, as one of the major goals for her first full year in office was the further development of the Museum's reading room into a full-service library, an attempt to update the services offered to patrons. Bragg's work with educational institutions also continued to expand, as she believed education to be the dominant ideal of every museum, equalizing "opportunities between the rich and the poor."[10]

The Museum now consumed even more of her energy and her time: "The work here is a morning, noon, night affair, and if I am to pull it off, I simply cannot make plans or think for anything else." She wrote to "dear, dear Dadda" later that year: "I have never worked so hard in my life—every hour full. But, oh, it is grand to be getting results. We have done more at the Museum this year than in any three or four before. I am getting every sort of honor and praise enough to ruin me but I pay for it. Yet it is my own desire for accomplishment that drives me, not my trustees, nor any one else."[11]

As evidence of her hard work, attendance at the Museum had increased from more than ten thousand visitors in 1910 to almost thirty-nine thousand in 1920, a 300 percent increase during the decade. She wondered if "all museums are feeling a renaissance, a new interest in educational work, and a new appreciation of the value of what the museum can give to the community." Was this the "result of Charleston Museum activities for the last ten or twelve years, or is it due to some awakening all over the country? The third possibility is that it is due to the awakening throughout the South."[12]

Two new galleries were completed during Bragg's first year, the South Carolina culture exhibit was installed in another wing of the building, and the Museum opened a public health department. She presented a plan in the *Bulletin* for further installations: "the main floor was to be the vertebrate hall, the front half occupied by the history of culture exhibit and entirely devoted to that of the highest of the vertebrates, man. In the second half of the hall, the vertebrate series is carried back, through the mammals, reptiles, birds, and fishes. All the minerals, shells, insects . . . will be taken to the north gallery."[13]

Bragg dealt directly with the city and county school superintendents, meeting with them at the beginning of the school term to discuss use of the traveling exhibits along with the nature study course outlines for each grade. The schedule for the traveling exhibits was prepared in collaboration with teachers of the first and second grades, while instruction was provided for other elementary students at the Museum. Her educational focus was not limited to students, but extended to county teachers also. She continued to teach a two-week summer course on nature work, home geography, and local history, and she arranged for college credit to be earned.[14]

Prompted by Bragg's Museum education program, the ladies' Civic Club announced plans to make a stand against illiteracy in 1922. Her fellow club members were so appreciative of Bragg's work that they passed a resolution extending "sincere thanks to Laura M. Bragg for her wonderful work she has accomplished in Charleston; and that all members will endeavor to assist her in the free library she has recently opened at the Museum." Upon hearing Bragg's response to the resolution, a Civic Club leader replied, "Too much cannot be said in praise of Miss Bragg, who coming as a stranger to the city, has endeared herself to all by her kindliness, and spirit of cooperation in everything that will help Charleston to grow. Her work at the Museum is wonderful. . . . and it is the duty not only of the members of the Civic Club but of all Charlestonians to give her their help at all times in her work."[15]

In 1920 the state was still significantly rural, with only 18 percent of the population residing in urban areas. Bragg wanted patrons beyond the county borders to learn the story of the Museum and the educational services it offered. She sent Helen von Kolnitz to the Tri-County Fair at Andrews and to the State Fair in Columbia to demonstrate the traveling exhibits and to showcase the Museum's programs. A huge banner proclaimed, "The Charleston Museum Brings the Life of the World to You, Help the Museum To Preserve a Record of Our South Carolina Life for the World."[16]

Helen estimated that between fifteen thousand and twenty thousand people viewed the banner and the booth at the fair in Columbia, thus alerting potential patrons to the Museum and its services. "Most of [them] knew nothing about the Museum," and since there was an "absolute lack of cultural advantages in certain illiterate sections of South Carolina," she thought it would be difficult for anyone to understand what it meant to those people to see the Museum's exhibit. While the fair-goers passed other display booths with only a glance, they lingered at the Museum's exhibit, finding it both fascinating and educational.[17]

Bragg's reputation extended beyond the state's borders. She had met and befriended the sister-in-law of one of the Museum's trustees, Charles Stevens. Caroline Sinkler was quite involved with the Philadelphia Museum and was also supportive of Bragg and her efforts in Charleston. Just a month after Bragg became director, Caroline sent three boxes of "Egyptian things excavated . . . from various place along the Nile. I think each item speaks for itself to your practiced eye." Bragg was so thrilled with the material, which included a stone vase, wooden models, and a piece of bronze, that she wrote in her reply, "I suppose I should write you a very dignified official letter of thanks . . . but I am so excitedly happy over it that this is impossible." While Bragg wrote, "I just have to keep this letter out of the files," she did not, and in it she outlined her plans for "working out the story of Egyptian life which I wish to tell by means of our exhibit." For Bragg the Egyptian materials represented her "deepest interest of making the history of the past live for the people of the present."[18]

Bragg sought contributions for the Museum's library from the North from John Cotton Dana, the Newark Museum Association, and also from Caroline Sinkler. In February, Caroline sent a box of books to Bragg, who wrote, "such expensive volumes and some of them out of print. I had simply not dreamed of being able to own them here at the Museum." She also sketched out for Mayor Grace her plans for the Museum's library. Hoping to make it the children's center in Charleston, Bragg recalled that "I was brought up in the north where there are public libraries everywhere, and, though my father had a modern library of several thousand volumes, I know that a big part of my education is due to the public library." She pointed out to Grace: "Perhaps you have always had plenty of books. . . . when . . . [the] story hours are over, the children clamor for books about the stories. . . . Do you know most of the children who come to the Museum for the story hours know nothing of the stories that are the heritage of our race, the old Greek myths, the stories of King Arthur, German folklore, Irish legends and the Norse sagas."[19]

Initially, Mayor Grace had his doubts about Bragg's ability to run the Museum and deal with funding issues. He wrote to one of her Museum colleagues, "I was very skeptical when Miss Bragg took up the work when he [Rea] left off." He further admitted that he was "by no means originally a friend of the Charleston Museum. While I have been always a friend of education, I did not at first regard the museum . . . as such a necessary part of our educational program as to be worthwhile." In her first appearance before the city's Ways and Means Committee seeking the Museum's yearly appropriation, she had been unable to answer Grace's questions about the division of funds from the Museum's three funding sources: city, county, and general. After what must have been a disappointing session for her, she wrote Grace, "I can show people what I am doing at the Museum but I do not know how to talk for it." She asked that he allow her to show him her plans for the library, and she wished to take him "around the building when there was a large crowd Sunday afternoon and have you see the types of people, their enjoyment, and what the Museum means to them."[20]

Bragg was eventually successful in garnering Grace's and other politicians' support; by May 1921 she knew she had the appropriation and that she had won over the members of the Ways and Means Committee. Several months later Bragg opened the children's free library, with Saturday mornings set aside for distributing books to children under eighteen years of age. Grace was now a friend of the Museum and of Bragg.[21]

Grace may initially have been unsure of Bragg's ability to raise funds for the Museum, but her poetry friends recognized her leadership skills. As active as her business world was at the Museum, Bragg's social world had taken on a different aspect once the two different poetry groups merged and began to meet as one at 7 Gibbes Street. At some point one of the group members suggested that they formally organize a poetry society. Some agree that it was Bragg's idea; she had corresponded with Harriet Monroe of *Poetry* and Jessie Rittenhouse of *Contemporary Verse,* two poetry society enthusiasts, long before any society was formed in South Carolina. With her passion for organization, as well as her community and social contacts through her work at the Museum, it would be natural for her to suggest formation of such a society. One of DuBose Heyward's biographers contends, however, that it was actually Heyward who suggested to Allen at Bennett's home that a society was just what they and the city needed. Responding to H. L. Mencken's blistering indictment of the South as "the Sahara of the Bozart," they were "predicting nothing less than a literary revival that would sweep the state and spread over the whole South like a forest fire."[22]

By the fall of 1920 DuBose Heyward, Hervey Allen, John Bennett, Helen von Kolnitz, Elizabeth Miles, Laura Bragg (Josephine Pinckney was absent), and their hostess Belle Heyward met and formally organized the Poetry Society of South Carolina. They decided upon an invited membership limited to two hundred—"one wag remarked that the members 'appeared to be one-tenth poetry and nine-tenths society'"—and they also established the structure and aims of the society. There were different committees, such as the one for entertainment chaired by Belle, the school committee with Bragg in charge, and others headed by other socially prominent Charlestonians. Prizes were awarded to assist and recognize the poets: the Blindman, named after Allen's war poem; Bragg's prize of twenty-five dollars for poetry that was about local color; and Caroline Sinkler's prize of one hundred dollars.[23]

All of the charter members of the Poetry Society had some connection to the socially prominent families of Charleston. The membership list brought together two hundred of the city's elite, drawing from artistic as well as social circles. Invitations to the meeting on 15 February 1921, at which Carl Sandburg read his poems, were sought and treasured by members of Charleston society. In preparation for that reading, Bragg recalled that she made a perfect nuisance of herself reading Sandburg's poetry aloud to people before he came to the city. She called his verse "radical" and "exceedingly modern" and declared that she "admired him greatly." Prominent authors and literary critics followed Sandburg, and the society meetings overflowed Society Hall. Charlestonians heard Amy Lowell, Harriet Monroe, John Erskine, Vachel Lindsay, Stephen Vincent Benét, and Robert Frost—all within the first few years of the society's founding.[24]

Bragg became Heyward's critic, writing about him to his aunt Caroline Sinkler and calling him *the* poet of Charleston. He sought Bragg's "verdict" on his poetry, once writing her, "the things you caught in the pirates I can now see sticking out a mile, although I missed them before." Not only did Heyward value her criticism, but he also called her a "Dear friend of mine," one he enjoyed having a good talk with in her aerie (her rooms were on the third floor of Belle's house, where she had a sitting porch). Heyward decided to call her "Laura" rather than the more formal "Miss Bragg," by which everyone else addressed her (except for Belle). He concluded "that there was no reason why you should place yourself in an older and presumably superior, generation by calling me 'DuBose' while I pulled the humble forelock and addressed you as 'Miss Bragg.'"[25] Bragg must have responded, for in a later letter Heyward wrote, "Names don't matter to me one bit. You are you to me, and it is all one whether you desire to be labeled Miss Bragg, or Cleopatra for that matter." He was not going to offer her the "filial devotion due you from one of your boys," because their relationship, in his eyes, had become "a fine comradeship of give and take between us and God knows this is about the finest thing that can happen to two people."[25]

Bragg's relationship with John Bennett, the other critic of the group, did not begin with such ease or even comradeship, though she eventually did gain both his respect and his admiration. Bennett wrote weekly letters to his family over the course of twenty-six years. It is apparent that within a three-month time span during 1921 just after the formal organization of the Poetry Society, Bennett did not particularly care for Bragg. Early on in their association he wrote his family that she was "all butter and smiles and affability's finer self." The following month he wrote of her again: "Miss Bragg wanted to talk about herself and tell us all she knows and how much she knew when a child." Two weeks later he wrote that Miss Bragg "has a nasty habit of paying folk sugared and fulsome compliment to their faces. She does this too much." Calling her a siren and preglacial, Bennett was certain that Bragg was jealous of the inner circle of the Wednesday-nighters (him, Heyward, and Allen). Bennett wrote his family that Bragg wanted to take Heyward away from the other men because he "seems the readier one to swallow her sweetened words."[26]

Bennett's attitude about Bragg did not sway him from introducing her to other South Carolina intellectuals. Through her association with Bennett and the Poetry Society she met Dr. Yates Snowden, a professor of history at the University of South Carolina. Calling her "the General," Snowden enjoyed poetry with Bragg, and he talked and fished for devilfish with her in the surf at Beaufort. He warned her, though, "It's dangerous about even for an Amazon like you." Another South Carolinian, James Henry Rice of Brick House Plantation, near Edisto Island, came to know her through her Museum activities. An admirer of Bragg, Rice had been sternly forbidden "to express my real sentiments about you and have held me so rigidly to formalities." He believed Bragg's work was noble "in elevating the tone of the community is visible."[27]

As fulfilling as these relationships were, the Museum and its activities consumed more and more of her time and energy. In November, Bragg's "long cherished plan" for a children's room was realized with the opening of the William M. Bird Boys' and Girls' Room. Bragg and the staff transformed a storage room that had large windows covered by shelves into a sunny room with pale green walls, and they filled it with bookcases and exhibit cases containing cultural exhibits from other countries. The center of the room held low tables where children made stage sets and learned clay modeling, block printing, and etching, taught by E. I. R. (Ned) Jennings. While this room provided enjoyment for the children, the objective was to educate, to teach children "to observe and to think with scientific accuracy. . . . To awake in the child not only interest and enthusiasm and to create a desire for learning."[28]

An event occurred at the Museum during her first year as director that truly marked Bragg as a Progressive, a reformer, and a missionary in the South—and ultimately as an outsider. With Mayor Grace's support, she crossed the imaginary and arbitrary color line by opening the Museum to black patrons on Saturday afternoons.[29] Before Bragg was director, no black adult could enter the Museum unless accompanied by schoolchildren. Now blacks were offered a sense of parity that had not existed before.

Mayor Grace's friendliness to blacks and Bragg's actions were not in sync with the city's political elite. By this time Jim Crow laws segregated the races on streetcars and in parks and waiting rooms and denied blacks the right to vote. "Segregation became evident in housing patterns . . . [and whatever] . . . new jobs created by the economic boom went exclusively to whites." The Great Migration northward had begun for blacks, and for the first time in two hundred years Charleston had a white majority population.[30]

By December, Bragg had informed Principal Cox at Avery of the Museum's Saturday hours for black patrons. And in her "Report of the Director of the Museum for the Year 1921" to Mayor Grace, which was published in the [Charleston] City Year Book, she included her first notation of black attendance at the Museum: "Total colored attendance . . . 2,057."[31]

Crossing the color line was beyond the pale, and her conduct provoked many white Charlestonians. One of Bragg's later associates recalled how upset people were when she opened the Museum to black patrons. While there were those who disapproved of her behavior, there were others in both the black and white communities who took a different viewpoint. Searching for information about the Museum's patrons after the Saturday openings began, Bragg employed a social worker to complete a survey among residents in the downtown area. In Mary Preston's report to Bragg she wrote, "but when one ran across the colored, one was struck by their satisfaction when they heard they were entitled to visit the museum. With encouragement many more than do now would attend . . . the remark of one lady had quite an element of pathos 'My nurse will always bathe and dress the children twice to get to the Museum.' Here in passing I should say that I heard no adverse criticism (from whites) of the fact that negroes were admitted." These comments were never published in Bragg's director's report to the mayor, thus sparing the white power structure from the impact of new thoughts and new ideas.[32]

Bragg had been planning to go home for the Christmas holiday in 1921 but wrote, "I can't, *can't* made [*sic*] it. I do so want a *white* Christmas with you and Mother. I want a real Christmas tree and to hear sleigh bells and to go snowshoeing. But work holds me." She hated letting herself "get so out of touch with home, but I don't know how to do other than I do."[33] And so she spent the season working at the Museum, installing exhibits and drawing up plans for future programs.

Bragg's work and her ambition again caused her to fall ill, and she was laid up for most of January 1922. During her illness she read the eight volumes that described the expedition of Caroline Sinkler's nephew, Eckley Coxe, in the Sudan. Bragg had also befriended Caroline's niece, Elizabeth Stevens Martin, who was "so kind to me since I have been sick." She and Elizabeth Martin enjoyed reading poetry together and having tea. Caroline was also related to DuBose Heyward, who had received the *Contemporary Verse* prize for "Gamesters All," a poem about blacks shooting dice on a river pier. Bragg called his award delightful in a letter to Caroline. She enjoyed her role as Heyward's critic and friend, which was proving to be advantageous for making more connections to Charleston society and beyond in the larger social world. Caroline also knew Belle, who was Heyward's cousin.[34]

At the annual meeting of the American Association of Museums (AAM) in 1922, Bragg extended an invitation to the group to hold its next annual convention in Charleston in honor of the 150th anniversary of the founding of the Charleston Museum. As a celebration of "the birth of the Museum Idea in America," she invited them to see Magnolia Gardens, the old houses of Charleston, and Fort Sumter; to enjoy a trip around the harbor and a house party at an old plantation; and to visit a "Cypress reserve where you could see the herons and the rare southern birds. . . and show . . . what the old time life was in the South." Her invitation met with applause, and though the museums of Saint Louis also issued an invitation, the AAM's governing board of councillors chose Charleston as the site for its 1923 meeting.[35]

Bragg had less than a year to ready the Museum and the city for an influx of what was hoped to be more than one hundred museum professionals. Even so, this did not alter her summer plans. She went from Buffalo to Epping to spend the month of June visiting with her family. As usual, she visited other museums on her return trip to Charleston, spending "a very pleasant day in Newark, another in Philadelphia, and then three wonderful days in Richmond."[36]

Tourism was just beginning to become an industry in Charleston during the early 1920s. Fueled by the servicemen who had spent time at the Navy Yard before and during World War I and by the ever-increasing numbers of affordable automobiles for the growing middle class, tourists were flocking to the Holy City. There were some hotels available, and the city did have a number of rooming houses. There was also the fashionable and expensive Villa Margherita on South Battery, an inn that would be convenient for convention-goers. The city, under Mayor Grace's leadership, supported the construction of a new hotel, the Francis Marion, on King Street. This was a possibility for Bragg's housing plans, since its supposed completion date was the end of January 1923.[37]

Returning to the Museum and to the work of planning the convention, Bragg and her secretary, Emma Richardson, worked late into the evenings that fall and winter, eating supper wherever they found themselves in the building. One of the Museum galleries was finished, with new exhibits installed, while old ones were brightened and repaired and the building was painted. Many owners of plantations along the Santee River (the Wedge, Fairfield, and Hampton) agreed to open their homes to the visitors, and Bragg wrote the president of the Santee Gun Club in December, asking "in the name of the trustees of the Charleston Museum if the Santee Gun Club would not extend . . . the very great courtesy of the use of its Club House for one night for the housing of a part of this gathering." Bragg's friends Josephine Pinckney and DuBose Heyward, along with Caroline Sinkler in Philadelphia and Caroline Rutledge of Hampton Plantation, helped to secure the Santee Gun Club for the convention.[38] While Bragg was concerned with convention plans, the Museum's educational programs continued to flourish.

The work of the Department of Public Instruction moved forward. In 1922 there were twenty-seven white schools in the county, and they received 234 traveling school exhibits every two weeks. All five white grammar schools in the city plus three of the four black schools received 270 exhibits for two grades. The Museum also supplied eleven private schools weekly with the exhibits. The benefit of the museum's educational programs, especially the traveling exhibits, was testified to by various teachers at a meeting of the Kindergarten Association in the fall of 1922.[39]

But the focus for Bragg and her staff was the convention. Getting ready for the meeting was "straining our strength and resources to their limit," Bragg wrote Caroline Sinkler in February 1923. Once she learned that the new Francis Marion Hotel would not be opened in time for the association's meeting, she settled on the Charleston Hotel as the central inn. The hotel's general manager was a trustee of the Museum, and he assured her that he would take reservations up to the hotel's capacity. She could then place the overflow with private families, telling the association's director, "I know this is not the most desirable arrangement . . . it is absolutely the best I can do in the height of tourist season." The Museum would serve as the registration site and headquarters for the meeting, with Bragg arranging for luncheon and supper every day at the Museum. She persuaded her friends with cars to provide taxi service, even though the trolley cars ran everywhere. Bragg's convention program was planned to provide for as many personal contacts as possible. She wanted the convention to create a favorable impression in the community. And she believed that if there was to be a museum development in the South, it would be launched by the Charleston Museum.[40]

With housing assured, the program in place, the house party arranged, and assurances from plantation owners that the guests would have overnight accommodations (though Bragg wrote one of the trustees, "I am rather upsetting the rest of the river"), Bragg's plans as outlined in her original invitation were falling into place. However, there was one local hold-out: owner Norwood Hastie would not agree to entertain the visitors at Magnolia Gardens. In his reply to her letter of 19 February he wrote: "the courtesies of the Garden shall only be extended to Charitable Institutions. The inmates of these institutions, and flower lovers who really cannot afford to pay the admission, are welcome at all times, but these are the only guests that we find practicable to entertain." Bragg complained that Hastie "was the only person in all of Charleston who refused to do anything for the American Association of Museums, and he is generally talked of as being the only person who broke the rule of Charleston hospitality." Another disappointment was the refusal by the commissioner of light-houses in Washington, D. C., to grant her request for a lighthouse tender to provide association members views of Fort Sumter and other historic points.[41]

As busy as Bragg was at the Museum, her longtime companion, Belle, was still very much a part of "dearest Laura's" life. A charter member of the Poetry Society along with Bragg, she was one of the 163 in attendance at the convention as a committee member. Though Belle did not attend the house party, Bragg was joined there by two other Poetry Society members, Hervey Allen and Josephine Pinckney, who served as driver and hostess, respectively, at Fairfield Plantation. Another Poetry Society member,

DuBose Heyward, wrote a brief skit called "An Historical Interlude," which depicted the founding of the Museum and was performed as part of the entertainment. Pinckney and Heyward participated in the skit by portraying their ancestors Eliza Lucas Pinckney and Thomas Heyward (Heyward, and Eliza Pinckney's son Charles Cotesworth Pinckney, were the founders of the Museum).[42]

Association members saw town mansions and rice plantations. During their visit museum professionals were invited to a series of receptions in five historic homes south of Broad, which were opened to visitors for the first time and where "they were permitted to inspect the rare furnishings." According to Bragg, that was what most people wanted: "people are perennially unsatisfied unless they are able to penetrate what seems . . . to be in the heart of Charleston life, that is, the interior of its homes."[43]

The trip to the Santee River and to the old plantations was a huge success. Association members went to the Santee Gun Club, where an oyster roast was held. The men in the party spent the night there, while the women stayed at other local plantations, including Harrietta, the Wedge, and Hampton. The entire group enjoyed a picnic on the grounds of Hampton Plantation. The guests saw workers threshing rice, making shingles, and weaving sweet-grass baskets. Bragg recalled that the museum professionals "were so moved by what they saw" and that "they had never seen the South." On the last day the Episcopal bishop conducted a service in the Old St. James Santee Parish Church. The Queen Anne silver—which had been given by the queen to the church when it was founded—was used to take up an offering. Bragg recalled "that John McIlhenney of Philadelphia put in a one hundred dollar bill, and the church had over four hundred dollars, enough to repair the church."[44]

Bragg's 1923 convention brought together people from twenty-seven different museums, with sixty-five association members in attendance. All heard Dr. Kollock, the president of the board of trustees, laud her as "a frail wisp of a woman, . . . her gracious manner and true appreciation of our country has made her one of us . . . she was unanimously selected . . . as director. . . . It is not necessary for me to tell how well she has succeeded, not a misstep has been made, not a minute has been lost." Not only was she recognized by the board of trustees for her leadership, but she also garnered a second round of praise from the women of Charleston, and this time they bestowed upon her their highest honor—they called her a Charlestonian. Mrs. Ashley Halsey was spokesperson for the women, and she presented Bragg with a watch. She read the proclamation to the audience: "Miss Bragg had the misfortune not to be born in Charleston, but as soon as she was able to remedy the mistake, she did so by coming and staying, and she has so endeared herself to all of us that we feel we are truly speaking of and to a Charlestonian when we address Miss Bragg . . . [she has] done a noteworthy work at this time, when the woman's movement has the attention and is demanding the thought of men and women all over the earth. Realizing and appreciating this, the women of Charleston are deeply grateful that their banner is carried by a woman of the type, ability, and character of Miss Bragg. . . . a little token of esteem and appreciation and of gratitude that our cause is in such worthy hands."[45]

Bragg's meeting was such a triumph that the delegates had barely returned home before she and the Museum began to receive note after note praising her and Charleston. Frederic Whiting, director of the Cleveland Museum of Art and president of the AAM, sent her a handwritten note, while others sent formal letters. The secretary of the association, Laurence Vail Coleman, wrote to congratulate her "upon the tremendous success. . . . Everyone appreciated what you did and we all agreed that it was the most notable meeting which we ever had, as a result almost entirely of your untiring efforts." Praise also came from a Charlestonian, Rebe Frost, living with the DuPont family in Delaware, where she was serving as the children's governess: "just to congratulate you on that wonderful program you have. . . . I fairly curled up when I read . . . of all those visits to the various plantations, what I have always wanted to do and never could get there. It is simply fine what you are doing and what you have done for the Museum. Charleston owes you a debt of gratitude."[46]

Bragg's deafness had plagued her during the meeting. Whiting, as president of the association, sat with her and wrote out what was taking place during the sessions. After the meeting she wrote Coleman about how she had missed so much of the "spirit of the whole thing" and asked that he send her a full copy of the minutes because "I could not hear things." He did so, and she read them with the greatest of interest, discovering in the minutes the AAM's intent to conduct a membership drive. This struck a chord in Bragg, who admitted, "I have never solicited a membership in my life."[47]

Little did she know that she would not only solicit memberships for the Museum but also search for funding for the building and for the traveling school exhibits both inside and outside the state over the next seven or so years. The signs of change in her professional and personal life began to manifest themselves during the first heady years of her tenure. Her hearing grew progressively worse, and her staff had to yell loudly for her to hear; she ordered an earphone from a Massachusetts company to help her deal with her deafness.[48]

Whiting proved to be both Bragg's and the Museum's friend. He wrote Mayor Grace, at her suggestion, a letter praising her and endorsing what the Museum was trying to accomplish. Bragg told Whiting, "you would probably save me a good many hours in working for my appropriation." Before the association meeting in Charleston, Grace seemed to think that the city would be the attraction and that no one from northern museums would think the Charleston Museum worthwhile. It was Bragg's estimation that Grace did not understand that the merit of a museum was not judged by its wealth or by its collections but rather "by the proportional service it gives the community."[49]

Grace had supported her, and Bragg knew she needed to continue to support him. He began the summer in high hopes of being reelected, unaware that Tom Stoney would be a political rival in the primary. Stoney, a Broad Street lawyer with ancestry dating back to the seventeenth century, came as a surprise entry in the primary. While she was sure that Grace would be reelected, she thought that "he will have to go through a bitter mud slinging because of his religion." The primary election was bitter, with the National Guard called out on election day to maintain order. Bragg was right about the mudslinging but wrong about Grace's chance of reelection, because "much to everyone's surprise," Grace lost to Stoney in the primaries.[50]

Bragg's destination after the association's convention was her country retreat, Snug Harbor, which was about ten miles north of Mt. Pleasant. Leased in 1920 from Anne King Gregorie's family, it sat on a high bluff that overlooked the marshes at Hamlin Sound. The three-bedroom house was casual and unpainted. Reached by boat, it afforded Bragg both the isolation from the city, which she needed, and the beauty of the salt marshes, which she had come to love. She spent the week after the meeting there refreshing her spirits, and she was joined by her "poetic and artistic friends." This group probably consisted of DuBose Heyward, Josephine Pinckney, and Hervey Allen, all of whom had helped her with the convention. Though Bragg was about four years older than both of the men and about twelve years older than Pinckney, Bragg recalled that the four of them spent many weekends together. One or other of the men would call her and invite themselves, picking up both groceries and Josephine for their weekend at Snug Harbor.[51]

The Poetry Society was in full operation at this time, and the Footlight Players, a symphony, and the Charleston Etchers Club were all active. Bragg was a founder of the former and a patron of the latter, having provided the artists with space for their press and meetings. Charleston had seen an explosion of art studios, and Alfred Hutty, Elizabeth O'Neill Verner, and Minnie Mikell, among others, drew scenes of the city and the lowcountry.[52]

The Museum welcomed two artists during the early 1920s, one who

was a guest and the other, a Bragg's boy, who became the Museum's curator of art. The more famous of the two was sculptor Dwight Franklin, who
had come to Charleston that spring for the AAM meeting and remained
to create an Edgar Allan Poe miniature group, which showed Poe at nineteen when he served at Fort Moultrie. It was placed in a lighted cabinet in
a corner of the Bird Children's Room. Ned Jennings also returned to the
city after graduating from Columbia University and studying stage and
costume design for a year at Carnegie Technical Institute. He had been
commissioned by Bragg to create ten stage sets, which were to highlight
the drama of white man's civilization and serve as a transition to Franklin's
new group. When Bragg proposed to Jennings the idea of "a series of
groups illustrating beginnings of civilization and their development in
Egypt," he was still at Columbia University completing his degree requirements. Having known Ned since he was eleven, she told him that the work
he was doing had "museum possibilities." She invited him to Charleston to
work out the sketches with her and then return to New York where "accu-
rate information is accessible." She had originally intended to call this
group the "Drama of Man," but it became better known as the "Drama of
Civilization." Jennings was one of those whose talents she nurtured and
developed for museum work.[53]

Bragg believed that museums help people assimilate ideas. According
to her, there are three types of people who visit museums: people who will
absorb, people who will read labels and remember a great deal of what's
read, and a "superior person who knows most everything any way." It was
this first group of people that she wanted to appeal to with Franklin's new
form of miniature grouping. She wanted such miniatures to show "what
otherwise cannot be told except through labels."[54]

After being placed in sunlit cases, Ned's exhibits were to have attached
labels helping to explain the connections. Bragg outlined her plans for a
museum colleague: "For instance one of our cases contains pottery and
copper from the pre-dynastic period in Egypt. Farther along . . . Aegean
Culture is introduced with pottery and copper produced through direct
Egyptian influence." Bragg estimated that not more than half the people
seeing the exhibit would understand the connection from reading the
label, "but surely very few would fail to get it if the copper and pottery of
Cyprus were exhibited beside a miniature group showing the coast of
Cyprus and Egyptian trading vessels labeled '3000 BC Egyptian ships trad-
ing pottery and copper in Cyprus.'"[55]

Bragg may have rested after the AAM meeting at Snug Harbor, but she
was "so done up" by the preparations that she was ill for much of the summer. She did not correspond with Coleman, the association's secretary,

until 30 August, and he wrote her, "I was glad to have your letter . . . for I have not heard from you for a long time. I do hope that you will continue to recover rapidly." She blamed her illness on the amount of preparation that had to be done for the meeting, writing the association's president, Whiting: "You see we had to do the normal work of two or three years in less than a year and I confess that, by the time the convention opened, I was dazed with weariness and have not felt fit for any work until recently."[56]

In what was to become a regular occurrence, Belle left for an extended trip to Europe on 2 August. She wrote Bragg from the ship after leaving New York harbor: "It was very sweet of you to send [a telegram] and it was good to feel you were saying 'good-bye' to me and to know you were missing me already. I don't let myself think how long it would be before I see you." On 23 September, Belle was in Florence and mailed Bragg a card for her birthday: "Laura dearest, I hope that this may reach you on your birthday." And on another card dated on Bragg's forty-second birthday, 9 October, Belle wrote, "Laura Darling, I have been thinking of you all day, wondering how you are and where you are and sending you my love with you by wireless and my good wishes across the thousands of miles that are between us." No doubt, their relationship was a loving one, for Bragg called Belle her "closest friend."[57]

Her year ended with what was the beginning of honors, awards, and acknowledgments for her success at the Museum and for the outstanding and memorable AAM convention she had staged. The Charleston Chamber of Commerce selected her as a member of the committee for the Woman's Bureau; Bragg's biography was published in the first edition of *Women in America;* and the American Association of Museums asked her to serve on the Fire Hazards Committee. While she was not anxious for extra work, she was most interested in this assignment, "as my next big work is to teach Charleston the necessity for a fire-proof building and proper protection for Museum material." Bragg's plans were to ask the new mayor, Tom Stoney, and his administration for a fireproof extension to the building in combination with a county public library. What she had written to her college chums back in 1920 as a promise was still her major interest— she was intent on getting a free library for Charleston.[58]

Once Belle returned from Europe, she and Bragg spent a good Christmas together, enjoying a can of honey from Reverend Bragg's bees. Belle cooked waffles in her electric iron for her family to enjoy with his produce. In thanking Reverend Bragg, Belle wrote of Bragg's pride in her father's farm and all that he raised: "But I feel sure that you feel that the best of your raising has been this child of yours, Laura. She certainly is a wonder—and the place she has made for herself here in Charleston is *really* surprising—for Charleston is a place very set in her ways, and Laura has won over everybody."[59]

Though Bragg's personal world was one of contentment and satisfaction, this was a time of difficulty for the Museum's financial sources. By the end of Grace's last term as mayor, the city's and region's postwar prosperity had come to an end; the price of cotton had dropped sharply due to the boll weevils, and this had led to layoffs in the cotton mills. Civilian workers were also being laid off at the Navy Yard. Living costs and taxes rose, while job opportunities declined.[60] Times were lean, and money grew harder to find in the city budget for the Museum and its programs.

As the Charleston economy deteriorated, Mayor Stoney worked to develop the tourist trade, coining the phrase "America's most historic city." Though he was a member of the elite class and understood how other elite Charlestonians felt, and though Yankee visitors from "off" may well have been the last people most city residents wanted roaming their streets and peering into their gardens, tourism became the city's biggest industry by the late 1920s. One aristocratic Charlestonian remarked somewhat prophetically, "Nothing is more dreadful than tourists, whether grasshoppers, boll weevils, or money-bagged bipeds. They will make Charleston rich and ruin her."[61]

The year 1924 began for Bragg with an additional acknowledgment of her leadership. The national Bureau of Information for Women Voters solicited her personal choice of the two Democratic candidates for president, Underwood or McAdoo, and wanted to know her assessment of the "general sentiment expressed among the women of your city." Bragg promptly replied that she greatly regretted that McAdoo had not been nominated four years earlier, as she strongly supported him, but she admitted that she had no idea as to the general sentiment of her community. Mrs. Day, the secretary of the bureau, immediately responded with the same request about the sentiment of other women, although this time she asked Bragg to provide "names and addresses of several Democratic women of your acquaintance in your own city, county, or state whom we may address with reference to the coming election." Whether Bragg replied or not, this solicitation of her opinion by a national political organization clearly signaled respect for Bragg's influence within the smaller Charleston community and its connections to the larger South Carolina political arena. Another honor for Bragg was a request to photograph her in the art of cooking, as part of the National Cooking Service of the Procter and Gamble Company. Given Belle's role in Bragg's life and Bragg's self-declared hatred of housekeeping, she must have chuckled as she replied, "I very seldom cook. . . . I confess it would be better for the people who go on my country house parties if I did, or rather if I could."[62]

What must have been a pleasurable beginning of the new year for her was a house party at Snug Harbor for "her boys." The group left town at noon on New Year's Day and stayed until the following Wednesday. Bragg brought together all the young men "who are or will be associated with the institution. . . . Rhett Chamberlain, and his twin, Burnham, Robert Whitelaw, Alexander Sprunt, and Ned Jennings."[63] Emma, Bragg's secretary, also was a part of the house party. All of "her boys" had been members in the Natural History Society, and it was these same young men who had transported bones and specimens from the college campus to Thompson Auditorium when the Museum moved into its new building in 1910. Her goal of interesting them in learning and in museum work had been successful.

One of "her boys" was missing from the house party. Ned Hyer, her first assistant director, had been forced to leave his position with the Museum in the months after the AAM meeting in April 1923, though Bragg knew as early as March that the trustees wanted to let him go. She and Paul Rea both had searched for positions for Hyer and his wife, whom she wrote of as having a "wonderful personality and very decided ability." Hyer, her first mentoring project, had married one of "her girls," Helen von Kolnitz, and their first child was Bragg's godchild. Calling Hyer her only tragedy at the Museum, she was forced to discharge him because of financial irregularities. Ironically, Ned's mother had once warned Bragg that Ned should not have anything to do with money because, as Bragg recalled, "he did not know the difference between thine and mine." Money had turned up missing, and despite Helen's pleading, Bragg had to let Ned go.[64]

What had to have been both a personal and a professional disappointment for Bragg did not prevent her attendance, along with Josephine Pinckney, at the AAM's nineteenth annual meeting in Washington, D.C., from 9 to 12 May 1924. They saw the National Cathedral, and Bragg shook hands with President Coolidge at a White House garden party. The wife of Dwight Franklin, the artist, presented Bragg with "an expression of appreciation" for the hospitality at the Charleston meeting, a lace collection as a gift to the ladies of Charleston. In her remarks Mrs. Franklin explained how the gift of lace had been decided upon as the house party was ferrying down the Santee: "it would be a beautiful and appropriate thing if each of the ladies there contributed a piece of old lace, as it seemed to me that old lace stood for Charleston."[65]

At the Washington meeting Chauncey Hamlin, the president of the AAM, appointed Bragg chair of the Southeastern States committee. She could choose the personnel for the committee, and they could elect their own officers at will.[66] But what developed as a result of an earlier trip she had made to Richmond determined the real importance of this committee assignment.

Bragg had visited Granville Valentine and his father's museum in Richmond in the summer of 1922. After her visit Granville's wife, Calvin, had written Bragg that she had "taught us so much and put fire in our ambitions." Those ambitions slumbered for more than a year, and it was not until September 1924 that the Valentine Museum contacted Bragg again, asking for her help in "expanding and rearranging on modern principles." Bragg was so overjoyed to receive the letter that she proposed to travel to Richmond if they were able to pay her expenses. If that weren't possible, she was willing to help them by letter. However, she was sure that her "experience in re-installing the Charleston Museum and developing its new exhibits would, perhaps, be of more value than the services of some Northern museum worker who would have less sympathy with our Southern program."[67]

Bragg, the northerner, now had a southern program for museums. Writing Valentine's secretary, she pointed out that the first item of business for the Valentine Museum would be to determine the scope of the museum, so that all development would be extension, rather than reconstruction. This allowed for "growth in any department without causing any vital change." It was her belief that "this should be done with even the smallest museum, if it was to be an efficient working institution." She ended this letter with a question important to her: "Do you plan to have a children's room?"[68]

Valentine agreed to pay her expenses, and Bragg made plans for a visit during the second week of October 1924. Bragg was pleased with this development, as it dovetailed with her work with the AAM's Southeastern States committee. She wrote Coleman immediately upon hearing from Valentine and proposed to him that she undertake part of his planned trip south to study the problems of small museums in concert with her trip to Richmond. Using some of the money from the Rockefeller grant that the association had received for the study, she asked that he "let me have some of the money from the fund . . . and let me visit and report to you conditions at Raleigh, Atlanta, Montgomery, and Savannah." Bragg asked him to write to each of the museums, letting them know that she was representing the AAM and that she was the "Chairman of the Southeastern Section," giving her visit a "double force."[69]

Coleman agreed to her plan, and Bragg began her tour of southern museums in Richmond (where she pronounced Valentine's museum dead) the second week of October, with the intent of returning to Charleston on 10 December. She sought answers to four questions: "Can a small museum cover Art, Science, and History? (In practice this is reduced to the question of whether there are enough broad-minded directors to be found?) What is wrong with the Historical Society? What is wrong with the College Museum? Can a museum advantageously find permanent lodgment in a library, and if so under what conditions?" Her plan for this journey was revised to include museums in Charlottesville, Lexington, Blacksburg, Raleigh, Atlanta, Birmingham, Tuscaloosa, Montgomery, Macon, Augusta, and Savannah.[70]

Bragg wrote Emma, her secretary, on 24 November that she had spoken in each city, "saw museum trustees, and scarcely breathing between. . . . Tell my trustees that this trip is going to mean the whole south this side of the Mississippi served by good museums and our museum doing preparatory work and planning installation for most of them. But I begin to feel tired though I weigh *121*— the most I have ever. . . . I want to come home but after all the expense it seems foolish to not make a thorough work of it." Her itinerary had expanded to include Frankfort, Jackson, New Orleans, and Mobile, and in each of the sixteen cities visited she talked about what the Museum was doing and shivered "over having people see what we have*n't*." Delayed because she "got poison and sick four days [in] New Orleans," Bragg returned to Charleston "after having been gone for ten weeks on December 13."[71]

However she felt physically, her emotional health was wonderful. She was pleased with the success of the trip and believed that "it is going to have far-reaching effects and from all the follow-up work I plan to do, I believe it will prove to have laid the basis for the development of museums in the south which will, during the next ten years, to set a working limit, carry what the modern system should provide to every smallest rural community in the south." During this trip she met a number of women who were working as curators or volunteers in the different museums she visited. Some of these women became "attracted" to her, "taking pleasure in showing hospitality to a stranger." When Bragg did not write to them upon her return to Charleston, they became concerned that she was ill. But, of course, it was her "busy life [which] makes me slow in expressing what I feel."[72]

The trip through the Southeast also foreshadowed one of Bragg's next projects. She noted that one of the needs faced by small museums was for trained workers: "I could place three today if I knew where to find them but I do not know where to turn for them."[73]

Other events during the latter part of 1924 augured changes in her personal life as well. One of the charter members of the Poetry Society, Hervey Allen, left the city rather quickly after an incident at Snug Harbor. On occasion he would borrow Bragg's country house, where he would spend weekends with his students from Porter and then from the High School of Charleston, where he had transferred after leaving the military school under a cloud of suspicion of improper behavior with his students. It was after one of those visits that a father confronted Allen about his advanced ideas about sex. The father had learned about the weekend's activities from his son's account of Allen speaking about "sex hygiene and cleanliness."[74]

Bragg recalled that if Allen were touched he would freeze. This was due to a World War I injury, when his knees were cut. He could not take being reprimanded and, unable to defend himself against the allegation, left Charleston for New York. He taught at Columbia University and later at Vassar College, marrying one of his students there. Bragg defended Allen when recounting this story many years later, saying that nothing had happened at Snug Harbor. She remembered him as too broad-minded for Charlestonians, who still thought sex was dirty and spoke of flower pistils and stamens, while Allen talked to his boys straightforwardly.[75]

The Poetry Society and Allen's friends were all saddened by his sudden decision to leave town. Bragg had been his critic, playing a similar role for him that she played for DuBose Heyward. She recalled much later in her life that Allen was very unlike Heyward about criticism, as he more willingly accepted it than Heyward. Allen asked her to read all he wrote, and she added nearly all of the needed punctuation for his poetry. In a presentation copy of Allen and Heyward's *Carolina Chansons,* Allen wrote to Bragg that she had "kept the arctic teal out of South Carolina poetry."[76]

The city was missing other Poetry Society members as well. Heyward and his new bride, Dorothy, were out of town, as was Bragg's friend Anita Pollitzer. Actively involved with the women's movement and the National Woman's Party, Pollitzer in late November sent Bragg a copy of Edna St. Vincent Millay's poem "The Pioneer," honoring three of the leaders of the equal rights movement. But the city gained Alfred Hutty, an artist and etcher whom Bragg had befriended. He was returning from the Northeast for the winter and sent Bragg and Belle his kindest regards in a note. He hoped "that you and Miss Heyward will be glad to have us as neighbors." And, of course, Belle was still at 7 Gibbes. Her handwritten message in her Christmas card to Bragg read, "There's a lane that runs from my heart to yours / That's always blooming with love. . . . / With a year's glad memories / All for you."[77]

Heyward was gone from Charleston much of 1924, and by May 1925 he and the Poetry Society had run their course together. With Allen gone and Heyward resigning his position, other charter members also moved on with their careers. When Bennett's doctor encouraged him to cut his activities, the Poetry Society became a literary organization that discussed novels more often than poetry and brought speakers to the city, hosting receptions for them. But that was not what Bennett wanted, and he approached Bragg about the revitalization of the society. He wrote his family: "Had a long talk with Miss Bragg to get her to take a hand . . . to set the Society to rights. . . . Of course Laura Bragg has her enemies . . . but, murrain on them—they are doing nothing: she does things."[78]

Losing old friends to scandals or to new ventures neither slowed Bragg's progress nor deterred her from her professional goals, which had become of paramount importance. The new year 1925 began as the old had ended, with Bragg's time consumed by the Museum in Charleston as well as her work with the AAM. Coleman asked her to lead a session at the annual May meeting in Saint Louis on the scope of a community museum. She countered with the offer of a paper, "Culture Museums and the Use of Culture Material." Her study of museum conditions in the South had convinced her that "what we mean by culture is a solution of the small community's problems. . . . asking the larger museums to utilize their culture material with a definite purpose of developing a better world feeling through sympathetic labels, docent service, lectures, and work with children in connection with their culture exhibits." She became the keynote speaker with about an hour and a half for her presentation and discussion. However, Coleman was still unsure about the title of her presentation and proposed an alternative, "Field of the Small Museum." Her remarks were published with her title choice.[79]

It was not until Coleman received Bragg's four-page letter in mid April that he finally understood that she meant "culture" to be a broad interpretation of history and that a culture museum told the story of man, "tracing his development in a series of exhibits, from his use of implements through the development of ancient civilizations, down to the cultures of the present time." Bragg's idea was to use culture material to "create, among our own people, a better understanding and appreciation of foreign peoples. As I see it, the white race finds itself in a new position as a race no longer so preeminently predominant as before the World War. Conditions are so changed as to bring us into closer contact with peoples throughout the world, and for our own ultimate good, require closer understanding. . . . appreciation, and sympathy, through knowledge, are so far as the human mind has yet discovered the best means of making them (wars) as infrequent as possible." Holding "no brief for the Nordic race theory," Bragg felt that culture museums can "change our supercilious attitude toward the rest of the world."[80]

She claimed to need only twenty minutes to present the paper, and asserting that her deafness would make it impossible for her to conduct the discussion, she asked that Coleman lead it. He suggested other possible discussion leaders—the new director at Rochester, or overworked Mr. Rea, or some other whose name would come out of the registration cards. However, he would do it if she saw fit to call upon him, although he did not want to be on the program if he could help it.[81]

Coleman gave her credit for coining the "happy term 'culture' to cover a broad interpretation of history. This interpretation I have continued to call history in the Manual which I am preparing. Herewith is a table of contents. . . . It may interest you." It did interest her, and she saw another opportunity, just as she had seen the possibilities that the Rockefeller grant presented. That money had provided the means for her to conduct the study of southern museums and eventually orchestrate museum development in the South from the Charleston Museum, accomplishing one of her objectives for the 1923 AAM Meeting (although four months after she returned home he had yet to see her report).[82]

Claiming "considerable diffidence," Bragg suggested that, "as I have as you put it, coined the term 'culture museum' and practically started the idea of that type of museum in this country, what would you say to having me write a brief chapter for your Manual on 'The Culture Museum,' and then you adopt the term throughout the manual." Since her term was more comprehensive than his "historical museum," she suggested that he utilize hers throughout his manual: "Yet I know you would scarcely care to adopt it without giving me credit for the present use of it. Numbers of southern museums have asked me for a printed article on what I mean by a *culture museum* and how to build up one. A chapter in your Manual in the form of an introduction or appendix would only add to the sale of the book." Graciously, he responded that he would "be glad to use some material from her pen." By this time, however, he must have suspected that she did not have the time nor the inclination to write anything. When Coleman's *Manual for Small Museums* was published, it did not contain a chapter by Bragg. However, Coleman did include one paragraph acknowledging her and her contributions to the field—the culture museum theory.[83]

Her leadership continued to bring her more recognition. The Public Libraries group wanted her name included in the second edition of *Who's Who among North American Authors,* with her claim as an author based upon the museum publications she wrote and edited. She was elected to the

Council of the Museum Association at the 1925 May meeting. A friend from Baltimore, Dr. Howard Kelly, congratulated her on the Museum's outreach programs beyond the community and into the rural areas of the state.[84]

Long ago Bragg had acknowledged to her father that she was no good at letter writing. Now, with the many professional letters her position demanded of her, she continued to be "no good" at it. During that winter in 1925–1926 many of her personal letters were typed business-style and contained opening paragraphs of both explanation and apology: "If I wait to write by hand, you will never hear from me"; and "If you will forgive this dictated letter I may get a word to you. I have delayed, thinking I was going to write you personally, and have failed to do so."[85]

During the 1923 Charleston convention Bragg had formed a fast friendship with the "charming" Henry Stephens Eddys and his wife and believed that she owed the couple a "disproportionate amount of the pleasure I had in the convention." The couple were friends of Coleman, and Henry Eddys was an artist whose paintings were exhibited at the Gibbes Art Gallery. Bragg liked them so much that she wrote to them: "you must know how warm a friend I am now, last year, and forever. I don't have to write to tell you that. When you come this way you will find me last as I was when you were here last. I do not entertain people that I am not pretty fond of, but my friendships develop best with people who will understand that and do not make me unhappy over my failure to write. Please just be good friends and take me as I am. . . . please never doubt me."[86]

Bragg had asked Coleman at that meeting in 1923 and on into the year to assist her in locating a woman trained in museum work who was "able to prepare nature study courses and go in the county, as well as the city schools and give nature study instruction." In addition to "executive ability," Bragg's requirements included "knowledge and personality."[87] Louise Smith from Knoxville had personality and executive ability, and she accepted Bragg's offer to work for the Museum in 1925.

Louise Smith would first hold the position as public instruction assistant, and if found to be satisfactory in six months time, she would be elected curator of public instruction. She would be succeeding Bragg as the curator, with a yearly salary of $1,500 for forty-two hours a week and a one-month vacation. Bragg wrote Louise that she was required to visit county and city schools, conduct nature study trips, and "plan and put through the public instruction work, new school exhibits to be made, stories to be written, talks on nature study subjects, games, and handwork in the Children's Room, Story Hours, and short talks in the Main Hall. . . . At summer school . . . will you try to get some fundamental biology, regular beginner's biology which will give you the classification of the world's birds and animals. . . . Please do not hesitate about your ability to handle this work. . . . I have a special gift for making people develop ability they did not know they had." Bragg had searched for two years, finally finding the right woman. Smith arrived in Charleston and at the Museum that year, making both her homes. Bragg was right again: Smith met her demanding standards and remained until she retired from the Museum and the curatorship in 1942.[88]

As a result of Bragg's keynote speech on culture museums at the May meeting in Saint Louis, Mr. Hamlin, the president of the AAM, appointed her chair of the committee on the use of culture material. As with other committees, she was allowed to choose the members and determine the scope of their work. One of the members she had chosen, E. K. Putnam, hoped that she would give the committee something to do. Bragg developed a questionnaire for foreign students and asked for committee members' reactions to it. She also requested that each of them provide a list of the foreign students at their respective state universities and also a set of notes on the peoples and cultures with which they were familiar. In a letter to another committee member, she mentioned Dr. Putnam's fear that she "would not give the committee anything to do. After this letter, I imagine you will think his fear unfounded."[89]

Evidently President Hamlin was Bragg's supporter. He appointed her to the committee and agreed with her suggestion later that summer in 1925 that she be designated "Regional Chairman, Southeastern States." This suggestion was one she made directly to Hamlin and not to Coleman, who was the secretary for the organization and in the past had been her contact for association matters. Bragg's sphere of influence had grown so that she felt comfortable enough to have her secretary write to Coleman and ask for "some association stationery so that she can write some letters in connection with her committee work."[90]

Bragg was now such a recognized leader in the association that at the November council meeting at the Yale Club in New York City, Hamlin agreed with her suggestion that the "country might be advantageously zoned on the basis of museum service rendered and that the Southeastern United States might prove to be a suitable region for a demonstration of regional development." This recommendation was a result of her long-awaited report on the survey of southern museums she conducted between October and December 1924. This report, as well as her educational work in the state, assured her the respect of her peers as an expert on museums and museum education. In five years as director she had breathed fire into the institution, and the Charleston Museum was now recognized as "an up and coming institution" by such people as John Cotton Dana, director of the Newark Museum Association.[91]

Bragg had become well-known throughout the state as the Museum's director. But even before attaining that post, Bragg's persuasiveness and keen eye for opportunity had led her, as well as her Museum, in several promising directions for preserving the state's cultural heritage. Bragg had first met Anne King Gregorie of Oakland Plantation at Porcher's Bluff in 1917, when Gregorie shared her investigation of the Sewee Indian tribe with Bragg. They worked together creating a paper based on Gregorie's work, with Bragg handling the necessary details before the paper was to be published. Once it was completed, Bragg thought it read "delightfully" and "was having a map cut to show where the Indian mounds were located" to accompany the published article. Calling her work a hobby, Gregorie decided in 1925 that she wanted to withdraw it from publication, as she would be mortified to have the "Notes sprung as a contribution to science." Bragg was upset when she received Gregorie's letter and replied that "it was quite too late to withdraw them. In the first place, you gave them to me; and in the second place, the Museum has spent too much in preparation for them. The paper for the printing and covers was already purchased, plates were being made."[92]

Bragg's letter pointedly expressed her disappointment over Gregorie's wish to withdraw the notes and with Gregorie's reluctance to provide the planned map. Bragg could not understand "how you could have time to wander about Washington, Georgetown, and Beaufort and yet have no time to finish the simple strip of country between Hamlin Sound and Mount Pleasant. I have now pretty well covered it myself so I know it is no great task." Bragg did, however, end the letter on a complimentary note: "Your paper finds its chief value in its interesting and thorough assemblage of the historical references to a particular tribe."[93]

Rather than addressing her as "my dear Laura," as her previous letters had done, Gregorie's response was written to "Director Charleston Museum." Her words were equally as sharp in protest of Bragg's actions: "I have already made you four maps and have neither time nor inclination for a fifth. My last map is an historical compilation unconnected with the field work of your state survey, and shows with reasonable accuracy every place mentioned in the text. Its omission is a distinct loss against which I enter formal protest."[94]

Bragg quickly responded within a day and wrote Gregorie that she recalled seeing only two maps. She acknowledged that Gregorie could have done four but not sent them to the Museum. While she had "handled too much detail to be able to remember everything," she and Emma both recalled that Gregorie "pleasantly carried off the last map, with Mr. Hyer's outline, for transfer." Eventually Bragg and Gregorie resolved their dispute, and the "Notes on Sewee Indians" were published in 1925 as a *Contribution from The Charleston Museum*. Bragg sent Gregorie twenty copies of the issue and a sonnet she had written to express what Oakland meant to her when she first saw it in 1917. Interestingly enough, at the same time, in a letter to a museum colleague in Milwaukee, she called the article "amateur, but it described a district and brought together historical data which I wished to have published."[95]

Gregorie, whose French Huguenot family was of the planter aristocracy, was an educated woman; she earned the first doctorate awarded a woman from the University of South Carolina soon after this disagreement. Like Bragg, her primary emotional relationships were with other women, and she lived the last thirty years of her life with another female. Gregorie's friendly association with Bragg ended once Gregorie came to see Bragg's actions as "very superficial and all for show. One of her most provoking peculiarities was to drive up to our door with a Ford full of guests and 'honk' me out with her horn and demand to buy eggs. I did not like to sell eggs personally, and generally gave them to her. But the odd thing was that she always thought she paid for them, and no amount of free giving ever stopped her from coming for more the next time. The better I knew Miss Bragg, the less I thought of her." When Gregorie was first impressed with Bragg's brilliance and her skillful flattery, she willingly turned over her work on the Sewee Indians for printing as a *Contribution from the Charleston Museum*. But the fact that Bragg kept the Indian notes for eight years before finally publishing the material and acted, according to Gregorie, in a high-handed and autocratic manner was too much for Gregorie to tolerate. Their close friendship ended with this episode. Women, such as Gregorie, immediately liked Bragg, but over time some changed their opinions of her. While some men (for example, Bennett) did not like her at first, they often came to admire and respect her.[96]

Through her association with Gregorie, Bragg had become interested in Indians native to the state and to the lowcountry, and she participated in excavating various Indian mounds around the area, planning to publish a survey of them. In 1925 she met Edward C. L. Adams of Columbia, who helped her with excavation of a mound there that resulted in the discovery of an Indian shell culture. Adams had made an inaccessible site reachable, and he took care of Bragg's personal comfort. In her thank you letter to Adams she expressed her wish that she had his "freedom for accomplishment . . . [and] leisure for concentration on an interest . . . but life's duties limit most of us."[97]

One of Adams's other interests was collecting Negro folklore, and Bragg invited him to read his prison songs and to bring a group of black men from his Columbia plantation to sing at the Museum. Adams had compiled "Negro Prison Picking Songs," which Bragg thought were folk poetry. She shared them with John Bennett, in whose judgment she had absolute faith. They both thought Adams's work was the "best stuff of its kind" and encouraged him to continue collecting material around Columbia. Because Bragg failed to publish his work in a timely manner, Adams wrote to ask about the publication of this material. Ultimately, even though Bragg had the material long before *The Reviewer,* that magazine printed Adams's work three months before it appeared in *The Charleston Museum Quarterly* in the summer of 1925.[98]

She thought Adams should create his own book of the "gems," but she also wanted to keep a copy on file at the Museum. She assured him that there would be a label stating that his work was not to be copied and was to be used for reference and study "as a part of a survey of South Carolina folk lore, accessible to any student." Bragg, ever the critic with the keen eye, wrote to Adams: "You will see from the book I am sending you and Mrs. Adams how carefully variations of a folk song should be treated. Your original stories will be the gems of your book but its value will be in proportion to its completeness. It might be made to cover more than your region by friendly cooperation and exchange with those interested here and elsewhere."[99]

Just days after writing Adams, she sent a copy of the songs, along with Adams's article about Negro folk songs and stories of South Carolina, to Harriet Monroe of *Poetry* magazine. Since Monroe knew both Heyward and Bennett through the Poetry Society, Bragg wanted her to know that she consulted them about the significance of Adams's work. Asking her what she thought of the songs as folk poetry, Bragg wrote Monroe that she could use the "Picking Songs," taking them from the context of the article. She suggested to Monroe that the descriptive part of the article would furnish the facts for explanatory notes.[100] Obviously her assurances to Adams about copying and usage did not apply to her.

Another example of the intersection of Bragg's role as Museum director with her relationships was her association with David Doar of Harrietta Plantation on the Santee River. Doar was a trustee of the Museum and had entertained some of her Museum associates during the 1923 AAM Charleston meeting. He, like Gregorie and Adams, was involved with exploring, understanding, and preserving early South Carolina culture. His contribution to Bragg's *Museum Quarterly* was to be an article on rice that he had written especially for her. "I consider it one of the biggest and nicest things that was ever done for me," Bragg wrote Doar. Even the Museum's trustees noted in their December 1926 minutes that his work "was written for the Director," but as late as 1929 the Museum did not have the funds to publish the work. When it was finally published in 1936, the dedication to Bragg was deleted from the manuscript.[101]

Doar, like Adams, was compiling material about the Negro experience in the state. Bragg wanted to publish the proverbs Doar had collected in the Museum's summer quarterly, in "a Carolina Folk-Lore Department" that she had "recently decided to introduce." By December 1925 the Museum had opened a South Carolina Culture Gallery, thus bringing to life her concept of the culture museum. But there was no additional money to publish Doar's works in either a *Contribution* or a *Quarterly*.[102]

While Bragg was creating her Museum to fit her concept of culture, America was beginning to more closely examine same-sex relationships. In the early years of the 1920s there was a bitter political struggle between women and men over women's sexuality; over women's romantic friendships that had been accepted as normal before the 1920s; and over the nature of the sexes and their respective roles in society. The rules had changed due to the "phenomenal growth of female autonomy during and after World War I and the American popularization of the [male] . . . sexologist[s] who cast widespread suspicions on love between women."[103]

Women who loved other women were now forced to view their romantic friendships from a distance where they could be attributed to the context of time and place. This must have been extremely puzzling to women who grew up in the late nineteenth and early twentieth centuries and who had understood and accepted love and affectionate expression between women. One such woman was M. Carey Thomas, president of Bryn Mawr. "Even though she enjoyed the conversation of men, the intimate companions of her adulthood were women . . . she understood herself as a passionate woman who loved women." Although Thomas had read the medical literature in the mid 1890s, as had Bragg, she continued to write of her relationship to her lover in terms comparable to those used in marriages. By the 1920s Thomas faced a different world, and she feared that the lesbian label "would make it difficult for women to form with each other the warm attachments they needed."[104]

The men who created this different worldview of same-sex love were primarily middle-class physicians, such as Richard Krafft-Ebing and Havelock Ellis. These sexologists began writing about homosexuality in the latter half of the nineteenth century, and it was their definition of sexual invert (their term for lesbian) that was first applied to women of the lower class who engaged in intimate relations with other women. Not many decades passed "before relationships between middle-class women (who were becoming entirely too independent) came to be seen by sexologists as similar to what they had observed in the lower classes." Labeling such behavior as degenerate, sexually inverted, and homosexual, the scientific community became the arbiters of society's mores. And so women's sexual behaviors were defined by male sexologists such as Krafft-Ebing and Ellis, who insisted upon the primacy of the body as the definer of public, social behavior.[105]

Although Krafft-Ebing continued to be a major influence on sexologists well into the twentieth century, Sigmund Freud essentially replaced him by the 1920s. While Krafft-Ebing believed that the invert was born with the condition, and thus that it was congenital, Freud maintained that lesbianism was determined by childhood. Women who loved other women were abnormal and were encouraged to seek medical help in order to be cured.[106] What once had been seen as natural was now viewed as neurotic and a mental disease.

Much later in Bragg's life one of her students from the Wednesday morning classes during the 1950s believed that Bragg had made her place in Charleston through the relationships she established with the young children who were members of the Natural History Society. Bragg mentored them, and they remained attached to the Museum and to her, even after they grew into adulthood. When she was forced to dismiss Ned Hyer, she also lost "one of her girls," Helen von Kolnitz Hyer. Bragg later expressed the belief that because of her treatment of Ned, this Helen was one of only two people she knew hated her.[107] As Helen Hyer left the Museum, Helen McCormack entered.

Helen McCormack was younger than the other "bright young things" Bragg had befriended in her earlier years at the Museum. She had not participated in the Natural History Society but first appeared at the Museum as a volunteer in 1923, while still a student at the College of Charleston. Helen was a product of the public schools, while the others had attended either Porter Military Academy (for boys) or Ashley Hall School (for girls). She was a member of Bethel Methodist Church, while the others were Episcopalians who attended Grace, St. Philip's, or St. Michael's. Called a little angel, Helen was a petite blonde with a sweet voice. She was quite shy; Bragg recalled that Burnham Chamberlain once said to her, "Miss Bragg, can't you do something about Helen McCormack? Even her voice blushes when she talks to a man on the phone." Helen was remembered as meek and withdrawn well into adulthood. Bragg, with her special ability to draw the best from people, believed that she gave Helen confidence "by only giving her work she was sure she could accomplish."[108]

By August 1925 Helen had graduated from the College of Charleston with a degree in English and was working at the Museum in the absence of the curator of children's work, Anne Porcher, who was ill. Once she joined the staff her responsibilities included "study and preparation of exhibits." She also was Bragg's friend and was invited to Snug Harbor for weekends. The times spent there with Bragg were so important to Helen that she recalled them in a poem written more than fifteen years later:

> Not this green marsh, these clouds, this sun, these voices—
> Not merely these compose the peace I know
> But long remembered marshes, other places
> I treasure in my heart from long ago.

And for Helen, "Moon and silver beams always call back my first memorable night at Snug Harbor and you, Miss Bragg." While Helen was becoming an important part of Bragg's life, Belle was in Europe for six months, having left in August.[109] By the time she returned in January 1926, Helen was on staff at the Museum and very much a part of Bragg's world.

The Merging of Spheres:
Making Connections in the Museum World

> Museum exhibits are for the purpose of creating understand-
> ing, not teaching facts.
>
> Laura Bragg to Langdon Warner, 4 October 1926

BY THE SUMMER OF 1925 BELLE was away again in Europe. Her relationship with Bragg had reached a stage not unfamiliar in many heterosexual marriages, in which the partners' interests have diverged with one
working all the time and the other seeking ways to fill the empty hours.
At this point in Bragg's professional life, Helen McCormack's role at the
Museum had increased in importance. Nearly every activity Bragg was
involved in or initiated was connected with the Museum, and the expansion of her ideas about museum principles became paramount. With her
companion no longer in Charleston to make her home, Bragg's home was
the Museum. There she exerted the most influence and was recognized by
her colleagues as an expert.

During the last five and a half years of Bragg's tenure as director of the
Charleston Museum, she was concerned with five main issues. These
included the personal relationships she focused on in her professional
world; her continual search for funding sources for the Museum's activities; her efforts at preservation of Charleston's heritage; a museum studies
course she taught at Columbia University, which was designed primarily
for women museum workers; and her involvement with the expansion of
museum activities across the Southeast. By the end of 1930 all of these
concerns had been resolved in some way and the time had come for her
to seek new work that would hold her interest.

Beginnings and Endings

During Belle's 1925 trip to Europe, she sent Bragg several cards. In one she
admitted, "I wished I could know how you were. I feel very far from home
and cut off from things." She remembered Bragg's family at Christmas with
cards and gifts from Paris. New Year's Day in 1926 found Belle still in
Europe and away from 7 Gibbes and Bragg. Her card to "my dearest
Laura" reminded Bragg that "It is 11 years today since you came to live
with us at 7 Gibbes Street—do you remember that? I do with very loving

remembrance of the years between then and now." Bragg remembered Belle while she was away with a card and letter at Christmas describing all that she was doing, including her plans to teach a museum studies course at Columbia University.[1]

Though glad to hear about her activities, Belle wanted to know if Bragg's plans for the upcoming summer meant that Bragg would not be traveling abroad on a seven-month sabbatical that had been granted by the Museum's trustees for study. Instead of traveling to Europe (an activity that Belle enjoyed), Bragg chose the opportunity to teach at Columbia and spread her ideas about museums. Her professional world (with Helen in it) had become more important than her personal one with Belle.[2]

Just a short time after returning from Europe, Belle had an accident with the instantaneous gas heater in her bathroom that heated the bathwater. Bragg had been away from Charleston and returned to their home at 7 Gibbes just in time to discover that her friend had been accidentally asphyxiated, due to gas. Bragg wrote her father, "It was very serious, she was saved by only the merest chance and the most skillful and persistent effort. . . . There will be no after effect so far as we can judge."[3] Belle left Charleston again for Europe shortly after the gas episode and was gone until just before Bragg's birthday in October.

While Belle traveled through Europe that spring into the summer and fall of 1926, she sent Bragg a series of postcards. All indicated that Bragg was important to her: "thinking of you constantly—always your loving Belle"; "I feel so much better really like myself again my love, with you as always . . . and looking forward to being with you once more"; and "I thought of you today and wished you could be with me today."[4] During this time Bragg was in Charleston and then later in New York with Helen doing museum work, with Bragg as the teacher and Helen as her student.

Before Belle returned to Charleston that fall, Bragg received word that her father was ill, so ill that she was compelled to return north in September 1926 to see him. After finding him better than she thought, she still hated "more than ever to come away this time." Her visit north followed the same pattern she had established during her earliest years in Charleston when going home to see her family in Epping. After checking on the health of her "Dadda dearest," she used the time to visit museums in Boston, Philadelphia, and Trenton. She visited museum friends, the Eddyses (Coleman's friends whom she had met in 1923 at the Charleston anniversary meeting) at Nantucket, and Miss Haynes, a botanist, in Highlands, New Jersey, who was completing work for the Charleston Museum.[5]

In a letter to her father she described the beautiful campus that she loitered about in Cambridge, the glorious monument to Washington in

Princeton, and the beautiful gothic refectory in Proctor Hall. Bragg vividly described where she went and what she did as she made her way back south to her Museum. And it was to him, as always, that she wrote of her dreams and her passion: " If only I could make it [the Museum] reach the thousands and thousands it cannot touch yet. . . . I need to know so much and to do and be so much. I want the power of the great minds in strong bodies—to do!"[6]

Belle returned from Europe in time for Bragg's forty-fifth birthday on 9 October and gave her a card that read, "For my very dear Laura, with much love and all good wishes for your birthday from Belle." But only eleven days later Belle was dead from yet another accidental asphyxiation in her home at 7 Gibbes Street and was buried at Magnolia Cemetery. Her death was so sudden and unexpected that her cousin DuBose Heyward did not hear about it until some time later. Though Belle's death was ruled accidental asphyxiation, Bragg called it a "murder" when speaking of it in 1971, naming Faber Porcher, a boarder and Belle's distant relative, as the murderer. Faber, according to Bragg, had made two other murder attempts prior to this one, and in all three instances Dr. Wilson, a Museum trustee, had treated Belle, though the last time he was unable to save her.[7]

Whether family murder, an act of God, or the suicide of a lovelorn woman, Belle's death shook Bragg's world. Josephine Pinckney scripted a play based upon murder as an explanation of Belle's death. However, an equally plausible explanation is that of suicide. While Josephine composed her play based on Bragg's assertions, she wrote Hervey Allen a different story: "I was wondering if you heard that poor Miss Belle Heyward turned on the gas for the third and last time. . . . Don't put it that way to Miss Bragg of course—she insists it was another accident. Has gone into deep mourning and seems crushed. Of course the whole regime at the little house is changed and it is very sad for her." John Bennett wrote his family that Belle was found dead in her bed by Faber Porcher from gas poisoning but that she had been "bright, well, and full of seemingly cheerful plans" just the night before her death. Bennett also saw Belle's death as traumatic for Bragg. He told his family that Bragg was staggered because Belle's death "had cut the foundation from under her," as Belle provided "home, care, and affection" to Bragg. Belle was more than that—she was Bragg's supporter and protector and had been her entrée into Charleston's political and social circles.[8]

Bragg received letters of condolence from relatives and other friends. Bragg's mother, Sarah, acknowledged Belle as "a dear companion and helper to you in many ways. . . . my loving thoughts will be with you in this sorrow that I know so well will not grow less as you miss the dear presence of your friend." Bragg received sympathy from her sister, Barbara, and her Aunt Anna in New York City, who called Belle's death an "irreparable loss" and "a blow [that] has been dazing for you. The sudden shock is very stressing, but the daily realization of the emptiness of life." And her friend Yates Snowden wrote, "We have thought of, and felt for you. . . . Ah, the pity of it all,—and the mystery!!!" No one knew the real story then, and it has remained a mystery.[9]

While their letters spoke of Bragg's loss of a friend, Anita Pollitzer's letter went to the heart of why it hurt so deeply. Pollitzer grieved for Bragg "because Miss Heyward is gone." Pollitzer wrote of Belle's recent trip to Europe, calling it full of beauty and life and happiness. During that trip they had admired Michelangelo's sculpture of a sleeping woman called *Night*. Pollitzer's eloquent description of the sculptor's loss of his dearest friend, Vittoria Colonna, used his sonnets to express her understanding of Bragg's relationship with Belle, "when they were both mature—when their friendship was the closest human friendship he'd ever had." Her words and the use of the love sonnets displayed Pollitzer's understanding of Bragg's relationship to Belle and the depth of loss that Bragg felt.[10]

Pollitzer, who graduated from Columbia University, was aware of female sexuality. She even wrote Bragg about the "days of Belle and Aphrodite," referring to the Greek goddess who practiced same-sex love. One of Bragg's favorite photos was of the Bartlett head of Aphrodite, whose hairstyle she emulated. In fact Bragg posed beside that photograph when Doris Ulmann, the famous photographer, took her picture while in Charleston. Bragg identified with the goddess "because she knew how to love," it was recalled.[11]

By the mid 1920s Freud and his theories of human sexuality had pierced America's consciousness, even as far south as Charleston. Freud was popular with the American public because his "views held out hope for the cure of lesbianism." It was this hope for a cure that prompted the writer Radclyffe Hall to embrace the congenital theory and to make it central to the story of Stephen Gordon, the mannish lesbian protagonist in her novel *The Well of Loneliness*. Like Bragg, Hall was a member of the second generation of New Women who saw autonomy from the family as a right and sexuality as the symbol for female autonomy. Hall "believed that her novel would provide lesbians with a moral and legal defense, that a woman's body was her unavoidable destiny, against a society which viewed same-sex love as immoral or curable." The novel provided a full-fledged development of the congenital-inversion theme, and there were probably few lesbians who were unfamiliar with it. The book "generally had a devastating effect on female same-sex love not only because the central character ends in loneliness but because the author fell into the congenitalist trap. . . . It reinforced the notion that some women would not marry . . . because they were born in the wrong body. To be born into the wrong body was freakish."[12]

Thanks to the male sexologists Krafft-Ebing, Ellis, and Freud, "by the 1920s social reform, as well as feminism was being dismissed as neurotic, masochistic, sadistic, and homosexual." These punitive labels were pinned on women who were resistant to fully adult sexuality with men and on "frigid" women, who were seen as immature and masculine. By comparing both the women's movement and love between women to masculine drives, it seemed that the goal of the sexologists was to discredit and to wage war on any form of women's bonding. Promoting feminist goals and campaigning for rights that had strictly been masculine privileges before the women's movement was good evidence that such women were abnormal and degenerate. Bragg's brief flirtation with the women's movement aside, it was her drive and ambition that were perceived as masculine. Coupled with her "Boston marriage" to Belle and her new romantic friendship with Helen McCormack, she came to represent a threat to the dominant male culture in Charleston.[13]

What once had been acceptable and desirable female friendships were now seen not only as spiritual relationships but also as sexual ones. And women who continued to live in Boston marriages were viewed as obstacles to heterosexual relationships. One way to control these "sexless termites, hermaphroditic spinsters . . . was to condemn their love relationships . . . [which] posed a threat to a system where the fundamental expression of power was that of one sex over another." Romantic friendships between women were now classified as homosexual by the medical profession.[14]

Thus women's sexual options were narrowed by the controversy over *The Well of Loneliness* and by the sexologists and their medical definition of right and proper sex. The open-ended confidence and playfulness of the 1910s and 1920s did not survive these pressures, and the women's movement became irrelevant nationwide and even more so in Charleston. The romantic friendships of the first generation of New Women and the second generation's flamboyant, experimental lesbians became, in the public's eye, representative of the deprived and depraved *"femme damnée."*[15]

Whether or not Bragg acknowledged her own sexuality and how it was now viewed, she continued to pour out her feelings to her father. Expressing the despair she felt as a result of Belle's death, she wrote: "I have no heart for letters and am still too numb to think. . . . I don't yet see anything as worth an effort." She spent time at Snug Harbor and "grew almost serene working out of doors, pulling weeds and having new paths cut out and little seats put up." She assured her father that Belle's death made no change in her living at 7 Gibbes, since Nan Porcher "made the home as she did while Belle was in Europe." But there was a decided change in her immediate finances, even with the several hundred dollars Belle had left her in the will.[16]

Even though she was dealing with the emotional distress of Belle's death, Bragg still had to confront her old nemesis, how to deal with her money responsibly. She did not have the money to meet her obligations to her father. She asked that he tear up her checks for her December and January payments on the four hundred dollars she owed him. Being her "loving father," he did just that. Her father knew that she was suffering, and he wrote, "It seemed so sad that you should lose one who in so many ways during the years past has been your most dependable friend and homemaker as well."[17]

Nan Porcher may have made the house at 7 Gibbes home for Bragg while Belle was away in Europe, but once Belle died and Nan inherited the house, Bragg was no longer welcome there. A family friend recalled that in the discussion over the estate there was an argument over some of Bragg's gifts to Belle, and Nan decided that Bragg needed to find somewhere else to live. Within six months Bragg would leave what she had considered her home for more than a dozen years, buying "a little house" on Chalmers Street in March 1927. Reverend Bragg sent her four hundred dollars when she wrote him of the purchase, which she accepted as a gift. "And if you care to lend me 600 I will be very glad to have that much but the second 1000 is more than I wish to borrow."[18]

She moved into her "new-old" house at 38 Chalmers after Albert Simons, the city's premier preservationist architect, made extensive repairs to her exacting specifications. Her house reflected the meticulous care that Bragg gave to her personal appearance (her hair was perfectly styled, and her clothes were in the latest fashion). Bragg was soon joined by her friend Josephine Pinckney, who bought the house next door at 36 Chalmers Street that same year.

Writing to Mildred Babcock, who had been one of her students at Columbia University, Bragg's words indicate her pride in her home: "The gate is up and beautifully painted red. New garden earth has been put down each side of the walk and violets are growing beautifully. . . . The kitchen is finished and it shines with brilliant enamel paint, ochre walls and ceiling and a wonderful blue floor. You can see yourself in the walls and you feel as if you were walking in the Gulf Stream when you cross the floor. . . . but the doors still lack latches and I can't find any of the right period, as yet."[19]

While Belle's death continued to cause Bragg sorrow, a new interest came into her life. She met a Chinese student who was attending The Citadel. Not a month had passed since Belle's sudden death when she wrote to John Maybank, a wealthy contributor to the Museum, that she had heard that a Chinese gentleman had visited him the previous summer. She wished that "you would let me know who he was. Chinese culture and Chinese history ought to be of special interest to us all these days and are particularly so to me." Maybank may have directed her to The Citadel or she may have found her Tsing Hua student on her own, but by Christmastime her "China boy," Chia Mei Hu, spent ten days at Snug Harbor with her. By March 1927 Bragg was informing people that she had, "in a sense, adopted a student who is at The Citadel."[20]

Chia Mei was not the only reason Christmas in 1926 was bearable. Bragg's father continued in the close supportive role he had always played in her life. After receiving his letter of condolence, Bragg was prompted to write him, "I treasure every word you write me and the sympathy of your card I know is heartfelt." Her friends gave her a basket of good food and two bushels of oysters and cooked her a ham and a turkey, while neighbors brought her eggs, milk, candy, nuts, and oranges. She and "her young men visitors" ate waffles along with her father's honey. But even with these tokens of sympathy Belle was still on her mind when she wrote, "Oh, life is full, but my heart wants my friend."[21]

In the same letter to her father Bragg wrote about their family ancestry. She wanted to "trace all our lines on the female side. . . . I am convinced that our Braggs were closely connected with Connecticut. . . . And surely we can trace our Pithin and Lyman connections. William Pithin was governor of Connecticut. The Lymans have been scholars." She told him about a book that would give him "glorious reading, something big ahead of him, enough to fill months with marvelous musings"—Spengler's *Decline of the West.*[22]

In this letter to her Methodist minister father she is quite open concerning her belief about Christ's birth. Even when confirmed by Mr. Wood at St. Luke's in 1916, Bragg was not sure how she reconciled Christ's birth with her own faith. This doubt and questioning plagued her, and though she moved her membership in 1920 to St. Philip's Episcopal Church, where Belle was a member, she was not a believer. She and a friend, Dr. Kelly of Baltimore, discussed faith during his visits to the Museum beginning in 1921, and he often sent her books and articles about Christianity, trying to win her "away from law into grace." This practice continued into 1927, when he sent her a "wee book called My Counselor . . . as a special personal gift for daily consumption." It was Bragg's belief that "if we had practiced love throughout the centuries, the theology would speak for itself," and she saw Christ's birth as a coming of love, but not theology.[23]

While she rejected her father's and Dr. Kelly's organized religion, she continued to explore Chinese culture and religion through her "China Boy." Chia Mei became increasingly important in Bragg's life, as she did in his. He wrote to her the week after Christmas vacation, "I was almost moved to tears on thinking of the motherly love you have shown me. . . . Visions of your charming house and the delightful Snug Harbor are before me as I write to thank you for the pleasure." He began calling her "Tama which is a common but respectable Chinese term to address women of the age of one's mother; 'Ta' means big, 'Ma' means almost life mother."[24]

Bragg's world tilted again with her father's death in April 1927. She was at Snug Harbor when the telegram arrived, and she did not receive word until the next day when a Museum worker carried it over by boat. In writing to a friend about his death, she said, "in the deeper things of life, though not in those from day to day, his loss is the greatest I can know." Just days before he died she received a letter from him that made her "cry with happiness," and she asked him in her reply, "Do you love me so?"[25]

Helen McCormack knew how close Bragg was to her father, and after his death she wrote Bragg in Epping, "He is that sort of person who does not die. He will go on living—always dearer and dearer to you, and spiritually near when you want him." Helen offered Bragg comfort as well as love in this letter: "Mamma and Alice [Helen's sister] send you their love and I—you must guess at how much I'm sending, for a mere letter can't contain it. Your Helen." Bragg's return to the Museum and Charleston took her through New York, where Helen sent her a letter: "It has been almost a week since I talked to you this way. But I have been thinking of you, of course." Chia Mei wrote her after learning of her father's death: "Words are too far away from explaining my deepest sorrow toward the death of your father. I wish you could see that every word appeared on the paper is a drop of tear."[26]

Helen was now Bragg's companion, but in a much different way than Belle had been. Belle had been older than Bragg; Helen was younger. Belle had belonged to the class of people that Bragg sought associations with and was a member of the Episcopal Church; Helen was Methodist. Bragg kept her own house at 38 Chalmers, while Helen continued to live with her family at 8 Bull Street. And Bragg and Helen shared their professional world, while Belle's social world and Bragg's professional world had merged only through the Poetry Society. Belle had never been a part of the hours consumed by the Museum. Helen's relationship with Bragg was deepened at Snug Harbor, while there is no indication that Belle ever went to Bragg's country house. Many of Helen's early letters and even some written in the late 1930s speak of that special night at Snug Harbor. While Bragg was in Washington for the 1927 American Association of Museums meeting, Helen wrote of the moon that special night, "that same moon who disregards the clouds at Snug Harbor—is just outside my window. I blow her kisses and tell her to take them to you.... I'm very, very glad you took me to see the Moon. She was so perfect and so beautiful, and we saw her in so many ways along the shore. Dearest I see so much beauty because of you."[27] This is a love letter from a young woman who was much in love with the person who had opened the world to her. Bragg had mentored her protégée, and Helen had fallen in love. Whether Bragg loved Helen in the same way is not clear.

Ned Jennings also shared Bragg's passion for culture and same-sex affection. He traveled to Paris under a Carnegie scholarship soon after Belle's death to study art for eight months. Before he left, he had produced a fantasy revue, "Show Box," for the Junior League of Charleston that met with mixed reviews. He also was the program and costume designer for the Society for the Preservation of Spirituals. Ned's eccentricity was evidenced in a production where women wore only fig leaves and on another occasion at a Charleston plantation party when he "is said to have danced around a bonfire to the music of a banjo, dressed in a blanket, and wearing a headdress of Spanish moss."[28]

Ned returned to Charleston from Paris in September 1927. He began another series similar to the "Drama of Civilization"; became an instructor at the Art School of the Carolina Art Association; led a study group on Greek mythology; and provided a mask illustration for the Poetry Society's *Year Book*. Though his professional life was productive, he seemed unhappy to some. John Bennett remembered: "Ned had taken himself from our quiet, although sympathetic ring, into the swift and cocktail-drinking set of younger people striving to be mature, and middle-aged men and women trying vainly to remain young; but he was not a drinking man, nor ever was; although he always drank a cocktail or more to stir his fancy for his dances—which were strange things."[29]

Not only did Ned return to the city in the fall of 1927, but Bragg's group of bright young things grew in number when five additional Chinese students joined Chia Mei at The Citadel. In her quest to learn about Chinese culture and all things Chinese, she carried on a "voluminous correspondence" with a friend of Chia Mei who attended a northern college and was a "rabid advocate of the Cantonese cause." These Chinese students were known around Charleston as "Laura's babies," and most people thought it was strange that she chose to adopt them as she did.[30]

Bragg poured affection and understanding into these relationships. The students cherished all that she did for them, and one wrote, "you really are the only one who are [sic] so kind to us ... in this country." Another Chinese cadet expressed his feelings: "your sympathy and thought for others, your care for your friends, and your spirit of sacrificing for others have been too strong for you to be balanced by the thought of your own welfare and health. . . . Whenever I think of your constant kindness and warm friendship toward me, I could not find enough words to describe my obligation and gratefulness to you."[31]

Chia Mei attended church events with Helen and escorted both her and Emma Richardson to other social occasions in Charleston. All of the Chinese students enjoyed using Snug Harbor and the house at 38 Chalmers Street while Bragg was away during the summers, when she was either teaching at Columbia or visiting her mother at Epping. They also drove Bragg's Chevrolet sedan around town and near The Citadel campus, which was located in a racially mixed residential area in the northwestern part of the city. Many young blacks who lived near the campus of the military school knew they were banned from the institution because of Jim Crow laws. They found it difficult to understand why the Chinese, who were also people of color, could attend an all-white institution while they, native Charlestonians, could not go to any white college in the city or the state.[32]

In the fall of 1927, just after the arrival of the other five Chinese students, it was rumored around town that Bragg had applied for Poetry Society membership for all her "babies." Bennett noted in a Sunday letter to his family that it was a "faux pas; there are too many who will take offense." Bragg must have been persuaded otherwise and instead attempted to open Charleston society to them through the formation of the Ta T'ung Club. Bennett noted it as a "Conversation or Discourse club for the young Chinese: Ned Jennings, Ned McCrady, Robert Marks, . . . Mary Pringle, . . . and the SIX celestials" were all members. Another Charlestonian, Mary Martin Hendricks, who was also a member, understood its purpose somewhat differently. She recalled that it was designed as a cultural organization to introduce the Chinese students to Charleston society and to teach white southerners about Chinese culture through lectures, given by the Chinese students or by Bragg. Eventually these club meetings would become more "high brow," as Bennett termed them. At these gatherings, Bragg was to provide insight into Greek culture and life while focusing on Ned Jennings's sculptures.[33]

Bragg set many tongues wagging in the homes on High Battery when she invited respectable young ladies to meet the Chinese cadets at her home or at picnics at Snug Harbor. Margaretta Pringle Childs, whose mother allowed her older sister, Mary, to attend the club meetings, recalled that at that time Charleston society was not broad-minded enough to accept the students, considering them "colored." It was believed that respectable young ladies would be contaminated if they talked to the Chinese. But for the Chinese students, the club cultivated a friendship that was "sacred or ideal . . . there is no other motive . . . except mutual understanding and mutual appreciation," and they saw it as "a remarkable and unprecedented event in the history of the Americo-Chinese friendship."[34]

Bragg chose to warn "her babies" about talking to "half-negro blooded boys." One of the Chinese cadets, Shu Chun Liu, first met these boys on Market Street. Then on a different day they appeared at the Museum and followed him into the lecture room, where they sat beside another cadet, Li-Sui An. Listening to the speaker, Shu Chun "felt embarrassed all the time when the lecture was going on. When the lecture ended, . . . they wanted to shake hand [sic] with us and say goodbye. What could I do?" It was Li-Sui who told Shu Chun how "much embarrassed" Bragg was over the incident. Writing her a letter of apology, Shu Chun remembered that she had "seriously told me sometime ago that I should not have anything to do with them and I promised you too. This is why I feel myself guilty."[35]

There can be no doubt that these Chinese students were aware of the "colored problem." When a Chinese laundryman was murdered on King Street by four black boys, Shu Chun's "sympathy was somewhat abated." However, his opinion of the four blacks changed after he read *Uncle Tom's Cabin*. When he thought about the murder of his countryman in light of the book, he wrote Bragg, "Now I am just thinking that maybe this is not their fault because they are ignorant and uneducated. 'Forgive them, because they don't know what they do.'"[36]

Among the most perplexing paradoxes that exist about Bragg's objective with the Chinese students and the Ta T'ung Club is her opposition to mixed-race relationships and marriages. While he was in pilot training Chia Mei met an American woman whom he thought he wanted to marry, but Bragg quickly changed his mind. After an exchange of letters, Chia Mei wrote Bragg, "Herewith I want to assure you from the bottom of my heart that I'll never marry Virginia because of various reasons as you know." One can only guess how she reacted to the news that two of the other Chinese students thought Helen was adorable and had acceptable virtues. Helen tried to dissuade one of them by explaining how she had put aside all thoughts of love and marriage due to the conditions at home (Helen's parents, according to her, were old and poor, and her sister was an invalid).[37]

As treasured as Bragg was by the other Chinese students, Chia Mei was like her son, for he truly had her heart. During the summer of 1930 Chia Mei was in training at Kelly Air Field in San Antonio when he was involved in a terrible plane accident. Bragg, in Washington at the time, was able to take a train to Texas via Jacksonville, and she spent her month's vacation nursing him back to health. Bragg wrote many letters from the hospital and spent her time at Chia Mei's bedside, where she planned how to get him back to Charleston to recuperate. She wrote to Robert Marks, one of "her boys," about Chia Mei's accident, expressing her feelings about her adopted son and his near fatal crash. Chia Mei was one of the few people in her life for whom she expressed her compassion and sympathy.[38]

Robert Marks was another brilliant young man whom Bragg mentored. Dismissed from Yale and disinvited to return to the College of Charleston, he would only study what he was interested in, rather than what the professors assigned. Bragg sent him to New York City with an introduction to Henry Canby of the *Saturday Review of Literature,* and Marks wrote reviews for that publication. He then returned to the Museum where he became curator of music instruction and used his own patented invention of an "instantaneous recording machine" to record speeches and music on metal disks for traveling music exhibits. He was also a great friend of the Chinese cadets and, as a result, wrote a history of Chinese musical instruments.[39]

Given her self-described missionary role, Bragg's memory of her relationship with these young Chinese, what she would call "the Chinese business," had to have been influenced by time when she recalled: "The Chinese business had great influence on my thinking. . . . I don't know if I opened the Museum to colored people before I met the Chinese. . . . I never believed in intellectual equality, but I did believe in equality of opportunity. . . . I know my feeling of fighting for the underdog developed when I was fighting for the Chinese at The Citadel."[40] As her father's apt student, she had witnessed his missionary work among black students in Mississippi during a time of great social upheaval. She saw him working for and with the underdog, blacks who had been freed but were still treated as if they were slaves in the New South. Bragg feared that the Chinese cadets would also face the same oppression and discrimination.

Bragg had grown so weary of museums and conventions that by August 1930 she had Coleman write the Guggenheim Foundation "to make an inquiry concerning the possibility of a research fellowship or scholarship in the case of a museum director who would like to pursue a line of inquiry in Europe." Writing the secretary of the foundation, Coleman identified Bragg as "the director of the Charleston Museum, . . . as well as whose influence upon museums throughout the South, is doubtless known to you." Bragg had an interest in "determining specifically the parts played by European cultures in shaping our own," which would be the focus of her study.[41]

The secretary replied to Coleman that Bragg was "the kind of person, with the kind of project that we would be glad to consider." Coleman forwarded the application forms to Bragg with a handwritten note, "Here you are. I'm delighted." Her completed application indicated that she intended to study ironwork, china, glass, furniture, architecture, and the evolution of culture during June, July, August, and September 1931: "For 25 years I have been studying the history of civilization by myself applying what I have learned to problems of the culture history museum or the culture history section of the general museum.... In asking for a fellowship ... I am seeking means for answering definite questions which have confronted me in my work as a museum director and which my study of culture history here in America has so far left me unable to settle.... The results of four months study in Europe would be utilized in exhibits and public instruction in the Charleston Museum, articles on culture history ... and in instruction to workers in the southern museums I seem to influence." Bragg returned the application to the foundation by 14 November 1930 but did not receive a Guggenheim Fellowship.[42]

The Museum's Programs and Activities and Bragg's Search for Funding (1925–1930)

At this point in her life Bragg believed that the acknowledgments and honors she had received were almost enough to see her through the tough financial times facing the Museum. By November 1925 she was involved in a membership drive, searching for new members who had money to give to the Museum. In a letter to a prospective member she wrote what were prophetic words: "The demands which people are making on us are now so much greater than I can meet, that if I did not have a good deal of faith in the future, I would want to throw every thing up and go north. Beside the need of new members, the city's not being able to pay anything for two months makes our condition rather more serious than it would be otherwise and you will be helping very definitely, if you are able to give us your generous subscription immediately." Three months later the financial problems for the city were no better; in fact, the county millage had been reduced from forty mills to thirty-six, with a "consequent reduction in our income." As a result, Bragg's home phone, which was "used entirely for Museum business," had to be disconnected "on account of a reduction in our [the Museum's] appropriation from the city." When Bragg was asked to chair a committee to raise money for another organization in the state, she replied, "we need money here so much more than they need it anywhere else so that it does seem tragic to try to raise for some other place."[43]

While Bragg was teaching at Columbia and dealing with her relationships, first with Belle and then with Helen McCormack, the Museum continued to grow and flourish without extra money for the programs and activities it offered Charleston citizens. Her next report to the mayor and the city indicated how successful the Charleston Museum was in achieving her goal of becoming the modern museum that visualized and interpreted the environment for the visitor. Museum attendance increased by over three thousand visitors from sixty-five thousand in 1925 to sixty-eight thousand in 1926. The public instruction department grew to include traveling school libraries.[44]

Bragg's work with the public schools had expanded far beyond those first traveling exhibits she sent out only to city schools in 1912. Thirteen years later the county schools received fifteen traveling school exhibits, as well as traveling libraries. The service to the city schools had also become more integrated, for the Museum's contribution to public instruction was more in line with the teachers' curriculum. Now individual students from the city's twelve public schools came to the Museum for classes and lectures, using the Museum's library as a public reference library. Boys and girls had their own library clubs and were allowed to check out books free of charge.[45]

In the nine city public elementary schools Bragg's nature study course was taught in the first, second, and third grades as a regular part of the curriculum. The Museum's Department of Public Instruction sent schedule cards each week to teachers that indicated the work for the following week along with the appropriate traveling school exhibit. Additionally, Bragg had made arrangements with the city superintendent that each teacher be required to bring her/his class to the Museum twice a year.[46]

The Museum distributed tickets to fourth- and fifth-graders so that they could attend a series of story hours offered by the Museum throughout the school year. Topics for these story hours, which were selected to stir the "imagination and thrill the heart," included, for example, the "Days of Knighthood," the Norse sagas, Greek myths, a "Child's Life in China," and Chinese fairy tales. Sixth- and seventh-grade teachers could request geographical, historical, and/or industrial exhibits— for example, "Modes of Transportation in China," which contained a scene in rural China with a fisherman "using a typical Chinese river boat . . . [while] a wealthy official rides in a sedan chair . . . a farmer rides a water buffalo . . . and another man walks."[47]

Working together, Museum staff and geography teachers developed special geography exhibits that students could produce at the Museum and for which they would receive extra credit. These projects took various forms of expression: painting, modeling, stage-set making, miniature group making, block printing, and creating costumes for dramas and plays, for example. Finally, teachers in secondary schools received the exhibits on request and visited the Museum by appointment. Through Bragg's efforts, every school in the city was part of the educational program at the Museum to some degree.[48]

Some of "her boys" were at the Museum helping Bragg. Ned Jennings, as the curator of art, conducted handwork classes and helped the students illustrate geography projects. Burnham Chamberlain headed the preparation department and mounted bird and animal skins. Art classes were taught by the new curator of prints, Elizabeth O'Neill Verner, who had joined the staff around the time that Bragg purchased Verner's childhood home on Chalmers Street. But for northern visitors as well as Charleston residents the most popular department at the Museum was the South Carolina Culture Department, which included the "valuation and purchase of South Carolina furniture and furnishings." Bragg placed Helen McCormack in this department and intended that she be trained as a specialist in South Carolina culture materials such as furniture, glass, porcelain, prints, textiles, and ironwork, not only for the Charleston Museum but also "for other museums in the South to which she can go on exchange."[49]

The Museum's appropriation was four hundred dollars less in 1926 than it had been in 1925; in fact, each year after 1924 the museum "had a constant shrinkage" in appropriation, even though Bragg spent much time at city council meetings pleading for money, just as Rea had done. There are several possible explanations for this decrease: the county's and city's deteriorating financial conditions; Bragg's gender, which framed the all-male council's reaction to her funding requests; or their inability and unwillingness to accept the Museum as an educational institution that served all citizens, regardless of color.[50]

The time had come to look to sources outside the city for funding the Museum's educational activities. For Bragg, the logical move was to appeal to the state superintendent of education for help in funding the traveling school exhibits, since they were now being used by teachers across the state. Since 1922 the Museum had responded to exhibit requests from teachers in Florence, Beaufort, Rock Hill, Chester, Greenwood, Georgetown, Sumter, St. Matthews, and Greenville. The cost of building the portable display cases, assembling the display materials, writing the teachers' stories, and paying the curator of public instruction's salary had been borne by the Museum through city appropriations.[51]

Writing to the Sumter superintendent of schools (who was also a member of the South Carolina Board of Education) in November 1926, Bragg asked to talk with him about the exhibits for the whole state and invited him to have lunch with her at the Country Club of Charleston (where the Museum had a membership), since she had been told that he was in the city every other week. On the same day Bragg wrote to State Superintendent J. H. Hope and proposed a similar meeting so that she could talk over her plan for the traveling school exhibits. She wrote Hope, "As a gentleman told me in New York, you may be very busy in the hours you are here, but you have to eat, and we could have our conference over luncheon."[52]

Bragg considered herself a businesswoman and the equal of any man. Confident and assertive as a professional museum director, she must have stunned those two native South Carolinians. It was quite possible that she was unlike any woman, southern or not, they knew. Even in the late 1920s and into the Depression years southern authors such as Herbert Ravenel Sass were writing about the "romantic ideal of Woman as being enshrined and set on high." Bragg was a lady, but not the southern lady enshrined on high, and she would not have tolerated being treated as one.[53]

In what was to be a long and ultimately fruitless search for funding, Bragg also went outside the state to organizations such as the Carnegie Foundation and the General Education Board. In writing to Richard Halsey of the Metropolitan Museum, she asked for his help in getting in touch with the General Education Board and with the Carnegie Foundation. She was sure that she could persuade them to assist the Museum in its education work and called the present situation almost tragic: "I have almost a confidence that if I could present the needs . . . before men organized to assist . . . that I could make them feel the need right here." She may have been confident about her persuasive ability, but the Carnegie Foundation declined to assist the Museum, as they had "decided pretty definitely to concentrate our efforts in the arts, for the present, in the colleges."[54]

The issue of funding for the school exhibits and for the Museum was a continual worry for Bragg. She wrote Coleman, "You generally see me with plenty of courage but I am down flat now from lack of money for expansion. There are great opportunities in every direction and financial depression here is so great that there is no chance of more money."[55]

In a letter dated 21 January 1927 she explained to Dr. S. H. Edmunds in Sumter, "probably there are politics involved [with Hope] and, as I do not wish to have anything to do with politics, I will just leave the matter with you, confident that you can straighten it out." Politics were involved as Hope wanted her to go to the Charleston County delegation to ask that they introduce a request for five thousand dollars for traveling school exhibits before the Ways and Means Committee, a message that Hope sent by way of another. Further, she was concerned that "if Mr. Hope were honestly in favor of this progressive piece of work it would be perfectly easy for him to follow my suggestion." Bragg did not understand Hope's behavior. What she found peculiar was that he told someone else that he had already turned in his budget by the time Bragg spoke to the state board. Even though he was supposedly in favor of her proposal, Hope was willing to let the whole matter slide. Bragg found all of this odd, as she "understood for the last two years that he wished to have the school exhibits."[56]

Also on 21 January 1927 she provided Hope with a clear explanation that the Charleston County delegation would have no interest in asking that "the Department of Education make the appropriation [of five thousand dollars,]" since that money was to be used outside of Charleston County. Bragg wrote quite specifically as to what she would do: "I am prepared to take no further action"; she was also specific about what she had requested of the delegation, which was "to do nothing except support you."[57] She ended this letter by suggesting how Hope might word the budget item request.

Bragg had a 24 January 1927 response from Hope, but it was not particularly positive nor did it address the issue of the delegation's role. In her return letter she again pointed out to Hope that the county delegation was taking no action at her request and—politically astute as she was—that the state board was neither progressive nor visionary in the matter of the school exhibits. She asked that Hope consider the future of education in the state: "I am quite sure that in twenty years from now, if you do become so, you will be very proud to claim credit for it. . . . I truly believe you will think of it as one of the most important things of your administration as State Superintendent of Schools." Dr. S. H. Edmunds pleaded her case with members of his delegation, who advised that it was best to postpone the question until the next session of the legislature.[58]

In 1926 there were 147 traveling school exhibits going out to thirty city and county public schools and nine private schools, and there were one hundred traveling school libraries. By the next year traveling school exhibits went out to all the schools in the city and the county, and for the first time they were systematically circulated to the county's black schools. With money donated by a Quaker philanthropist to the General Education Board, the Jeanes Fund assisted rural black schools by providing itinerant teachers who did extension work in the industrial arts, and the Jeanes teachers carried the exhibits from school to school.[59]

Charleston was still an extremely isolated county. A photographer from Maine noted the societal conditions upon her visit to the South Carolina lowcountry in the late 1920s as she took pictures of many young black children. Bragg understood the effects of isolation and poverty, and expressed sorrow over the condition of southern people, who were in her estimation, "in need of a better comprehension of modern science, a greater understanding of foreign peoples living today, and some approach to an appreciation of the fine arts as applied to life. In spite of the educational efforts of the last few years, people outside the centers are more backward than those of the north, and there is at present, along with an awakening of spirit and desire for knowledge, a reactionary tendency which is inclined to direct this spirit conservatively." Bragg's points were valid. In the 1930 census more than 78 percent of the residents of South Carolina still lived in rural areas, and the public education system in the state had proven woefully inadequate well into the first decades of the twentieth century."[60]

Bragg's and the Museum's involvement with the black community was limited to the Saturday openings, but an incident showed her to be more open and liberal than her southern friends. This incident also demonstrated how separate the two races were. Mayor Tom Stoney had visited the studio of Edwin Harleston, a black artist who had graduated from Avery Institute and Atlanta University and had also studied art at the Boston Museum of Fine Arts. Pronouncing himself favorably impressed with Harleston's work, Stoney believed that the general "citizenship would be interested to know that Charleston, the cultural center that she is, has so affected a member of the colored race that he has gone out and perfected himself in the art of painting and crayon drawing." He suggested to Bragg that she would be rendering a real service to a "worthy individual of the opposite race" if she could arrange an exhibit of some of his work.[61]

Upon seeing Harleston's work, Bragg agreed with Stoney and made arrangements for an exhibition of his portraits in oil as well as some of his sketches. In her letter to Stoney she pointed out, "As the south is frequently criticized for its supposed lack of appreciation of the attainments of the Negro race, you may be glad to be able to point to this exhibit during the meeting of the Foreign Trade Council." But Bragg knew that the Museum "under normal circumstances . . . would not think of having a one-man show of modern oil paintings." Wanting to keep peace with the Gibbes Art Gallery and "knowing that showing an exhibit of modern art, particularly oil paintings, are the province of the Art Gallery rather than the Museum," she wrote to the gallery's secretary, Tom Waring, and offered the Art Association the opportunity to have the exhibit.[62]

Ten days after Bragg sent this letter to Tom Waring, the Museum's trustees met in a special session. While they were unanimous in desiring to exhibit Harleston's work, they voted to defer it with reluctance. Unforeseen circumstances had intervened (local artists had pressured Bragg and the Museum's trustees to abandon the idea), so Bragg and Mayor Stoney both decided that the exhibit would hurt Harleston. The letter informing Harleston of the trustees' actions and the decision made by Bragg and Stoney was sent to the wrong address, that of Harleston's aunt, who was out of town. It was not until seven days later that Bragg realized the mistake, for Harleston sent her a letter with the catalogs from his previous exhibits and a list of the ministers of the city's black churches whom he wanted notified of the Museum exhibit. Calling it an "unhappy thing" that she was "terribly distressed about," Bragg assured him that deferring the exhibit was to his advantage. Harleston would never exhibit his work at the Charleston Museum, although his work was later shown at the Gibbes Art Gallery.[63]

Bragg made a third attempt in 1928 to become directly involved with the Negro community by securing books for use in the Negro schools. She and Clelia McGowan, an active clubwoman, had written letters to the county board requesting that they contribute seventy-five dollars for books to be used in the Negro schools. "The Board agreed to the proposition, provided the plan was legal. . . . These books will be the property of the County Board and kept either at the home of the colored superintendent or in the office of the County Superintendent to be distributed to the schools by the colored supervisor."[64]

Whether dealing with the mayor, the school board, or the Museum's trustees, Bragg was not one to give up or be daunted by adversity. Knowing how little money there was for the Museum and its extension programs, she continued her schemes for funding the expansion of the traveling exhibits. She wrote to the director of the Educational Museum in Saint Louis in June 1927 that she was "planning for a series of traveling exhibits to go to all the states of the South and to serve as an initial step in providing a system of traveling school exhibits for each state. . . . The General Education Board is considering giving me assistance for it." Bragg was playing fast and loose with the truth, as she had just written a six-page letter requesting the aid of the board for a three-year program: twelve thousand dollars for the first year, fifteen thousand dollars for the second, and twenty thousand dollars for the third. The money would be used for the design, construction, preparation of teaching materials, and distribution of the traveling exhibits. There is no record of response to this request.[65]

In early January 1928 Bragg began looking again for support of the bill concerning funding for the traveling exhibits. She wrote one of the wealthiest and most influential members of the Museum's board of trustees, J. L. Coker of Hartsville, a wealthy cotton broker and an inventor. She asked that both he and his wife contact all of the men they knew on the Education Committee and that they, if possible, attend a committee meeting on 25 January at which she planned to speak. Sending her thanks for his help in a later letter, she seemed hopeful that the committee would be able to get together at least one thousand dollars. In her mind this would be evidence that "the idea was taking—we could persuade the Superintendent of Schools to include the item in his budget next year. At present, he is passing the buck."[66]

Bragg's appearance before the committee was successful, for a concurrent resolution was approved that cleared both the House and the Senate, and the entire General Assembly voted in favor of the Museum's request. Sam Rittenberg, a Charleston County member of the state legislature, offered her hope that "next year [1929] will bring you the desired appropriation so as to enable you to extend the benefits of your undertaking to all schools of the State." Bragg recognized the leverage of this powerful support for the exhibits and wasted little time before writing to Superintendent Hope: "I know that you are as pleased as I am with the concurrent resolution . . . I thought it would please you because it gives you just the backing you need and you can have no further hesitation about including the five thousand dollars in your budget next year."[67]

By 1928 there were 160 traveling exhibits circulating regularly in the city schools (white, black, and private) and in the county schools. Created by the Museum's curators, such as Burnham Chamberlain, Ned Jennings, and Louise Smith, they included: "the nature study exhibits (which included mounted specimens of small mammals and nearly every bird native in the state), the Forestry Exhibits (which included models of a tract of land before, during, and after good and bad foresting) and the Culture Groups." Every county school also had a traveling library each month during the school term.[68]

Given her own handicap of deafness, Bragg recognized the importance of touch as "a real asset in teaching." In an interview conducted late in her life Bragg spoke of the need for every child to touch and handle the items in these exhibits as a way of learning. (Birds and other animals were regularly replaced in the exhibits as they were petted to death.) She was to emphasize this need in a letter to the educational department of Newark Museum Association: "I do not approve of exhibits hidden behind glass with nothing that children could touch . . . I believe that tactual value of visual instruction work is as great as the ocular."[69]

Bragg must have received some response from Hope because later in December 1928 she corresponded with a teacher who had requested information about the exhibits: "Mr. Hope has promised that the item will be put in his budget this year. I hope he has done so." Always one to recognize an opportunity, Bragg understood the power of a teacher's letter to the superintendent and suggested that the teacher write Hope to ask how soon she "would be able to obtain exhibits as a result of that ... resolution ... I think he would be glad to know of your desire. . . . He needs to know, however, that the different teachers want the exhibits so that he may the better advocate the appropriation."[70]

Bragg did not hear from Hope again after their May exchange of letters, when he had requested that she write him again in October to tell him "clearly as to what she wished." (She complied with this request and sent a copy to Sam Rittenberg.) The new year arrived without word from Hope, even though another county delegation member, Senator Legare, had also written him asking for "assurance that the $5,000 had been included in his budget." Bragg was not without charm and used flattery with her ally Rittenberg. She called him a friend to the exhibits. Complimenting his political skills, she pointed out that she had decided to "leave the matter completely in your hands, feeling confident that you can handle it as ably as you did the passage of the concurrent resolution last year."[71]

The money to build the exhibits (construction costs were estimated to be fifty dollars per box) was coming from an ever decreasing Museum budget with increasing demands for services. Bragg had seen the last few years as discouraging financially and ended her January 1929 letter to Rittenberg by asking him about the hope of an increase in the value of the county property values, which would have a "consequent slight increase in the Museum appropriation."[72]

Bragg's relationship with Hope turned into a battle of wills. Even though Hope had replied to Senator Legare's letter on 20 December and indicated his desire to include the item in the State Department budget, Bragg wanted Hope to understand that the Museum would be unable to do the work: "the only fund from which the Museum is willing to receive the money for this work is that under your control. The Museum will positively refuse to do the work under any special appropriation or bill since it feels that this is properly a part of the work of the Department of Education. So that there can be no question of any bill being introduced in the Senate."[73]

Luckily for the exhibits (and later for the Charleston Free Library), Bragg's professional association with a young man, Clark Foreman, led to the funding of the exhibits. Foreman wrote Bragg in February 1929 that he was working with the Rosenwald Fund of Chicago, which was "particularly interested in education and health." Given that the Rosenwald Fund provided financial support to educational and social service institutions throughout the South, Foreman believed that there was a match between its goals and Bragg's work. Since he and other Rosenwald Fund officials would be in Charleston, they wanted to hear from her about the Museum's library service and educational extension work. He asked that she bring together some of the "more outstanding supporters in the white group and some of the more educated colored leaders" to meet Mr. Embree, the president of the Rosenwald Fund.[74]

On their visit Foreman and Embree saw the Museum and visited Dart Hall, which contained the library of Reverend J. L. Dart. They met Dart's daughter, Susan Dart Butler, who managed her father's collection and made it available to the black community. At the Museum, Bragg and her work must have impressed Embree because not only did he pledge $80,000 in support of a free library for the county (with certain conditions as to matching funds from the delegation), but he also recognized the "great educational value of the exhibits and pledged one thousand dollars of the [library] funds in any one year or each year used for extending the Museum exhibit service." As wonderful as this news was to Bragg, she was still discouraged and wanted some direct help for the Museum. She knew that the library would only add to the financial burden and responsibilities of the already struggling Museum, so she asked for a "few thousand dollars to extend what we are already doing."[75]

Tying the library money to the Museum money from the Rosenwald Fund was not the only issue with which she was unhappy. Even though Foreman had written in the last sentence of his February letter, almost as an afterthought, "that the Rosenwald Fund does not limit its help to either race," Bragg clearly did not want to deal with the "colored problem." She wrote Foreman, "As it is, I very greatly appreciate your good will and what may come from this, I nevertheless feel that the burden of handling the colored problem is much a serious one that the harm to the Museum in the struggle will more than offset any benefit."[76]

The struggle for political, social, and cultural parity during the Jim Crow era had encouraged black patrons to seek even greater equality. Several years after the Museum provided Saturday hours for black patrons, Bragg recalled that "certain tax paying negroes wrote to our Mayor and remonstrated because they were limited to Saturday afternoon. . . . We gradually let leaders among the negroes know that admission could be had by appointment." As a result of this request blacks were admitted on days other than Saturdays, attending lectures and meetings such as the American Ornithological Convention in 1928.[77]

By 1929 Bragg had ceased reporting "colored attendance" in her yearly report to the mayor and city council. The last reference had come in her 1926 director's report, in which she noted its decrease. With black

Charlestonians confronting the color line more openly, local as well as national conditions had deteriorated for them. Handling the "colored problem" had become more than she could deal with, given the funding problems confronting the Museum. It is possible that Bragg had come to understand that just as southern women supposedly had to know their place, blacks also were expected to remain subservient to white men.[78]

Money worries were all-consuming during these years at the Museum, so Bragg ended her May letter to Foreman with a plea: "Why is it that the big funds make it so hard for us to get help? The additional tax for the library will probably reduce the Museum's appropriation because the city literally has not the money. Therefore I am exceedingly discouraged but I would not be selfish enough to stop working for the library and I just trust that the Museum is taken care of somehow or other. Mr. Foreman, you people from the foundations have no idea of the courage you could give people and the actual help you could give if you would be willing to spend a few thousand dollars here and there without conditions." The Rosenwald Fund gave Bragg five thousand dollars for the traveling school exhibits. They also acknowledged her work in the "development of museums and museum extension work in the Southern States" by giving her two thousand dollars for traveling expenses associated with this work. President Embree called Bragg's work remarkable and praised her for furnishing "such brilliant leadership that it is an honor to be associated with your work." She now had the money to produce the exhibits for the state schools and, for the first time as director, she had an expense account, which would fund her goal of museum expansion activities throughout the South.[79]

As wonderful as this news was for Bragg, for the Museum, and for her educational program of traveling school exhibits, greater financial trouble was on the horizon for Charleston and the nation. Following the stock market crash in October 1929, few northern tourists had the money to visit Charleston any longer, and that trade along with the truck-farming industry evaporated. There would be no extra money for the Museum in the city budget, and at the State House no funding source appeared for the traveling school exhibits.[80]

While Bragg was successful with the Rosenwald Fund, she was less so in convincing the state's political leaders of the traveling exhibits' educational value. In December the State Budget Commission refused to approve the appropriation, with a member of that body writing that it "must necessarily come through the General Assembly, originating with Charleston delegation." This was exactly what Bragg did not want. It seemed that her careful explanation written to Hope earlier in the year had been misunderstood, and politics were still an issue of who would ask for the state dollars to fund the initiative. Bragg returned to her ally Rittenberg in January 1930, and he appealed directly to the governor, who refused to "approve any appropriation for that purpose."[81]

Rittenberg's letter had to have been disappointing for Bragg, and his suggestion for getting the appropriation through was time-consuming and difficult. He recommended that Bragg start a campaign through the individual counties by selling the "teaching and educating bodies . . . on the proposition, they could get their respective county delegation to include as appropriation in their general county supply bills for covering the cost of bringing those exhibits to their schools. Based on the amount asked for a state campaign, the average county cost would not exceed $100, a comparatively small sum and easily obtained from any delegation by proper coaxing."[82]

Bragg's dogged determination would not allow her to give up, and in February she took Rittenberg's advice. She spoke to the county teachers' conference in Meggett and before the administrators' meeting, asking both groups "to endorse our program for introducing traveling school exhibits into the schools of the state. . . . We want the endorsement of all the teachers of the state so as to push it hard."[83] She spoke about the 175 traveling school exhibits, which included natural history exhibits, industrial exhibits, cultural exhibits, and picture exhibits.

Bragg continued to work with the Rosenwald Fund throughout 1930 and wrote to its president about the increased services to the seventeen black schools (twelve of which had been built with Rosenwald money) outside the city. The Museum acknowledged the funding by marking each traveling exhibit and each book as a gift of the Rosenwald Fund. While state political leaders could not see the educational benefits of the exhibits, museum professionals recognized their potential. L. C. Everard, of the American Association of Museums, understood the educational value of the exhibits and asked Bragg to send him the plan, description, and photograph of the "Charleston Museum Type."[84]

In addition to the traveling school exhibits Bragg had a dream of a free library for all of Charleston's citizens, but this was still to be realized. The original 1929 library proposal of $80,000 from the Rosenwald Fund was a five-year proposition, which Bragg and Mayor Stoney both believed was too good for either the city or the county to turn down. Though six years had passed since Bragg had made a similar funding request for a free library, the lawmakers had not changed their minds. Museum trustees spoke against the Rosenwald plan, calling a library "unnecessary." Charleston legislators too did not think the city needed a library, especially one that would serve both black and white citizens. In December 1929 Bragg wrote to Helen that "everything possible has gone wrong" with the library proposition for the county.[85]

The rejection by lawmakers mobilized the community. Bragg's educational work had been appreciated, and now various civic organizations representing different social and economic groups endorsed the free library: Civic Club, Chamber of Commerce, Catholic Women's Organization, Rotary Club, Council of Jewish Women, Federation of Women's Clubs, Charleston Garden Club, Central Labor Union, Graduate Nurses Association, Bennett School PTA, James Simons PTA, and the Society for the Preservation of Old Dwellings. Another women's group, the American Legion Auxiliary, announced its intent to promote the extension and development of library services for former military men and their families. This was followed by the Education Committee of the Chamber of Commerce's endorsement of the Rosenwald Fund's gift to Bragg.[86]

Along with Bragg, other community leaders mounted a campaign to obtain several thousand signatures, including those of prominent Charlestonians and educators who supported the funding of the library. It was not until 1930 that the delegation eventually approved the library appropriation and the way was cleared for the establishment of the library at the Museum. Bragg was a trustee and an incorporator, and she was to be the librarian when the Charleston Free Library opened on 1 January 1931.[87]

After all the years of asking for money for the Museum, its activities, and its traveling exhibits, her pleas to the Carnegie Foundation for help finally bore real results when the foundation learned of the Rosenwald Fund's intent to fund the Charleston Free Library. This came about through the efforts of Dr. Foelsch, the president of the library's board of trustees, who informed officials at the Carnegie Institute about the need for library facilities for Charleston. The president of that institute replied to Foelsch, "I shall seek an early opportunity of bringing your letter up for discussion. . . . for conference with the Corporation trustees." Support also came about because of the activities of local community leaders, such as solicitor Sidney Rittenberg and clubwoman Clelia McGowan, who not only conducted the petition drive but also successfully "concentrated their efforts on the County Delegation." Once the delegation's ten-thousand-dollar matching appropriation was assured, the Carnegie group was willing to appropriate thirty-five thousand dollars in the spring of 1930 to be used for the purchase of books, "contingent upon the actual establishment of the library here."[88]

The Rosenwald money for the library and the Carnegie appropriation represented major professional accomplishments for Bragg that allowed her to use the library skills learned during her years at Simmons. She had been the impetus behind the drive to create a free library, a long-held goal that she had first broached to the Museum's trustees in 1920.[89] But without the assistance of Dr. Foelsch and other local civic leaders, lawmakers would not have matched the Rosenwald grant.

This money also allowed Bragg to bring back to Charleston one of the students, Margaret Hightower, she had taught at Columbia during the summer of 1928. Margaret had spent the fall of 1928 and the spring of 1929 working at the Charleston Museum as an apprentice and living with Bragg at 38 Chalmers Street. She developed programs for the Girl Scout troop, which used the Museum as headquarters, and worked with the nature study course in the public instruction department.[90] But with the Museum's ongoing financial problems, Bragg had not had the money to continue paying her salary.

Bragg had then sent Margaret to the Newark Museum to work for half a year. She had not wanted to, noting in her July 1929 introductory letter to that museum's director, "I have decided that it is greatly to her advantage to go to you. But please, I want her back when you have trained some one else to take her place. Do not let her get married up there or so wedded to your museum that she will not want to come back to me." Bragg had grown so attached to her that she wrote Hightower's father, "I do not like to think of next year without your Margaret. I shall miss her so."[91]

With the Rosenwald Fund money for the public library almost assured by June 1930, Bragg thought that she would have enough money for Margaret to return to the Charleston Museum for public instruction work. She wrote to the Newark Museum requesting that Margaret be kept on there until January, at which time she would return to Charleston. Bragg definitely wanted her back in Charleston by January 1931 because she could now afford to pay her with the Rosenwald money.[92]

Bragg's focus on the library funding issue had not dissuaded her from looking for other financial sources for the school exhibits, as well as for the extension of them in other southern states. If the prospects were not favorable within the state for the traveling school exhibits, they were elsewhere. Due to her own work in North Carolina and Virginia, she identified both as possibilities for expansion of that work. Bragg had become acting director of the Valentine Museum during its reorganization, and the owner had promised her fifteen hundred dollars toward the work. She had traveled to Wake County, North Carolina, to speak before the board of education, whose members became so enthusiastic over the educational value of the exhibits that they sent three of their teachers to Charleston to learn how to make their own exhibits.[93]

Bragg was so encouraged by these developments outside the state that she wrote to her young champion Foreman, asking the Rosenwald Fund to "undertake to help in the development of traveling exhibits in all of the southern states." In April she spoke in New Orleans at the Southern Museum Conference on her ten-year plan for the traveling school exhibits. Bragg had decided that she had an "ambition to reach every child in the southern states within ten years. As I could not get any help from the Carnegie or the Rockefeller people, I am going ahead independently."[94]

By September 1930 Bragg knew that traveling school exhibits would be established in museums in Richmond, Virginia; Atlanta, Georgia; and Birmingham, Alabama; and they had already been established in San Antonio, Texas, where 350 natural history exhibits were in circulation. In a letter to E. R. Embree, president of the Rosenwald Fund, she outlined her ten-year program for the extension of traveling school exhibits, making the Charleston Museum a center "from which assistance could be given in organization, production, and distribution of school exhibits while each state was establishing its own center."[95]

Superintendent Hope also reappeared with the possibility of state funding for the exhibits in November 1930, when he again contacted her through someone else to let her know that he was including a request for "the $5,000 toward the extension of traveling school exhibits work by the Charleston Museum for the State Board of Education." Bragg was so pleased with this news that she offered to travel to Columbia to appear before the State Budget Commission and to have a special interview with the governor.[96] Whether Bragg made an appearance at the State House or before the governor is uncertain, but the Museum never received any money from the State Department for the traveling exhibits.

Preserving Charleston's and the State's Heritage

With or without additional funds, the Museum's work during these years continued to be multipurpose: to preserve, illustrate, and interpret the natural and cultural history of South Carolina as well as that of other people in various parts of the world. Museum exhibits were planned according to the most current anthropological scholarship based on Darwinism, reflecting Bragg's scientific training and background. Charlestonians and other visitors to the Museum were encouraged to view their world through a cultural context of investigating and understanding other cultures.[97]

At first the Museum had no focus, as it had a reputation as a place where folks could leave their junk. Bragg wrote late in her tenure, "turning over junk to the Museum became a mild kind of joke in Charleston. . . . [but] there has come to be preserved . . . the most representative culture of a single locality . . . in the United States." This reputation did not change overnight, but the impetus began when Bragg decided to create a place within the Museum where "articles of priceless worth" could be housed. She knew that historical material was passing into the hands of northern collectors and museums, so she appealed to Charleston citizens to give or to lend their possessions to the Museum.[98]

When Bragg was named Museum director in 1920, her first preservation efforts were to install the woodwork, furniture, and fixtures of a Charleston drawing room and to set up the interior and equipment of Apothecary Hall, which was the original pharmacy on King and Broad. Assisted by John Bennett, it took the Museum staff almost four years to install the exhibit of the phases of pharmacy history.[99]

Bragg was no different from other preservationists in that she saw the past and the future in her efforts to preserve Charleston's and the state's cultural heritage. But she was the Museum's director, and while some Charlestonians came to accept her as one of their own, there were others who did not. In seeking a larger role for the Museum in the city's cultural life, Bragg created some jealousy within the preservation community. Members of the Society for the Preservation of Old Dwellings (SPOD), established the same year that Bragg became director, were of the opinion that their organization should be the front-runner in this movement, rather than Bragg and/or the Charleston Museum. Founded by Sue Frost, suffragist leader and real estate developer, the group included many of Bragg's friends and associates, but she was not a member.[100]

Bragg had first become aware of the fever to sell "articles of priceless worth" when visitors in town during World War I were buying pieces from the old plantations. She learned how to value furniture, glass, and china and was constantly invited to dinner parties in order to appraise the antiques in people's homes. Bragg's critical eye was so good that Josephine Pinckney crafted a character in one of her novels on Bragg. *Splendid in Ashes* was set in Charleston, with museum director Jessica "always on the lookout for angels for her pet, the museum, faithfully stalking the least angelic people. . . . Jessica took swift advantage . . . to get in the really important idea she had to plant. Under museum operation, the house and the collection would be beautifully kept up [and] preserved to posterity."[101]

Josephine once alerted Bragg that a museum curator from the Agassiz Museum was going to visit one of the Pinckney plantations, Runnymede: "I don't know how valuable this junk is; maybe you have appraised it and don't want it, but on the chance you do want some of it, I decided I would warn you of the deal."[102] Bragg was thoroughly familiar with the overwhelming desire to acquire antiques at advantageous prices, but unlike other collectors, she wanted them for the Museum.

By the last four years of Bragg's tenure as the Museum's director, there was a real fever among visitors to take away with them a piece of the city. With the transformation of Charleston into a tourist city, more and more local citizens began to emphasize the need to preserve its inheritance from the past. It is no accident, then, that beginning in 1927 South Carolina culture exhibits were given special attention, with the Museum preserving culture material, "including the implements of plantation life and industry throughout the state."[103]

The Museum gladly took the lead in preserving the city's culture, receiving as gifts the interior woodwork of three rooms from the mid-eighteenth century and two rooms from 1804. One of these rooms, from a city tenement, was set up as a memorial to Thomas Pinckney, Josephine's father and the first president of the Museum after incorporation. The second room was from Elmgrove Plantation, which Bragg found in a dilapidated state and from which she had the woodwork removed for preservation. She knew, however, that the gifts were not representative of what was being stripped from the city by collectors and other museums. She wrote to the Carnegie Foundation president: "But as wonderful as those gifts were, there is another side to the shield and that is the sad story of Charleston heirlooms being sold. . . . the sums realized . . . however, are mere messes of pottage and produce a real impoverishment of the state. . . . The Museum . . . is working for a fund with which to salvage choice floating bits from the wreck of the ancestral ship." Bragg's hopes and dreams of a true culture museum within the state rested with preservation efforts and with the Museum's ability to present a "panoramic picture of life in South Carolina. . . . for the casual visitor, . . . for the intelligent tourist . . . and for the education of our own people."[104]

As Museum director Bragg wanted to preserve the heritage of the city and the state. But that took funds, and she was not shy about using her contacts within the larger museum community to serve as introduction to the New York foundations. There she would find the large sums necessary to accomplish her preservation plans. She claimed that "raising money or asking for contributions" was difficult for her. Difficult though it may have been, she sought funds to preserve a "very fine old house . . . adjoining St. Michael's churchyard. If it comes to be known . . . how fine the house is, I am sure the interior woodwork of at least the great drawing room will be purchased outside of Charleston." She was right, as the hand-carved woodwork in the Mansion House was sold for two thousand dollars and then resold later for ten thousand dollars. The drawing room of this showcase would be completely reconstructed in the DuPont-owned Winterthur Museum. Bragg also asked the Carnegie Foundation for money to purchase and preserve the Adam-period Radcliffe-King House, which once housed the High School of Charleston. The house was demolished, but the Museum did receive the staircase, the steps, and the ironwork from the Board of School Commissioners in 1927, which was then given away by Bragg's successor, Milby Burton, and used in the restoration of the dilapidated Planter's Hotel into the Dock Street Theatre.[105]

Bragg's most visionary plan involved the soon-to-be-formed National Forest preserve outside Mount Pleasant, which covered acreage in both Berkeley and Charleston counties. While it was not created until 1936, there had been talk of the National Forest since the turn of the century. Once South Carolina formed its own state forestry commission in 1927, the way was clear for a state agency to purchase property in the area. It was the creation of this agency that prompted Bragg's dream.[106]

This area was visited by the AAM members in 1923, where they saw the old rice plantations of the South Santee River delta. She dreamed that the National Park Service would purchase the old plantation houses and then administer them as museums. And she wanted the plantations to come under the Museum's educational program. She was sure that some of them could be purchased for preservation. "There are four old houses on the river and a beautiful ruin of the home of Thomas Lynch. . . . Fairfield, the oldest house (owned by Josephine Pinckney) could not be purchased; Hampton I believe could, for a museum . . . the Wedge is for sale and Harrietta, possibly. . . . The Santee Gun Club. . . . has a cypress swamp rice reserve which contains one of our most beautiful heronies." All of the plantations Bragg named were very old and very historic, and their owners still attempted to live the southern antebellum lifestyle derived from rice and indigo production. Fairfield was completed about 1730; Hampton was constructed five years later with one of the few grand ballrooms outside of Charleston; the Wedge was built about 1826; and Harrietta took the longest to complete—over fifty years from 1800 to 1850. Bragg's fear, which was well-founded, was that these grand houses would either be dismantled or sold to northerners. Another of her fears was that the Forestry Service would only be interested in the trees and take no interest in the preservation of the cultural heritage.[107]

By 1928 Charleston had become a "field of exploitation for dealers in antiques and for connoisseurs of beautiful architectural details." Given her prior unsuccessful efforts, she appealed to Josephine Pinckney's uncle, Dr. William Heard Kilpatrick of Teachers' College, an influential education professor at Columbia University, for help with the Carnegie Foundation. Bragg wrote, "Quite tragic things have happened here lately. Woodwork which we were trying to secure funds to purchase and retain here in Charleston has been bought by outside agents. . . . Much of the finest woodwork and furniture in Charleston is going North these days and we are helpless to preserve it."[108]

Discouraged and in despair, Bragg wrote Caroline Sinkler that "apparently every other active, hard-working museum can get adequate support except for ours. But I will try not to be too discouraged and hope it will break for us some day." And so she continued her appeal to the General Education Board of the Rockefeller Fund: "While I realize that in the march of progress many of Charleston's ancient landmarks must be swept into the discard, yet I believe that posterity will blame us if we do not take some foresight and salvage what we can of those things that are beautiful and historic. . . . there are others . . . who are driven either by necessity or by greed to sell away from the city even its most treasured heirlooms." Bragg believed that the city was virtually being looted by its own citizens, and the irony was that she was a northerner trying to preserve it. She wrote a northern collector, "The determined effort of northern collectors to ruin this atmosphere [of the city] is making the preservers disheartened."[109]

She also sought help from William Sloan Coffin, a trustee of the Metropolitan Museum of Art who was influential in New York City, as was Kilpatrick. Both had many contacts on the philanthropic boards, such as the General Education Board of the Rockefeller Fund and the Carnegie Foundation. In a series of letters back and forth between Bragg and Dr. Richards of the General Education Board, she became exasperated with him and his explanations as to why they would provide no help to the Museum. She expressed this in a letter to Coffin: "In regard to the General Education Board: Dr. Richards speaks to you of a Southern Museum Wing at the Charleston Museum, then writes me that the request I have made for practically the same thing is not within the definite activities of the Board. Last fall they turned down my request for help in circulating traveling school exhibits throughout the south saying the action was 'largely based upon the fact that the projected activities do not fall within the scope of activities adopted by the Board.' I cannot discover what its activities are." Calling her hope "deferred," Bragg wondered if she ought to resign and "try to get someone here who knows how to raise the money. But I cannot imagine any one else caring or working for the Museum as I do."[110]

Coffin's reply to her tart letter was accompanied by copies of letters from the president of both boards, neither of which was positive. However, President Keppel of the Carnegie Foundation wrote that the Charleston Museum project would be brought up next fall, "and I don't see how we can do more meanwhile than to express interest and sympathy to anyone who would like to know our opinion." Coffin thought it best if Bragg would provide him with "a definite proposition of exactly what you do want, . . . if the opportunity presents itself your friends in New York may know just what your programme is."[111]

After many letters from Bragg and from others in support of Bragg's requests, the presidents of both the Carnegie Corporation and the General Education Board were not only responding to her but also noting her actions in their internal memorandums and corresponding with each other about her and her requests for the Museum. In 1928 Keppel noted in a letter to a Bragg supporter and fellow museum professional, H. W. Kent, that he found Bragg appealing; however, just one year later he wrote a terse memorandum about Bragg that said, "She was dispirited that people don't do things the way she thinks they should be done." C. R. Richards of the General Education Board reviewed one of Bragg's letters to Keppel and found her proposal for the southern expansion of the traveling school exhibits interesting. But Richards pointed out to Keppel that the request would be better served if it came from the AAM, since then "assistance and guidance of men like Paul Rea . . . and others would be insured."[112]

While Bragg was putting time, energy, and effort into her preservation campaign, she was also facing a similar battle with the Museum's leaky roof. Over the years the roof had been patched so many times that the city council had finally agreed to replace it, with a special appropriation of five thousand dollars. But the spring and summer of 1928 brought numerous storms. Rain poured into the building and threatened the exhibits. The staff of the Museum spent much time moving cases and puttying their tops to prevent water from soaking through and damaging both the cases and the exhibits. In September a major hurricane destroyed the roof, damaging and discoloring the walls and the ceilings. As a result the Museum was closed from September 1928 through March 1929 while the staff cleaned and refurbished cases and a new three-ply roof was put on in the middle of December. The Museum reopened that spring, and attendance figures for 1929 surpassed those of all previous years.[113]

Bragg had identified another need for the Museum back in 1923. She had written Coleman, the secretary of the AAM, then that she was going to educate the city about the need for a fireproof building, asking Mayor Stoney and city council for the funds to construct one. The Museum building was of steel construction with plastered brick walls, wooden floors, and roof sheathing, but it was not fireproof.[114]

Bragg apparently either did not ask for the money or, knowing the dire financial circumstances the city was in, chose not to follow through with the idea. Rather, she again turned to the major players, such as the Carnegie Foundation, in hopes that they would recognize the need for fire protection for the exhibits and grant the Museum $240,000 for a fireproof extension. Using as an example the assistance she understood was provided to the University of Pennsylvania Museum, she was hopeful that Keppel, president of the Carnegie Foundation's board, would "come to see that our request is quite in line with the spirit of what you are doing elsewhere." Keppel failed to see the similarity, and his response was negative: "it is written under a false impression so far as any promise by us to any Pennsylvania museum is concerned. We have promised nothing to any museum . . . that we will have to put the whole matter over until another fiscal year."[115]

In this matter, as in the preservation issues facing the city and the Museum, Bragg turned to Josephine Pinckney and her uncle, William Heard Kilpatrick, for assistance. Kilpatrick sought the assistance of Columbia University's president, who knew F. P. Keppel. Kilpatrick asked President Butler to intercede on behalf of the Museum, which Butler agreed to do. But Butler did not indicate his support of the issue or "intimate what reception he thought it might have." Butler did have Keppel's ear because not two weeks later Bragg had another letter from him stating that the board had "put off the whole question of participation in the educational services of museums."[116]

Rebuffed at every turn, Bragg tried a new tack in 1929. She wrote letters to the members of the AAM who had visited the city during the 1923 meeting. Appealing to their memories of the visit and asking for their help in seeking any sources of financial support they might have, she pleaded with them to help her save the plantations that were being sold to northerners. Bragg's favorite of these homes was Harrietta. When it was optioned, she wrote to Frederic Whiting at the Cleveland Museum of Art, "Can't you do something to get someone to buy it and give it to the Charleston Museum to be maintained as an 'out-door museum' to represent the life of antebellum times. . . . If you could help about this, wouldn't I be grateful!" She also told him about the $150,000 fund for the "Southern American Wing" that she wanted to create for housing South Carolina material. Bragg's letter was filled with Museum needs, and she unabashedly ended with, "I do not hesitate to ask you to help, if possible."[117]

Harrietta was sold to a northerner, and Bragg wasted no time in contacting him once she learned that he was going to preserve and restore the plantation: "the Charleston Museum will be only too happy to help you so far as it can." In her letter Bragg included the history of the plantation and its name, hoping to persuade the new owner, Horatio Shonnard, to retain the plantation's name and not denude it of its "historic value." She suggested that he commission the Museum to secure the right period furnishings, adding, "We constantly have people offering us things which we are unable to purchase and unhappily much of the old stuff goes to people in the north."[118] She did not want the antiques to leave the state, so having them at Harrietta was an acceptable option for retaining South Carolina's cultural material.

Shonnard graciously replied to Bragg's letter, informing her that he had furnishings from the right period (he listed a number of pieces of Chippendale, Sheraton, and Duncan Phyfe) and so was not in need of the assistance offered by Bragg. She was successful, however, in persuading him not to change the plantation's name; after reading Bragg's explanation of its historical significance, he had "now definitely abandoned any idea of changing it."[119]

Preservation of the city's image became more personal for Bragg when Standard Oil decided to build a gas station at the corner of Meeting and Chalmers Streets. Since her house abutted the site, she fiercely protested its construction to Mayor Stoney by reminding him that such a building "near St Michael's would be a crime and that Charleston would be accused of having lost its traditional culture." Bragg's appeal was successful. When the service station was finally built, it looked unlike any other in the city. City council and Standard Oil came to an agreement that the building would be of a colonial revival design and would use historic materials in its construction.[120]

While there were not thousands of dollars available for Bragg's larger preservation efforts, the sum of five hundred dollars did form the foundation for the first museum house in the city and what ultimately became the Museum's first community preservation project. This donation came from New Englander Frances Emerson, whose architect husband knew Albert Simons, the local preservation expert. Frances Emerson gave Simons a check, which he then turned over to Bragg. This gift, along with Simons's admiration for Bragg and her preservation efforts, persuaded the Museum's trustees to have Bragg take an option on what came to be known as the Heyward-Washington House.[121]

Bragg understood that what was "a preservationist's nightmare" was actually a historic property that the city could not afford to lose—particularly the Georgian interiors. The house was built about 1770 for Thomas Heyward Jr., who was a signer of the Declaration of Independence. Another claim to fame was that George Washington slept there when he visited the city on his historic trip through the South in 1791. What had been a grand city townhouse now housed Fuesler's bakery on its southwest corner, which had been lowered to street level. The rest of the house, including its woodwork, was ripe for some collector or museum to claim. Unlike past efforts of preservation, Bragg now had the money in hand to prevent another of Charleston's historic homes from being stripped of woodwork and then sold out of the community.[122]

The house was purchased through the combined efforts of Bragg as the Museum's director, The Society for the Preservation of Old Dwellings, and Albert Simons with a down payment of ten thousand dollars. Bragg sought help from all of the Museum's friends to make payment on the interest. She asked Whiting, president of the AAM, to solicit some of his friends to help the Museum restore the House. Bragg's friend and Philadelphia benefactress Caroline Sinkler participated in raising seventeen hundred dollars from her friends in that city with a benefit dinner party. The contributors of the first five hundred dollars asked their relatives to contribute additional money. Bragg's Chinese students contributed, and there was a plantation tour held at Harrietta and Hampton Place as a benefit for the fund. Once the house was cleared of debt, it would belong to the Museum.[123]

Simons directed the reclamation of the property and called it the most satisfying of his career, partly because of Bragg, who he said was "extremely cooperative and pleasant to work with." By January 1931 the house was opened for visitors, with furniture borrowed from several antique dealers. Members of SPOD donated period furnishings that sparsely filled the second-floor rooms. Josephine Pinckney loaned the Museum a rug for the drawing room, while Bragg looked for curtains to hang there. With the garden beds laid out and no plants, Bragg hoped to collect the proper plants at a plant exchange day sponsored by the Museum. But the visitors did not come in crowds.[124]

Various groups and individuals representing a cross section of the community rallied in support of the preservation of the Heyward-Washington House. With the tie to George Washington, the state Society of Cincinnati contributed twenty-five hundred dollars, and both local papers, the *News and Courier* and the *Evening Post,* offered extensive coverage of the effort. In order to support the house, SPOD held its first house tours in 1931. According to an essay written by Bragg the same year that the house tours began, "people are perennially unsatisfied unless they are able to penetrate what seems . . . to be the heart of Charleston life, that is, the interior of its homes."[125]

With her critical eye for both style and substance, Bragg's preservation efforts extended farther and wider than to historic houses and hand-carved moldings. Over the years she purchased many items, including knife boxes and urns for silver flatware, and the Museum was given a Revolutionary War–period bed and iron pieces by Christopher Werner as well as woodwork and iron from three demolished historic houses at the corner of

Church and Broad Streets. During this time she also made extensive notes about Charleston ironwork with the intention of publishing the material in the future. While Bragg was the initiator of the effort to save the Hey-ward-Washington House, what may be her most successful effort at preser-vation did not involve a house or a piece of carved wood or iron, but rather South Carolina pottery. Bragg's ability to recognize the rarity of a literate slave and his work led her to collect as many pieces of Edgefield pottery as the Museum could afford at the time.[126]

In 1919 the first inscribed jar made by an enslaved African American potter named Dave was given to the Museum. This forty-gallon storage jar is the largest slave-made vessel known. Paul Rea, who was the Museum's director at the time, wrote a few months after the jar arrived at the Museum that the "jars should be collected . . . in the hope of ultimately identifying them. . . . it is the hope of the Museum to obtain . . . information [about] the work to prepare a history of the old potteries." While Rea made a visit to the region where Dave lived and worked at Miles Mill Pottery, he did not purchase any other Edgefield pottery. It was not until late 1927, when the deposit of the first Dave jar was questioned by a relative of the initial depositor, that Bragg was drawn to Miles Mill Pottery and Dave's jars.[127]

John Bennett noted that, as with all of her collecting, Bragg plunged into the collection of Edgefield pottery, "as she does so remarkably, into the history of . . . glassware and pottery. . . . She has indubitably brains; and almost daily increases their scope by some new knowledge; that's more than the rest of us do regularly." His wife, Susie Smythe Bennett, accom-panied Bragg to Orangeburg on one of her collecting trips, which Ben-nett noted in a Sunday letter to his family. This time Bragg bought "a really fine lot of Carolina pottery. . . . One jar bore an inscription by the 'unknown potter,' a negro named DAVE, who appears to have been one of [the] most expert potters."[128]

Bragg's earlier experiences as an appraiser of antiques provided the foundation for her understanding that Edgefield pottery was unprece-dented in the South since it was decorated. As with other "articles of price-less worth," she wanted to prevent the pieces from being sold out of the state. For three years she scoured South Carolina from Orangeburg to Union to Aiken looking for Dave's work and bought every piece of Edge-field pottery that the Museum could afford, purchasing over one hundred articles during this time.[129]

In 1930 on a visit to Edgefield County, Bragg talked at length with two African Americans who recalled that they knew the one-legged pot-ter, Dave, who had worked at Miles Mill Pottery. This account has survived at the Museum and tells us about Dave. He was an enslaved African American who lived and worked around Edgefield from 1834 until about 1870. This was during the period when it was illegal for any black to learn to read and write, and it was also illegal for a white person to teach these skills to a black person.[130]

For more than thirty years Dave made huge vessels, some holding as much as forty gallons. Dave is now recognized as the most outstanding African American potter of his time because of his technical skill coupled with his unique poetic compositions. His mammoth jars are still among the largest utilitarian vessels made in the United States and have survived time and nature. The Edgefield pottery collection at the Museum is a testament to Bragg as a preservationist; she saw the future and the past in a clay jar made by a poetic slave who inscribed his works with information about his family, the customers, and the climate. Bragg offered an article about the history of South Carolina jug and jar pottery for *International Studio,* which had just printed her work on the Valentine reorganization, but the pottery piece was never published.[131]

The preservation of such objects as jars, furniture, and woodwork would have been pointless if the Museum had burned, but fortunately it did not. While Bragg's hopes for a fireproof wing had been dimmed by her failure to procure funds, they had not been completely destroyed. In October 1930 Paul Rea, the former director of the Museum, paid a visit to Bragg and the Museum. He was now a consultant to the Carnegie Corporation, and he knew that conditions had not been favorable when she had made the earlier application for the wing. He wrote her, "I know, however, that the Trustees are very favorably disposed toward the Charleston Museum." In Rea's opinion Bragg and the Museum needed to develop a grant "that will both meet with their approval and provide substantial aid."[132]

Rea cautioned Bragg that he was writing her of his own initiative, but still her reply to him was one of hope: "[your] letter fills me with courage." He again wrote her, asking that she "not allow yourself to build too confidently upon the hope that I have held out to you. It will be wise not to allow your hopes to concentrate upon any particular project." But Bragg did build her hopes on Rea.[133]

Creating a Network of Museum Professionals

During the eighteenth and nineteenth centuries people who worked in museums went by a variety of titles, including, for example, curator, keeper, director, and conservator. In many cases they had no uniform training and shared few of the same duties. In many museums responsibility for a collection could pass from the original collector to others when the museum was incorporated, when it was transferred to government control, or when the institution began to maintain longer hours of operation. The first museums were usually run by women volunteers and amateurs. As museums gained in popularity, new pressures created the need for new positions, such as museum educators and community program coordinators who would be more concerned with their specific patrons' needs.[134]

Early museum workers received their training in traditional academic subjects, such as art, history, or science. Since museums were so highly individualistic, it was quite common for many staff members to have academic degrees. During the first decades of the twentieth century it was common practice for them to learn the nuts-and-bolts side of museum work on their first jobs. As museums became more popular, there developed a growing need for professionally trained workers with specialized skills. There were early training courses, such as the one developed by Homer Dill, who provided training in taxidermy and exhibition techniques at the University of Iowa in 1908. Unfortunately, little is known about the two courses set up as early as 1910 by women, which preceded Paul Sachs's course at Harvard by several years. Wellesley College offered a course taught by Myrtella Avery, and the Pennsylvania Museum offered one by Sarah York Stevenson.[135]

By 1925 the need for trained museum workers was critical, and Bragg recognized this need from her earlier trip across the South for the AAM. Thus when John Coss, director of the summer session at Columbia University in New York City, visited the Museum that summer she recognized the opportunity to spread her views. He was impressed with Bragg's work as a museum educator and administrator. Writing her that fall, he asked if she thought a course in museum administration had merit and if she, or some "competent" member of her staff, would be interested in teaching such a course during the next summer session. He saw the purpose of the course as providing instruction to people interested in "opening small general museums in connection with historical societies, town libraries, school systems, or other public institutions."[136]

Calling it an "interesting experiment," Coss wanted her help in encouraging as many people as possible to enroll in the course. But Bragg was adamant about not encouraging people to start museums based merely on a summer class: "We have to contend particularly with inadequate preparation in would-be directors and with trustees who cannot realize the necessity or importance of preparation of any kind." Bragg was interested in the students' personal qualities and their temperamental suitability for museum work. And she wanted to use Coleman's book as an accessory textbook, claiming to have written "certain pages in it."[137]

Offered a stipend of five hundred dollars to teach the course, which entailed presenting a "one hour lecture, five days a week, with considerable time spent in consultation and museum work," Bragg accepted Coss's offer because it would give her "a chance to spread my own ideas of museum service."[138] And the course was an answer to one of the concerns Bragg had identified during the study of southern museums she conducted for the AAM—too few trained museum workers to fill the demand of museums. It was possible that she could help solve that problem for herself and other museum administrators by teaching the course.

Bragg spent several days alone at her country home, Snug Harbor, in late November 1925, and she wrote her father that she had cooked her supper over an open fire and that there was "such sunshine during the day—so hot I was sunburned." She also wrote him about being asked to teach the course at Columbia the next summer. In his reply Reverend Bragg pointed out to her, "Your engagement for next summer at Columbia University is significant of attainments and reputation already acquired and I trust you will be able to fulfill the engagement with credit to yourself and to your museum," and he signed his letter "Yours with a father's tender love." Her friend John Bennett also noted her work at Columbia, writing his family, "certainly she is qualified to speak expertly." Bennett saw the course offering as a compliment to the South and to the Museum, calling it a "good piece of publicity. . . . I wish it could persuade wealthy Charlestonians and Carolinians to lend some financial assistance [to the Museum]."[139]

Bragg had written Coleman about her eagerness to teach the summer course in 1926 and how he could, in her opinion, help the movement have "better trained workers if he included an editorial word urging the custodian of a small museum to fit herself for real curatorship" by taking the Columbia course. This letter contained the text of the course announcement, in hopes of attracting a number of women who were "already working in smaller museums. . . . There are so many museum workers who need special knowledge." With Coleman's help the course at Columbia University was advertised, using Bragg's text, on the front page of the AAM's newsletter, *Museum News.* She later wrote Coss that in her estimation the course could not have had better publicity. She had "heard a great deal of talk about the course" at the Federation of Arts meeting in Washington and the American Association of Museums meeting in New York.[140]

Bragg's announcement for the course outlined both her museum ideas and her philosophy of education. Not surprisingly Bragg used the announcement and then the course to promote her beliefs about the work of small museums: "The possibilities of the small museum are receiving more and more recognition. Some of the best museum work is today being done by the small museums." Calling the development of museums "a powerful force in America," she believed that there was an "impetus towards further development" and that the movement needed trained workers "fired with the spirit of museum service." Bragg named her course's five "aims":

1. To make clear the ideals of the modern museum and the potential scope of its activities and influence.
2. To give training in approved museum methods of administration, covering organization and reorganization; financing and bookkeeping; staff ethics; cataloging and care of collections; publications; publicity; and cooperation with other institutions.
3. To teach the principles of installation and their application to different collections whether classed as natural history, culture history, or art.
4. To outline the nature of museum public instruction work: first within the museum, and second, carried outside to schools, libraries, clubs, etc., of town, of city, county, and state.
5. To take up the museum problem of each student in the course and assist him or her to a solution which shall create a museum center of influence, strong locally, and reaching out to touch contiguous centers.

As a means of achieving Bragg's five aims, the students also visited museums of New York City. Additionally she gave "special emphasis to trailside work, and part of the class visited [a] nature trail."[141]

Along with Helen McCormack, her protégée from Charleston, the other students in the class included Louise Connolly of the Public Library of Newark; Theodora Rhoades, a New Yorker; and a Chinese student, S.Y. Liang. Each was important to Bragg for different reasons. Helen's professional importance grew because she was specializing in American decorative arts, which she studied during the six weeks at Columbia. It was Bragg's opinion that she was "going to make an excellent student of the subject." When she returned to the Museum that August she was to become curator of the South Carolina Culture Department, which was Bragg's special focus. Her personal significance was due to the deepening of her relationship with Bragg, a relationship that was noticeable to Connolly, who wrote Bragg, "What did your little blonde study at the Metropolitan?"[142]

Connolly was nearer Bragg's age than the others. She wrote Bragg before the class began and called herself "something of a student of the woman who runs the details of the man's job, and I have long thought of you as more than usually intelligent and normal at it. Maybe it is because you are somewhat picturesque in your going south and making good and finally succeeding." She admired Bragg; it was not the normal student-teacher relationship but rather one of an adult who can appreciate the character of another: "You were sincere; that's the vital matter between friends. . . . You did not mean to offend. . . . I am very much tickled by the psychology of you. I have never before seen a northern woman . . . assimilated by the south. . . . So many people just slip into classes. It's the individual specimen that interests the collector." Connolly also worked with John Cotton Dana, a nationally known museum authority, at the Newark Public Library. Dana was Bragg's colleague and was considered preeminent in the field. She was interested in learning his museum techniques and principles. Dana had called the Charleston Museum an up-and-coming institution after her election to the AAM's governing board.[143]

Rhoades and Liang shared Bragg's love of Chinese culture. Liang was Chinese and a graduate student at Harvard studying archaeology in preparation for his work in a museum at Nanking. Rhoades had a "decidedly broad knowledge of things Chinese and of Chinese students and specialists in this country." Bragg considered Rhoades's work "fine" and asked Coleman if museums could not capitalize on her knowledge of Chinese and use her as a specialist working with several museums. She was so impressed with Rhoades's plan for a Chinese culture exhibit, developed during the six-week course using Bragg's principles, that she wanted to present it at the next association meeting. Rhoades evidently returned the admiration, continuing to work on labels for her Chinese culture exhibit into September. She corresponded with Bragg about her plans for an American Indian exhibit and sent her warm regards: "You certainly did improve New York's social climate."[144]

Bragg believed that her principles would assist museums that did not have specialists to prepare exhibits of different cultures. Seeking advice from an expert about China, she wrote Langdon Warner, a professor at Harvard, to let him know that she knew Caroline Sinkler, the Museum's benefactress. Using Sinkler's name as a means of introduction, Bragg asked that he review Rhoades's Chinese culture exhibit. She wanted his comments and suggestions about Rhoades's plans, which she had prepared using Bragg's principles:

1. Museum exhibits are for the purpose of creating understanding, not teaching facts.
2. The exhibit should be for the interpretation of an idea rather than for the display of an object.

3. A museum exhibit should be a good composition following the laws of pictorial composition.
4. A section or group of related exhibits should carry a progressive story, displayed not necessarily chronologically but with continuity of idea and each of the separate exhibits of the group or section should be combined as to form a single composition—well composed, of course.[145]

The American Association of Museums published a landmark report, *Excellence and Equity*, in 1992 that reaffirms the many contributions museums have made and continue to make to the educational needs of the nation. *Excellence and Equity* "submits that the missions of museums should state unequivocally that there is an educational purpose in every museum activity."[146] This mission is reflective of Bragg's own philosophy as exemplified in her museum principles and in the aims of her museum studies course at Columbia University.

Writing Coleman about her class, Bragg judged it to be a success, and Coss (the summer session director) agreed with her, inviting her back for the next summer term in 1927. She also wrote that though the class was "small it was constructive. . . . I see how I can make the whole thing so much more efficient and tie up the course with other classes suitable for art, science, or culture history students. Columbia seems to be the great international educational center and, therefore, just the place that I should be considering my interest in the culture movement. . . . I can foresee this course growing into a really broad museum school at Columbia." Coleman's reply to Bragg was both positive and supportive, calling her an extraordinary woman and her progress "quite thrilling." Further, he agreed with her suggestion that having specialists, such as Rhoades, to do specific jobs was "thoroughly sound" and an idea whose time would come.[147]

Bragg's second venture into higher education at Columbia in the summer of 1927 saw little change in her objectives, though the course was moved out of the business department and placed with other fine-arts courses. She taught more students, bringing several with her, including Helen, Mary Ford Pringle, and Edward McCrady from the Museum and Catherine Auld from Mount Pleasant. They were joined by others from Ohio, New York, Virginia, and Oregon, for a total of ten students.[148]

She was pleased with the results of the 1927 course. One of her students, Mildred Babcock from Ohio, was named curator of the museum at Winthrop College, where she "revolutionized teaching methods in our state normal college through her emphasis on museum cooperation and visual instruction methods." Another one of Bragg's students was "a public school principal and a member of the South Carolina State Board of Education and has been as active and as influential as myself in getting through an appropriation for traveling school exhibits for the public schools."[149]

Not all of Bragg's time in New York during the summer of 1927 was spent at Columbia or with Helen. She also visited with Anita Pollitzer, who took her to see two paintings by Georgia O'Keeffe at the Brooklyn Museum and at Alfred Stieglitz's studio. "Stieglitz, the photographer, publisher, and avant-garde entrepreneur, was Anita's mentor," and he later became O'Keeffe's lover and husband. Anita wrote "Pat" (the name she called O'Keeffe), "She [Bragg] knows all & is a grand judge of fine things in old Art & now tells me your two paintings . . . gave her a real 'thrill.' . . . I'd like you to spare time to have tea with her & me." Of the visit to Stieglitz's studio, where Bragg saw the Cloud Photographs, she said, "Anita you didn't ½ tell me ever how great these paintings are. . . . I have never seen such things. They are cosmic."[150]

It is possible that Bragg tried to attract more students to the 1928 course by broadening its appeal. She changed the name of the course to "Museum Training and Public Instruction." Also she arranged with both Coss and George Cox, chairman of Columbia's fine arts department, to have Anita Pollitzer at Columbia with her. Pollitzer was to teach a course on principles of museum installation through "a series of progressive exercises" that would teach the students how to handle arrangement in line, dark, light, and color.[151]

Bragg knew that more and more museums were training their own assistants and that museum studies courses were offered by other colleges and universities, such as the Wellesley College Art Museum and the University of Iowa. She offered a subtle warning to Coss: "We must realize . . . that a six weeks course can only be considered as introductory to museum training." As a museum administrator, she had agreed to have two girls serve as apprentices the next winter at the Museum. The AAM was to offer a course in museum work, and Bragg anticipated the trend of longer training sessions. Knowing what the association intended to do, Bragg proposed to S. A. Barrett, chairman of the Museum Training Committee, that they "work together a little more in this matter. . . . Knowing the museum field as I do . . . I could easily form a school here at the Charleston Museum, and would have to do so if I could not persuade students to go on to Columbia. . . . If we could get certain museums in New York City to give special courses under Columbia University in the Museum Training Department and could cooperate to get enough pupils to make it seem worth while, we could give the general work in New York, and then distribute students for practice work." Barrett was interested in her proposal and suggested to Bragg that she contact Hamlin, president of the AAM, and Coleman directly, explaining "the importance of your work at Columbia, as well as the desirability of cooperation between your department there and the museums in New York. . . . I am tremendously interested in your report of the fine progress your course is making." Bragg also approached John Cotton Dana at the Newark Museum, but he did not see her plan as feasible.[152]

Bragg was more aggressive that spring in searching for students to enroll in the course. She wrote letters to the American Library Association, the New-York Historical Society, and the Museum of Natural History at the University of Rochester informing them of both courses and pointing to the specific application to each organization. She received letters from prospective students in Gaffney, South Carolina; Milledgeville and Dublin, Georgia; Wichita, Kansas; Brooklyn and Oakfield, New York; New Haven, Connecticut; and Northampton, Massachusetts; and another Charleston girl, Anna Wells Rutledge, would also join the class.[153]

While Bragg was in New York during the summer of 1928, Helen was a specialist on loan from the Museum to what would become a biological research museum in Highlands, North Carolina. She went there with Edward McCrady, an assistant curator from the Museum. He was gone by 19 July, when Helen wrote Bragg, "I'm weeping from loneliness for you and nobody knows." Soon thereafter she was concerned about Bragg's health, as Bragg had been quite ill earlier that winter with time spent in the Baker Sanatorium. Helen wrote, "Hoping that you are, but fearing that you are not [healthy], I am—anxiously, devotedly, your Helen." And, of course, she wanted Bragg with her. One night in the mountains she climbed to a rock and watched "a flaming gorgeous sunset. . . . Oh! I wanted you so. I thought of the pale sunsets we had watched on the Hudson, and the bright lovely ones at Snug Harbor. I wanted your arms around me, I wanted to hold your hands in mine." Helen loved Bragg and sought to remind her of their shared experiences. No doubt Helen hoped that the desire was reciprocal.[154]

Though the number of students enrolled had increased with each session, her course "perplexed" John Coss. By early October he decided that "we ought to wait until we have a larger public on whom to draw. . . . and the growth of your own work is a great satisfaction to all of us. . . . For 1929 I think we ought not to offer any courses." While Bragg did not teach again at Columbia, Coss viewed her as an expert whose opinion he valued. He wrote her about two courses that would be taught during the 1929 winter session, "one dealing with the relations of schools and museums in education; and the other in the preparation of museum exhibitions for school use," and asked her to suggest the teacher.[155]

It was not possible for Bragg to leave the Museum during the winter months since she was using her sabbatical summer leave to work at

Columbia. Instead, Bragg sent her curator of public instruction, Louise Smith Barrington, to Columbia to teach the two courses. Though Barrington had no college degree, Bragg called her an excellent teacher. In recommending her as the instructor, Bragg described Barrington as "a Charleston type, quite exquisite, quiet in manner, with charm, and is very good looking. . . . her practical knowledge is so much greater [than Anita Pollitzer's] of the exhibits themselves. . . . This preparation of the school exhibits requires knowledge of a special technique." This emphasis on personality reflects how feminized the museum profession had become. Similarly, these characteristics were the same ones sought in professional librarians.[156]

Bragg made one last attempt at creating a center for museum training at Columbia University. In a January 1929 letter to Coss she wrote that although she was "simply not strong enough to be in New York," the work was started "too well to let it drop and there is too great a need of workers." Asking to be left in charge and willing to work without a salary, she suggested that funding yet again be sought from the Carnegie Corporation for the training school for museum workers proposed by the AAM, which would be housed at Columbia University. Bragg and four others were to compose a committee of sponsors and advisers to the work. One of the advisers was to come from the Newark Museum, whose director, John Cotton Dana, was opposed to her plan. Instead Dana went to Coss directly with his own plan and suggested that the Newark Museum apprentice course "be accredited . . . for the training of graduate students who wish to learn the business of running a museum. . . . the course would be given by us in Newark and would be the same as that is already in operation here."[157]

By early summer Bragg learned of Dana's actions through Alice Kendall, also an alumnus of Simmons College, who was employed at the Newark Museum. Though Coss acknowledged Dana's letter, nothing came of Bragg's last attempt to place a course at Columbia. Both the Charleston Museum and the Newark Museum offered a museum apprenticeship program, but Bragg did not teach another museum training course at a university or college.[158]

Bragg's Expansion of Southern Museum Work

With her trusted staff in place, Bragg was able to promote the expansion of museums in the South. One of the first events she organized and participated in was the Southern Museum Conference, which was held at the Museum in April 1927 following the three-day session of the Southern States Art League. The objective of this meeting was to help the participants visualize the museum work that was going on the South. A secondary objective was to discuss cooperation among the southern museums. Bragg thought that one method of encouraging this cooperation was for each museum to train specialists in different lines, with each museum receiving "the benefit of the work of these . . . specialists through exchange."[159]

One of those specialists was Bragg's former student Theodora Rhoades. Bragg had recommended Rhoades to Dr. Wheeler at the museum in Birmingham, and there Theodora installed the Chinese culture exhibit that she had created in the 1926 summer course at Columbia. But Bragg still wanted the exhibit for Charleston, and she wanted Rhoades to allow her to present it as part of her report at the association's May meeting in Washington: "I would rather demonstrate it and use it as an object lesson rather than for you to read it as a paper. Do you mind letting me do this?" Rhoades asked Bragg to reconsider her request, "as this Chinese interest is my only major asset and you, Laura Bragg, have so many major assets." Persuasive as only she could be, Bragg won out, and Rhoades's plan for the Chinese culture exhibit was a part of her report at the meeting.[160]

During 1927 Bragg's work on behalf of museum expansion included four southern states. In Alabama she and Dr. Wheeler cooperated in studying the problem of the interchange of services and the circulation of traveling school exhibits. In Chapel Hill, North Carolina, she directed the finishing of the room that housed the Geology Museum and planned the cases to hold its collection of minerals and rocks with the university architect. In Greensboro she found that the Historical Society had accomplished a great deal since her visit two years earlier and in her opinion was "ready for the interpretative state." She also was asked to give advice to the Ozark Natural Research Society in Arkansas. Bragg's dream of museum development in the South, with the Charleston Museum at its center, was being realized.[161]

Bragg's southern expansion activities took a different course in 1928. She sent her employees to Birmingham and to Highlands, North Carolina, to work with fledgling museums. Through the AAM and Coleman's recommendation, she also became involved with a group in Florida that was attempting to start a museum.

During this same time period she was approached by a summer resident of Highlands, a resort in the foothills of the Appalachian Mountains in North Carolina, to help start a museum that would "arouse the interest of more of the children in the natural history of the place and to make a laboratory that would be attractive for scientists." Clark Foreman wanted someone who was willing to spend vacation time at the museum to get it started. Bragg was so interested in his proposal that she agreed to "let you have a member of our staff for two months, if that will do or, if you want to keep it open longer, one member for two months and a second for the third." After consulting with her staff Bragg decided to send Helen, who would work with the Indian material and was described as "quite wonderful with children," and Edward McCrady, who "will help you with your natural history work as well as with culture work," for the summer while she was in New York.[162]

Ned McCrady left after a month, and Helen was there on her own until the end of August. She did not want to stay and wrote to Bragg's secretary: "this dreadful thing, which I am so reluctant to mention is that I've got to stay in this place until the end of the month. From a voice crying in the wilderness." Helen was homesick and wrote Bragg directly, "I used to wonder why I never got homesick in New York. But it does not seem strange now. I had you there, and I haven't here." Bragg did not send for her, and Helen gained the invaluable experience that Bragg intended, cataloging and developing public instruction work. This prepared her for her next "on loan" assignment at the Valentine Museum, where she was sent in September 1928. Bragg's connection continued with the Highlands museum as a member of the 1930 advisory committee. In Foreman's opinion, "I feel that the Highlands will always be attached to the Charleston Museum and will hope to cooperate with it in any way possible."[163]

In the fall of 1928 Bragg was invited by Donald Blake and the Florida Federation of Arts in Tampa to create a cooperative plan for organizing the different societies in Saint Petersburg, Jacksonville, Miami, Palm Beach, Orlando, and Gainesville. Suggested by Coleman as a speaker and museum expert, Bragg readily agreed with Blake's request and was willing to go to Florida for "a series of conferences and addresses . . . if you will pay my expenses." In preparation for her visit, she sent him copies of the Museum's constitution and charter and also provided information about funding sources.[164]

Bragg wrote to Coleman after she had spent a week during the winter of 1929 in Florida and reported that people there were doing "pretty good work." She and Blake made plans for a museum movement in the state. He impressed Bragg, and she saw him as "the only redeeming feature," as he had a "really broad idea of a museum and is very teachable." Blake was impressed with her also—he wanted to employ her full-time as the director, a post she was not at all anxious to have, as she was "already overburdened." However, she offered to serve as the acting director while training him for the post.[165]

Due to the generosity of Caroline Sinkler and the Rosenwald Fund for her museum expansion work, Bragg was able to travel for five weeks across the South and into Texas and Mexico, where she purchased items for planned Mexican exhibits. She visited museums in Atlanta; Birmingham and Tuscaloosa, Alabama; Laurel and Jackson, Mississippi; New Orleans; San Antonio, Austin, and Dallas, Texas; and Mexico. Bragg was "confident I learned more in my five weeks' trip through the southern states, Mexico, and Yucatan than in any former year, or you might say, two years of my life"[166]

Once she arrived in Mexico, Bragg found that "the Mexican government would not allow antiques to be taken from the country, so I turned to the same type of material which Homer St. Gaudens collected for the Carnegie Corporation exhibit now at the Metropolitan Museum." The items purchased for the Museum included "serapes (collected among different tribes of Indians), cut lacquer ware, including a beautiful black and red chest and small boxes and trays, from the state of Guerrere, as well as items from the Mexican Free Air School," which Bragg planned to use in traveling school exhibits on Mexico.[167]

When Granville Valentine, owner of the Valentine Museum in Richmond, Virginia, learned of her trip, he contributed four hundred dollars toward purchases and her travel expenses, with the understanding that there would be an exhibition at the Valentine of the Mexican items. But he warned her that she was trying to do too much by proposing to cover so much territory that "only a globe trotter would attempt." Bragg decided to go on to the Yucatán peninsula, though "she did not tell the Mexican consul that when she got the passport. In fact, she did not decide to go there until after she had told him where she intended to go." Bragg enjoyed her trip much more than conventions: "I did love my Mexican trip. Frankly I am getting so tired of museum conventions."[168]

Granville Valentine's invitation for Bragg to direct the reorganization of the Valentine Museum in Richmond had been the impetus for her trip through the South during the fall of 1924. She had spent a week in Richmond that October, and Valentine had agreed with her idea that the museum would become a culture museum and that his secretary would be trained by Bragg in museum fundamentals at the Charleston Museum. But time and other obligations had interfered with those plans, for Valentine became involved in the publication of Edgar Allan Poe's letters, which were owned by his museum, and he helped to raise the money to finance a World War I Carillon Memorial for Virginia.[169]

Money was a crucial issue in the reorganization. Valentine was concerned over the cost of returning the main building to its original condition in the early 1800s. Other concerns were the cost of repairing and installing exhibits in two historic homes that would also comprise the Valentine Museum. Asking Bragg to "think over the whole matter carefully," he sent her drawings of the buildings in preparation for his visit to Charleston.[170]

In 1926, two years after Bragg's first trip to Richmond, Valentine, along with his "whole family" and several friends, visited her at The Charleston Museum and discussed what was needed at his museum. Bragg made the week-long visit memorable. They met Mr. and Mrs. Charles Stevens (he was a member of the Museum's board of trustees) and visited Snug Harbor with Bragg's "very pretty friend" Helen. Accompanied by John Bennett, they saw Magnolia and Middleton Gardens, Goose Creek Church, and the nearby Oaks Plantation. The Valentines also attended a Poetry Society meeting at which Louis Untermeyer spoke on modern British poetry.[171]

Since this was a business trip, Bragg made sure that she and Valentine determined a definite plan for the reorganization of his museum. Bennett assisted Bragg in explaining and convincing Valentine of the proper methods to use while adapting the museum to an educational focus. He then returned to Richmond to convince his mother and his brothers that their museum was out-of-date (Bragg has actually pronounced it dead) and a disgrace to its founder, Mann Valentine. In contrast to their time in Charleston, the family meeting did not go well: "Mr. Valentine looked very down"; and Mrs. Valentine wrote Bragg, "If we could only transport all the brothers to the Charleston Museum I feel the game would be won."[172]

By 1927 Valentine had three buildings ready for exhibits, his family and the staff were looking through the material that had been put aside for years, and they were moving slowly "on account of the money question." Granville Valentine's uncle Eddie was a sculptor, and he had placed all of his artworks, casts, letters, and prints on the first floor of the building, which he had appropriated as exhibit rooms for his work. Knowing this, Bragg was still thrilled that she would have the opportunity "to start afresh with nothing in the building."[173]

Bragg re-created the Valentine Museum using her museum ideals; including having a curator who could write labels for the specimens, with each specimen related to every other one and then fitted into a constructive story. It was her experience that only a brilliant student, such as Helen, was capable of label writing. She also knew that the placing of objects, or installation, is "art in itself and requires a knowledge of color, lighting, composition, psychology, history, and art, which only a study of art and psychology can apply."[174]

Valentine knew that Bragg would "put new life in me regarding this undertaking." Four long years after she first visited the Valentine Museum he agreed to Bragg's offer to take charge of the installation, and one of her assistants would work in Richmond for six months under her supervision. He had "$10,000 in hand" for the installation and wanted Bragg to review the plans carefully with him.[175]

Bragg's reply from New York, where she was teaching at Columbia University, was one of excitement, pleasure, and pride and shows Bragg as an astute woman who knew her worth: "I shall be glad to undertake the directorship of the installation of the Valentine Museum. We will arrange terms when I see you. I will want to budget the $10,000 and decided how far it can carry us. You know you are to let me be the director for the work or I could not think of doing it. There would not be enough mental interest in it for me to make me willing to take the time. I accept the remuneration because this will be a serious piece of work and I could not do it for love since I am not free financially to do so. But we will discuss and plan this on paper." Once Bragg and Valentine knew that she was going to direct the installation, their letters seemed happier, lighter. At last there was to be forward movement. "You are going to make it as lovely for this day and generation as it was for its own when first installed," Bragg wrote Valentine from Epping, where she had gone to visit her mother after her summer in New York. He relayed his hopes for the museum: "It will be the greatest satisfaction to me if the Valentine Museum can ever be started along the lines for the good of the people generally. I hope some day we may get citizens interested in a City Museum."[176]

Again the trained curator "on loan" was Helen, who was to leave Charleston for Richmond and reorganize the Valentine Museum following Bragg's directions. She waited in Charleston at the Museum for Bragg to return from the North, writing her, "I am so glad you want me to spend the night with you the first night you are home. I have so much to tell you I am counting the days and the hours and the minutes til Tuesday at twelve forty. Lots of love to you. Helen"[177]

That fall of 1928, after arriving in Richmond, Helen was homesick for Bragg, as she had been at Highlands. An accession slip from the Valentine Museum, completed by Helen in her handwriting, shows that she saw herself as Bragg's "accession": the information filled in by hand indicates that Bragg had collected her "From her parents," to be returned by the Museum "Never," with a price of the accession as "Invaluable."[178]

No matter how desolate she may have felt about being in Richmond and away from Bragg, Helen had impressed Valentine, and his uncle Eddie, the sculptor, was quite taken with her. Valentine wrote Bragg that he hoped Helen had taken notes about everything Eddie was saying about "objects he has and those in the museums. The history of each piece of sculpture modeled by him will in the future be of great interest to the public." While acknowledging that Bragg was in charge, he still wanted her to talk over carefully with Helen what had already been done and what her future plans were for the museum. Valentine sent Christmas wishes for both Bragg and McCormack, "May you & Miss McCormack have a most happy Season, in so beautiful surroundings as Charleston."[179] Just as Connolly had recognized that Bragg and Helen were a couple, Valentine understood the relationship.

After the holiday season Helen returned to the Valentine Museum and worked so diligently that by early March 1929 she was ill. She wrote Bragg and asked for a month's unpaid leave of absence: "Please may I have a month's leave from all my jobs? You remember I haven't taken an honest to goodness vacation, one entirely free from responsibility, since I finished college." Helen wanted to come home and desired to "lie down by the marshes and while I am home we may get a chance to talk over our plans for this museum, which is impossible when we are here."[180]

Helen wrote her seven-page plea to come home on 6 March, and Bragg's reply of seven days later—"Surely you may have leave of absence. Expecting you tomorrow. LMB"—expresses no sympathy nor asks any questions. It is in marked contrast to Helen's neediness: "The prospect of a letter from you every day is thrilling but don't add another to the responsibilities you already have. I know you are thinking of me. You are working much too hard."[181]

Calling herself disheartened over Helen's sickness, Bragg chose to express her feelings to Valentine, but her letter to him was primarily about the business of the museum; including electrification problems; the placement of the furniture from the home of his recently deceased brother, James Marie Valentine; and the money—money for a Chinese painting that a Chinese student, who was a friend of Chia Mei, had sold to the Valentine Museum for $325 and money for Bragg's work as acting director. Bragg envied James Valentine and his death, writing his brother: "just to rest and be free from the pressure, the terrible constant pressure of having to do more than there is time or strength for."[182]

"Bragg's boy" with the cleft palate, Ned Jennings, was curator of art for The Charleston Museum, and he was working on a Valentine House group similar to the Drama of Civilization series he had created for Bragg. In May 1929 he was found dead from a gunshot wound to the head. The official ruling, by suicide, is what most people believed. But Bragg recalled in 1976 that a "detective had told her that Ned's body had been moved, and so he could not have shot himself," and she was "completely convinced that Ned's male lover had murdered him."[183]

As with Belle's death, Bragg insisted that it was murder, rather than the more sinful suicide. With murder the fault lies with the killer, while the act of suicide draws society's examination of the role of family and friends. Regarding both deaths Bragg chose not to accept that two people she cared for had chosen to end their lives. Hearing about Ned's death from her mother in Charleston, Helen wrote Bragg: "It is so hard to believe. I can't believe he did it. I wish I could think that he did it because of some moment of bright ecstasy. But I know that all the gaiety, the fantasy and beauty that he put into life are living things. And those things were really what I called 'Ned,' and so he is living, too."[184]

Bragg's spirits had been low already, but Ned's death and the funding problems only compounded her depression. Her friend Howard Kelly was in town during May, and he noticed her despair: "You need a close intimate absolutely dependent friend whose song fills your life and makes the difficulties appear microscopic. Christ, our living Savior is such a Friend; there is no other."[185] But Bragg no longer attended church, even though she remained a member of St. Philip's Episcopal, which she had joined because of Belle.

Bragg spent much of that summer in Richmond working with Helen and Anna Wells Rutledge installing the exhibits at the Valentine Museum. Helen enjoyed having her there, and though Bragg seemed well, there was "a nervousness which evidences itself in a terrible itching." Helen kept Emma, Bragg's secretary, posted about Bragg's progress, at the same time asking for various museum supplies.[186]

Just a month later Bragg had a serious gastrointestinal attack while still in Richmond and was hospitalized for four days, having tests on her stomach and metabolism as well as X rays. The end result of the visit was a new diet of six meals a day and having to sleep with the foot of her bed elevated. When Bragg finally wrote Emma herself, she admitted to being "not at all well and life is a perfect drag. Sometime later on I have to have a major operation," she envied "Miss Gilchrist," who died, "no more troubles for her, poor dear."[187]

Bragg sold other pieces of Chinese art to Valentine that fall. Calling a selling price of five hundred dollars very reasonable, she offered him a Chinese painting from the Ching dynasty and a roll painting from the Yuan dynasty. These works of art were owned by a Chinese student at Columbia University, Miss Liu, who had owned the first painting he purchased. Bragg told Valentine that when the student asked her father for money to pay tuition, he would send her a painting to sell. Since she had no way of disposing them, she asked Bragg to sell them for her. Liu acknowledged Bragg's help in "rendering my financial position a little easier and thus extending to your people the knowledge of what Chinese art really is."[188]

Personal financial issues continued to play a part in her dealing with Valentine. Bragg's initial retainer for her work at his museum was $1,000. Further, her agreement with him called for an additional $750 for her services during 1929. She had such financial difficulties during that year that she borrowed money from DuBose Heyward, and when Valentine was late with a payment, she sent him a reminder: "Please, I hate to mention money for myself. According to our agreement I should have had $250 on March 15th. I shall be in a hard place if it does not come." Knowing her money worries, Valentine wrote her later that year and asked if money were due her by the first of August. She replied that the $500 she was expecting would be used for payment on her house on Chalmers Street.[189]

The reorganization work at the Valentine Museum proceeded throughout the winter and spring of 1930. Though Anna Wells Rutledge, another of Bragg's protégées from Charleston, was to help Helen with the work, she had returned to Charleston to complete the writing of exhibit labels according to Bragg's exacting standards and principles. Valentine wrote Bragg that he had doubts about Anna working in Charleston, possibly because he wondered if she would do the work. However, he left the matter to Bragg, since she was in charge.[190]

By September the exhibits had been installed and the Valentine Museum was ready for an October opening. But Valentine preferred delaying it until the beginning of the new year: "I feel sure that the delay will be most advisable for our people—generally with the drought over Virginia, are greatly depressed and have no thought other than 'bread and meat' and all of us must do our part to help everything [be] ready for a time that will be fuller of sunshine that at the present."[191]

Bragg's handwritten five-page reply pointedly opposed Valentine. Asserting herself and her principles of museum work, she outlined five points of disagreement:

> First: The principle of museum work is progressive installation. A finished museum is a dead museum. Second: I explained to you that I would have to resign the first of November. You do not realize the impossible amount of work I am pledged to in regard to this new library and my own museum. The library is the fruition of seven years of work for me. I must not fall down on the realization. Third: Helen is quite able to carry on the museum but she has not (as yet tho it will develop) the external force to make people do as she thinks wise. She is small and people treat her too much as a sweet child. She needs me to open and get her started. Of course she always has her position here and I will never completely relinquish her. My desire is for her to be the director

at Richmond (she will make a splendid one because she has the true comprehension of the museum ideal for the 20th century).   Fourth: Publicity is already started. Fifth: The financial depression will not affect peoples attending a free institution. People are most pleased when they can say, "you have made changes since I was here last."—There must be change or the museum dies.

Bragg ended this letter with praise for Valentine's breadth of vision and receptivity to new ideas, adding that she would abide by his decision but hoped the museum would open on 13 October. Bragg got her points across to Valentine, and though the museum did not open on 13 October, it did open seven days later. Helen was named director of the Valentine Museum. She would remain in that position, and far away from Bragg and her beloved Charleston, for ten long years.[192]

Helen administered the Valentine Museum in the same manner that Bragg directed The Charleston Museum, with story hours and traveling exhibits for children and other exhibits that came from Charleston, such as the Mexican exhibit. The bronze plaque on the front of the building proclaimed it a "culture history museum. Its collections show the fine and folk arts of many peoples and many ages. It places particular emphasis upon the elements in world culture which have contributed to the making of Virginia." Helen McCormack had been Bragg's apt student, as Bragg had been her father's.[193]

1931 and the Opportunity to Go Home to New England

As diligently as she had worked over the past five years, there were few individual professional accomplishments for Bragg by 1931 in Charleston. One accomplishment was the creation of exhibits at the Museum, which were organized so that they told the story of man's development and served as background for South Carolina culture, fitting her concept of the culture history museum. The exhibits were arranged to trace the development of that culture—"through European, Egyptian, Tigris and Euphrates cultures to Central Asia and primitive man; then turning eastward to the Indian, Chinese, Japanese and the South Sea cultures, with the union of eastern and western in the contacts between the American Indians and the Europeans."[194]

The second of her accomplishments was realized when the Charleston Free Library opened at the Museum on 1 January 1931. Within six months branch libraries were opened in Mount Pleasant, McClellanville, Saint Paul's Parish, and Edisto Island. A museum colleague wrote her, "Southern museums and libraries already owe you a great debt and I hope they sometimes say so." But the accomplishment was not hers alone; civic leaders participated in the effort. Without the Rosenwald Fund and her relationship with Clark Foreman, neither the library nor her third accomplishment, the funding of the traveling school exhibits, would have been possible. The last of her hard-won achievements was her work, along with many others, of preserving the Heyward-Washington House.[195]

Even with these achievements to her credit, Bragg, the Museum, and the Charleston community still had huge financial burdens due to the Depression. The city had a tremendous municipal debt and by 1931 teetered on bankruptcy. Receiving a monetary gift from "Miss Carrie [Sinkler]," Bragg wrote that she needed "to keep the second check for the Museum as this will probably be a hard year. There are numbers of new resignations and no new members." Later that same month she let Rea know that even though city council had given the Museum the same appropriation as the year before, there was a "great agitation on the part of the citizens for a revision of the city budget and a reduction all along the line. The tax payers are determined on state retrenchment and so naturally, the legislators are starting with the educational institutions and have brought in a bill to cut the teachers' salaries 20 per cent. The Museum has not yet been mentioned but even members of our own board of trustees, Mr. Hagood for example, say that they are willing to have the Museum's quarter mill cut if it will lower taxes." Since Rea had also dealt with city council over the lack of funding, he well knew what Bragg was facing. If the Museum were allocated less money in the budget, there would probably have to be a reduction in services as well as in staff.[196]

Bragg appealed to Rea to try to get assurance before the end of February about the new building. She wanted to be able to tell the members of the county delegation "that there is every prospect and that we would be able to put a large sum of money into Charleston for . . . a new building in the not distant future." Rea replied that he would be unable to get the matter of the new building before the trustees of the Carnegie Corporation until April, and again he offered her a caution: "It is not going to be entirely easy to convince them . . . a building is the right thing to do. . . . I shall do everything in my power to put it in the strongest and most favorable light possible."[197]

Rea was also concerned about the depressed financial situation and wrote that the "present conditions of business . . . do give me considerable concern with the project for a building." However, there was an advisory group meeting for the Carnegie Foundation on 20 February, and he assured her that if his recommendation about the Charleston building was adopted, he would write her immediately. It is the outcome of this meeting and Rea's follow-up letter that gave Bragg real hope that the Carnegie

Corporation would fund the new building. The advisory group members regarded his recommendation "as clearly demonstrating the need of the building, . . . and that the record of the Museum both in the past and at present abundantly warrants special aid. . . . I have reason to believe that the project has now been put in a favorable form, and I hope that ways may be found to bring it to a successful conclusion. In any event, it has successfully passed the first stage in negotiation. I cannot give you any assurance of the ultimate outcome but I am not without hope." In Rea's opinion Bragg was "quite justified" in letting the city council members and county delegation know of the possibility of a new building.[198]

By early March, Bragg had been approached by Zenas Marshall Crane from Pittsfield, Massachusetts, with an opportunity to return to her native state. Crane had spoken with Rea and had contacted the American Association of Museums, asking for advice about his family's art museum. Both Rea and Coleman referred him to Bragg. At Pittsfield she would have carte blanche to turn his "old man's attic" of a museum into an educational and cultural institution. In undertaking this work, she saw the chance "to do the reorganization work which I have so much enjoyed in Charleston and in doing over the Valentine Museum and in helping other museums in the south and particularly the prospect of building up a large extension work with traveling school exhibits traveling up and down the Housatonic Valley."[199]

She visited the Pittsfield Museum and on her way home stopped in Richmond, where she saw Chia Mei, who was flying for the air corps in Texas. They spent the weekend with Helen. It must have been an unpleasant time for all three, as Helen later wrote Bragg, "I'm terribly sorry that you felt as you did about your weekend here . . . I thought all along that it was I who was hurt. . . . it probably explains what you took to be coldness and lack of hospitality in me. But I found Chia Mei so changed. He was not all as I remembered him. . . . I decided sometime between last October and now never to have more emotions. Work and emotions don't combine very well for me. . . . Please do not feel that there is no hope and joy for you in the future. A big new field is opening up for you whether in Charleston or Pittsfield. It is only because we love each other so much that we can hurt each other so. But I believe that the hurts wear away and are forgotten but the love goes on. Yours as I have always been, Helen."[200] Chastised by her mentor Bragg, Helen, the protégée, assumed the blame for the unhappy visit to Richmond. Helen was Bragg's apt student again— learning not to combine emotions and work. It was a lesson that Bragg had taught her when she sent Helen away from Charleston, the Museum, and most important, from Bragg herself.

Bragg was emotionally torn between what seemed an incredible opportunity to continue her work in Charleston or to reorganize the museum at Pittsfield. She wrote to Dr. Buist, president of the Museum's trustees, from Miss Carrie Sinkler's home in Philadelphia that the Carnegie building was "to be a matter of five hundred thousand dollars and it seems to be possible. . . . the Carnegie [people] say I must not resign at Charleston, and I also must not be deprived of the present opportunity at Pittsfield. . . . They [the Carnegie people] are prepared to tell him [Crane] that I am the only museum person who can reorganize his museum. . . . Won't it be wonderful if we get the building. . . . Oh, I have worked so long and hard for this that I can scarcely believe that I am to see the realization of my dreams."[201]

Bragg's "peculiar methods of finance" had come into question by several Museum trustees at this point, but she brushed it off, calling "the matter of the handling of the treasurer's account petty and unimportant." Somehow the Rosenwald Fund money had become mixed up with funds for the Heyward House. In an exchange of letters between Buist, the president of the trustees, and James Hagood, the treasurer, it was apparent that neither understood her methods and looked askance at the "whys and wheres" of her accounting procedures. Indeed, it became the opinion of the treasurer that Bragg was "the proper custodian" of the Rosenwald Fund, since "it was given with the condition that she should disburse it . . . this problem can be solved by having the Board turn over the entire amount to Miss Bragg." Her personal nemesis had now become a professional one, but Bragg was dismissive of treasurer Hagood's concern. She wrote Buist that the Carnegie people found the trustees' method of paying the bills to be "archaic. So I'm enough of a woman to be satisfied that I was right. After all the work of the people is the great thing, not the small detail of method."[202]

Instead of hearing directly from Bragg about her decision to leave Charleston, Helen heard about it from Robert Whitelaw, another of Bragg's "boys." He had assumed Ned Jennings's position as curator of art after Jennings's death and was in Richmond at the Valentine Museum dropping off another group from the Drama of Civilization series that he had created for them. Whitelaw told Helen on 23 March that Bragg had definitely decided to take the Pittsfield Museum job. Left "breathless" by Bragg's leaving, Helen saw it as a great loss to Charleston. In an outpouring of emotion Helen wrote Bragg that what she had done for the Museum would be left to the trustees and their resolutions, but she would tell Bragg what Bragg had done for her: "Do you remember how shy I was when I first went to you—and nobody thought that I would ever amount to very much? But you taught me to swim by sort of pushing me in—

persuading me to do things by letting me think I was doing them for your sake. And have you any idea of the number of things I know and love, whose knowledge I owe to you? Greek plays, Georgia O'Keefe's (*sic*) pictures, Snug Harbor—and oh, so many lovely, lovely things. And do you by any chance know how much I love you, love you—and always will—no matter where you go—love you and love you? Surely some little things I did for you that I would have done for no one else and will never do for any one again, must have told you that I love you."[203]

While Whitelaw was in Richmond letting Helen know Bragg's news, Bragg was writing to another trustee, J. L. Coker of Hartsville (she already had endorsements of her plans from two other trustees), asking for his support. In a letter full of hope and supplication, Bragg informed Coker, "I must not definitely resign but must maintain connection with the Museum." She asked him for his assistance in her plan to remain as director of the Charleston Museum while she went to Pittsfield on a five-year leave of absence.[204]

Dauntless, Bragg believed that she could direct the Museum from an advisory position in New England, but she also knew that she could not bear to leave Charleston permanently. She wrote Coker that the plans for a new type of museum, an "ideal building" as Bragg called it, were to be worked out by a national committee of group of northern architects. Thus, she felt that "I can help with this better from the north and I also believe that from this northern museum I can have more influence in securing the cooperation of the northern people who are buying homes down here."[205] Bragg ended this letter by writing that if it seemed best to him and the other trustees that she resign and sever her relations with the Charleston Museum, she would do so.

The board of trustees met on Monday, 30 March 1931 and granted Bragg's request for a five-year unpaid leave of absence while she was employed at the Pittsfield Museum of Arts and Sciences. Unable to attend the meeting, Coker, Dominick, and Sinkler all sent word of their support for Bragg's plan. With a vote of nine to two, Bragg retained her post, and it was her suggestion that Milby Burton, an insurance salesman and a trustee, be named acting director. The two trustees who voted "no," Frederick Horlbeck and D. E. Huger, both felt "that the Museum should not be tied up for such a length of time." The minutes of this meeting also reported on the conference that Bragg and Rea held with Keppel, who had assured her that her absence would not interfere with the plans for the new building, and included this statement: "The Carnegie people consulted felt that Miss Bragg should not sever her relations with the Museum and that an acting director should be appointed."[206]

Bragg must have written Helen shortly after the trustee meeting, because her "little note" made Helen sad. Bragg had asked her to do something, possibly to come home to Charleston for a visit, but for Helen "the very things you yourself have done for me—have taught me—make it impossible for me to do what you now ask me to. But, darling, please remember that I'm thinking of you every day—every minute just now—Though I haven't my arms about you as I have so often in reality—my love is there like a warm mantle around you. Can't you feel it dear? I have loved you, dear, as I have loved no one else. With you I have touched heights that otherwise I would never have known. I am deeply conscious of my indebtedness to you—And neither time nor space can come between us. . . . Remember that I love you always and always—your Helen."[207]

Bragg may have been leaving the South, but she took one last trip to Kentucky on behalf of her culture museum theory and the southern museum expansion activities she so ardently favored. Instead of attending the AAM's annual meeting in Pittsburgh, she went instead to Bowling Green to help the Western State Teachers College with plans for a culture history museum. Writing both Rea and Coleman about this trip, she also let them know of the trustees' actions in granting her leave of absence. Bragg's letter to Rea included a reminder that since the "trustees are deeply interested in the progress of the prospective new building," he should "not let this fall."[208]

Bragg and Margaret Hightower, her protégée from the museum classes and a library worker, left Charleston on 1 July in a worn-out Chevrolet ("never using second gear," Bragg recalled) first bound for Scranton, Pennsylvania, and due to arrive in Pittsfield on Sunday, 5 July. They were joined a month later by another Charlestonian, Mary Martin, the granddaughter of a trustee and Miss Carrie's grandniece. While her adopted home would never be far from her thoughts, Bragg was going to a situation where she would have fewer money worries, as the budget came primarily from one man's pocket, and not from city and county appropriations tied to the wealth of the populace. She would have money, and she would be "free to develop the Museum [in Pittsfield] so that its reorganization shall make a definite contribution to the history of museum development in America."[209]

Citadel student Chia Mei Hu, 1928 (Citadel Archives and Museum, Charleston, S.C.)

Meeting of Ta T'ung Club at Snug Harbor, 1928 (Citadel Archives and Museum, Charleston, S.C.)

Chinese cadets: Hu, Tseng, Liu, An, Tu (Citadel Archives and Museum, Charleston, S.C.)

Catherine Auld (far left), Helen McCormack, Jen Tao Li (left) and Shu Chun Liu at Snug Harbor (Citadel Archives and Museum, Charleston, S.C.

Christmas 1928 at 38 Chalmers Street, Charleston (Citadel Archives and Museum, Charleston, S.C.)

Chalmers Street garden. Front row: L.S. An, S.C. Liu, Margaret Hightower, Laura Bragg; standing: Wen-Jo Tu and Catherine Auld. (Citadel Archives and Museum, Charleston, S.C.)

Heyward-Washington House (87 Church Street, Charleston), c. 1770, before restoration (Courtesy of The Charleston Museum, Charleston, S.C.)

Heyward-Washington House after restoration (Courtesy of The Charleston Museum, Charleston, S.C.)

Paneled drawing room of the Heyward-Washington House, where President George Washington was entertained in 1791. (Courtesy of The Charleston Museum, Charleston, S.C.)

The Valentine Museum, Richmond, Va., ca. 1922–1925 (Valentine Museum and Archives, Richmond, Va.)

Photograph of Laura Bragg by Doris Ulmann, ca. 1928–1929 (Gene Waddell, Charleston, S.C.)

This 1859 forty-gallon alkaline-glazed stoneware jar, donated to the Charleston Museum in 1919, sparked Bragg's interest in collecting pottery for the Museum. Incised script: "Lm May 15, 1859/Dave & Baddler" (front, upper shoulder between handles), "Great and Noble jar, /hold sheep, goat and bear" (opposite). (Courtesy of The Charleston Museum, Charleston, S.C.)

The Berkshire Museum, Pittsfield, Mass.

Ellen Crane Memorial Room, Berkshire Museum, 1937

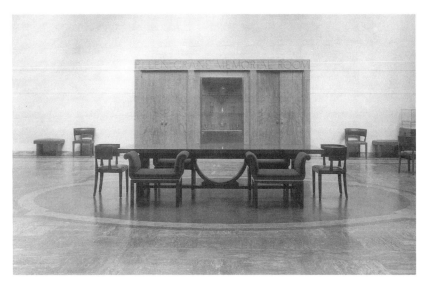

Furniture in Ellen Crane Memorial Room designed by Miss Gheen of New York City. These pieces featured the Berkshire logo, created by artist Anna Heyward Taylor of Columbia, S.C.

Ellen Crane Memorial Room, 1937. North view of fireplace, whose wood carvings were designed by Stirling Calder.

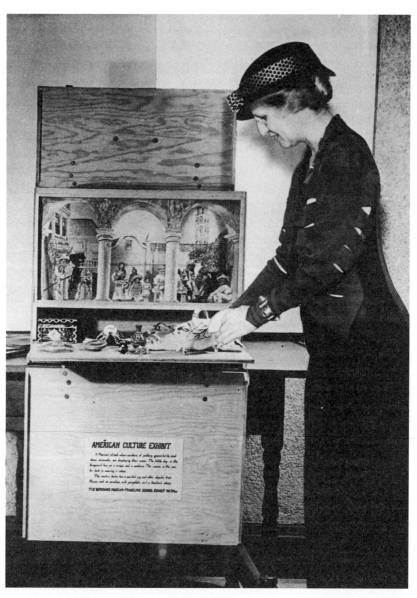

Bragg with an American Culture Traveling School exhibit.

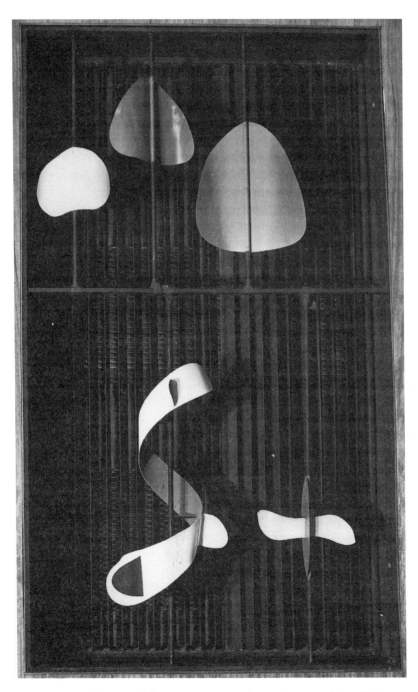

Alexander Calder's *Mobiles* (1937) was used as architectural installations to mask the ventilation system of the Berkshire Museum's new auditorium in 1937.

Laura Bragg with one of her many cats, all named "Guido" (Miriam Pope Herbert, Charleston, S.C.)

The Berkshire Museum
As a Progressive Institution

A museum's proper function is to broaden horizons
as well as to interpret the familiar.

Laura Bragg, museum director's report for 1933

AT FIRST GLANCE, PITTSFIELD AND CHARLESTON appear to be markedly different cities. Pittsfield, nestled at the foot of the "Purple Hills," or Berkshire Mountains in Massachusetts, boasts among its early residents literary figures such as Nathaniel Hawthorne and Herman Melville and wealthy industrialists such as Zenas Crane. These well-known men attracted others like them, and by the end of the 1800s a group of wealthy individuals were making their homes in the Berkshires. In 1929 Pittsfield was a confident city. General Electric, the city's major industry, increased its employment force by fifteen hundred workers in one year; other local industries were flourishing; and plans were drawn for a new hotel. At the same time, however, agriculture and textiles were depressed and farmers had financial troubles, with rural banks failing. While industrial production increased, so too did the number of unemployed. But when Bragg arrived in 1931, the city had not felt the Great Depression as sharply as had other communities, such as Charleston. As the city's largest employer, General Electric still had many large orders to fill, and several large construction projects were going forward in the city, which slowed the layoff of workers.[1]

In contrast, Charleston was a seacoast city and home to planters of aristocratic lineage. While the city's industrial base had slowly increased after World War I, its economy was still primarily agricultural. By 1929 the city was not financially solvent and money issues were troublesome. Bragg knew that there was no rosy future to look forward to at the Museum or in Charleston, as there was in Pittsfield at the new museum she was to direct.

With the improvement of roads and the increasing use of the automobile by 1928, tourism had become one of the largest industries for Pittsfield and the surrounding Berkshire area. Highways and cars had contributed to Mayor Stoney's decision in the early 1920s that Charleston would seek tourist dollars in hopes of bolstering the city's economy. In both cities, while most people approved of tourism because of the needed money, there were still some who resisted it. As in Charleston, historic homes were demolished in favor of progress. In Pittsfield—for example, three of the oldest homes in town were dismantled to make way for construction of the New High School.[2]

When People's National Bank collapsed in Charleston, it took the city's payroll with it. To cover the emergency, the city paid its employees with scrip. Their salaries and the operating budgets of city offices were cut. In Pittsfield unemployment increased when General Electric reduced its working schedules and many small retail stores went bankrupt. The city budget was also unstable, with city employees not receiving their paychecks on many paydays. Schools were affected as no new teachers were hired and all school employees took a 10 percent salary cut. The two cities may have appeared to be different, but the Great Depression had proven to be an equalizer.[3]

A common feature shared by the Charleston Museum and the Berkshire Museum was that Bragg was the first full-time director at both, while few other similarities existed between them. Not only were the buildings entirely different in style and purpose, but one was old and the other young in the museum world.

The Charleston Museum had been a cavernous auditorium in its first life, before Bragg installed the stored exhibits that transformed it into a museum facility. Founded in 1773 by a group of planters, it was the oldest museum in the country. Bragg's efforts to educate the citizens and to preserve the culture material of the area brought a change in the focus of the Museum during her tenure. While it began as a scientific museum, with its incorporation in 1915 it became a municipal institution. This meant that its yearly income was primarily derived from public funds allocated through city and county budgets. Tying the financial resources of the Museum to the city's and county's fortunes brought the effects of the Depression directly to bear on what was already a meager budget. The Charleston Museum's expected income for 1931 was just over seventeen thousand dollars.[4]

In marked contrast, the Pittsfield museum's commitment had always been to educate the public of the county about the past and the future and to reach wealthy summer visitors. The fireproof museum building and a major part of its collections had been gifts from Zenas Crane to the people of Berkshire County in 1902. The Italian Renaissance-revival building had an exterior of gray Roman brick with Indiana limestone trimmings. The interior was quartered oak with carved Italian overmantel doorways. The wrought iron staircase to the second floor was in a sunlight-flooded hall with windows that overlooked the interior courtyard.[5]

Furthermore, the museum in Pittsfield had a reputation as a repository of old masters. First named the Pittsfield Museum of Natural History and Art, it was directed by the same man who oversaw both the town's library, the Athenaeum, and the Natural History Museum. Zenas Crane's art collection on the second floor of the building formed the core of the museum's exhibits. Crane also had an interest in natural history, and those exhibits were housed on the first floor of the building. Funded by an endowment and by gifts from other Crane family members, the budget was thirty thousand dollars yearly.[6]

Perhaps a bit disingenuously, Bragg said later that she arrived in Pittsfield as a teacher and that the Crane family wanted her to teach them how to create a museum out of their father's collection. There can be little doubt, however, that she was primarily attracted by the promise of a freer hand into deeper pockets. The Crane family chose her because of her reputation as a progressive museum administrator and educator, and also because Coleman and Rea, as her supporters, had directed Crane to her. But there were other connections that drew the Crane family to Bragg. Zenas Crane's son, Z. Marshall Crane, owned Hope Plantation outside of Charleston near the small town of Jacksonboro. His new plantation house was designed by Albert Simons, Bragg's architect friend, who had helped the Charleston Museum save the Heyward-Washington House. And Ned Jennings, Bragg's protégé, had drawn a pictorial map of Crane's properties showing the location of hunting preserves on Crane's three-thousand-acre plantation. He would have had opportunities to become aware of her work at the Charleston Museum before he approached Rea and Coleman.[7]

Another strand in the web that drew Bragg home was her reputation as a progressive reformer, through her education department at the Charleston Museum. This educational work had caught the attention of Mrs. W. Murray Crane, a sister-in-law of the museum's original benefactor. Mrs. Crane was an advocate for progressive education and a founder of the Dalton School, a private school in New York City that served primarily middle-class students. She was firmly committed to progressive education and understood the museum's role of providing educational opportunities for all. Thus, Bragg and Mrs. Crane held similar educational philosophies.[8]

In June 1931 the wife and son of the original benefactor, Zenas Crane, offered the institution an additional twenty thousand dollars, beyond the yearly endowment funds, to increase the staff and expand the institution's activities. At the same time they asked that the board of trustees consider the separation of the museum from the Athenaeum, with a full-time director to be employed to oversee the increased demands made upon the museum.[9] Upon acceptance of this gift, the trustees cleared the way for Bragg to be named director of the Pittsfield Museum.

Bragg's appointment and most of the eight years she spent at the museum in Pittsfield were not without controversy. Initially, the conflict was not because of her personally but because her tenure represented change to an institution that had remained virtually the same since it had been founded. Mr. Ballard, the librarian who had overseen both the Athenaeum and the museum since 1903, wrote to Bragg before she arrived. "He evidently has no idea that I am to be director of the Museum, separately incorporated," Bragg wrote Crane in astonishment. "Do please get this matter straightened out," she directed. Bragg's appointment brought a new staff and three new departments. The staff had consisted of an assistant curator and the head of the children's department, whose salary was paid by Mrs. W. Murray Crane. Bragg brought Margaret Hightower, her Charleston apprentice, with her to be curator of science (they shared an apartment at the South Street Inn); Mary Martin, the new art assistant, who arrived in August; and her secretary, Margaret Sizer, who came up from New Jersey. Bragg also hired Stuart Henry as curator of art.[10]

What set the stage for real misunderstanding was the decision to change the name of the museum. It was Bragg's wish that it be incorporated as the "Pittsfield Museum of Natural History, Culture History, and Art and keep the general name as the Pittsfield Museum without the additions," as she wrote Crane before she arrived. However, the name was changed to the Berkshire Museum, and the change was attributed to her.[11]

In Bragg's first interview with a local paper, *The Berkshire Eagle,* she spoke of the Charleston Museum's influence on the establishment of other museums. And in her comparison of Pittsfield to Charleston, she revealed her devotion to her adopted city by calling Pittsfield the "Charleston of the North." Bragg told the reporter that it was her belief that people came to Pittsfield for the same reasons that they traveled to Charleston: artistic, historical, and literary pursuits.[12]

The reorganization of the museum was supposed to broaden its community focus through extension work, for Bragg believed that museums represented both cultural resources and educational centers for all. She had accepted the directorship because Crane and his sister, Mrs. Samuel Colt, had pledged to her "that I shall be free to develop the Museum so that its reorganization shall make a definite contribution to the history of museum development in America."[13]

Bragg's lifework, her ambition to make a name for herself, was not in botany or the classification of ferns, as she had once written her father, but in the development of American museums. A northerner, she developed a plan for southern museums that she spread across the Southeast. (Bragg wrote Crane about those who accepted her ideas as "progressive": "I suppose I think them progressive because they accept all my ideas but that it is one of the little ironies of human nature.") Bragg had now returned home to contribute her plan to the Berkshire Museum, where she wanted to do something truly progressive.[14]

Bragg made an impact on two fronts almost immediately upon arriving in Pittsfield. She instituted an extensive educational program at the same time that she was breaking new ground with modern art exhibits. The educational expansion work was not controversial, as it had been in Charleston, but the modern art exhibitions were not well received locally. However, they made a splash outside the area, garnering considerable publicity in *The New Yorker* and *Art News*.[15]

Even before she left Charleston, Bragg had been in contact with Edwin Barrie, director of the Grand Central Galleries, about an exhibit of contemporary art paintings to be held at the Berkshire Museum soon after her arrival.[16] She had not been able to pursue this interest in modern art in Charleston for two apparent reasons: lack of money to mount loaned exhibits and the conservative aesthetic nature of the city. Bragg's interest in art had been fostered long before, during her four years at Simmons College, from her many visits to art museums in New York City, and through her relationships with Anita Pollitzer and Georgia O'Keeffe. Now she had the Cranes' money and proximity to New York and Boston to pursue her learning, and it was Bragg's intent to provide the opportunity for others to learn about modern art as well.

The Grand Central exhibit was held in conjunction with the trustees' reception welcoming Bragg to the city and the museum. The guest list for the reception included two famous painters, the social elite of the Berkshire community, and numerous art and science devotees. Margaret Hightower wrote to Bragg's former secretary at the Charleston Museum, Emma Richardson: "The opening of the Grand Central Exhibit and Miss Bragg's reception was most successful. Everybody says that it was an enormous success as far as Pittsfield is concerned, because the people very seldom ever come out to things like that. The exhibit really is lovely, though, and the galleries that Miss B. did over are beautiful—I do wish you could see them." This was the first time contemporary art had been shown in Pittsfield. The exhibit and the opening reception (a custom Bragg inaugurated) also established her entrée, as the museum's director, into the network of the upper classes, who were familiar with the New York modern art world. Bragg also inaugurated another practice (which was far more questionable) with this exhibit: the paintings and sculpture were for sale. The local newspapers commented on the show and encouraged their readers to purchase and collect contemporary art, assuring them that the Berkshire Museum would not profit from the sales.[17]

Sixty-five leading contemporary American painters and twenty-three sculptors were represented in this exhibit. The display of so many different pieces provided the Grand Central's director of education, Wesley Wiseman, the opportunity to teach the museum's patrons about them. His talks were so popular and drew so many patrons that Bragg extended them beyond the original three days, scheduling an evening talk for members of the business community who were not able to attend the day speeches. On the third day *The Berkshire Eagle* reported that the drop of a pin could not be heard and that Wiseman's audience had more than doubled in size.[18]

Wiseman generously contended that it was Bragg's commentary on *Supper Eternal,* by Luis Mora, that stole the show. Bragg was familiar with all six of the great teachers represented in that work: Christ, Moses, Buddha, Lao-Tzu, Confucius, and Zoroaster. The local paper agreed with his assessment, exclaiming, "Miss Bragg will have to do this over and over again for the benefit of the public. No one can do it as she can. No report can begin to do justice to her inspired interpretation."[19] Bragg's continuing study of theology had proven useful in the delivery of her interpretation.

The modern art exhibit was not the only show mounted that fall at the Berkshire. Several local artists were featured, and Bragg also arranged for a South Carolinian, Anna Heyward Taylor, to display her block prints, watercolors, and textiles at the museum. In a press release to a local paper the Taylor exhibit was presented to Berkshire residents as "an opportunity to know intimately the beauties of the Carolina coast region."[20]

Bragg entertained Taylor with a reception that all residents of Berkshire County were invited to attend, and she again extended the hours of the museum day to accommodate businesspeople. As she had done with the Grand Central exhibit, Bragg made the Taylor artwork available for purchase. However, this time 20 percent of the selling prices for the artwork came to the museum. Selling articles exhibited at a museum was a questionable practice, but it was one that Bragg continued throughout her time at the Berkshire.[21]

Bragg honored another South Carolinian, her protégé Ned Jennings, by mounting a memorial exhibit of his paintings and masks. From the Berkshire Museum she sent the exhibit to the Currier Gallery of Art in Manchester, New Hampshire. Bragg wrote the director there, "I have been astonished to find how large is the number of people who feel a strong sympathy for Mr. Jennings. It requires a highly cultivated and somewhat sophisticated mind and also a certain type of temperament. Unimaginative people would not get him." Later she sent the exhibit to the Brooklyn Museum, but she was "greatly discouraged because the exhibition seems to have yielded no critical comment. . . . I am convinced of its fine imaginative quality . . . I am going to let the exhibition go back to Charleston and be cared for as Mr. Jennings' family see fit."[22]

Pittsfield's proximity to New York and Boston, and a larger salary (considerably more than double her Charleston salary), encouraged Bragg to buy a car with only a few hundred miles on it. It was a dark green coach Chevrolet two-door and came with a new car guarantee. Helen wrote Bragg after learning of the purchase, "You like being able to get to such exciting places, don't you?. . . I love you lots—as always Helen."[23]

Bragg's innovations extended beyond the physical reorganization of the museum and included new staff and the renovations of galleries. Besides lengthening the museum's hours to accommodate the business community and exhibiting art pieces for sale, Bragg, with Margaret Hightower's help, opened the museum on Christmas afternoon for the first time in the museum's history.[24] She spent that first Christmas of 1931 in Pittsfield with Margaret, rather than going to Epping to see her mother.

Bragg's success in the North went unnoticed, as the Charleston Museum's acting director, Milby Burton, traveled north that first November after she left the city. He went first to see Paul Rea in Haverford, Pennsylvania, and then to New York City to visit Dr. Keppel, president of the Carnegie Foundation. It became apparent to Burton that Rea had done "nothing regarding the expected gift from the Carnegie Fund since last January. Mr. Burton then interviewed Dr. Keppel, who is the chief administrative officer of the Carnegie Fund. Dr. Keppel stated that not only was there no possibility of the Carnegie Fund presenting funds to the Charleston Museum for a building, but there never had been any such possibility; that the Carnegie Fund has not engaged in any building operations since the World War, and has no intention of considering a policy of donating buildings." Burton's report to the trustees was in direct conflict with what Bragg had presented to them not eight months earlier. Based on her assurances, they had agreed to her request for a five-year leave of absence, allowing her to return to her position as director at the end of that time. Not only did Burton tell the trustees of his discovery, but he also reported Keppel's "refusal to help the Museum with funds for the new building" to Paul Rea.[25]

When Burton informed the trustees on 9 December of his discovery, treasurer George Buist wrote the paragraph quoted above. It was inserted into the trustees' minutes, eliminating any reference to a resolution in praise of Bragg. (The original minutes are no longer part of the record, and

the trustees' actions stand as above.) Buist adamantly insisted that the minutes include the results of Burton's meetings with Rea and Keppel: "I
object very seriously to this omission, because the supposed assurances
from the Carnegie Fund have loomed very large in the actions of the
Museum during the past several months." On 13 January 1932 Milby Burton was elected director of the Museum, and "the title of honorary director was conferred upon Miss Laura M. Bragg."[26]

Bragg received this news from the secretary of the board, Mabel Pollitzer, who had been ill and absent from the meeting when the board took
the action. Before writing Bragg, Pollitzer phoned the president of the
trustees, Dr. Buist, for an explanation. His response to Pollitzer was
included in her letter to Bragg: "The trustees felt that we are now passing
through a most crucial period. . . . We must turn more and more to outside help. It was the sense of the meeting that to have an acting director
was a distinct handicap to the Museum. When Mr. Burton approached
people with money, it was a decided advantage that these moneyed people should be seen by a director and not by an acting director. . . . Dr. Buist
and the board felt that this change was for the good of the museum—*your*
museum." The Pollitzer letter outlined the desperate financial conditions
that the city and state were facing as a result of the Great Depression. City
council "will appropriate *not a penny* and even should the county delegation still give the one quarter mill, it will yield *much less.* Many members
have resigned." Burton's report and the trustees' subsequent action certainly
call into question Bragg's credibility, with the Great Depression a convenient reason to use in answering possible questions about the change in
Burton's and Bragg's positions.[27]

While the Charleston Museum and its new director went about dealing with the effects of the Depression in the Holy City, Bragg continued
her reorganization of the Berkshire Museum. The Crane family had given
Bragg an explicit mandate to open the museum's educational program to
all social classes.[28] Certainly that was one of her accomplishments in
Charleston, and it was one of the primary reasons why the Cranes sought
her expertise. Bragg implemented the same innovative ideas in Pittsfield
that she had used in Charleston.

In Bragg's opinion, it was through education that the museum became
accessible to everyone. Bragg believed, and had firsthand experience to
support her beliefs, that education was a successful tool for bringing the
public into the museum. To increase community awareness of the
museum's services, she took the educational programs into the schools,
again coordinating them with the geography and natural history curricula.
Bragg spread the word about the exhibits by speaking to teachers and prin-

cipals. She also held public receptions at the museum, where the traveling exhibits were displayed.[29]

The primary mechanism employed by Bragg in Pittsfield, as in Charleston, was the traveling school exhibit. The exhibits, built in boxes, opened like stage sets to display the different subjects, such as period rooms, cultural history, geography, natural history, industrial topics, or Berkshire County. Each included a teacher's story and items for students to handle. For example, in the whaling exhibit there were pieces of scrimshaw that were passed around in the classes. The materials used in the exhibits came from various places, including the museum's storage closets and basements. Along with Margaret Hightower, Bragg brought in Robert Whitelaw to work on the school exhibits, just as she had in Charleston and at the Valentine Museum when she had been the acting director during its reorganization.[30]

Since she intended for the museum to be seen as a county institution, Bragg adopted the principle that the educational extension work should reach rural children first, since they could not visit the museum as often as students who lived in the city. In 1932 Bragg estimated that the fifty-one traveling exhibits were seen by more than seventeen thousand children in the eleven schools in Pittsfield and the other forty-two Berkshire County schools. Fifteen additional exhibits were added the next year. They were put to use thirty-three thousand times. In two years the use of "Bragg boxes" had expanded across all of Berkshire County into every town, with sixty-six exhibits used forty-seven thousand times.[31]

Bragg boxes, as they came to be known at the Berkshire Museum, served as a window on the world for children who rarely came to the museum. The boxes represented progressive social reform, as a means of educating and socializing rural and immigrant families to the prevailing American social values. Since they were recognized as such, Bragg was invited to speak to the national Progressive Education Association (PEA) meeting in Baltimore in February 1932. She titled her speech "The Charleston Museum Type of Traveling School Exhibits," as it was her intent to give Charleston credit for the stage-set principles utilized. Bragg boxes had been adopted by six other museums and one county public school system. They were displayed at the meeting with labels announcing their locations. In the summary of the forty-one museum educational programs prepared for the sectional meeting at which Bragg spoke, her type of traveling school exhibit was the only one listed.[32]

Bragg boxes were unique. Her invitation to speak before the PEA indicates acceptance by the educational establishment of her extension programs as examples of progressive educational reform. Educational reform was one of the major points of the progressive movement that had run its course as a political movement. Progressive education was called an attitude and a belief in experimentation and was distinguished by its commitment to the education of all children and to democracy in schools.[33] Bragg boxes were an attempt to do that both in the South for the rural poor and in the North for the immigrant.

At the same Baltimore meeting George Counts, another progressive educator, delivered his famous address "Dare Progressive Education Be Progressive?" He spoke forcibly about his belief that many progressive educators considered themselves to be members of a superior breed. Counts challenged listeners to confront the social issues that the Great Depression had made visible. For ten years Counts had critically examined American schools and found that American education had been serving the selected few. Troubled by the effects of America's social structure and its impact upon public schools, Counts believed that "democracy notwithstanding, access to . . . education was contingent on social and economic standing." His Baltimore speech became a rallying cry for progressive educators and stirred their imaginations. It also brought encouragement to them, for at that time control of the organization rested with headmasters of private, exclusive schools. After the 1932 meeting the PEA was never the same, as professors of education wrested control away from the upper-class schools, giving the organization a different philosophy.[34]

One of Bragg's champions was Mrs. W. Murray Crane, who was a founder of the exclusive Dalton School, which proclaimed to be progressive and based its principles on John Dewey's philosophy that "schools should provide an education that balanced the children's interests with the knowledge of adults, that engaged children in cooperative active work and that integrated social learning." Two questions could be raised: How did Bragg reconcile Counts's charges against the movement with her own actions as a museum director? and What were Bragg's thoughts and how did Counts's speech affect her? Bragg had provided the same educational services to blacks and whites beginning in 1913, opened the Charleston Museum to blacks in 1921, and believed that the purpose of education was to "fit man to sustain harmonious and helpful relations . . . to people with whom he is directly or indirectly in contact." But at the same time Bragg did not believe in mixed marriages or relationships, and she mingled easily with the social and culturally elite in both Pittsfield and Charleston.[35]

Bragg employed a total of seven artists on various projects that included building traveling school exhibits. Five of the artists produced Bragg boxes with a Japanese street scene, an Irish village, and camels and the Egyptian desert. When the museum displayed the work of the artists, Bragg commented in the local press, "they have created works which should awaken a creative impulse and understanding among school children and others who use them."[36]

Traveling school exhibits were the major focus of the museum's activities at this time, as reflected in Bragg's 1934 director's report opening: "Topping all other museum activities in 1934 was the circulation of traveling school activities. Every town in Berkshire County received the exhibits."[37] Her educational outreach programs at the Berkshire Museum had extended faster (in only three years) and further (throughout the county) than had her initial efforts in Charleston, where the county schools had to wait almost seven years before receiving the exhibits on a regular schedule.

By 1936 *The New York Times* was reporting on Bragg's innovation and her belief that a museum must go to the people if they cannot come to the museum. The exhibits and their contents had evolved to include "History, geography, nature study, home economics, and conservation lessons." A new type of exhibit with a social message had also been added—it depicted familiar surroundings that had been neglected as well as those that had been "made attractive by grass, flowers, and trees." Another example of this exhibit was a "burned out forest scene in contrast with a tidy public picnic area or the gas stations and roadside stands that are inviting to customers by their neatness and attractiveness, shown in opposition to crude and unkempt buildings." With the Depression and hard times in Pittsfield and across Berkshire County, Bragg, as a progressive social reformer, understood the great impact these visual scenes would have on children, teaching them middle-class values. In addition to the other museums using the traveling school exhibits, the American Museum of Natural History now adopted Bragg boxes for use by the New York City schools as well as other museums in New England.[38] Written about in *The New York Times* and adopted by museums in many sections of the country, Bragg boxes had become nationally recognized.

In addition to Bragg's educational program, the Berkshire Museum extended itself beyond the modern art and old masters exhibits. She sought community involvement by soliciting objects for a "Time of Washington" exhibit as an observance of the bicentennial of George Washington's birth. They included "paintings and papers of Washington; furniture and house furnishings . . . , silver, china and glass, and textile and costumes." Bragg and her committee gathered objects from more than one hundred people—enough items to fill six galleries of room displays, "showing three drawing rooms, a dining-room and a bed-room." While many prominent people received invitations, more than twelve hundred guests attended the opening. During the three weeks of its display more than nine thousand people visited the exhibit, viewing galleries and hearing speeches about the displays. Bragg's exhibit reached the ordinary citizen through the posses-sions of the upper classes, who had lent their furnishings to the museum.[39]

Another exhibit that caught the public's attention was a collection of Chinese paintings. The purpose of this exhibit was to show the influence of Oriental art on painters in the Western world. There were forty-nine roll paintings, one of which was fourteen feet long, and several Oriental porce-lains were displayed. Some of the paintings had previously been owned by Bragg's Chinese friend Miss Liu. Liu, who was now at the Chinese Library of Harvard University, presented a talk at the opening and a story hour for the children.[40]

There were two other noteworthy exhibits at the Berkshire Museum that summer, both bringing in large crowds. One presented contemporary art, with eighty-nine paintings by artists from twenty-one countries. Bragg opened this exhibit with a public reception attended by 650 guests. The local newspaper's account included the reaction of the crowd to the paint-ings, calling them a mystery to many. This exhibit drew a strong reaction. Bragg had redecorated the gallery that contained Crane's old masters, and it drew ahs. But the gallery that held the modern art inspired only ohs, or so the *Eagle* noted. One of the punch pourers asked a guest, "Have you come far to see these horrors?"[41]

The fall exhibit was far removed from modern art and its ability to shock. Bragg presented an exhibition of Shaker furniture, textiles, and domestic objects. Local interest was strong, as there were three Shaker communities located near Pittsfield: New Lebanon, Hancock, and West Pittsfield. Bragg had arranged for seven members of the Shaker communi-ties to be present at the opening, two of whom gave talks about Shaker life. In the two weeks the exhibit was on display, it had more than ten thou-sand visitors, some of them from museum circles: Juliana Force of the Whitney Museum, Charles Sawyer of the Addison Art Gallery, and an offi-cial of the New England Society for the Preservation of Antiquities. Thirty-four hundred schoolchildren along with their teachers also attended. The Shaker exhibition was written up in *The New York Times.* "Quite swell, you are, rating that," Helen wrote Bragg.[42]

The Berkshire Museum, once a repository for old masters and Indian relics, had become a living, breathing part of the community. More than sixty-six thousand people visited during 1932, more than double the thirty thousand that was the average for the years before Bragg's reorganization. A former employee, Bart Hendricks, remarked of Bragg, "She got the museum to wake up."[43]

No doubt she did, and both the social elite and the working classes in the community had taken notice. In a local newspaper account an art critic and fan of Bragg reported her conversation with a taxi driver, who told her, "Yes, I've been to the museum. A small town like this is pretty lucky to have such a museum. Any town, big or small, would be pretty lucky." The Berkshire Museum touched commoner and blue blood alike.[44]

As astonishing as the attendance figures were for 1932, no one could have been prepared for the thousands of new visitors who descended on the Berkshire Museum for a series of Sunday international programs and exhibitions in January and February 1933. Delegating responsibility, Bragg assigned each of the staff members a Sunday program. Each had to find someone of a specific nationality to speak and arrange the program for that day.[45]

Italian day drew a crowd of one thousand; fifteen hundred attended Polish Sunday; another fifteen hundred were there for Ireland's Sunday; and six hundred came to hear spirituals and a speech on "The Aspirations and Progress of the Negroes" on a Sunday in February. Other scheduled countries or cultures included the Scandinavian countries, Syria, and a Hebrew art exhibit. Bragg could not have mounted such a program in Charleston. Maybe she had heard Counts's plea in Baltimore after all.[46]

The Sunday afternoon programs brought thousands of new visitors to the museum—people who had never before entered its doors. They came to hear about their cultures or to learn about those different from their own. Bragg understood that it was "human nature to be most interested in things belonging to oneself and associated with one's immediate interest . . . and to attend . . . programs of local . . . interests." However, she recognized that unless the museum found a way to bring the people back "again and again for smaller gatherings and for exhibitions and talks about the unfamiliar," then the effects of the Sunday programs would have no permanent value.[47]

Bragg believed that "a museum's proper function was to broaden horizons as well as to interpret the familiar." With the Sunday programs she began the process of broadening horizons. Her aim at the Berkshire was "for the day when the largest attendance will be at exhibitions which bring new ideas and new visions of what human effort has aspired to."[48]

Another of Bragg's major goals was the reorganization and redecoration of the galleries—which would contain art to broaden horizons. One of her principles was that "in a living museum nothing is ever completed."[49] For two and a half years at the Berkshire Museum there was an almost constant state of renovation, painting, and refurbishing, with nothing, or so it seemed, completed.

The first area of the museum to receive treatment was the administration offices, which were a gift of Z. Marshall Crane. The redecoration of the upper hall was also a gift from Crane and his mother, Mrs. Zenas Crane. Two Sèvres vases, gifts to the museum, held palms in this hall. The galleries on the second floor of the museum featured the tremendous devotion to detail and the exacting perfection for which Bragg was noted.

The Earliest Known Cultures Gallery, or Gallery One, contained the story of western civilization's first cultures. Bragg replaced a gallery of curios with an exhibition of materials from Egypt, Asia, India, Persia, the Tigris-Euphrates Valley, Syria, and Palestine. Bragg bought a Persian fresco from a palace in Ispahan for this room. Here, as in all the newly renovated galleries, the walls received dramatic color treatments. They were of "burnt limestone . . . cornices, an Egyptian red-orange and Egyptian blue, the color of the pottery glazes." In the Classical Gallery, or Gallery Two, the story of man's civilization progressed from the Aegean, through Greek, to Roman culture. Displayed here were two Cyprus jars on loan, other pieces of marble and pottery on loan from the Metropolitan Museum of Art, and original sculpture from Palmyra and Cyprus from the museum's permanent collection. The walls were "the tone of weathered, creamy marble with overhead mouldings, cases, and pedestals, in a typically classical Pompeiian red." Both of these galleries opened in the spring of 1933.[50]

The European Culture Room, or Gallery Three, told man's story in the period of the Renaissance through the eighteenth century. Once the old masters' gallery, the room was redecorated "in a rich gold color . . . that brings out the tones of the paintings."[51] A new miniature group of Michelangelo painting the Sistine Chapel was created by Robert Whitelaw (from the Charleston Museum) for this gallery. It also contained all the gifts of the museum's founder, Zenas Crane. According to the paper, works by Rubens, Van Dyck, Frank Dobson, Ponty, Murillo, George Morland, Edward Hopper, and Thomas Lawrence were exhibited there.

The first stage of renovation and redecoration was completed during the summer of 1933. With neutral colored backgrounds for displaying paintings, the three galleries housed early American artists in the Berkshire County Room and in the Nineteenth Century Gallery. The latter exhibited a large number of paintings from the Hudson River school of art. Purchased by Zenas Crane, they were part of the museum's permanent collection. Early American art was exhibited in Gallery Four, which included works of Charles Wilson Peale, Rembrandt Peale, Gilbert Stuart, Henry Inman, Thomas Sully, and Matthew Harris Jouett. The Berkshire Room displayed a John Singleton Copley portrait as well as Chippendale and Hepplewhite furniture.

Gallery Seven, or the Twentieth Century Gallery, was formerly the old Sculpture Hall. Bragg's plan was to use this gallery for modern painting exhibitions, as the walls had special panels "prepared for constantly changing exhibitions of prints." The museum owned a few examples of modern art, most notably *The Night March* by John Allan Wyeth.[52]

The Night March was a gift of a former resident of Pittsfield, Mrs. Eliot

Watrous, who had made an earlier gift to the museum of the painting *Port Vendres* by Henri Verge-Sarrat. In Bragg's opinion, the gift was an important milestone. With its addition to the collection there were now seven works of art in the museum painted after 1900. This painting would help the museum move its patrons closer to an understanding of contemporary art. It was Bragg's intent, she wrote Watrous, to work toward the present in art fashions: "I am hoping to make the transition to the freer forms of today by means of Chinese painting. Those who can see beauty in the Chinese convention, so different from the Western, I am hoping may be led to find beauty also in the break with convention of our modernists."[53]

In 1933 Bragg exhibited the work of four Berkshire residents: Alexander Calder, George Morris of the Fifth Avenue cubists, Calvert Coggeshall, and Alma de Gersdorff. While his family summered in the Berkshires, this was Calder's first exhibit in the United States. Calder gained fame in Paris, where he used simple iron wire as his medium, twisting it into varying curves and forms. Calder was considered a pioneer in his use of industrial materials and fabrication processes. In the opinion of many art experts, much of contemporary sculpture has been influenced by his work. Bragg purchased two of Calder's early modern sculptures exhibited at this show for the Twentieth Century Gallery. In an *Art Digest* article about Calder's work, written just after the purchase, Bragg said: "They succeed in giving freshly creative form of motion devoid from representation. Whether or not they are the introduction of a new art form, I am sure they have real significance. I have watched with curiosity their effect upon the general public. People sit quietly before them, apparently stilled and quieted by something, perhaps merely by the rhythm of the movement. But we have found it easy to make a Sunday afternoon crowd understand 'abstract' motion where they would be blank before abstract painting." Bragg was the first American museum director to recognize Calder's genius with her purchase of two motorized sculptures, *The Arc and the Quadrant* and *Dancing Torpedo Shape*.[54]

The eighth large gallery, with cream and vermilion walls, was not designed for exhibiting paintings. However, it was completed in time for the Loan Exhibition of Painting and Sculpture in the late summer of 1933. The residents of Berkshire County lent the artwork to be displayed, which spanned a wide sweep of Western art: Dürer, Titian, Holbein, Sargent, Manet, Pissarro, Matisse, and Picasso. Even Bragg was surprised by the wealth and range of art that existed in the area.[55]

This gallery had been designed to display the art of Oriental cultures, particularly Chinese and Japanese. The first exhibition was of pottery, including a gift of a Neolithic jar from a dealer in Chinese antiquities.

Other pieces exhibited were "some most marvelous reproductions of Chinese paintings from a portfolio purchased from the Boston Museum of Fine Arts."[56]

With the opening of these last galleries, Bragg pronounced the art department reorganized. The end of 1933 marked the conclusion of two and a half years of reinstallation of the art galleries and the development of the public instruction department. Before she turned her energies to the first floor and science and natural history exhibits of the museum, Charleston beckoned her return.

Though Bragg had hoped to return to Charleston and the South for a visit in 1932, she became ill again with gastrointestinal problems, which necessitated a hospital stay in Boston at the Leahey clinic. As early as January of the next year she had written Josephine Pinckney that she was coming home for two weeks in the spring. In her reply to Bragg's news, Josephine wrote Bragg about her reduced ("about 75%") circumstances due to the Depression. Bragg must have asked Josephine about the social register, which Josephine seemed to find rather curious, given what she was dealing with in the real world of Charleston's depression: "About your social register—it must have been years ago that you saw one at our house. I have been trying to find out who the agent is and where—have industriously inquired of everybody who might know but nobody has any idea where he is to be found. The only person who seemed ever to have heard of the Social Register thought Charleston was dropped. . . . [Find someone in Pittsfield] and let them pass the word on to this district to list you again in the Charleston section." The rest of Josephine's letter returned to the issue of the Depression and its effects upon the Charleston Museum and the city. For Josephine, whose family lineage was as old as Bragg's, ancestry had lost its prominence in the wake of financial disaster. Josephine, the Museum, and Charleston had changed, while seemingly Bragg had not lost her deep-rooted need to be with the "right kind or people." Tellingly, Bragg's interest in her family ancestry and her social standing was as much a part of her life in Pittsfield as it had been in Charleston.[57]

Bragg had spoken to a few groups in Pittsfield about southern literature when she first arrived. But with the winter of 1933 she began to obsess about the South, as there was a dramatic increase in the number of speeches she gave at the museum and the newspaper coverage given to southern topics. In January she spoke on DuBose Heyward's new book, *Peter Ashley,* using readings from the book and from Allen and Heyward's book of poetry, *Carolina Chansons,* and displaying etchings of the locations described in *Peter Ashley.* She also talked about Hervey Allen's *Anthony Adverse.* The local paper noted that Allen "was one of a group who organized the Poetry

Club (*sic*) of South Carolina at Miss Bragg's home....What Miss Bragg has to say will be of great interest as she was the guest of the author and his wife at their summer home at Cazenovia, N.Y. only last month."[58]

In early April she attended the Southern Conference of Museums in Birmingham, and she was reelected chairman of the group. Meeting consecutively with the museum conference, Bragg also attended the Southern States Art League. She was interviewed by the local paper as someone who "knows more perhaps about museums than any other individual in the country." Bragg believed that Birmingham was handicapped as a city without a museum building. Her suggestion to the reporter was that President Roosevelt put the "unemployed to work on a splendid museum building, it would remove them from the ranks of charity. . . . People who are employed are far happier than those who accept charity."[59]

Knowing that Helen had no money and wanting to see her, Bragg paid for her to attend this meeting, using the Rosenwald Fund money that had been given to Bragg in 1929 on behalf of the development of southern museums. Bragg worked for another three years to bolster the Southern Conference of Museums and continued to serve as chairperson. She wrote her Birmingham colleague in 1934, "You know my heart is in the southern work and I want to come right back into it two years from next summer." By 1935 attendance numbers had dropped considerably at the conferences and the Houston host for the next year's conference was "not optimistic about the fate of the Southern conference," claiming that the South was too large geographically and was too unwieldy.[60]

Following the conferences in Birmingham, Bragg spent two weeks in Charleston, staying at Josephine's house. Charleston welcomed her home with teas, dinner parties, and luncheons during her visit. In an interview with a local paper, she declared herself still a South Carolinian: "For twenty-four years I have felt that Charleston was my home and I am looking forward with pleasure to the time when I will return again for good."[61]

On her return trip to Pittsfield she stopped in Richmond, staying with Helen for several days. With only the brief time in Birmingham, there had been no visit between the two in their new homes since Bragg had returned north in 1931, even though Bragg had been in Baltimore in 1932. Since Margaret Hightower was in Pittsfield with her and Helen's economic circumstances did not allow her to travel, Bragg and Helen had drifted apart. However, after Bragg's visit the flame was still there for Helen, who wrote Bragg: "You came and went so quickly. . . . Please come to see me soon, again. I need to see you, often. . . . I shan't ever again go anywhere except Charleston probably. So it is lucky that it should be the place of all the world that I like best. You must come back to it, too."[62]

While Bragg was being feted in her adopted home, the Great Depression with its despair and destitution was at its zenith. Pittsfield had its share of unemployed during the Depression. As part of the New Deal, Roosevelt and Congress had established various relief projects for writers, artists, and other professional people. Through the creation of the Federal Public Works of Art Project of the Civil Works Administration, artists were provided with work projects decorating public buildings. As part of their service they also had to swear an "Oath of Office" to support and defend the Constitution of the United States upon accepting the appointment. In December 1933 the Berkshire Museum was selected as one of eight art centers in New England, and Bragg served as a member of the New England Regional Executive Committee.[63]

Each center had a quota of people (Bragg's was ten) for which work could be provided. Since she knew the area's artists and their abilities, she was forthright in sharing her assessment of who could do what in her response letter to the chairman of the New England Committee. In her estimation there were no artists in Pittsfield or in the county "who were capable of doing a historical frescoe or a frescoe of any kind. . . . As to paintings to be hung in hospitals, Mr. Francis Day was in my mind. His paintings might give much pleasure to convalescents. People of good taste . . . have them in their guest rooms. . . . but I do not accept them for the museum. . . . Probably both of the above could be used as assistants in some major mural project, but I do not imagine they would be especially valuable." Bragg eventually employed a total of seven artists on three types of projects. Francis Day, the artist whose work hung in people's guest bedrooms, completed an oversize canvas painting for the town hall of Lanesboro. Five of the artists (including one of the two who "could be used as assistants") produced traveling school exhibits such as a Japanese street scene, an Irish village, and an Egyptian desert, among others, for the museum. The other artist deemed appropriate to serve as an "assistant" painted a mural canvas of the Mount Greylock Beacon.[64]

The establishment of this arts program, the meetings in Boston and Pittsfield, and letters and telegrams back and forth occurred near the Christmas holiday. That year Bragg did not remain in Pittsfield but left the museum on the day before Christmas Eve, traveling to Epping to see her mother and sister. Margaret Hightower, however, was left to answer the phone and close the museum at the end of the day. Certainly Bragg was not expecting Mr. Taylor, chairman of the New England Committee, to call her. Margaret's letter to Bragg with the messages from Taylor's phone call reveals the relationship she shared with her "Darling Boss": "Your 'nothing' sent me into ecstasies when I got home from the museum this morning—I never saw so much, really. Thanks heaps, I feel too flattered to get so many when you had such a multitude of people to remember. Loads and oodles of love for you, darling, from your little 'funnyface.'"[65]

As quickly as the opportunity for government service developed in December, it disappeared within a month when the artists' project was cut. Taylor informed Bragg, "It has been decided at Washington to cooperate on major mural projects and reduce the number of workers in the interest of furthering these." But Bragg saw the other side, writing Taylor, "This whole affair seems most unfortunate." However, measured in dollars the project was a success: "Disbursements for the Project up to the end of the fourth week totalled $5000 of which 92% paid out in salaries to artists and 8% for administration."[66]

In late spring of 1934 Bragg held an exhibit at the museum of the works created by artists through the government's Public Works of Art project. Technically the works belonged to the federal government, but they were distributed to Berkshire County schools and towns. The exhibit included "posters, charcoal sketches of historic buildings, traveling school exhibits, and a chart showing the story of paper making." Though Bragg called the art contemporary, she was not particularly complimentary about the artists in her final report: "There were no unemployed geniuses among the artists of Berkshire County. The Project was . . . as manna from heaven to six of the seven men who were . . . employed."[67]

Bragg concentrated the next phase of her reorganization plans on the museum's first floor. Using a budget of just over two thousand dollars, she reconstructed the natural history section of the museum. It was Bragg's plan to follow "broadly the order of evolution on this earth, [and] the beginning was made among the inorganic minerals and will progress through the lower forms of life, rising, higher and higher, to man."[68]

Another of her museum principles was that every installation must be made over at least once every thirty years, and Bragg personally believed that few exhibits retained their vitality beyond fifteen years. The first room on this floor to receive Bragg's touch was the mineral room. Here were displayed the more than two thousand mineral specimens collected by Daniel Clark, a prominent Pittsfield citizen, and donated by him to the combined museum and library in 1900. These minerals were exhibited in the same manner as they had been when first acquired thirty years earlier, which made them ripe for change according to Bragg's museum principle.[69]

Bragg believed that change was the master word in museum psychology. To alter the mineral room she first eliminated the cherry cases the minerals were displayed in, replacing them with glass. Then she gave Margaret the task of cataloging the minerals and assigned the former head of the children's department, Frances Palmer, to help her. Palmer resented the assignment and later recalled that Bragg "seemed to think it was her duty to stick up her nose at everything we had here." After the cataloging was complete, two-thirds of the original Clark mineral exhibition were placed in a study collection, while the other third was displayed.[70]

Though the modern art exhibits had stirred the community, Bragg was not deterred from her next goal of having a lecture on evolution presented by Dr. Richard Lull, who was a professor of paleontology at Yale. In her invitation to him she asked that he not make any "reference to religious considerations or thought of fundamentalist feeling." His lecture was to help the museum take "another definite step toward liberalism in its teaching," and it would help introduce the natural history section of the museum.[71]

Lull's lecture traced the development of man through five hundred thousand years, claiming that "man is a primitive mammal with many things in common with the ape." Lull used slides to illustrate his speech, "Evolution as the Scientist Sees It." Using the skulls and skeletons of apes and men, he explained the similarities and differences in structure. In Lull's opinion, there would be no further physical evolution of man. But he ironically pronounced that "with the development of a super-environment, man would have a greater immunity to disease and our greatest progress would be largely mental and moral."[72]

The modern art exhibits, the changes in staff responsibilities, and the focus on the evolution of man for the science department eventually led to increasing controversy over Bragg and her leadership. Her protégée Mary Martin Hendricks recalled that although Bragg was universally admired in Pittsfield, she was criticized for her liking of modern art: "they thought anyone who did understand or like it was a little queer. They didn't understand her—she was brilliant." Hendricks also remembered her as "always teaching and interesting people in things they would never have known about." When asked to name those with whom Bragg had shared time, her assistant recalled that the trustees were Bragg's friends.[73]

Bragg's life at the Berkshire Museum may have been fulfilling professionally, but it was difficult, and her personal life was not any less difficult. She lost Margaret to marriage after all. Margaret met Donnel Dixon MacCarthy, an engineer at the General Electric plant, and married him in June 1934. Helen, another protégée, was simply no longer close to Bragg. In May she wrote Bragg, "I haven't heard a word from you since [last] November. . . . They [Bragg's new projects] seem to be nearer to you than anybody except Margaret and Mary."[74]

As disappointing as these episodes were in Bragg's life, the death of Chia Mei, the Chinese student who was like a son to her, was the most crushing blow that summer. After traveling in Europe for the latter part of

1931, Chia Mei had returned to China the next year, where he was a captain and a chief instructor in the Chinese air force at Hangchow. He had married a Chinese professor of English literature, who came from a well-to-do family, as he did. In June 1934 Chia Mei was practicing aerial combat during a training flight with another plane when the two planes collided. Chia Mei's plane crashed, killing him instantly. The aviation school was then named for him, and his family received a pension of twenty thousand dollars from the Chinese government of Gen. Chiang Kai-shek. The general had known Chia Mei and mourned his loss for the country and for the air force. Bragg received the crash details from the aviation adviser to the national government of the Republic of China two months after it happened, but only after she requested the information.[75]

Bragg's mother also died that year, on 12 September in Epping. She had been an invalid and seriously ill since February. Bragg's two emotional anchors, Chia Mei and to a much lesser degree her mother, were now gone. The relationship with her mother was never close. Her mother had once written Bragg, "When you care to tell me of your inner life, I shall care to listen." There is no record yet to be found that Bragg ever shared her inner life with her mother.[76]

Seeking comfort, Bragg wrote Helen in January 1935 about Chia Mei's and Mrs. Bragg's deaths. Helen accepted the blame for their drifting apart and in her reply admitted that she was ashamed that she had not written to Bragg during much of the past year. Bragg's letter set off a stream of memories for Helen of when she had first come to the Museum: "the happiest times I've ever had were the first years I worked at the Museum. I can remember walking to work in the mornings my heart would sing with gladness. . . . And most of what I learned and dreamed through and from you." There were also powerful and memorable experiences Helen and Bragg shared at Snug Harbor: "Do you remember the first time you ever took me to Snug Harbor? . . . It was so lovely, the place—your trees and the water—your house and you. . . . you took me to a hidden sheltered place that you called the 'Earth Moods' place. . . . we used it for a box seat at the gorgeous pageant of a sunset. There were so many lovely times we had together. Just the two of us." Other memories were of Chalmers Street and Christmas parties with many people, and of Ned as a part of their lives. Expressing her feelings to Bragg, Helen wrote, "But my silence didn't mean that I haven't been thinking of you and loving you—ever & ever so much—Helen."[77]

While she had to have been pleased with the progress of her progressive plans, Bragg surely did not find any personal comfort at the museum. Controversy and conflict were part of almost every undertaking during the last four years of her tenure. A Gertrude Stein lecture set off a storm in the community; her sale of a painting for much less than its worth was publicly denounced in the local paper; and Bragg's grand plans for the second phase of renovations to the museum building were called into question by the community and staff members. It was not just in Pittsfield that she faced opposition. In Charleston the Museum's board of trustees was reexamining the activities she had conducted during her last year of tenure and their agreement with her about returning to the Museum as director. Her professional career as a museum innovator was nearing its end, and she believed that she had yet to do something truly progressive at the Berkshire Museum.

Gertrude Stein's visit could not have come at a worse juncture for Bragg. Bragg was already viewed as controversial as the museum's director, and Stein was viewed as strange. Stein was called the "question mark of literature," and her writing was a puzzle to most literary critics because of her innovative uses of syntax and punctuation. She had lived abroad for thirty-one years, returning in the fall of 1934 to the United States to give a series of lectures. Somehow Bragg had been able to secure an engagement for the Berkshire Museum during Stein's short two-and-a-half-month tour. Bragg knew of Stein. She had read *transitions* long ago when one of "her boys," Robert Marks, brought her a copy. She had attended the premiere of Stein's *Four Saints in Three Acts* in New York, which ran for only a short time due to the controversial reaction it received from the audiences. Someone who knew Bragg late in life called her "exotic," and most would agree that the same word could also be used to describe Stein.[78]

In her lecture Stein declared that paintings have a life of their own, an independent life. Picasso received her highest praise, for in her opinion there were no great American painters. She dismissed the artists Thomas Hart, Diego Rivera, and James Whistler, those most recently exhibited at the museum, as being not very good and called Rivera just a local disturbance. Hart and Whistler were local favorites, and her dismissal of them was not pleasantly received by the Berkshire residents.[79]

Stein offered an explanation as to why most people did not like modern paintings. (Quite possibly she knew about the community's dislike of Bragg's contemporary art exhibits.) In her opinion, observers of modern paintings were annoyed by the manner in which the objects, people, or landscapes are presented. For several days after Stein's lecture local papers reported on Stein's mental state. One speaker who gave a lecture at the YMCA claimed that Stein was too old to be psychoanalyzed, and an American medical journal asked if Stein were facetious or sick?[80]

Next came the ill-advised sale of a treasured painting, which fed the flames of discontent over Bragg's leadership style. Her intent to reorganize and renew what she considered to be a dead museum led her to clean out closets, attics, and storage areas. In 1934 she determined that a George Caleb Bingham painting, *Raftsmen Playing Cards*, "was not in line with our work. Its historical value was not equal to the other things which we could get." So she sold it to the City Art Museum of Saint Louis for fifteen hundred dollars. The sale was conducted with the full support of the president of the board of trustees and the donor of the painting, an Italian countess. With the money realized from the sale the trustees voted to purchase a fragment from the Acropolis, a Chinese painting from a dealer friendly to Bragg and the museum, and a collection of Chinese prints. This purchase represented the bulk of the museum's collection of Chinese objects.[81]

Henry Francis, president of the museum's board, and other trustees knew of the sale, but Z. Marshall Crane, Bragg's financial backer and son of the museum's founder, did not. When he read about the sale in the newspaper, he called a cousin, Charles Kitteredge, who was also a museum trustee, asking for an explanation. Kitteredge then wrote Bragg a letter, reminding her of the assurance she had given him that Crane's sister did know about the sale of the painting. As a result of the sale of the Bingham painting, Crane now wanted a list of all the items Bragg had sold and their purchase prices. The list was to include the titles and names of the artists, as well as when each piece had been acquired.[82]

The sale of the Bingham painting created a furor in the local press, and Bragg drew sharp criticism for her action. A Pittsfield resident who had first admired the Bingham work when it was displayed at the Berkshire, saw it again in an exhibition at the Museum of Modern Art in New York City. In a letter to the local newspaper he publicly questioned Bragg's decision to sell the painting. Further, he claimed that only "second-rate Slavs" had been displayed at the museum while the best modern art was kept away from the town. Bragg's defense was that she was focusing the collection and that "the canvas was not in line with our policy for showing the development of American art."[83] Bragg's discerning eye apparently had failed her, and Pittsfield's museum-going public, as well as her financial mentor, questioned her judgment as a result of this fiasco.

While Bragg's tenure as director at the Berkshire Museum had been fraught with conflict, her twenty-two years at the Charleston Museum had been professionally rewarding and had garnered national recognition. Bragg had been revered in Charleston, and the trustees called her an "exceptionally competent director" until Burton's report. However, in the spring of 1935 the trustees of the Charleston Museum appointed a committee to reexamine the organization of the Museum. This group investigated several matters: the directorship; the relationship between the free library and the museum; and the operating costs of the Heyward-Washington House. In each case the committee recommended what would have been sweeping changes and were in direct opposition to Bragg's actions when she was the Museum's director.

The committee recommended that Milby Burton immediately be elected director and that Bragg be offered the title of director emeritus (this was not done). It further recommended that the Museum needed to sever its connection to the free library because, in their opinion, "it has been and now is of disadvantage to the Museum. . . . That all physical means of access to the Museum from the Museum should be securely locked. . . . on no occasion should the Museum receive money for the free library, as has been done in the past, or accept an appropriation from the legislature for the purposes of the free library." (The free library moved into a historic house at 95 Rutledge Avenue in 1935.) Since the Heyward-Washington House was a financial drain, the committee recommended that the Museum sell the property. (The Heyward-Washington House is still a Museum property.) Ultimately the committee achieved two out of the three recommendations. Burton was elected director, and the free library was separated from the Museum, free to find its own support.[84]

On 10 May 1935 Buist informed Bragg of the trustees' decision to name Burton the Museum's director. Buist provided a copy of his letter to other trustees, and one, James Hagood, thought the letter was "a masterpiece." Buist's reply to Hagood reveals his true feeling about Burton's appointment and Bragg's continued association with the Museum: "I must admit that the situation was a delicate one and I am glad that it terminated in the way that it did."[85]

Two weeks after the date of Buist's letter Bragg met Helen in Washington, where they saw a great deal of each other at the national museum conference. Helen wrote Bragg's former secretary, Emma Richardson, that Bragg seemed "to think that she wants to stay in Pittsfield some time longer." A week after that Bragg and Helen spent "four delightful days in Williamsburg." No doubt Bragg was distressed by the news from Buist, which quite possibly prompted the two to meet again. They had been together only three times in the four years Bragg had been in Pittsfield— once in Birmingham, during a short visit on Bragg's return to Pittsfield in 1933, and just the week before in Washington. Helen thought that their time together in Williamsburg was "another incarnation. . . . one is vouchsafed glimpses into that former incarnation, and can experience again its delights, and be thankful. Forever after, the odor of honeysuckle will bring back our togetherness. Forever after, twilight will recall our ride from Yorktown along the water's edge. Forever after, Williamsburg will seem a personal treasure. . . . Loads of love darling, and thanks—thousands of them—for a grand time. Ever–Helen." In times of sorrow, as with Chia Mei's and her mother's death, Bragg sought solace from Helen, who was always there, waiting to fill the role of Bragg's admirer and supporter.[86]

Not one to hide behind conventionality or seek cover from conflict, Bragg was dauntless in her continued focus on contemporary art for the major exhibits during this pivotal time at the Berkshire Museum. Bragg was intent upon moving the museum and the community along in their acceptance of liberalism, as she had written the Yale professor of paleontology when inviting him to lecture about evolution in early 1934. Almost two years later she wrote, "Much of the work of the year has been devoted to teaching the county that art is something more than naturalistic reproduction."[87]

The year 1935 began with an exhibition of a newly discovered artist who was seventy years old. Louis Eilshemius was one of the few American modern painters accepted by other modernists. Bragg held the first one-man exhibit of his work in the country as a loan exhibit through the Valentine Galleries of New York City. Some art critics called his pictures "poems." They were the artist's "sonnets about nature as seen with keen observation and a deeply poetic imagination. All of nature— the sea, earth, and water was portrayed romantically," according to the local paper. The Berkshire Museum did not purchase any of the thirty paintings exhibited, possibly because their prices ranged from $250 to $2,000 or, even more likely, because the museum's trustees and the Berkshire public did not like modern art. Bragg already owned two, which she loaned the museum for the exhibit. Months after the show closed Bragg wrote Eilshemius, telling him about the paintings she owned and asking if he would tell her about them. She ended her letter to him by appealing to his pride: "Every once in a while I drop into the Valentine Gallery for the pleasure of looking at your paintings and as I visit different museums I make a point of seeing what they own of yours."[88]

She may have erred with the Bingham painting decision, but her critical eye had found another of the rising stars in the modern art world. With Alexander Calder and now Louis Eilshemius, Bragg's reputation as a forward-thinking museum director was established. Lewis Mumford, social philosopher and the art critic for *The New Yorker,* claimed that Bragg had the capacity "to invent, to stir up," and Elizabeth McCausland, another art critic, cited her courage in bringing modern art to the Berkshires.[89] Bragg succeeded in changing the artistic direction of the Berkshire Museum from an unimaginative approach to one that was visionary and innovative.

Bragg then purchased three works by Alfred Maurer, the first bought by any museum. (Bragg also acquired a gouache of a single head for herself.) In her review of the exhibit McCausland wrote that Maurer's art reflects a sensitive man doomed to frustration and tragedy, but with a talented creative spirit. *Two Heads,* the oil painting, displays a distorted image of one or two or even three heads. In the critic's opinion, "All those who see nothing in so called abstract art should take a good long second look at this painting, and then a third, and then a fourth. If they still see nothing in it, that only proves they like their food predigested and their art prefabricated." The Berkshire Museum public had accepted the exhibition of Eilshemius paintings, but Maurer's work was another story. There was much controversy over his paintings, so Bragg's approach was to educate the public. She frequently lectured about his modern art at the museum and to civic groups, trying to stifle the debate. Even though the trustees approved purchasing Maurer's work, they appointed an Art Advisory Committee, possibly in reaction to the controversy.[90]

The last big function scheduled before the onset of the final remodeling project was the Whitney collection exhibition. According to Bragg's letter to the curator of museum extension at the Whitney, "The whole object of this exhibition is to educate our people as to what is best among the American painters." Using Holger Cahill and Alfred Barr's *Art in America in Modern Times* as a textbook, Bragg put together a list of forty artists whose works she wanted in the show. She specifically requested Georgia O'Keeffe's *The White Flower,* which was hanging in Julianna Force's office at the time. Additionally, she wanted to show Eilshemius again, although his one-man show had roused no enthusiasm among the Berkshire residents or among the trustees. Bragg intended to use the Whitney exhibit as another chance to educate the public about modern art.[91]

The opening of the exhibition was held during the week of the Berkshire Symphonic Festival, when the area was full of visitors, and the guest list for the opening reception included two thousand names. There were 134 paintings from the permanent collection that filled five galleries of the museum for the guests to view. Reported in *The New York Times,* the exhibition and reception were a coup for Bragg.[92]

In contrast with the modern art exhibits, the museum also held a table-setting exhibit that fall. The display probably did not draw the art crowd, but it did bring in the social elite of the Berkshire area. They came to see their own possessions displayed at the museum and to see the other table settings. Bragg asked Mary Martin Hendricks, her former secretary and now resident of Pittsfield, and Mrs. Wendell Ahearn, wife of a trustee, to assist her in gathering china, glass, and tables to create an exhibition of table decoration of the past two hundred years. "Lovely old families

donated lovely old things. . . . Miss Bragg had to have my help to work the
exhibit out. She knew that I knew the people who had the china," Mrs.
Ahearn recalled.[93] The display included Shaker tables, a Queen Anne table
set with Canton china dating from George Washington's day, an Empire
table, and other objects from various periods.

Between the two of them Mary Hendricks and Carolyn Ahearn
found just what Bragg wanted, but the Empire table was more difficult to
locate. "Struggling day in and day out to locate one," Carolyn finally discovered someone who had an Empire table and was willing to loan it to
the museum. Yet when it arrived at the museum, Bragg covered it with a
tablecloth that went all the way to the floor. Carolyn recalled: "We worked
hard to get that table and when I saw her put that tablecloth over the
whole thing, I thought 'that's just too much.' We laughed over it, she was
great that way. She was very exacting. . . . she was so particular. . . . everybody admired her, she was very capable. We were so fortunate to have her.
It was really something to work that hard. That was why she had such a
good reputation, because she was so particular."[94] This was the last exhibition before the addition to the museum was begun. It was also the only
time that Carolyn Ahearn assisted Bragg with an exhibit.

Many residents of Pittsfield and the surrounding county were wealthy
(as evidenced by the loaned contributions to this exhibit), but no family
had as much wealth and influence as the Cranes. When Z. Marshall Crane
and his sister, Frances Crane Colt, first approached Bragg about coming to
the museum to direct its intellectual reorganization, they enticed her with
a twenty-five-thousand-dollar gift to the museum. The sum provided for
an increased staff and helped to finance the expansion of museum activities into the community. Other Crane money poured into the museum the
following year with Charles Crane's bequest of fifty thousand dollars. The
largest funds for the museum's use came from the estate of Ellen Crane, the
wife of Zenas Crane, on her death in 1934. Her will contained a one-hun-
dred-thousand-dollar bequest for the general purposes of the museum and
for the purchase of "suitable and appropriate exhibits." Renovations and
plans for a memorial room dedicated to Ellen Crane led to the ensuing
controversy over Bragg's high-handedness.[95]

Bragg discussed her plans for the building renovation with Charles
Kitteredge, a Crane family member, over the telephone. He offered her a
cautious written response after discussing her plans with Z. Marshall
Crane: "While I can appreciate the need for better working quarters for
the staff, I think it would be very undesirable to in any way spoil the
entrance to the museum by a narrow, restricted passage. . . . I think before
the Trustees definitely approve or disapprove such changes we should have

pretty definite plans and sketches as to what this will look like when completed. . . . I understand our plans are rather elastic as to how the money will be spent toward the future reorganization. . . . In other words I feel that all these matters need and deserve more thought and study on everyone's part before making any definite decisions than have so far been given to them."[96]

The original museum building, as well as the additions, had been designed by a local architectural firm, Harding and Seaver. First opened in 1903, the building cost $250,000. Additions designed by the original firm were completed at three different times, with the final addition creating a rectangular building with a central courtyard surrounded by four sides of the building. Seaver recalled Z. Marshall Crane telling Bragg in his presence that his firm would redesign the building in the future. Within six months of receiving Kitteredge's letter, however, Bragg chose another firm of architects.[97]

Bragg had admired a modern building, the Avery Memorial in Hartford, which had been designed by Morris and O'Connor, a design team from New York City. She met with them and chose them to renovate the museum. After that meeting with the New York architects Bragg presented the plans to Crane and his sister, seeking the money to carry them out. These plans contained Bragg's progressive contribution to the museum, a memorial room that would make Ellen Crane's name become the "symbol of the ideal of the modern museum. No museum of its size in the country will be better equipped for carrying out modern museum ideals." The Crane children agreed with Bragg. In a special meeting of the trustees held two weeks later they agreed to "defray the entire expense of said addition, and improvements to the existing building and the furnishing and decoration of the addition, providing that the total gift of either of us shall in no event exceed $75,000." And of course the budget, presented by the architectural firm Morris and O'Connor at the same time as this letter from the Crane children, was for $150,000, exactly the sum the Crane children said they would pay for the desired memorial to their mother. Upon taking bids, the building committee (Bragg was not a member) found that the architect's estimate was exceeded by $33,000. Bragg went back to the Cranes, who donated that additional amount to the museum, providing funds that "shall in no event exceed $91,500."[98]

Bragg's announcement of the museum renovations to the community via *The Berkshire Eagle* included a sentimental description of Mrs. Crane's last visit to the museum as well as an account of the gallery, "the hearthstone of the museum's life. Luxuriously furnished, it will have an open fireplace, with a central table and high hanging tapestries, inset shelves for books and cabinets for exhibitions." The second major phase of the plan was an auditorium with a projection room for motion pictures, a stage-lighting room, and dressing rooms.[99]

Seaver was furious when he learned of Bragg's use of a New York design team. In several letters written to various people during the 1936 construction, Seaver pointed out what he saw as Bragg's flaws: her age (she was fifty-five) and her feebleness, which would shorten her tenure (Bragg had been ill frequently); her lack of real museum training; and her destruction of Zenas Crane's gift. Seaver alleged that Bragg told one of the architects, who then reported to him, that Seaver and his architectural plans were not to be consulted. In Seaver's opinion, "So, it seems . . . that Miss Bragg was bound from the first to make a modernistic museum and tear out all evidence of Mr. Crane she could." Seaver claimed that Bragg "did not like what Zenas Crane had bought nor the building he had built, nor the name of his museum. Things were changed, removed, quartered oak painted, cases were painted, rooms closed for long times and some for all time." He felt that she had changed it all to suit her modernistic taste and that "she bossed it from first to last though they [the trustees] purposely did not put her on the building committee. . . . By the way, . . . do you realize they spent money on these two rooms like a drunken sailor . . . I have heard so much about it from the various contractors." Throughout the period of construction Seaver was unhappy and tried to find allies in the community and on the museum staff in his protest over Bragg's plans.[100]

With time on her hands and the storm clouds gathering, Bragg again sought out Helen. Having received a Rockefeller grant to study museum methods at the Brooklyn Museum (Robert Whitelaw had helped her to receive the grant), Helen was nearby and handy to offer Bragg support and comfort in dealing with the growing animosity in Pittsfield. Just after she arrived in New York, she wrote Miss Bragg, as she continued to call her (Bragg was fifty-five and Helen was thirty-three at the time), "Let's do some of the things we like when you get here. Being together in New York can't possibly be like being together in Williamsburg, but at least it will be together. With great expectations and lots of love, Helen."[101]

Helen then went to Pittsfield in response to a telegram from "Miss B.," who wired her "to come, for the woods are lovely with autumn color just now." Writing her family in Charleston after this October visit, Helen described the time spent with Bragg, disclosing the type of relationship they shared: "I had a perfectly lovely time at Miss Bragg's. . . . The sun sifting down through the leaves made the whole place luminous, so that I had the feeling of floating in all that gold. . . . On Sunday night Miss Bragg lit a fire. . . . [and] expounded to me the cause of the 17th earl of Oxford. . . . On

Monday we were lazy in the morning (I slept for the first time since getting here in peace and quiet.) Then we went to Miss B.'s museum which is all torn up for some alterations. Then we called on some friends of hers who are keen on the Shakers." More revealing perhaps is her bread-and-butter note to Bragg: "I had a wonderful weekend! So many things about it were lovely—wood smoke, sleep, and the Hudson and best of all you."[102]

There can be no doubt that Helen's visit was just a diversion, because it was the Ellen Crane Memorial Gallery that held Bragg's interest during her last two years in Pittsfield. The founder's children financed the fifth and final addition to the Berkshire Museum, the Ellen Crane Memorial Gallery and auditorium, which opened to the public in June 1937. While the building's exterior remained one of a Renaissance-revival classical building, Bragg transformed the central core into purely art deco style.[103] The two-story addition was placed in what had been the open courtyard in the center of the building, with the new auditorium on the first floor and the new Ellen Crane Memorial Gallery on the second. Sunlight no longer flooded the stairwell.

Here "the furniture was custom designed, as were the fountain and the simple carvings around the fountain base and doorways." Stirling Calder, Alexander's father, designed the marble fountain and the bas-relief wood carvings. The swan, turtle, and water-plant motifs used were favorites of Mrs. Crane. But what caught the attention of the national art press was the use of Alexander Calder's mobiles as architectural sculptures, masking the ventilation system in the new auditorium. They were the first of their kind in the world. The museum renovations were reported in *The New York Times, The Art Digest, The Art News,* and *Magazine of Art,* and Bragg was praised for her visionary use of the younger Calder's work.[104]

Among the noteworthy accessions displayed during this week was the recent gift of Albert Gallatin. He donated five modern paintings from his Museum of Living Art. They included works by Bissiere, Halpert, Hartley, Lapicque, and Beaudin, and all were contemporary. The fifty Chinese block prints that Bragg purchased with the money from the sale of the Bingham painting were also exhibited. At the time most museums did not have such prints in their collections. Art critics pointed out that Bragg's foresight in purchasing examples of these and seeing their value marked her as a pioneer. There was also a loaned exhibition of forty landscapes from the sixteenth to the twentieth centuries, organized by Stuart Henry, who was the museum's curator of art (he later succeeded Bragg).[105]

The architects Morris and O'Connor oversaw every detail of the work. The custom-designed furnishings of the Ellen Crane Memorial Gallery included wall cabinets and other pieces of furniture from Miss Gheen, Inc. of New York. The furniture featured the museum's logo, designed by South Carolinian Anna Heyward Taylor in 1931, in exotic woods. The fireplace andirons were designed by the functionalist architect Walter Baerman. *The Arts News Reporter* stated: "The gallery is forty feet wide by sixty feet long and is twenty feet high, lighted by daylight. The end walls are paneled in English oak. A fireplace is at one end of the great room, with a semi-elliptical recess set around an elliptical pool. The long walls are of plaster painted gray, being violet over a coat of strong chrome yellow. Swedish green marble and a Georgia marble called Rosepia add to the richness of materials used."[106]

The reopening of the museum brought out the elite of the Berkshires. House parties were held for guests from all over the East. There was a dinner party at the Pittsfield Country Club and a reception at the museum, with a thousand invited guests. Frances Crane Colt hosted a garden party at her home for several hundred guests.

Frank Crowninshield, editor of *Vanity Fair* and editorial adviser to *Vogue,* spoke on Presentation Day about the development of the collections at the museum. As a member of the Art Advisory Committee at the museum, he was well aware of how modern art had been received by the community and some of the trustees. Philip Youtz, director of the Brooklyn Museum, spoke that same day when the newly renovated museum was presented to the community. He discussed the use of museum facilities for the public benefit, as had occurred at the Berkshire Museum under Bragg's leadership. Other events were for the ordinary citizen: an open house was held on Sunday afternoon; the children's room was reopened; the Town Players performed "Death Takes a Holiday"; and teachers were invited to see an exhibition of Bragg boxes.[107]

Bragg's truly progressive contribution did not come without a cost, one that was dear both professionally and personally. There were fourteen motor-driven fans to cool the memorial room in the summer, with 17,500 watts of electric lights. The room was too hot in the summer, and rarely did the temperature rise above fifty-four degrees in the winter. The roof of the memorial room needed special treatment when it snowed. The auditorium had a huge stage, but the height was low. And the cost was exorbitant—$183,000 in 1937.[108]

While the New York press celebrated her great success, Bragg announced her resignation just three months later. It was almost the end of her professional career as a museum director, but there was unfinished business with the Hall of Man in the science wing still to be completed. Further, she intended to mount one last modern art exhibit before she left in 1939. It would prove to be the exhibit that angered and provoked the most controversy in the community and among the trustees. Her pioneering spirit was not daunted by the criticism she had faced in the community. However, she was very much aware of it and ended her 1937 director's report with this statement: "From personal contacts and letters received, the staff cannot but feel that the reorganization authorized by the Trustees is considered outstanding by all but a few individuals who have not yet grasped the ideology of the present day museum world."[109]

With her major contribution to modern museum thought complete, Bragg now returned her energies to the science wing. She had begun her reorganization much earlier in this area in 1934 with the opening of the new mineral room and with Dr. Lull's speech on the evolution of man. This work was halted in favor of the major renovations of the gallery and the auditorium. In a way, she set the stage then for the final piece of the intellectual puzzle she was completing at the Berkshire Museum. The first-floor improvements were the last large-scale project Bragg initiated at the museum before her departure in October 1939.

With a two-thousand-dollar budget, the mural artist Helen Tee-Van completed mural paintings depicting life's evolutionary process. Planned by Bragg, Tee-Van's role was to draw Bragg's understanding of current scientific thought on man's evolution. The plan, as executed by Tee-Van, called for drawings of one-celled plants and animals up through the evolution of plant and animal life to man and his accomplishments in art and science. Several pictures of Tee-Van's mural were published in the 30 August 1938 issue of *Life*.[110]

As with other vanguard artists, such as Calder and Maurer, whom Bragg had embraced, Tee-Van was also out of the mainstream. She and her husband accompanied Dr. William Beebe on his deep-sea exploration trips in a bathosphere, where she painted pictures of the underwater life of British Guiana.[111] Two of Bragg's associates from South Carolina had also accompanied Beebe, Robert Whitelaw and Anna Heyward Taylor. Tee-Van was the daughter of the famed conductor Frank Damrosch, who was a summer resident of the Berkshires, as were Alexander Calder and his father. Through the social circles at the Berkshire Museum, Bragg possibly had made the connection with these artists. Once she learned of Tee-Van's exploits and talents, she commissioned her to paint the mural.

Given Bragg's ability to draw unusual people to her, she and Tee-Van developed a friendship over the course of the several years Tee-Van worked at the museum. Bragg visited her in New York, and Tee-Van lived across the hall from Bragg's apartment when she was in Pittsfield. By late fall of 1938 Bragg knew Tee-Van's mother and was planning a trip into the city to visit with her family: "John and I are thinking already of how to find an amusing dump to take you to and Mother says you must come there for dinner one night and do I think you would rather go to the theater or have a few people to meet you at dinner???" Once Tee-Van completed the mural, Bragg missed her friend, writing her: "It would be impossible to tell you how much I miss you."[112]

Bragg received a gift of over four thousand dollars from Frances Crane Colt, which she used to complete the biology room. This gift, along with additional money from the trustees, enabled Bragg to hire Tee-Van again. Bragg wrote, "I shall look forward to your coming eagerly." Tee-Van was to create the zodiac on the ceiling, wall paintings in the Hall of Man—everything she and Bragg had discussed. In the summer of 1939 Tee-Van completed the paintings that illustrated the different stages of man in human culture. And Bragg had young Charlestonian William Halsey, a former student of her beloved Ned Jennings, paint frescoes in the arches of the mineral room. With these projects completed, Bragg's plans for the natural science wing were virtually achieved before she left Pittsfield for Charleston.[113]

Much of what Bragg had set as goals for herself and for the Berkshire Museum in 1931 had been accomplished by 1939. Her modern art exhibits reaped attention both in the local press and in the larger art world of New York. The Whitney Exhibition in 1935 had put the Berkshire Museum on the art map. More and more tourists were making their way to the Berkshires for culture—either at the museum or at the music festival. Bragg's major art exhibits opened the same week as the Berkshire symphonic festival, held at Tanglewood every summer. While begun as an experiment in 1934, the festival, along with the Berkshire Museum, helped to institutionalize the area as a cultural center during the 1930s. Through the modern art world, Bragg had come to know Elizabeth McCausland, the art critic, and her companion, the photographer Berenice Abbott. She was aware of the intimate relationship between the two women, and she closed many of her letters to McCausland by asking that she give her love to Berenice. When Abbott gave a lecture at the museum in the summer of 1938, the local paper called her "an intimate friend of Bragg's."[114]

Bragg and McCausland planned Bragg's final art show at the museum for over two years. In early February 1939 Bragg and Stuart Henry made the decision that McCausland's show would serve as the museum's opening exhibit for the season. "The Problems of Today or whatever we decide to call it" would be the Berkshires' answer to the New York World's Fair, which was also going on that summer. Bragg even suggested the wording of the advertisement: "visitors who wish to see something really choice should motor up to the Berkshires for the most carefully selected and choicest exhibition to be seen, etc., etc., !!!!?"[115]

Renamed "The World of Today," the theme of the exhibit was to showcase the problems, ideas, creative forces, and crises of the real world. In organizing the exhibit McCausland tried to select work of "excellent quality, but also with content. . . . Do you [Bragg] object to social subject matter, as housing, lynching, children playing in city streets, mine disasters?" Bragg replied, "No objection to social matter. Let's not have more than one lynching! Duplicate on any other problem you wish. Pile up the agony, but as the world also has a few pleasant things, include at least two pictures that are not heart rending!" Bragg saw the show with its portrayal of social problems as a fitting conclusion to the reorganization of the art department.[116]

By early June, Bragg's resignation was finally announced publicly, and she thought it had been handled "amply and pleasantly" by the local press. She repeated what one newspaper had printed about the sharp criticism she had received, asking McCausland, "What would the art page say to this? Would it regret the sale of naturalistic cows and sheep and serenaders? The Trustees, however, have authorized all the changes, and the Board includes several of Mr. Zenas Crane's own family, so I am not bothered." McCausland knew her exhibit would not be liked by those who pined for naturalistic cows: "they may not like what the progressive, forward-looking men and women are doing in painting and print making . . . I don't believe they will be indifferent to the work."[117]

McCausland's words were prophetic. They weren't indifferent—quite the opposite. The exhibit of abstract, realist, and surrealist works mostly done by artists involved with the New Deal's Federal Art Project contained fifty paintings in all manner of mediums—including watercolors, oils, gouaches, prints, and drawings. The exhibit was dedicated to Bragg: "Because she has the vision to perceive art's function and the courage to act on her vision, this exhibit is dedicated to Laura M. Bragg—a fearless progressive and humane museum director."[118]

But the public thought the paintings and drawings were frightful and contained labels "criticizing the government and the capitalists for the treatment of the poor." And the trustees were "violently opposed to the use of the name of the Berkshire Museum in connection with the circulation of the 'World of Today.' The labelling of this exhibit, as you know, refers to matters other than Art alone." Bragg told McCausland how distressed she was by the trustees' action and the public's response: "I am nearly worn out with all the troubles and anxieties of these last few weeks. . . . The antagonism to our World of Today exhibition is a grief to me and has made me very depressed. . . . There are evidences all around that bringing works of art to people before they are hackneyed is inspiring to certain people, but Mr. Henry says my fault as a director is that I give people things before they are familiar with them. So in spite of teas and parties, I feel depressed. I think that five years from now Pittsfield people will be accepting the things that I have tried to give them." The exhibit was to have circulated to other museums, with the arrangements made through the National Art Society. While it went on to Vassar, where they too thought it was radical, it was not shown anywhere else.[119]

Besides the parties and teas, Bragg was also honored with a dinner given by the museum's trustees before leaving Pittsfield. They offered her praise, and they were grateful in their appreciation of her work. They believed that Bragg had "extended the usefulness of the museum and enlarged its contribution to community life. . . . and quickened its significance." McCausland wrote a two-page article in *The Springfield Sunday Union and Republican* about Bragg's accomplishments, calling her a pioneer: "Bragg believes with all her heart that it is more important to reach and enrich the lives of people than to contribute learned essays to weighty tomes. . . . the period of reorganization from 1931 to 1939 [w]as one of revolution. . . . but one is inclined to believe that her generous and affectionate interest in other human beings, all kinds of human beings goes deeper—to a profound and humanizing ethical conviction."[120]

Bragg's future plans, she said, included going to China to "help in developing museums there." She had received an offer from the consulate general of the Republic of China, and after serious consideration she was "willing to take up the work." She had remained active in her support of the Chinese, having organized a boycott of Japanese goods and heading up a China relief group in 1938. But Bragg did not go to China. Instead she returned to her home in Charleston on Chalmers Street, where she became the grande dame of the city. Her career as a museum administrator was over, but a new life awaited.[121]

6

Always a Teacher,
Always a Learner

Be an opener of doors for those who come after you.
Attributed to Laura Bragg, 1 July 1997

IN 1939 BRAGG RETURNED TO A CITY that was more hopeful than it had been in 1931, when she left to go north. Charleston had benefitted from Roosevelt's New Deal programs and enjoyed good relations with the county, state, and federal governments. Other signs of prosperity included the opening of a new movie theater, the Riviera, an art deco building only several blocks from Bragg's home on Chalmers Street. There were two radio stations and two newspapers enjoyed by the citizens, and the city was visited by more than three hundred thousand tourists in 1939. As one of those visitors accurately observed, "tourists were welcomed but not wanted." With the outbreak of the war in Europe, the Charleston Navy Yard employed more workers, having received an increased demand for more ships. The Intracoastal Waterway channels were opened to shipping, with watercraft passing near Porcher's Bluff and Bragg's old country home, Snug Harbor.[1] The city still did not readily welcome interlopers or outsiders.

However, the outward appearance of prosperity disguised a city still "marked by poverty and neglect." Homes along the Battery still needed painting. And the smell of sewer drains had been joined by the odor of the chemicals from the fertilizer plants in the north area of the city. The city's appearance had suffered from another August hurricane that flooded the streets and uprooted trees and telephone poles.[2] To knowing eyes, Charleston had changed very little.

Bragg's return to the city was celebrated with several interviews in the local papers. She was honored because of her career as a museum director and because she was an adopted Yankee who chose to live in the South. In Charleston her experiences with the modern art world, her vast knowledge, and her home with its vivid colors (the kitchen floor and moldings were painted turquoise) made her seem exotic to the young people she met through her morning culture classes and her Sunday evening salons. Whether she planned to stay at home, travel to China, or write her museum autobiography or an illustrated southeastern botanical field guide, Bragg was welcomed back to the city by her old friends. Josephine Pinckney lived next door at 36 Chalmers, and Helen returned to the city in late 1940, living with her mother at 8 Bull Street. Another old friend, Marshall Uzzell, who taught at the High School of Charleston, visited her frequently at her home, bringing his children. She ate every Christmas dinner with the Uzzell family at their home on Orange Street after her return to the city.[3]

But she was not welcome at the Museum, as Milby Burton, her successor, had made it absolutely clear to the people who worked there. Some thought that he was insecure around her, and he went out of his way to avoid her company. Before Bragg chose him to be the acting director, Burton was an insurance salesman and a trustee with no museum training. He did not have a college education, and Bragg's intellect threatened him, or so her supporters believed. For him, "Miss Bragg did not exist."[4]

While Burton may have been concerned about Bragg as a threat to his power and position as the Museum's director, her photographs at this time depict a woman who appears to be in poor health. When considering the post in China, Bragg had written the Chinese consulate that she needed to go home and rest for the winter in order to be ready to travel in the late spring or early summer. She was concerned about her health and whether she would be "strong enough to do the work [in China] without getting sick." Her first surgery was during her junior year at Simmons, and by all accounts in her letters to her father in the years following, Bragg was never a physically strong woman. Mary Martin Hendricks, her assistant, recalled that she was ill much of the time while she was in Pittsfield.[5]

Later in life Bragg told Gene Waddell, who worked at the Museum before entering the College of Charleston, that she had a breast removed while living in Massachusetts. She said that the surgery had not prevented the cancer from spreading and that her physician told her she only had a short time to live. (Her assistant at the Berkshire Museum, Mary Hendricks, was unaware of this illness.) This news had prompted her to resign as director of the Berkshire Museum and to return home to die in Charleston. But Bragg did not die for almost forty years after returning to Charleston. Outliving all of her immediate family and her closest friends— Josephine, Anita, and Helen—Bragg was almost ninety-seven when she died in 1978.[6]

Finances continued to be a problem for her, as her salary had ended. Not two months after leaving Pittsfield, Bragg appealed to the trustees of the Berkshire Museum to review her salary that had been reduced in 1933. They took no action on her request, as they considered the matter closed. Possibly she was in hopes of some retroactive funds. There was no pension from her years at the Berkshire Museum or at the Charleston Museum. Social Security was not available for her because she had been much younger than the mandatory age of sixty-five at the time of her retirement, and the system had not been in place long enough for her to have paid in enough to qualify. Bragg had little money to spare and was forced to live carefully within her budget. This was far different from the heady times in Pittsfield when she had a generous salary.[7]

Bragg also sought financial help from the young men she had befriended during her years in Pittsfield. One of them, Norman Lunsignan, her former secretary at the Berkshire Museum, owed her $105. Four others also owed her money. Citing all that she had done for him, Lunsignan helped her locate them: "I'm afraid I don't think very much of any of them for I think, to put it bluntly, they used you for all they could and when you didn't have any more they just dropped connections." By June 1941 Bragg must have needed money badly, as she assumed the directorship at the Highlands Museum in North Carolina, although she remained in the mountain community for only that one summer.[8]

Back in Charleston, she settled into a routine. In July 1940 Bragg began teaching cultural classes for the wives of the city's professional men, such as lawyers and doctors. The suggestion had come from Mrs. Joseph Henry Moore, who wanted Bragg to help her understand why the Alfred Maurer painting was such a wonderful picture. She earned money for teaching the classes, and they gave her something to do. On Sunday evenings she held salons for members of the artistic and cultural community. Here she did not lecture but rather guided or directed the conversations. Occasionally she spoke to a book club or a civic organization about one of the many different topics she knew well. Lucile MacLennan recalled first meeting her when she spoke to the Moncks Corner Book Club. Another speaking engagement was in Orangeburg, where Bragg spoke to a civic group of black women. It was only the second time she had been in a black person's home, she noted in an interview. The first time was just after she arrived in Charleston in 1909.[9]

Through the years at Christmastime Bragg received cards from old friends in the New York art world and the museum community, and from others whose lives she had touched, such as the Chinese cadets. (Three of the Chinese cadets were in touch with Bragg, but after the Communist takeover of the country in 1949 that correspondence ended.) She heard from Elizabeth McCausland, the art critic she had befriended while living in Pittsfield, several times about her Maurer gouache. Bragg had some famous visitors, including Gertrude Stein, Stein's companion Alice B. Toklas, and Carson McCullers. When the American Association of Museums met in Charleston again in 1959, Bragg was invited to the opening luncheon as an honored guest. According to Laurence Vail Coleman, she stood "as a Charleston symbol of the meeting-to-meeting cycle."[10]

But for a three-month trip to Europe in 1952 (funded by "people who took up a purse") and a short trip north in 1961 to see the exhibition of Chinese paintings at the Boston Museum of Fine Arts, Bragg's life was centered solely around 38 Chalmers Street and the little bit of cultural life the city had at that time. There Bragg could be the alpha and omega of culture, since Charleston was in many ways the same cultural desert it had been when she arrived in 1909. With her tremendous amount of knowledge she could be a source for, and have influence on, people who were interested in such topics.[11] One of "her boys" believed that she returned to the Holy City because there she could be the grande dame and the center of attention without any competition: "She brought the outside world into Charleston . . . new ideas, avant-garde ideas. . . . and interesting people from the scientific world."[11]

Later in the 1960s and early 1970s, as Bragg lost her hearing completely, she ceased teaching the culture classes and became dependent upon the evening salons for her intellectual stimulation. Someone who attended the culture classes recalled thinking that toward the end of her life Bragg existed for the salons, and that they were what kept her alive. The salons were expanded until she held them almost every night before her illness and death.[12]

The classes and salons met in Bragg's upstairs drawing room at 38 Chalmers, which was filled with her books and light streaming through the tall windows overlooking Washington Park. This room also overflowed with many cats and plants. The cats walked a plank from the service-station roof next door to get into Bragg's house through a bedroom window. She fed them all, whether they belonged to her or were strays.[13]

Her drawing room was small, as was everything else about the three-story house. When Bragg bought the place in the spring of 1927, it needed a great deal of work, first to make it livable and second to meet Bragg's exacting standards of perfection. Just as in her dress (every hair was in place, and her jewelry always matched her dress), her home had to suit its time and place. The house was built in 1844 and sat right on a street paved with cobblestones in one of the oldest sections of the city. The front door faced a narrow passage on the side, and Bragg wanted the house to be like that of her neighbors. She had the noted Charleston architect Albert Simons complete extensive renovations, adding Georgian and federal architectural details, before moving in during the fall of 1927. She had lived in the house a little over three years before accepting the Cranes' offer to go to Pittsfield.[14]

Bragg's living quarters were on the second floor, while she rented out both the downstairs and the third floor as apartments to either College of Charleston students or professors. Some of the women recalled that on the wall of the second-story landing hung one of Bragg's modern drawings, a work by Miro. ("Her girls" thought it was a depiction of male genitalia.) To the left of this landing was the little sitting room, accommodating only fifteen people at a time. There Alfred Maurer's gouache hung over the mantel (according to one of the girls, this work was horrid: "it was so anguished.") Every corner and nook was filled with books, and Bragg needed no other diversions. Even when television became a common household appliance, she never owned one. And she had no air-conditioning for the brutal summers. Using open windows and fans as everyone else did, Bragg survived the torrid, sultry heat of Charleston.[15]

Her bedroom, with her bath, was to the right of the landing. Helen's picture, the only one on her desk, was placed where she could see it from her bed. On the other side of the bedroom was a tiny kitchen. One of "her boys" recalled that it was especially small, with what seemed to him was a two-burner hot plate. Bragg rarely cooked and seldom entertained. Whenever she needed food, she would call Burbage's, a local grocery store that delivered. The delivery boy would put the groceries on the kitchen shelf for her. She usually ate something that was already prepared, if she was not going out for the evening.[16]

The little house on Chalmers was a mecca for the ladies from south of Broad Street. Students in Bragg's morning culture classes learned about the classes either by word-of-mouth from friends or from advertisements in the newspaper. The classes met for two hours with no refreshments, since "it was not a tea party. We were there to learn." The students, Bragg's "girls," were housewives who wanted to learn about other countries, other cultures. They had to be interested in what she had to offer, since Bragg chose the topics and books.[17]

Bragg was always the teacher, and some of her students recalled how cold and distant she was with them. She rarely shared tales about her personal life, never speaking of her parents or of those years in Mississippi or of her success as a museum administrator either in Charleston or in Pittsfield. She maintained a personal distance with a wall separating her from the students. It was a part of that imperiousness and presence learned from her father that set her apart from the rest of the world. When asked if she loved "Miss Bragg," one of the "girls" admitted that while she admired her, love and warmth were simply not part of "Miss Bragg." She was more interested in the intellectual than the emotional and simply did not express her affection. As true as that was of Bragg's personality in the twenty years or so before her death, it was also true in the 1930s. A daughter of a trustee and a recent graduate of Mt. Holyoke, Harriett Wilson worked in the free library with Bragg until she left for Pittsfield. In her opinion, Bragg was "cold, austere, and hard to warm up to. . . . She was probably more respected and admired than loved."[18]

Only in her letters to her father or when writing about Chia Mei is any expression of emotion apparent in Bragg's correspondence. She expressed her love for Reverend Bragg quite freely, calling him "dadda dearest" and writing, "How I love you . . . I am afraid to show it as much as I feel, but these last years, it has grown so strong it hurts sometimes."[19] It is interesting that only a few of the letters he wrote to her survive. Her expressions of love or affection to others, such as Belle or Helen, have not been found. Belle's sudden death was hushed up, and her family decided what correspondence would be saved once Bragg moved from 7 Gibbes. Helen was an intensely private woman, and she saved the letters she wrote to her family while she was away but little other personal correspondence. None of Bragg's letters to Josephine Pinckney, Anita Pollitzer, or DuBose Heyward survived or were saved by the recipients.[19]

"Her girls" were married, and as proper southern ladies they were willing to be lectured to and willingly "sat" at Bragg's feet. Bragg was cognizant of gender roles and expectations for women in the South, as well as the shift in society's approval of sexuality. When "her girls" questioned her about marriage, she shared a story with them about her engagement to a Russian scientist who worked at the General Electric plant in Pittsfield. The story made her seem more like them. K. K. Paluev and Bragg were supposed to marry after he retired, Bragg claimed, and they were planning to make their home in Charleston. However, the marriage never happened. (Bragg was fifty-eight when she retired; Paluev was forty-five, thirteen years her junior.)[23] When her assistant was asked about this engagement, Mary Martin Hendricks was quite definite in answering that Paluev was not Bragg's fiancé but rather her friend.[20]

During the twenty or so years that Bragg first lived in Charleston she would not have needed to tell such a story. Her long-standing relationship with Belle was still socially acceptable as a friendship between two spinsters. Few of the educated in the city (Bragg was one of those few) had read anything about female sexuality, sexual inversion, or lesbianism. But with the changing notions of psychology and the popularization of Freud, societal support for women who loved women was undermined. And by late 1939, when she returned to Charleston, sexual knowledge had come to the city. Bragg was aware that it was much less acceptable to be unmarried or to be without male suitors in her past.[21]

Bragg's story of her engagement is important on several levels: one, she rarely shared anything about herself personally with the girls; second, word of her unsuccessful engagement garnered sympathy; and third, she was offering a socially acceptable explanation for her unmarried status. Interestingly, one of the girls from the later years thought Bragg was an attractive and interesting woman who did not need or want a man.[22] A man or a husband would have gotten in her way.

As much as Bragg desired to be different, she also wanted to be accepted. She chose to tell "her girls" another story to put herself in a more favorable light. She accused Burton of "stealing her position." Bragg told them that she thought she would reassume her position at the Museum when she returned to Charleston in 1939. In 1971 she chuckled as she told Waddell in an interview that she resigned from the Museum in 1933, "or they put me out, I don't know which."[23] Yet she knew the truth of the matter, as she had received all the correspondence from the Museum's board of trustees after leaving in 1931. She knew that she could not return to the position, especially given her embellishment about the prospects of funding from the Carnegie Fund. Further, she wrote the board's president, Dr. Buist, from Pittsfield in May 1935, "Your letter was not a surprise to me as I have known since the first letter I had from Milby after I left Charleston that he would wish this result."[23] There can be no doubt that Bragg knew the truth, and yet she chose to tell a tale that would make her seem to be the injured party.

When her falsehood was discovered by Burton and reported to the trustees, they quickly moved to name him director. Dr. Keppel of the Carnegie Fund supposedly told Burton that there had never been any hope for a building; however, Rea's letters to Bragg are encouraging, though cautionary, about her not becoming too hopeful over the prospects of the new building. There are two letters from March 1931, both written by Bragg to different people, that explain her plans for a new fireproof wing. But if Rea supported Bragg's story when Burton visited him, the correspondence (which is solely Burton's letter to Rea after his December 1931 visit) does not indicate that. Finally, there is nothing in the Museum's library/archive to document Bragg's meeting with a Mr. Cornelius from the Metropolitan Museum about the fireproof wing. Burton may or may not have also concocted a tale. What Burton did was to frame Bragg and her story in the worst possible way, making him seem more attractive to the trustees. As the result, he received the directorship.

There are those who believe that Burton "stole" her position or "did her in." Burton's gender, his proximity, and his wife's family connections (she was a Pinckney and her family owned a plantation, Runnymede) all may have made him more attractive to the predominantly male trustees. Bragg's dear friend Josephine Pinckney was a trustee at the time, and she abstained from the vote giving Burton the position. However, Bragg made a poor choice in attempting to assure herself of the director's position at the end of a five-year leave of absence. While it is not as easy to fault Burton, there is no evidence in the Carnegie Archives to support the statements he made to the trustees, though neither is there any that supports Bragg's assertions.

Bragg's story that her position was "stolen" from her was not the focus of the culture classes. Her lectures came from her own knowledge, covering one topic at a time. Her favorite quotation was "Be an opener of doors for those who come after you," one of the students remembered. Not only did she have an inquiring mind, but she also had a photographic memory, representing great depth and width of knowledge in almost every field. She knew many subjects, such as art, minerals, literature, botany, and astronomy. Even though one of "her girls" thought the classes did not seem to be structured or organized, she found Bragg to be stimulating as a teacher. Whatever Bragg chose to talk about was interesting to the students because she would go into great detail, one student remembered.[24]

Bragg's skill as a teacher was her ability to communicate how she felt about knowledge. She was always learning, studying intensely. For example, Waddell recalled that she studied Egypt for ten years and did the same for Shakespeare. For Bragg, the classes served several purposes: she earned money; she continued learning; and they provided her with the companionship of people who needed her and recognized her worth as an authority, an expert. She saw learning as a continuing process for herself and for the people around her. Life was always under construction, and so was understanding. It was about making connections with old learning. For Bragg, learning was opening doors and seeing what was out there in a constant search for knowledge. That is what she shared in her culture classes.[25]

One of her students believed that that was also how Bragg viewed her position as a museum director. As someone who was to open doors for others, she provided the same opportunities that she had been afforded by her parents and by her education. In this student's opinion, that was the reason Bragg worked so hard to open the free library for all the citizens in Charleston.[26]

It was common knowledge in the small community south of Broad frequented by these women that Bragg had been controversial when she lived in Charleston earlier. They were aware that she had been aggressive about admitting blacks to the Museum. They had heard about how persistent she was in establishing the free library, working twenty years to achieve that goal. Many people viewed her as an interloper with her extraordinary ideas. Bragg was independent, articulate, and educated, and they knew she was quite unlike them. For example, in Charleston in the 1920s a southern woman did not get into a car and go as Bragg did. They also understood that she did not see herself as like other woman, and she refused to let her gender stop her from doing what she set out to achieve. Both "her boys" and "her girls" understood that Bragg would not tolerate being deferred to because she was a woman.[27]

During the later years Bragg spoke with authority because she had a great wealth of knowledge, one student recalled. She was seen as definitive, never hesitating over anything. A woman who knew Bragg through Helen saw her as autocratic: "She held court where she talked to you, not with you. . . . [Bragg was always] in the teaching mode as a purveyor of information and ideas. She knew best and of course she brooked no argument. She totally controlled the group. . . . And you could take it as the gospel, the gospel according to St. Laura."[28]

Whether autocratic or authoritarian, many of those who knew her agreed that Bragg had presence. She was regal, calm, and serene, with a poise and a dignity about her. "I don't think Miss Bragg was ever surprised by anything. She was a woman of the world. C. S. Lewis said, 'You can't surprise the greatest saint or the greatest sinner.' Everything was under control. She was never taken off guard, never."[29]

First held on Tuesday mornings, the classes were later moved to Wednesdays. During the two hours of each session she lectured on Chinese culture and art, Japanese art, or the literature of France, England or America. Using her notes from the Hall of Man creation at the Berkshire Museum, she lectured on "man and evolution." She gave discourses on Albert Camus, Jean-Paul Sartre, Aldous Huxley, Gertrude Stein, and Simone de Beauvoir. She spoke about the members of the South Carolina Poetry Society, including Josephine Pinckney, DuBose Heyward, and Hervey Allen. She talked about modern painting, calling Maurer a pioneer; and in Bragg's opinion, the greatest painter since Michelangelo was Paul Cézanne.[30]

She was not interested in discussing religion. "She was not a believer," recalled one of Bragg's "girls." Bragg did not seem to be a religious person: "She knew so much about Confucius, Tao, and all of the different philosophies. . . . She knew everything she wanted to know about orthodox religion and it wasn't enough for her." Bragg never ceased to question, though, for on one occasion she turned to Waddell and asked, "What if I am wrong and there is a Hell?"[31]

In many of the morning sessions Bragg lectured on Chinese excavations, literature, and art. In 1946 she wrote one of the Chinese cadets that she had lectured to the culture classes nineteen times on China. One of the students years later remembered Bragg as being fascinated with that country. She was also charmed by Italy and its art and literature. (Italy was the objective of her three-month European trip in 1952.)[32]

Bragg's heroine was an Italian noblewoman, Isabella d'Este, who was educated in the arts and trained in diplomatic and political skills. Scholars have written that she, among all the fifteenth- and sixteenth-century princesses, personified the Renaissance, calling her the "first lady of the world." She collected manuscripts, statues, paintings, and jewelry. And she corresponded with all the famous personalities of her day, who sought her friendship. Baldassare Castiglione, an Italian diplomat and writer of the early sixteenth century, visited her court at Mantua. His *Book of the Courtier,* whose heroine is Isabella d'Este, is based on his observations of court life and describes the acceptable behavior for an ideal courtier. Identifying with the Italian lady and her classical education, Bragg conducted her salon much as Isabella had. Both were women, and just as Isabella had been the center of her intellectual circle and was entertained by courtiers, Bragg was the center of knowledge and directed the conversations in her classes and salons. She even named many of her cats over the years Guido, after the male character Guidobaldo in Castiglione's account of Isabella's court.[33]

Bragg was such a night owl that she spent most of her days in the house, sleeping in until midmorning. She ate lunch every day across the street at the old St. John's Hotel (now the Mills House Hotel). Whenever she had an invitation to an affair at the Gibbes or some big party, she would be escorted by one of "her boys." She was described as "absolutely elegant, with a substantial amount of jewelry with an impressive amount of tales behind it. She wore a long black skirt, with lace or silk, or some fine top . . . always carrying a cane (she had several with silver tops). . . . She was quickly ushered to the seat of honor and people would be brought in to see her. . . . Standing there by her side, you would get to meet these exciting people. . . . It was quite dazzling to be with someone who was the Grand Dame of the city."[34] Some of the cultural affairs were held at the Gibbes Art Gallery, where Helen was now the director. As with many of the places important in Bragg's confined world of Charleston, the Gibbes was quite nearby—just a block from her home.

There were a few special friends in Bragg's circle, one being Helen, who now lived with Alice, her mentally handicapped sister, across Washington Park in the Confederate Home for Widows and Orphans. Every week Helen had one special night when she visited Bragg alone with no one else there. Surely they talked and laughed as dear friends do, but Helen also mended Bragg's clothes. Whenever Helen attended other occasions at the house, Alice came too. Usually Bragg had one of "her boys" take care of Alice so that Helen could enjoy herself. Helen did not attend the morning classes but was part of the Sunday salons, at which she said almost nothing.[35]

Another special friend was Marshall Uzzell, who taught at the High

School of Charleston. Bragg had known him well before his marriage in 1928. By the time she returned to the city in 1939 he and his wife had several children, all of whom loved to go to "Miss Bragg's." Uzzell had his own special night each week; he was her "handyman," making repairs around her house. His wife attended neither the morning classes nor the evening salons. She was a graduate of Wellesley busy raising children and was comfortable sending her husband to Bragg's without her.[36]

Gene Waddell also had his special night with Bragg. Waddell had worked at the Museum during the summers and on weekends before he entered the College of Charleston in 1962. He saw Bragg's name in archaeological notes, but Bragg and her work were never spoken of at the Museum. It never occurred to him that she might still be alive because no one ever mentioned her name. He was surprised to meet her one day in 1964 at the Book Basement, where she was working in order to qualify for Social Security. She was eighty-three years old and could still walk across town from her house on Chalmers to the bookstore at the corner of College and Green, just on the outskirts of the College of Charleston's campus.[37]

After their meeting at the bookstore, she invited him to her Sunday evening salons "because people dropped by." Waddell and Bragg developed a friendship that lasted more than fifteen years until her death. On his visits they spoke about their interests and what they were currently reading. He lived in her third-floor room during one year while he was completing college. Waddell made arrangements in New York for the sale of her modern art when she became so ill that she was placed in a nursing home just months before her death.[38]

Bragg also enjoyed a larger circle of casual friends and was continually adding to it. Waddell brought other young men to her home, who then became "Bragg's boys." Two were his classmates at the College of Charleston, Gregg Privette and Hal Norvell. Privette accompanied Waddell to Chalmers Street for his "audition" one Sunday evening. He recalled that "I, of course, did not think of it that way at the time. But it is perfectly clear later on that is exactly what was happening. If you weren't up to snuff, reasonably bright, of a certain age, and interested in the world then you wouldn't be invited back."[39]

Bragg liked to have a certain number of young people around to keep her sharp. She believed that she got new ideas and discovered new possibilities from young people, so she enjoyed having them around, especially at her Sunday salons. The young people who attended had to be reasonably civilized, and Bragg had to see a spark because she did not waste her social time with conventional people. Once they passed the audition interview, they then received a call asking them to attend other salons. Those who did not pass the test did not get a call to return. With the mix tilted toward young people, the ones who had passed the audition understood its importance, though none of them said a word to each other about it.[40]

As a helper at the salons, Privette was assigned the task of making highballs, "nothing particularly difficult, just bourbon and water." Bragg liked to serve pepper jelly on Bremner wafers with the drinks. But it was not the food or liquor that brought people to Bragg's. It was the company and the conversation. She wanted people to think, to ask questions, and she pushed them to expand their thought processes. The discussions were centered on meaning and importance. Since her home was considered the center of the artistic and cultural community within the city, it seemed appropriate that a newspaper article about Bragg was headlined "Lady Bragg, Cultural Bountiful."[41]

Anybody who was of interest or note who passed through Charleston was brought to her home for the salons. Robert Frost spent a weekend and read poetry to the Sunday gathering. Frequent guests at Bragg's guided conversations included Henry Miller, Robert Marks, Richard Coleman, and William Halsey.[42]

The salon was mostly attended by men. One of "her boys" believed that Bragg really did not care much for typical south-of-Broad women: "she thought they weren't too bright or articulate." Over the years only a few women attended regularly, including Helen, the writer Kitty Ravenel, Anna Wells Rutledge, and the artist Corrie McCallum, who was Bill Halsey's wife. (Josephine was no longer next door, as she died suddenly of cancer while in New York in the fall of 1957.) "Her girls" from the morning classes rarely attended, and the husbands were not interested in Bragg, as one of the students remembered. One of these husbands, a physician, remarked that "Miss Bragg was the most intimidating woman I ever met."[43]

Hal Norvell was another of those bright young people Waddell invited to the salons. Though her physical problems were apparent to him, at eighty-three she seemed ageless in 1964 when he first met her. She used her hearing aid (it was a bone conduction type) to her advantage, ignoring conversation when she chose. She also knew how to make it squeak on command. And she would joke about having had cancer, shifting her breast prosthesis around from to time, whenever it got out of place.[44]

Norvell's most vivid memory of Bragg was her ability to make him laugh: "She had a wonderful sense of humor, with a great laugh." Bragg enjoyed laughter and once remarked in a letter to McCausland about a New York play, "if I were in New York now, I would go to see Falstaff, and get a masculine belly laugh instead of a sophisticated, feminine chuckle."

Norvell thought Bragg could be quite naughty in her sense of humor, goading people and using a snide comment in her appraisals of them. Interestingly, one of the women from the morning classes felt almost the opposite about Bragg, whom she credited with a sweet, gentle personality. She thought Bragg never said a nasty thing about anyone because she did not have it in her to be critical or condemning.[45]

In Norvell's opinion, Bragg knew how to go beneath a person's facade because she was observant of human traits. He said, "Being invited into her home was an assessment of my potential. She accepted me and made me a part of her life. . . . she was always encouraging me. She always asked my opinion." At the same time she was always teaching. Bragg taught him "how to look at art, . . . how to be perceptive about art . . . how to accept nothing on face value."[46]

Her astuteness and perception were always part of her relationships. Uzzell had retired from the public school system and was teaching at a local private school. Through him Bragg met Ralph Nordlund, a gentle, soft-spoken teacher, who attended a few of her salons. After observing him on those occasions it became apparent to her that he was reclusive and shy in social situations. She suggested that he come back when there were only a few people. On these visits, besides their conversations, she would give him tasks and errands to do for her. Finally Nordlund came to understand that she wanted him to take Uzzell's place as her handyman. He repaired a bookcase and picked up ice cream and white grapes for her (two of her favorite foods).[47]

Though Bragg gave Nordlund some whiskey to loosen his tongue, she did much of the talking. She talked about the Chinese cadets, about her strong dislike for Milby Burton and his not honoring her work, about the Poetry Society and its members, and about art—from Renaissance to modern. And she told him she saw herself as a missionary when she came to Charleston, helping a "backward area." In his opinion she felt superior, even though she devoted her life to improving the cultural life of the city. "She tried her best to bring in the culture of the outside world," he felt.[48]

What Nordlund saw when he spoke with Bragg was her mind and her almost total recall of what she had read. Since she spoke as the equal of any man, he could not imagine her putting herself in the role of wife. Strong and independent, Bragg really was the equal or better of any man and simply could not be submissive. It seemed to him that their conversations, though frank, were not as those between a man and a woman, though some of them occurred in her bedroom.[49]

One time Bragg asked that Nordlund perform a simple task for her. When he did not perceive the real purpose behind his assignment, which was to buy a new can opener, she became disappointed with him and asked that he return some books she had given him. But she did allow him to keep a valuable painting. This is probably one of the few instances when Bragg's ability to manipulate people was unsuccessful. Privette was unaware of this example when he said, "I can't think of a single example when she did not get her way." He believed that Bragg used her charm to get people to do things voluntarily for her. It was a great skill, manipulating people, and she was good at it.[50]

For Bragg's "boys" and for the women in the culture classes Bragg was always a teacher. She opened the world to them, waking them up to see it, to see what else was out there beyond the immediate, and to understand that there were other possibilities. Privette compared her to Auntie Mame, "Open a new window, open a new door." MacLennan believed that Bragg taught her mind to travel and greatly influenced her pursuit of knowledge. Bragg inspired her to visit museums in Europe and to seek out archaeological sites in France—to open doors and to see what was out there.[51]

Bragg's most successful student was Helen, and while Helen's career remains as her greatest achievement, in later life her influence was most apparent with Waddell, whose career has been solely in the field of museums and curatorial work. Among his professional positions Waddell has been director of the Florence Museum in South Carolina; curator at the Getty Center for the History of Art and the Humanities in Santa Monica, California; and director of the South Carolina Historical Society.[52]

Waddell thought Bragg's greatest influence on him was introducing him to great writers and the best scholarship. She also caused him to deepen his own knowledge in topics that were already of interest to him. In his opinion, Bragg had the ability to interest people in learning because she was interested in so many subjects. She shared the possibilities she saw and her own unbounded enthusiasm in learning for learning's sake.[53]

Bragg was also generous to the "boys." She shared her eighty-fourth birthday party with Privette (their birthdays were the same date, 9 October) and insisted that the party at her home was for both of them. He invited guests, only a few, and all the others who attended came for her, to honor the grande dame. She threw a party for Norvell when he graduated from college, filling her bathtub with ice and champagne.[59] Her generosity also extended to "her girls." Before her final illness Bragg decided who would inherit her possessions, writing their names on the items. Her home was willed to Marshall Uzzell's youngest son, Jamie, with whom she was particularly close. Jamie was legally blind, and Bragg spent much time with him as he grew into a young man.[54]

In March 1973 Bragg, at ninety-one, was awarded an honorary degree

from the College of Charleston. After that her age and poor health prevented many outings as she neared her ninety-fifth birthday. Burton had
retired from the Museum, and the new director, Don Herold, invited
Bragg to the Museum to see the exhibits. He made Bragg a lifetime member of the Museum, recognizing her seniority there. Herold also made sure
that Bragg saw the architect's plans for the new building.[55] The Charleston
Museum was still housed in the same building in which she had installed
exhibits sixty-five years earlier. As wonderful as the visit to the Museum
was, how bittersweet it must have been for her to see the plans for the new
building.

As Bragg grew older, her hearing failed completely, leaving her totally
deaf. Her eyesight also deteriorated, and she was unable to read without
strong magnification. Lonely in her wonderful home filled with books, she
was totally dependent upon friends to sustain her emotionally and physically. During one particularly rough period one of "her girls," Mary
Hagerty, moved Bragg into her home for several weeks. Toward the end of
her life no one seemed to be in charge, as Helen had died of cancer in
1974. Other of "her girls" brought in food from time to time, with some
wondering how Bragg managed.[56]

Over the years her blood pressure had been a problem, and she suffered from dizzy spells. About two years before her death in 1978 she fell
in her home, breaking her hip. The surgery at St. Francis to set her hip was
successful, but she suffered a stroke during the operation and never walked
again. Bragg needed full-time care, but she was virtually penniless. Waddell
had the modern art drawing by Miro auctioned at Sotheby's to pay for her
final years in a nursing home, where she died on May 16, 1978, when she
was nearly ninety-seven years old. Bragg's body was cremated, and her
ashes were scattered over the Santee River delta, one of her favorite places.
"Her girls" from the cultural classes and the "boys" from the salons com-
memorated her life and her memory with a memorial service at St.
Philip's.[57]

Several months after the memorial service, Bragg's friends from the
classes and the salons organized a memorial fund to present a bronze bust
of her to the Museum. The announcement of this tribute was made on the
editorial page and carried the by-line of the editor, Thomas R. Waring. He
closed his article by honoring Bragg: "Though deaf from childhood, Laura
M. Bragg had a gift for communication. She had a command of language
and the ability of a born teacher. Her influence on Charleston is beyond
measure. It is now being transmitted through the generations from those
who grew up under her guidance. In recognition of her gifts to this community, it is fitting that a bronze likeness be placed in the Charleston

Museum's new building. . . . The owners of the memorial fund hope that contributions will come from a broad cross section of the community that Laura Bragg ornamented, enriched, and cherished."[58] The bust was presented to the Charleston Museum, and Bragg had finally come home to her Museum.

In Retrospect

We shall not cease from exploration
And the end of all our exploring
Will be to arrive where we started
And know the place for the first time.

                                    T. S. Eliot, "Little Gidding"

LAURA BRAGG'S STORY IS ABOUT GENDER, as all stories about women are; it is about race, racism, and class and how this early feminist confronted those issues; and it is about Bragg's sexuality and her ambivalence about it. It is a story about a woman whose passion was her work and whose passion was redefined and redirected each time a new opportunity presented itself. And, finally, it is a story of a disremembered university-trained woman who helped to construct and carry out a reform agenda in the Progressive Era.[1]

As an early feminist, Bragg was one of many women in the forefront trying to reform governmental and social institutions in the Progressive Era. These women were working to gain autonomy while taking on the responsibilities of public life and seeking the right to vote. Bragg was among other white middle-class women who considered themselves feminists but chose to act as individual social reformers rather than addressing the specific problems of women through collective organizations.[2]

As a movement in both the North and the South, progressive reforms touched the cultural, social, and political institutions of both regions. Spanning thirty years in the North and almost forty years in the South, the Progressive Era and its reformers created new agencies that would reshape life across the nation.[3] One of these agencies was a re-created museum as a public institution, which responded to the great educational needs of immigrants and the rural poor.

At the beginning of the Progressive Era museums had reawakened to public demands. For many years they had been mausoleums of preserved relics, viewed as institutions for the educated—the social and cultural elite of the community. Just as the Progressive Era brought changes to other social and political institutions in the country, it also led to changes in museums and their focus. With the tremendous influx of immigrants from other countries, who came with their own languages and customs, museums began to serve as social institutions in Americanizing these immigrants. Thus museum directors and curators had to change their methods of installations and exhibits to adapt to museums' educational role.[4]

Bragg came to understand this as she visited museums around Boston during college and her first years as the Charleston Museum's curator of books and public instruction. She saw northern museum personnel respond to the challenges of newly arrived immigrants. They altered their focus by writing new exhibition labels in language that could be understood by the average person—words that would both illuminate and instruct. Since the goal was to Americanize immigrants, the information presented and the language used were specific to that goal. All of this was part of the growing professionalism of museum work, one of the hallmarks of the Progressive Era.[5]

Early museums were run by volunteers with little specialized training, as there were few courses specifically designed for museum studies. The first salaried workers in museums had some college training in academic subjects such as art, history, or science. As museums became more popular, new pressures created demands for new positions.[6] With Bragg's college degree and her appointment as a museum director, she was in a unique position to transcend the societal limits placed on women. Her position and power as a museum director provided Bragg with an avenue to open new horizons for herself and other women in her reorganization of the Charleston Museum, the Valentine Museum and the Berkshire Museum.

Using the knowledge she gained from the reorganization and reinstallation of exhibits at the Charleston Museum, she developed a museum studies course for the summer school session at Columbia University that was specifically designed for women curators. She also mentored the women she taught and helped them find positions in museums. By creating a network of museum professionals, she extended her influence and her museum principles beyond her own museums.

Bragg used both the Charleston Museum and the Berkshire Museum as social and cultural institutions. Her broad educational programs were designed for ordinary citizens, providing them with Progressives' definitions of uplift and progress. Seeing the museum as an engine for social change, Bragg turned both museums into social settlement houses by offering plays, lectures, art classes, and educational programs. In both museums she employed progressive social ideals, working for the betterment of the citizens.

While there were few new immigrants in the South in 1909 when Bragg arrived in Charleston, there was great poverty and ignorance among blacks and whites. As a missionary and social worker, Bragg recognized the possibilities for social change, even though she had come to the city intending to be a librarian and botanist. The impoverished city virtually existed as it had since the years after the Civil War, with the same families ruling the social power structure. Though there were reforms being enacted at the state level, much of the state's population was basically illiterate and impoverished. The citizens were thirsting for the knowledge she offered. Through the educational programs instituted at the Charleston Museum, Bragg attempted to give Charlestonians the same opportunities she had experienced growing up in New England. She wanted to Americanize the southerners who did "not know even the heroes and myths of our culture," as she wrote Mayor Grace on one occasion.[7]

With Museum director Paul Rea filling two faculty positions at different institutions of higher learning, Bragg was presented with the perfect opportunity to transform a scientific, academic museum into a public institution dedicated to education. In the long view, she could be viewed either as doing good for ordinary people on a massive scale or as attempting an intellectual revolution through the traveling school exhibits, libraries, art classes, lectures, films, music, and other aspects of the educational programs she instituted.

Revolutions "have always been limited by the social settings in which they take place."[8] In the Holy City, Bragg's intellectual revolution was framed by class, race, and gender. Race was not dealt with directly at the Museum until 1917, when the trustees passed a resolution allowing classes of black students accompanied by their teachers to visit the building, while denying admission to black adults. The Charleston Museum was an institution for whites only until Bragg opened it to blacks one afternoon a week. By then Bragg had already circumvented the Jim Crow rules by first sending traveling school exhibits into the city's black schools in 1913. These black schools were overcrowded, substandard to the white schools, and offered fewer textbooks and other educational materials for students and teachers. The Bragg boxes were truly windows on the world for the black students.

As a social reformer, Bragg understood the tremendous impact of the traveling school exhibits. These exhibits, as part of Bragg's museum educational programs, are among her greatest accomplishments. Through these windows on the world she was able to expose children to countries, cultures, and nature they would never have experienced. As a means to an end, they accomplished her primary goal, which was to bring adults into the Museum. But viewed from the perspective of eighty years later, they are examples of progressive social reform. Bragg boxes were an attempt to end the apathy and ignorance of schoolchildren. She hoped that they would become educated adults who would visit the museum and bring their children.[9]

As a "quiet feminist," Bragg made a personal attempt to mold her world, and at the same time her actions helped her achieve a measure of independence. Her struggle to define herself, to take chances and risk failure while developing her career, did not come without costs in both her personal and professional lives. Her choices and her path, as she defined them, were not the prescribed passive, subservient ones that society saw as appropriate for women at that time, especially southern women. By living her life as she did, Bragg challenged and in many instances overcame many of the restrictions that limited women's options during the first decades of the twentieth century. These actions mirror those of other American women during this time period, such as Lucy Sprague Mitchell, founder of the Bank Street College of Education in New York City. Mitchell's biographer, Joyce Antler, contends that through her struggle for individual autonomy, Mitchell and others like her exemplify "feminism as life-process" rather than "a self-conscious political strategy." Like Mitchell, Bragg and other women were alive in their own lives, passionate about their work and willing to risk themselves to achieve their goals.[10]

The compelling forces in Bragg's life that shaped who she was as a person were her relationship with her father and her educational advantages. By spending time with her father, watching him, and learning from him he, with his controlling personality and his world of books, became her role model. His manner and his bearing, imperious and impervious, became hers. She appeared cool and distant to those who did not know her well. Because of her self-control, nothing visibly surprised her or caught her off guard. Detached and seemingly without emotion, she seemed always in command of her passions and any situation in which she found herself.[11]

In examination of every other relationship in Bragg's life, except possibly the one with Rea, Bragg's role seems always to have been dominant and controlling. As Rea was her superior, Bragg could not dominate him, but given his other activities he was often away from the Museum. In her dealings with him she met him as her equal, as a New Woman would. Bragg also had important relationships with "her boys" and "her girls," who rotated in and out of her life. They were always much younger than she, and her role was as the dominant one, that of teacher to student. Though she treated the "boys" of the salons differently from the "girls" in the cultural classes, Bragg was always in control.

Bragg was rarely deferential to anyone. She did not defer to men, nor did she expect to be deferred to because she was a woman. Bragg was never a southern New Woman who believed her place was in the home. Most southern New Women became teachers, social workers, or nurses—in the tending, caring professions. Few were mavericks, and it was not until about 1930 "that Southern culture permitted more diversity in female roles."[12]

Bragg's gender and the role expectations for southern women

bounded whatever she attempted at the Museum. Bragg was a progressive New Woman whose determination, forthrightness, and vision of educating all children distinguished her from many other women in South Carolina. While she asserted her rights and her "personhood" quietly and definitively, she did not fulfill the prescribed gender roles as expected of women at the time. Thus, she was unsettling to the status quo of the patriarchy in Charleston. Using leadership behaviors, she aggressively set forth her agenda, making the necessary social and political connections while forging alliances both professionally and personally to assure its success. With Belle Heyward's death, Bragg lost her protector, her supporter, and her entrée into the inner circles of power. Ultimately this loss, along with her inability to be a typical southern lady, affected her fund-raising for the Museum and her educational program. In the five years between 1925 and 1930, state superintendent of education J. H. Hope frequently used intermediaries to communicate with Bragg, rarely responding directly to her letters.

Bragg boxes could have reached more children if the power structure of the General Assembly and Hope had not chosen to stonewall her every effort to seek state funding. Historically, South Carolina's lawmakers were slow to reform anything, and since the exhibits were being sent into black schools, racism could very well have been a part of the politicians' game. In passing her request from the State Department of Education to the Charleston delegation back to the department, these men (except for legislators Rittenberg and Legare) did not want to deal with her and the Bragg boxes. Even though the General Assembly passed a concurrent resolution praising the exhibits, the state's financial support never materialized.[13]

Bragg's gender also played a part in her inability to gain funding for the Museum's fireproof wing during the nation's prosperous years of the 1920s. In every attempt to work with philanthropic boards of large corporations, Bragg met resistance. Even with influential friends and supporters, such as William Sloane Coffin and William Heard Kilpatrick, she was unable to secure funds for any of her schemes at the Charleston Museum. The Rosenwald funding for the traveling school exhibits and for the free library came through her professional relationships in the museum world, not from any social or political ally.

Swayed by wealth, she wanted to be a part of the elite in both Charleston and Pittsfield. Bragg's own social position was decidedly middle-class, and her religious heritage was quite definitely Methodist—both her father and grandfather were Methodist ministers. From 1909 until she finally joined the Episcopal Church in 1916, she spoke at length about conversion with her father and finally rationalized it away. Being accepted in the city's social and power circles was important to Bragg. If that meant joining a church other than the one of her family, she would do it. By 1916 Bragg's questioning about theology had led her almost completely away from orthodox religion. With her conscience clear and a strong enough rationalization about conversion, she easily joined St. Luke's Episcopal Church, which her friend Hester Gaillard attended. Just a few years later, after she had begun her relationship with Belle, she moved her membership to St. Philip's Episcopal Church, where her new partner was a member.

Social class determined who belonged to the Museum and participated in the activities. It also determined the early members of the Natural History Society. Anita Pollitzer, Josephine Pinckney, Ned Jennings, and Burnham and Rhett Chamberlain were all young adults whom Bragg worked with and mentored, beginning in 1909. Bragg's relationships with these younger people continued throughout their lives, with her outliving them all. Yet she was their teacher and was always "Miss Bragg" to them.

As the Museum's director Bragg was accepted into the largest mansions along Charleston's High Battery. Many of the children who lived in them were her "bright young things." They came to her home at 7 Gibbes and then to Chalmers Street, and they enjoyed the beauty of Snug Harbor's marshes. By 1926, when Bragg met her first "China Boy," she was firmly ensconced in the city's powerful social circles and was able to openly flaunt Charleston's racial barriers. Determined that her "Chinese babies" would be accepted by Charleston society, she formed the Ta T'ung Club, inviting many of the daughters of the upper class to socialize with the Chinese cadets, either in the city or in the country. Horrified, some families refused to allow their daughters to attend, believing the Chinese to be "colored."

In her search for status and social standing, Bragg was similar to other members of the newly created professions of this era in their response to the confusing industrialized world of the early twentieth century. With her educational programs, she shared with these Progressives a faith in progress and a vision as one of serving the masses, "those the Museum had yet to reach." Morally sincere, Bragg sought to reform, democratize, and Americanize the very southerners by whom she wanted to be accepted.[14]

Frustrated by the lack of continued financial support for her Museum plans, by her personal failure to receive a Guggenheim fellowship, and by the worldwide depression in 1931, Bragg understood the tremendous financial problems facing the Charleston Museum. Because she was ready to move on, the offer from the Crane family came at a critical juncture for Bragg. Poor financial management had always played a part in her personal business as well as her professional life. The Crane family fortune, as a

resource for the museum and with its generous salary offer for herself, persuaded her to return to her home state. Instead of convincing a mayor and
council or a state legislature full of men, she needed to work with only one
man whose family wealth endowed the museum.

While she attempted to bridge the gap between the social classes in
Pittsfield with the educational programs, Bragg's modern art shows at the
Berkshire Museum were for the cultural and social elite of the Berkshire
community. Beginning with the reception welcoming her to the Berkshire
Museum, Bragg sought out the upper classes of the community. Held in
conjunction with a modern art show from Grand Central Art Galleries in
New York, this reception and art show set the tone for her tenure there.
Since Bragg liked parties, whenever there was an opening for an exhibit
there was a reception, with hundreds invited.[15] Bragg thought that modern art was wonderful, and she was intent upon teaching others about it.
Lectures preceded and followed other modern art exhibits from the
Museum of Modern Art and the Whitney Museum and then her final
exhibit of social realists.

The Berkshire Museum was used as a gathering place, with receptions
held for the upper class from the community as well as the cosmopolitan
visitors who made the Berkshires their home during the summer season.
Once the grand Ellen Crane Memorial Room was opened, it served as a
fitting space for parties and "the heart of the Museum's life in the community." These receptions became major social occasions and were
reported in the society and art pages of newspapers as far away as Chicago.
The New York Times society page reported the closing of an art exhibition
in 1936. Art exhibits and museum information were rarely reported in the
society page at that time.[16]

The importance Bragg placed on social class and money also affected
her personal relationships. Soon after moving to Charleston she met Belle,
and several years later she moved in with her, leaving behind a sad woman
(Hester) who needed her support. Belle's home was a happy household,
where Bragg was the receiver and Belle was the giver. At 7 Gibbes, Belle
played the feminine role, providing the home and the emotional support
that Bragg, the dominant or masculine partner, needed to sustain herself as
she unofficially directed the Museum. Belle's role as Bragg's helpmate was
recognized by her parents and others who knew them. The cards and letters she sent Bragg over the eleven years of their relationship are full of her
love, expressed openly and freely. It was an intense and long-standing relationship that was socially acceptable for a privileged, educated daughter of
the middle class.

As an early-twentieth-century woman Bragg had grown up in a society where love between women was not condemned. Emotional love was the norm in these relationships, and if sex entered into them, the partners were not concerned enough to worry over the implications. At that time American society had not focused on the issue of female sexuality. Bragg's family viewed her romantic friendship with Belle, and later with Helen, as an ideal alternative to a lonely life of spinsterhood. With Bragg's ambition for a full professional life, there was little room, if any, for a man, marriage, and a family. Belle's and Bragg's personal lives were filled for a time with Bragg's illnesses and then with Bragg's "girls" reading poetry and the formation of the Poetry Society. Bragg needed Belle first as a nurse and then as a gracious hostess. Once Bragg was named the Museum's director, with her own country home at Snug Harbor, the two women settled into a type of relationship not unfamiliar to many heterosexual couples—living together but having separate lives.[17]

This separateness along with Bragg's public achievements led to her relationship with Helen McCormack and the merging of the public and the private in Bragg's world. With the tremendous success of the American Association of Museums annual meeting in Charleston, Bragg's star was on the rise nationally. Belle left soon after on what was to become one of several European trips between 1923 and her death in 1926. The trips were with other female friends, leaving Bragg to be the Museum's director and leaving her alone.

During the summer of 1923, while Belle was away, a new girl with a sweet voice came to the Museum as a volunteer. Petite, shy, and bright, Helen caught Bragg's eye and mind. Eager to learn, she readily accepted Bragg in the dominant role and became her apt student over the next two years. By the time she graduated from college in 1925, she was as much a part of the Museum's staff as she was Bragg's life.

Belle was gone throughout the summer of 1925, while Helen went to Snug Harbor for what was a life-altering weekend with Bragg in August. It was in the winter of 1926 that Belle's first recorded accident with gas is discussed in Bragg's letters to her father. Possibly there is a connection between this event and Helen's permanent arrival in Bragg's life. Once nursed back to health, Belle hurried back to Europe with friends. Her cards to Bragg indicate that she had regained her composure: "I feel so much better—really like myself again."[18] She was gone from February until just before Bragg's forty-fifth birthday in October. Within days she was dead, her death ruled an accidental asphyxiation.

Belle's death was hushed up, and much later Bragg chose to offer a story of murder in place of a possible suicide as the explanation. Possibly Bragg wanted to deny that Belle's death was suicide. If Belle, her romantic partner and the woman she called a lesbian, had been unable to accept that she was supplanted by Helen in Bragg's affections, then her suicide would have been for love. The murder explanation Bragg offered was a cover for Belle, for the Heyward family, and for Bragg herself. By offering this story in the 1960s, Bragg had come to understand that love between women was not acceptable. Sexologists and scientists had successfully defined proper sexual behavior, and her romantic friendships were now seen as lesbian relationships, though Bragg would never have called herself a lesbian.

Bragg's last long-term relationship was with Helen and began as one of teacher-student, as did all the later ones in her life. For Helen, the relationship was one of unashamed passion and tenderness, as her letters to Bragg attest. Whether there was a physical side to their relationship or not, Helen was Bragg's emotional partner for the rest of her life, even when Bragg had moved on to other women. Throughout their lives together Bragg's role of the dominant partner and teacher to the submissive student remained the same with Helen.

One of Bragg's "boys" claimed that she was incidentally a woman. Her gender never defined her actions because she saw herself as a person who was dominant and controlling but also sensual—she loved beauty, clothes, jewelry, art, food, liquor. Indeed, Bragg never denied herself any pleasure. But Bragg did not see herself as being a woman as society defined her gender. She had always been the dominant one, the one in control.[19]

Neither romanticized nor presented as infallible, this story of Bragg's life shows her, with all her faults, to be a person of unique accomplishments. She changed the course of history through her actions and her will. Guided by her father's socialization and her education, Bragg was channeled into a role that emphasized her intellectual capabilities, allowing her to be an active participant in history. Bragg was ahead of her time not only in Charleston but also in Pittsfield, and she was a catalyst for change. She seemed to have a talent for recognizing the appropriate moment for change, a premonition that the times and people could almost bear the changes she was ready to make at the museums with which she was associated.

As different as she was from those with whom she chose to associate, she also wanted to be accepted, especially in the later years of her life. That is why returning to Charleston was for her the best way to frame her personality and to showcase her intellect. In the Holy City she could be different and accepted at the same time.

Notes

Prologue

1. Anne Firor Scott, *The Southern Lady: From Pedestal Politics 1830–1930,* 25th anniversary ed. (Charlottesville: University of Virginia Press, 1995), 287.

2. Directors' Correspondence, American Association of Museums 1919–1931; South Carolina Department of Education 1921–1938; Chamber of Commerce, Charleston Museum Library/Archive, Charleston (hereafter cited as CMLA).

3. Margaretta Pringle Childs, interview by author, tape recording, 10 July 1996, SP.

4. Lewis Mumford, "The Art Galleries," *New Yorker,* 14 September 1937, and Elizabeth McCausland, "The Reopening of the Berkshire Museum," *Art News,* 12 June 1937, Museum Clipping Book, The Berkshire Museum, Pittsfield (hereafter cited as BM). Mumford credited Bragg with providing him "timely help and encouragement when I most needed them"; — she showed "professional dedication . . . in the service of the mind," he said. Mumford, *Sketches from Life: The Autobiography of Lewis Mumford, The Early Years* (New York: Dial Press, 1982), 426.

5. "Museum Acquires Calder's Art in Motion," *Art Digest,* November 1934, Museum BM; Marion Grant, "Alexander Calder at The Berkshire Museum," 17 May 1990, unpublished manuscript. I am deeply grateful to the author for sharing this work with me. For clippings from the Museums' scrapbooks, publication and date information has been transcribed as noted here. Often written by hand, this information is sometimes incomplete.

6. "Carrying Art to the Schools," *New York Times,* 22 March 1936, Museum Clipping Book, BM.

7. Jacqueline Dowd Hall, "Lives Through Time: Second Thoughts on Jessie Daniel Ames," in *The Challenge of Feminist Biography: Writing the Lives of Modern American Women,* ed. Sara Alpern, Joyce Antler, Elisabeth Israles Perry, and Ingrid Weinther Scobie (Urbana: University of Illinois Press, 1993), 144

8. Leon Edel, "The Figure Under the Carpet," in *Biography as High Adventure: Life Writers Speak of Their Art,* ed. Stephen Oates (Amherst: University of Massachusetts Press, 1986), 24.

9. Estelle Freedman, "The New Woman: Changing Views of Women in the 1920s," *Journal of American History* 61 (1974): 393.

Chapter 1

1. Harold Norvell, interview by author, tape recording, 16 June 1997, SP; Laura Bragg, interview by Gene Waddell, 30 October 1971. Copies of these tapes are in the author's possession.

2. Copy of record of birth, 1881, vol. 324, p. 325, no. 94, Massachusetts Archives, Boston, Mass. Inexplicably, Bragg adopted Mary as her middle name sometime after she moved to Charleston and began living with Belle Heyward.

3. *Exeter Newsletter,* April 1927, Exeter Library, Exeter, N.H.; Ralph Nordlund

interview by author, 29 May 1997 SP; and Barbara Belknap, interview by author, 29 May 1997 SP; Jack Leland, "Laura Bragg, Cultural Lady Bountiful," *News and Courier,* 10 October 1976, vertical files, Charleston County Public Library, Charleston (hereafter cited as CCPL).

4. *Memoirs, Official Journal of the 99th Session of the New Hampshire Annual Conference of the Methodist Episcopal Church* (Lancaster, April 11–15, 1928), vol. 12, part 1, 78–81, General Commission on Archives and History, United Methodist Church, Drew University (hereafter cited as DU); Matriculation book #1, p. 36, Boston University School of Theology Library, Boston (hereafter cited as MBU-T); New Hampshire Conference Records of the Methodist Episcopal Church, MBU-T; New England Conference Records of the Methodist Episcopal Church, MBU-T; Duane L. Robinson, *General Catalogue of Middlebury College* (Middlebury, Vt.: Middlebury College Publications, 1950), 199–200; Laura Bragg, interview by Constance Myers, 27 March 1974, Dacus Library, Winthrop University Archives, Rock Hill, S.C.

5. Laura Bragg to A.J. Buist, Undated Correspondence, Laura Bragg Papers, CMLA.

6. William A. Link, *The Paradox of Southern Progressivism, 1880–1930* (Chapel Hill: University of North Carolina Press, 1992), xi; Jacqueline Dowd Hall, "Partial Truths: Writing Southern Women's History" in *Southern Women: Histories and Identities,* ed. Virginia Bernhard, Betty Brandon, Elizabeth Fox-Genovese, and Theda Perdue (Columbia: University of Missouri Press, 1992), 26.

7. Susan F. Semel, *The Dalton School: The Transformation of a Progressive School* (New York: Peter Lang, 1993), 7.

8. Link, *Paradox,* xi–xii.

9. Mary Martha Thomas, *The New Woman in Alabama: Social Reforms and Suffrage, 1890–1920* (Tuscaloosa: University of Alabama Press, 1992), 2–3; Janet Zollinger Giele, *Two Paths to Women's Equality: Temperance, Suffrage and the Origins of Modern Feminism* (New York: Twayne Publishers, 1995), 146.

10. Carroll Smith-Rosenberg, *Disorderly Conduct: Visions of Gender in Victorian America* (New York: Knopf, 1985), 245.

11. Ibid.; Esther Newton, "The Mythic Mannish Lesbian: Radclyffe Hall and the New Woman," *Signs* 9 (1984): 561.

12. Smith-Rosenberg, *Disorderly Conduct,* 177.

13. *Memoirs,* 79, DU; Document of membership for Lyman Bragg, Laura Bragg Papers, South Carolina Historical Society, Charleston (hereafter cited as SCHS); and *Exeter Newsletter,* 6 November 1914, Exeter Historical Society, Exeter, N.H.; Sarah Bragg to Belle Heyward, 28 September 1920, Laura Bragg Papers, SCHS.

14. *Memoirs,* 81, DU; Neil R. McMillen, *Dark Journey: Black Mississippians in the Age of Jim Crow* (Urbana: University of Illinois Press, 1989), 98–99.

15. James D. Anderson, *The Education of Blacks in the South, 1860–1935* (Chapel Hill: University of North Carolina Press, 1988), 240–42.

16. McMillen, 77, 75, 100; Ralph E. Luker, *The Social Gospel in Black and White: American Racial Reform, 1885–1912* (Chapel Hill: University of North Carolina Press, 1991), 17; and Levern Hill, ed., *Black American College and Universities* (Detroit, Mich.: Gale, 1994), 386.

17. J. Lawrence Brasher, *The Sanctified South: John Lakin Brasher and the Holiness Movement* (Urbana: University of Illinois Press, 1994), 10; Luker, 16.

18. Luker, 85; Booker T. Washington, "A Cheerful Journey Through Mississippi," *World's Work,* February 1908, 115; McMillen, 231.

19. Luker, 90; *Memoirs,* 81, DU.

20. Sarah Bragg to Laura Bragg, 27 January 1928, Laura Bragg Papers, SCHS; Eleanor P. Hart, "Weighing Her Merits," *Preservation Progress,* January 1965, Hinson Clippings, Charleston Library Society, Charleston (hereafter cited as CLS).

21. *Exeter Newsletter,* April 1927; Laura Bragg to Lyman Bragg, 10 December 1918, Laura Bragg Papers, SCHS.

22. Laura Bragg to Lyman Bragg, 19 February 1914, Laura Bragg Papers, SCHS; Lois G. LaFlamme, "Adventures of Mind Provided by Books," *Charleston Evening Post,* 27 July 1967, vertical files, CCPL; Lucile MacLennan, interview by author, tape recording, 1 July 1997, SP.

23. Laura Bragg to Lyman Bragg, 13 May 1912, Laura Bragg Papers, SCHS; Myers interview; Laura Bragg to Lyman Bragg, 15 December 1911, 8 April 1914, 2 June 1914, Laura Bragg Papers, SCHS.

24. Sarah Bragg to Laura Bragg, 27 January 1927, Laura Bragg Papers, SCHS; *The First Class of Simmons College Yearbook, 1902–1906,* College Archives, Simmons College, Boston (hereafter cited as SCA); Emma Reed to Sarah Bragg, 6 May 1927, Laura Bragg Papers, SCHS; Laura Bragg to Lyman Bragg, 3 October 1911, Laura Bragg Papers, SCHS; Myers interview.

25. Lillian Faderman, *Surpassing the Love of Men: Romantic Friendships and Love Between Women from the Renaissance to the Present* (New York: Morrow, 1981), 187; Suzanne Fields, *Like Father, Like Daughter: How Father Shapes the Woman His Daughter Becomes* (Boston: Little, Brown, 1974), 29; Olive Banks, *The Social Origins of First Wave Feminism* (Athens: University of Georgia Press, 1986), 33.

26. Banks, *Social Origins,* 44; William Halsey, interview by author, tape recording, 16 September 1997, SP.

27. Faderman, *Romantic Friendships,* 188; Laura Bragg to Lyman Bragg, 3 October 1911; Myers interview; Kenneth L. Mark, *Delayed by Fire: Being the Early History of Simmons College* (Concord, NH: Rumford Press, 1945), 31; Hart, "Weighing Her Merits."

28. Philip Bergen, *Old Boston in Early Photographs, 1850–1918* (New York: Dover Publications, 1990), x–xii; Peter Vanderwarker, *Boston Then and Now* (New York: Dover Publications, 1982), 22; Myers interview.

29. Jessie M. Watkins, "The First Twenty-Fifth Reunion," reprinted from *Boston Evening Transcript,* 10 June 1931, 133.

30. Laura Bragg, "History of the Class of 1906," *Simmons College Yearbook,* 1906, SCA; Laura Bragg to Alice Norton Dike, 14 March 1923, Bragg, Laura 1923 File, Laura Bragg Papers, CMLA.

31. Mark, *Delayed by Fire,* 31; *First Annual Catalogue of Simmons College, 1902–1903,* 24, SCA; Watkins, "The First Twenty-Fifth Reunion," 134.

32. Watkins, "The First Twenty-Fifth Reunion," 134.

33. Bragg, "History of the Class of 1906."

34. Ibid.

35. Laura Bragg to Bernice J. Poutas, 11 November 1961, SCA; Mark, *Delayed by Fire,* 44.

36. *First Annual Catalogue,* 21–22.

37. Laura Bragg to Lyman Bragg, January 1904, Laura Bragg Papers, SCHS.

38. Ibid.; Laura Bragg to Lyman Bragg, 2 February 1904, Laura Bragg Papers, SCHS.

39. Laura Bragg to Lyman Bragg, 11 April 1927, Laura Bragg Papers, SCHS; Gene Waddell, personal diary (in possession of writer; author has copy), 16 July 1976.

40. *Second Annual Catalogue of Simmons College, 1903–1904,* 32–33, SCA; Bragg, "History of the Class of 1906."

41. Bragg, "History of the Class of 1906."

42. Ibid.

43. Watkins, "The First Twenty-Fifth Reunion," 134; Hart, "Weighing Her Merits."

44. Mark, *Delayed by Fire,* 65, and Laura Bragg to Lyman Bragg, September 1904, Laura Bragg Papers, SCHS. There is no indication of the nature of the surgery, though Bragg stated later in life that she had three operations for cancer (Waddell, personal diary, 11 August 1966). It is possible that cancer was the reason for this operation. See Lyman Bragg, September 1904, SCHS.

45. Laura Bragg to Lyman Bragg, September 1904, SCHS.

46. Sarah Bragg to Lyman Bragg, 19 September 1904, Laura Bragg Papers, SCHS; Laura Bragg to Lyman Bragg, 3 October 1904, Laura Bragg Papers, SCHS.

47. *Third Annual Catalogue of Simmons College, 1904–1905,* SCA; Mark, *Delayed by Fire,* 65; Watkins, "The First Twenty-Fifth Reunion," 136.

48. Laura Bragg to Lyman Bragg, 3 February 1905, and 14 June 1905; grade reports, Laura Bragg Papers, SCHS.

49. Laura Bragg to Lyman Bragg, 12 January 1905, Laura Bragg Papers, SCHS.

50. Ibid.

51. Ibid; *Fourth Annual Catalogue of Simmons College, 1905–1906,* 100, SCA.

52. Laura Bragg to Lyman Bragg, 21 August 1906, Laura Bragg Papers, SCHS; Laura Bragg to Florence Junior, 7 July 1924, Bragg, Laura 1924 File, Laura Bragg Papers, CMLA.

53. *Third Annual Catalogue of Simmons College, 1904–1905,* 91–92, SCA; Laura Bragg to John Cotton Dana, 4 February 1921, Directors' Correspondence, Newark Library, CMLA; Laura Bragg to Lyman Bragg, September 1905, Laura Bragg Papers, SCHS, and *Fourth Annual Catalogue,* 37; Laura Bragg to Clifton Gray Norman, 25 January 1926, Bragg, Laura 1926 File, Laura Bragg Papers, CMLA.

54. Rowena Tobias, "Laura M. Bragg, Rejuvenator of Museums, Returns to Charleston After Retirement," *News and Courier,* 28 January 1940, Hinson Clippings, Charleston Museum, CLS.

55. Laura Bragg to Lyman Bragg, September 1905, Laura Bragg Papers, SCHS.

56. Ibid; Laura Bragg to Lyman Bragg, 20 November 1905, Laura Bragg Papers, SCHS.

57. Laura Bragg to Lyman Bragg, 20 November 1905, Laura Bragg Papers, SCHS.

58. Laura Bragg to Lyman Bragg, 15 January 1906, Laura Bragg Papers, SCHS.

59. Ibid.

60. Mark, *Delayed by Fire,* 89; Watkins, "The First Twenty-Fifth Reunion," 136.

61. "Class Prophecy," *The First Class of Simmons College Yearbook, 1902–1906,* SCA.

62. Faderman, *Romantic Friendships,* 179; Smith-Rosenberg, *Disorderly Conduct,* 247; Duncan Crow, *The Victorian Woman* (London: George Allen and Unwin, 1971), 326; Estelle Freedman, "Separatism as Strategy: Female Institution Building and American Feminism," *Feminist Studies* 5 (1979): 518.

63. Hart, "Weighing Her Merits"; Myers interview.

64. Tobias, "Laura M. Bragg, Rejuvenator of Museums"; Orr's Island Library Register, Orr's Island, Maine; Laura Bragg to Lyman Bragg, 30 July 1906, Laura Bragg Papers, SCHS.

65. Laura Bragg to Lyman Bragg, 30 July 1906, Laura Bragg Papers, SCHS.

66. Ibid; undated biographical sketch, Bragg, Laura, Undated Correspondence, Laura Bragg Papers, CMLA; Laura Bragg to Lyman Bragg, 6 November 1906, Laura Bragg Papers, SCHS.

67. Laura Bragg to Lyman Bragg, 6 November 1906, Laura Bragg Papers, SCHS.

68. Waddell, personal diary, 13 June 1976.

69. Laura Bragg to Bernice Poutas, 22 November 1961, SCA; Tobias, "Laura M. Bragg, Rejuvenator of Museums,; Laura Bragg to Lyman Bragg, 6 November 1906, Laura Bragg Papers, SCHS.

70. Laura Bragg to Lyman Bragg, 23 February, 1907, Laura Bragg Papers, SCHS; Hart, "Weighing Her Merits"; Robin Muncy, *Creating a Female Dominion in American Reform 1890–1935* (New York: Oxford University Press, 1991), 68.

71. Laura Bragg to Lyman Bragg, 30 July 1906, Laura Bragg Papers, SCHS; Hart, "Weighing Her Merits"; Laura Bragg to Lyman Bragg, 27 November 1906, Laura Bragg Papers, SCHS.

72. Laura Bragg to Lyman Bragg, 1 September 1906, Laura Bragg Papers, SCHS.

73. Laura Bragg to Lyman Bragg, 3 July 1907, Laura Bragg Papers, SCHS; Laura Bragg to Lyman Bragg, before Thanksgiving 1907, Laura Bragg Papers, SCHS.

74. Laura Bragg to Lyman Bragg, 21 January 1908, Laura Bragg Papers, SCHS; Laura Bragg to Lyman Bragg, 24 April 1908, Laura Bragg Papers, SCHS; Sarah Bragg to Lyman Bragg, 9 February 1908, Laura Bragg Papers, SCHS.

75. Laura Bragg to Lyman Bragg, before Thanksgiving 1907, Laura Bragg Papers, SCHS; Laura Bragg to Lyman Bragg, 4 December 1908, Laura Bragg Papers, SCHS.

76. Laura Bragg to Lyman Bragg, 1 January 1909, Laura Bragg Papers, SCHS.

77. Ibid.

78. Ibid; see *Bulletin of the Charleston Museum* 3 (March 1909): 3 and *Bulletin* 6 (October 1909): 53; Laura Bragg to Lyman Bragg, 23 February 1909, Laura Bragg Papers, SCHS.

79. Waddell, personal diary, 12 November 1975.

80. Laura Bragg to Lyman Bragg, 7 July 1909, Laura Bragg Papers, SCHS.

81. Ibid.

82. Albert Sidney Thomas, *A Historical Account of the Protestant Episcopal Church in South Carolina, 1820–1957* (Columbia, S.C.: R. L. Bryan, 1957), 702, and 1910 *U.S. Census,* prepared under the supervision of William C. Hunt, Chief Statistician (Wash-

ington, D.C.: Government Printing Office, 1916), 591; Walter J. Fraser, *Charleston! Charleston! The History of a Southern City* (Columbia: University of South Carolina Press, 1989), 347–348.

83. Laura Bragg to Lyman Bragg, 13 August 1909, Laura Bragg Papers, SCHS.

Chapter 2

1. Henry James, *The American Scene* (New York: Harper Brothers, 1907), 414.

2. Laura Bragg, interview by Miriam Herbert, 2 June 1972, Laura Bragg Papers, SCHS, Charleston; Robert Molloy, *Charleston, A Gracious Heritage* (New York: D. Appleton-Century Company, 1947), 2; Fraser, *Charleston! Charleston!*, 344; Mildred Crum, *Old Seaport Towns of the South* (New York: Dodd, Mead and Company, 1917), 125.

3. Fraser, *Charleston! Charleston!*, 344; Herbert interview; Molloy, *Charleston*, 6–7; Hart,"Weighing Her Merits."

4. Stephen O'Neill, "From the Shadow of Slavery: The Civil Rights Years in Charleston" (dissertation, University of Virginia, 1994), 75, 56.

5. Ibid., 57; Idus A. Newby*, Black Carolinians: A History of Blacks in South Carolina from 1895 to 1968* (Columbia: University of South Carolina Press, 1973), 82.

6. Doyle Willard Boggs,"John Patrick Grace and the Politics of Reform in South Carolina, 1900-1931" (dissertation, University of South Carolina, 1977), 11.

7. Dewey W. Grantham, *Southern Progressivism: The Reconciliation of Progress and Tradition* (Knoxville: University of Tennessee Press, 1983), 54–55.

8. Ibid; Walter Edgar, *South Carolina: A History* (Columbia: University of South Carolina, 1998), 472–473.

9. Fraser, *Charleston! Charleston!*, 347.

10. Ibid., 349.

11. John Joseph Duffy, "Charleston Politics in the Progressive Era" (diss., University of South Carolina, 1963), 22.

12. Ibid., 18–20; O'Neill, "From the Shadow of Slavery," 20.

13. Karl E. Taeuber and Alma F. Taeuber, *Negroes in Cities: Residential Segregation and Neighborhood Change* (Chicago: Adline Publishing, 1965), 45–47.

14. O'Neill, "From the Shadow of Slavery," 42.

15. Herbert Blumer, "The Future of the Color Line," in *The South in Continuity and Change,* ed. John McKinney and Edgar T. Thompson (Durham: Duke University Press, 1965), 322.

16. Fraser, *Charleston! Charleston!*, 351; Waddell interview, 30 October 1971; 1907 *City Year Book,* 35–36, CCPL.

17. 1907 *City Year Book,* 35–36, CCPL; *Information for Guides of Historic Charleston* (Charleston: Tourism Commission, 1985), 390–391.

18. Herbert interview; *Bulletin* 6 (October 1909): 53.

19. *City Directory* for 1910 and 1911, CCPL; Laura Bragg to Lyman Bragg, 23 September 1909, Laura Bragg Papers, SCHS, Charleston.

20. *Bulletin* 7 (November 1909): 63.

21. Laura Bragg to Lyman Bragg, 24 October, 1909, Laura Bragg Papers, SCHS, Charleston.

22. Laura Bragg to Lyman Bragg, 14 February 1910, Laura Bragg Papers, SCHS, Charleston.

23. *Bulletin* 7, no. 1 (January 1911): 5.

24. Paul Marshall Rea, *The Museum and the Community* (Lancaster, PA: The Science Press, 1932), 183; *Memorandum on the Report of the Advisory Group on Museum Education* (New York: Carnegie Corporation, 1932), 7.

25. *Bulletin* 7, no. 1 (January 1911): 7.

26. Laura Bragg to Lyman Bragg, 14 February 1910, Laura Bragg Papers, SCHS.

27. Laura Bragg to Paul Rea, 28 June 1910, Bragg-Rea Correspondence, Laura Bragg Papers, CMLA.

28. Rea, *The Museum and the Community,* 18.

29. Edward Alexander, *Museums in Motion: An Introduction to the History and Functions of Museums* (Nashville: American Association for State and Local History, 1979), 13.

30. Kenneth Yellis, "Museum Education," in *The Museum: A Reference Guide,* ed. Michael Shapiro (Westport, Conn.: Greenwood Press, 1990), 169–170.

31. Jean Weber, "Changing Roles and Attitudes," in *Gender Perspectives: Essays on Women in Museums,* ed. Jane Glaser and Artemis Zenetou (Washington, D.C.: Smithsonian Institution Press, 1994), 34; Albertine Burget, "A Study of the Administrative Role of Directors of Education Departments in Non-School Cultural Organizations" (dissertation, Loyola University, 1986), 19.

32. Lillian Miller, introduction to *Gender Perspectives,* 10; Kendall Taylor, "Pioneering Efforts of Early Museum Women," in *Gender Perspectives,* 13.

33. Eilean Hooper-Greenhill, *Museum and Gallery Education* (London: Leicester University Press, 1994), 9; Yellis, "Museum Education," 168–69.

34. Alexander, *Museums in Motion,* 13; Yellis, "Museum Education," 169.

35. Paul Rea to Barbara Bragg, 11 March 1911, Bragg-Rea Correspondence, Laura Bragg Papers, CMLA; *Bulletin* (1913); Laura Bragg to Lyman Bragg, 3 October 1916, Laura Bragg Papers, SCHS.

36. *Bulletin* 7, no. 4 (April 1911): 31; Waddell interview, 30 October 1971; *Bulletin* 8 (January 1912): 8, 16.

37. Waddell, personal diary, 15 August 1976 and May 1977.

38. Laura Bragg to Paul Rea, 29 June 1911, Bragg-Rea Correspondence, Laura Bragg Papers, CMLA.

39. Paul Rea to Mary Vardrine McBee, 7 July 1911, Directors' Correspondence, Education Department, CMLA; Mary Vardrine McBee to Paul Rea, 13 July 1911, Directors' Correspondence, Education Department, CMLA.

40. Laura Bragg to Paul Rea, 11 July 1911, Bragg-Rea Correspondence, Laura Bragg Papers, CMLA; Paul Rea to Mary Vardrine McBee, 10 October 1911, Directors' Correspondence, Education Department, CMLA; Mary Vardrine McBee, 10 October 1911; Mary Vardrine McBee to Paul Rea, 26 October 1911, Directors' Correspondence, Education Department, CMLA.

41. Laura Bragg to Paul Rea, 11 July 1911; Laura Bragg to Paul Rea, 3 August 1911, Bragg-Rea Correspondence, Laura Bragg Papers, CMLA; Laura Bragg to Paul Rea, 9 August 1911, Bragg-Rea Correspondence, Laura Bragg Papers, CMLA.

42. Laura Bragg to Paul Rea, 3 August 1911; Laura Bragg to Paul Rea, 9 August 1911; Paul Rea to Laura Bragg, 7 July 1911, Bragg-Rea Correspondence, Laura Bragg Papers, CMLA.

43. Laura Bragg to Paul Rea, 9 August 1911, Bragg-Rea Correspondence, Laura Bragg Papers, CMLA.

44. Ibid; Fraser, *Charleston! Charleston!,* 353.

45. Laura Bragg to Paul Rea, 2 September 1911, Bragg-Rea Correspondence, Laura Bragg Papers, CMLA.

46. *Bulletin* 7, no. 6 (October 1911): 44.

47. Laura Bragg to Paul Rea, 2 September 1911.

48. *Bulletin* 8, no. 1 (January 1912): 14–15; Laura Bragg to Lyman Bragg, 18 December 1911, Laura Bragg Papers, SCHS; *Bulletin* 7, no. 8 (December 1911): 63.

49. Laura Bragg to Lyman Bragg, 13 May 1912, Laura Bragg Papers, SCHS; Laura Bragg to Paul Rea, 29 March 1912, Bragg-Rea Correspondence, Laura Bragg Papers, CMLA.

50. Laura Bragg to Lyman Bragg, 13 May 1912.

51. Ibid.

52. Laura Bragg to Paul Rea, 27 July 1912; Laura Bragg to Paul Rea, 31 August 1912, Bragg-Rea Correspondence, Laura Bragg Papers, CMLA; Laura Bragg, to Lyman Bragg, 8 August 1912, Laura Bragg Papers, SCHS.

53. Laura Bragg to Paul Rea, 2 August 15, 14 July 1915, Bragg-Rea Correspondence, Laura Bragg Papers, CMLA; Laura Bragg to G. P. Putnam's Sons, 15 June 1915, Laura Bragg Papers, CMLA.

54. Amy Woods to Barbara Bragg, 26 August 1912, Bragg-Rea Correspondence, Laura Bragg Papers, CMLA; *1910–1911 Civic Club Program,* 13, Box 824, Office of Records and Archives, Charleston County School District, Charleston (hereafter cited as CCSD).

55. *Bulletin* 8, no. 8 (December 1912): 70–71.

56. *Bulletin* 3, no. 5 (December 1907): 80; *Bulletin* 4, no. 5 (December 1908): 74.

57. *Bulletin* 8, no. 8 (December 1912): 70–71.

58. A.B. Rhett to Laura Bragg, 29 November 1913, Directors' Correspondence, Education 1910–1970, CMLA; Grace Dobbins, interview by author, 10 February 1998.

59. William A. Link, "Privies, Progressivism, and Public Schools: Health Reform and Education in the Rural South, 1909–1920," *Journal of Southern History* 54, no. 4 (November 1988): 641; South Carolina State Department of Education, *Thirty-Second Annual Report, 1900* (Columbia, 1901), 12–13; Division of Instruction, *History and Development of Negro Education in South Carolina* (Columbia: South Carolina Department of Education, 1949), 7.

60. Ernest McPherson Lander, *Perspectives in South Carolina History: The First 300 Years* (Columbia: University of South Carolina Press, 1973), 127–28; Kirby, 103; Newby, 86.

61. Leon F. Litwack, *Trouble in Mind: Black Southerners in the Age of Jim Crow* (New York: A. A. Knopf, 1998), 52–113; Fraser, *Charleston! Charleston!,* 329; Jack Temple Kirby, *Darkness at the Dawning: Race and Reform in the Progressive South* (Philadelphia: J. B. Lippincott, 1972), 100, 103.

62. Edmund Drago, *Initiative, Paternalism, and Race Relations: Charleston's Avery Normal Institute* (Athens: University of Georgia Press, 1990), 180; Lander, 128–129; O'Neill, "From the Shadow of Slavery," 84.

63. O'Neill, "From the Shadow of Slavery," 175–76, 180; Fraser, *Charleston! Charleston!,* 349, 360.

64. Duffy, "Charleston Politics," 18–20; see Drago, *Initiative, Paternalism, and Race Relations,* 175–76 for a full description of this episode; Laura Bragg to Wallace Rogers, 18 June 1930, Directors' Correspondence, Attendance, CMLA.

65. Lander, 123; Asa Gordon, *Sketches of Negro Life and History in South Carolina,* 2d ed. (Columbia: University of South Carolina Press, 1971), 106–108; Louise Allen, "Laura Bragg's Intellectual Revolution: Bridging the Color Line at the Charleston Museum," paper presented at the annual meeting of the South Carolina Historical Association, Columbia, S.C., March 1999.

66. *Bulletin* 8, no. 8 (December, 1912): 72–74.

67. Laura Bragg to Paul Rea, 3 September 1912, Bragg-Rea Correspondence; Laura Bragg Papers, CMLA.

68. Sarah Bragg to Lyman Bragg, 28 July 1913, Laura Bragg Papers, SCHS; Francis Weston to Paul Rea, 25 July 1913, Directors' Correspondence, Francis Weston, CMLA; 1914 *City Directory,* CCPL; Elton Littell to Paul Rea, 14 August 1913, Bragg-Rea Correspondence, Laura Bragg Papers, CMLA; Paul Rea to Elton Littell, 20 August 1913, Bragg-Rea Correspondence, Laura Bragg Papers, CMLA.

69. 1914 *City Directory,* CCPL; Belle Heyward to Laura Bragg, 4 August 1913, Laura Bragg Papers, SCHS.

70. Barbara Bragg to Paul Rea, 12 September 1913, Bragg-Rea Correspondence, Laura Bragg Papers, CMLA; *Bulletin* 9, no. 6 (October 1913): 51.

71. Laura Bragg to Lyman Bragg, 20 October 1913, Laura Bragg Papers, SCHS.

72. Sarah Bragg to Laura Bragg, 3 January 1928, 27 January 1928, Laura Bragg Papers, SCHS; Laura Bragg to Lyman Bragg, 14 September 1918, 7 October 1918, Laura Bragg Papers, SCHS; Ernest Bragg to Laura Bragg, 12 February 1928, Laura Bragg Papers, SCHS.

73. Laura Bragg to Lyman Bragg, 23 November 1913, Laura Bragg Papers, SCHS.

74. Martha Vicinus, "They Wonder to Which Sex I Belong: The Historical Roots of the Modern Lesbian Identity," *Feminist Studies* 18 (1992): 482; Waddell diary, 15 August 1976.

75. Lillian Faderman, *Romantic Friendships,* 205, 187; Newton, 561.

76. Smith-Rosenberg, *Disorderly Conduct,* 278; Vicinus, "They Wonder," 476; Lillian Faderman, "Nineteenth-Century Boston Marriages as a Possible Lesson for Today," in *Boston Marriages: Romantic But Asexual Relationships Among Contemporary Lesbians,* ed. Esther Rothblum and Kathleen Brehony (Amherst: University of Massachusetts Press, 1993), 30.

77. *Bulletin* 10, no. 1 (January 1914): 14; Laura Bragg to Lyman Bragg, 18 December 1911, Laura Bragg Papers, SCHS.

78. Laura Bragg to Ned Hyer, 8 January 1914, Directors' Correspondence, Edwin Hyer, CMLA; "A Charleston Sculptor," *The Post,* 5 October 1915, Museum Clipping Book, CMLA.

79. Laura Bragg to Lyman Bragg, 19 February 1914, Laura Bragg Papers, SCHS.

80. Bulletin issued by the first class of Simmons College, May 1914, 4, RG 14, LOC 129, SCA.

81. Laura Bragg to Lyman Bragg, 8 April 1914.

82. Laura Bragg to Lyman Bragg, 2 June 1914, Laura Bragg Papers, SCHS; *Exeter Newsletter,* 31 July 1914, Exeter Historical Society, Exeter, N.H.; Laura Bragg to Paul Rea, 28 July 1914, and Paul Rea to Laura Bragg, 12 August 1914, Bragg-Rea Correspondence, Laura Bragg Papers, CMLA.

83. Laura Bragg to Paul Rea, 28 July 1914, Bragg-Rea Correspondence, Laura Bragg Papers, CMLA, and Laura Bragg to Lyman Bragg, 3 September 1914, Laura Bragg Papers, SCHS.

84. *Exeter Newletter,* 31 July 1914, and Laura Bragg to Lyman Bragg, 1 October 1919, Laura Bragg Papers, SCHS; Barbara Bragg Ottum to Mary Hollings, 27 June 1978, personal copy.

85. Paul Rea to Laura Bragg, 9 September 1914, Bragg-Rea Correspondence, Laura Bragg Papers, CMLA.

86. *Bulletin* 10, no. 8 (December 1914): 67.

87. Ibid.; *Bulletin* 11, no. 1 (January 1915): 9–10.

88. *Bulletin* 11, no. 1 (January 1915): 8.

89. Joseph F. Kett, "Women and the Progressive Impulse in Southern Education," in *The Web of Southern Social Relations,* ed. Walter J. Fraser, R. Frank Saunders, and Jon L. Wakelyn (Athens: University of Georgia Press, 1985), 168.

90. Ibid., 171–73; H.O. Strohecker, *Present Day Public Education in the County and City of Charleston 1929* (Charleston: Charleston County Board of Education, 1929), 21; Laura Bragg to J.H. Hope, 8 October 1928, Directors' Correspondence, State Department of Education, CMLA.

91. Martin S. Dworkin, ed., *Dewey on Education* (New York: Teachers College Press, 1959), 43; Link, "Privies," 637; Herbert M. Kliebard, *The Struggle for the American Curriculum, 1893–1958,* 2d ed., (New York: Routledge, 1995), 233.

92. Link, "Privies," 637, 641; Kett, 173–74.

93. George Thomas Kurian, *Datepedia of the United States, 1790–2000: America Year by Year* (Lanham, Md.: Bernam, 1994), 145; Albert Sanders, interview by author, 13 May 1997, SP.

94. Myers interview.

95. Abbie Christensen to Laura Bragg, [9 December 1914], Undated Correspondence, Laura Bragg Papers, CMLA; 12 February 1915 Program, Laura Bragg Papers, SCHS. Also see Monica Maria Tetzlaff, "Cultivating A New South: Abbie Holmes Christensen and the Reconstruction of Race and Gender in a Southern Region, 1852–1938" (dissertation, University of Pennsylvania, 1995).

96. Sidney Bland, *Preserving Charleston's Past and Shaping its Future: The Life and Times of Susan Pringle Frost* (Columbia: University of South Carolina Press, 1999), 28–30.

97. Hall, "Partial Truths," 15; Anne Firor Scott, *Making the Invisible Woman Visible* (Urbana: University of Illinois Press, 1984), 220; Freedman, "New Woman," 377.

98. Mary Martha Thomas, 2–3.; Scott, *Invisible Woman,* 219; Scott, *Southern Lady,* 225.

99. Bland, *Preserving Charleston's Past,* 57.

100. Myers interview.

101. Ibid; Darlene Gardner, "Though Different, Sisters had Same Goals," *News and Courier,* 7 October 1984, Hinson Clippings, CLS.

102. Francis Brenner, interview with author, tape recording, 1 March 1999.

103. Laura Bragg to Bragg family, 11 February 1915, Laura Bragg Papers, SCHS; Brenner interview.

104. Brenner interview; Laura Bragg to Lyman Bragg, 25 February 1915, Laura Bragg Papers, SCHS.

105. Brenner interview; Frank Durham, *DuBose Heyward:The Man Who Wrote Porgy* (Port Washington, N.Y.: Kennikat Press, 1965), 3, 5.

106. Paul Rea to Francis Weston, 19 June 1915, CMLA; Paul Rea to Laura Bragg, 1 May 1915, Bragg-Rea Correspondence, Laura Bragg Papers, CMLA; College of Charleston Academic Affairs, Museum Financial Statements, Special Collections, College of Charleston Library, Charleston, S.C. (hereafter cited as COC).

107. "Agreement Adopted by the Board of Trustees of the College of Charleston at a meeting held March 9, 1915," 1, College of Charleston Academic Affairs, Museum-Resolutions, Box 145, Folder 10, COC.

108. *Bulletin* 11, no. 3 (March 1915): 21-26; Alexander, *Museums in Motion,* 13; Minutes of the Charleston Museum, May 1917, CMLA; "4,000 Students in University Here," *The Post,* 10 May 1915, Museum Clipping Book, CMLA; "Nature Study at Museum," *The American,* 3 July 1921, Museum Clipping Book, CMLA.

109. Laura Bragg to Paul Rea, undated letter, Bragg-Rea Correspondence, Laura Bragg Papers, CMLA.

110. Laura Bragg to Paul Rea, 24 August 1915, Bragg-Rea Correspondence, Laura Bragg Papers, CMLA.

111. Ibid.

112. Paul Rea to Laura Bragg, 4 September 1915, Bragg-Rea Correspondence, Laura Bragg Papers, CMLA

113. Faderman, *Odd Girls and Twilight Lovers: A History of Lesbian Life in Twentieth-Century America* (New York: Columbia University Press, 1991), 35; Waddell, diary, 16 June and 15 August 1976.

114. Faderman, *Odd Girls,* 35; Faderman, *Romantic Friendships,* 228, 230.

115. Faderman, *Romantic Friendships,* 187; Smith-Rosenberg, *Disorderly Conduct,* 46, 278–79, 283; Blanche Wiesen Cook, "Female Support Networks and Political Activism: Lillian Wald, Crystal Eastman, Emma Goldman, Jane Addams," *Chrysalis* 3 (1977): 48; Faderman, *Romantic Friendships,* 291.

116. Laura Bragg to Lyman Bragg, after 9 October 1915, Laura Bragg Papers, SCHS.

117. Laura Bragg to Madeline Spigner, 1 March 1915, Directors' Correspondence, Education 1910–1970, CMLA.

118. Laura Bragg to Lyman Bragg, 23 February 1916, Laura Bragg Papers, SCHS.

119. *Bulletin* 13, no. 1 (January 1917): 5, and *Bulletin* 15, no. 1 (January 1919): 8; Laura Bragg to Lyman Bragg, 23 February 1916, SCHS.

120. Laura Bragg to W.G. Pearson, 31 March 1916, Directors' Correspondence, National Association of Audubon Societies, CMLA; 1916 *City Year Book,* CCPL;

Memorandum of Educational Work of Charleston Museum, 10 November 1916, 1, Directors' Correspondence, American Association of Museums (cited hereafter as AAM) 1916, CMLA.

121. Memorandum of Educational Work of Charleston Museum, 10 November 1916, 2-3, 10, Directors' Correspondence, AAM 1916, CMLA.

122. Laura Bragg to Lyman Bragg, 26 June 1916, Laura Bragg Papers, SCHS; Laura Bragg to Lyman Bragg, 3 October 1916, Laura Bragg Papers, SCHS.

123. A. B. Rhett to J. R. Guy, 31 July 1916, Box 866, Letterpress Book, 1911–1919, CCSD; Paul Rea to Laura Bragg, 27 July 1916, and Laura Bragg to Paul Rea, 31 July 1916, Bragg, Laura, 1914–1916 Correspondence, Laura Bragg Papers, CMLA.

124. Laura Bragg to Lyman Bragg, 3 October 1916; St. Luke's Canonical Register, L-2, 113, Vault of the Parish Hall, Cathedral of St. Luke's and St. Paul's, Charleston; Laura Bragg to Paul Rea, undated letter, Bragg, Laura 1914–1916 File, Laura Bragg Papers, CMLA, and *Bulletin* 12, no. 6 (October 1916): 50.

125. Laura Bragg to Paul Rea, undated letter, Bragg, Laura 1914–1916 File, Laura Bragg Papers, CMLA, and *Bulletin* 12, no. 6 (October 1916): 50.

126. Fraser, *Charleston! Charleston!*, 360–361; Duffy, "Charleston Politics," 279–280, 355; Bland, *Preserving Charleston's Past,* 56.

127. James T. Sears and Louise Allen, "Museums, Friends, and Lovers in the New South: Laura's Web, 1909–1931," *Journal of Homosexuality* 40, no.1 (Summer 2000), 120.

128. Laura Bragg to Lyman Bragg, 22 February 1917, Laura Bragg Papers, SCHS; Lyman Bragg, 22 April 1917; Laura Bragg to Lyman Bragg, 29 December 1919, Laura Bragg Papers, SCHS.

129. Laura Bragg to Lyman Bragg, 22 February 1917; Laura Bragg to Lyman Bragg, 26 June 1916, Laura Bragg Papers, SCHS.

130. Laura Bragg to Lyman Bragg, 22 February 1917, and 22 April 1917, Laura Bragg Papers, SCHS.

131. Laura Bragg to Lyman Bragg, 3 September 1917, Laura Bragg Papers, SCHS.

132. Laura Bragg to Anne King Gregorie, 25 June 1917, Anne King Gregorie Papers, SCHS.

133. Ibid; Anne King Gregorie, 23 March 1918, Diary 1913–1918, Anne King Gregorie Papers, SCHS.

134. Laura Bragg to Lyman Bragg, 3 September 1917; Laura Bragg to Anne King Gregorie, 22 August 1917, Anne King Gregorie Papers, SCHS.

135. Minutes of the Charleston Museum, May 1917, CMLA.

136. Benjamin Cox to Paul Rea, 17 May 1917, Directors' Correspondece, Avery Institute, CMLA.

137. Eugene Graves, personal communication with author; March 1998; Waddell interview; Fraser, *Charleston! Charleston!*, 372.

138. Grace Dobbins, 10 February 1998, interview with author; Laura Bragg to Wallace Rogers, 18 June 1930, Directors' Correspondence, Attendance, CMLA.

139. Fred L. Brownlee, *New Day Ascending* (Boston: Pilgrim Press, 1946), 135–136; Burchill Richardson Moore, "A History of the Negro Public Schools of Charleston, South Carolina 1867–1942" (thesis, University of South Carolina, 1942), 40; Drago, *Initiative, Paternalism, and Race Relations,* 119.

140. *Bulletin* 14, no. 2 (February 1918): 16; Laura Bragg to Lyman Bragg, 1 February 1918, Laura Bragg Papers, SCHS, and Simmons College Review, November 1918, 33, SCA.

141. Laura Bragg to Lyman Bragg, 1 February 1918, Laura Bragg Papers, SCHS. The most common reason for this procedure is endometriosis, which causes intense abdominal pain. Dr. Worthington, personal communication with author, 14 August 1997; Dr. Meyer and Dr. Wilson, personal communication with author, 13 August 1997.

142. Smith-Rosenberg, *Disorderly Conduct,* 258–59; Florence Milligan to Laura Bragg, 16 October 1920, Laura Bragg Papers, CMLA.

143. *Exeter Newsletter,* 5 April 1918, Exeter Historical Society, Exeter, N.H.; Laura Bragg to Lyman Bragg, 14 April 1918, 1 July 1918, Laura Bragg Papers, SCHS.

144. Laura Bragg to Lyman Bragg, 4 September 1918, 8 September 1918, Laura Bragg Papers, SCHS; Laura Bragg to Anne King Gregorie, 24 September 1918, Anne King Gregorie Papers, SCHS; Fraser, *Charleston! Charleston!,* 363.

145. Laura Bragg to Lyman Bragg, 9 October 1918, 25 November 1918, 10 December 1918, Laura Bragg Papers, SCHS.

146. Lyman Bragg to Laura Bragg, 20 January 1919, and Laura Bragg to Lyman Bragg, 21 February 1919, Laura Bragg Papers, SCHS.

147. Laura Bragg to Lyman Bragg, 21 February 1919, Laura Bragg Papers, SCHS; Laura Bragg, "Oakland," 16 March 1919, Laura Bragg Papers, SCHS.

148. Laura Bragg, interview by Ralph Nordlund, Charleston, S.C., ca. 1971, SP; Harriett Monroe to Laura Bragg, 18 December 1919, Laura Bragg Papers, SCHS; Headly Morris Cox, Jr., "The Charleston Poetic Renascence 1920–1930" (dissertation, University of Pennsylvania, 1958), 16–17, Caroliniana Library, University of South Carolina, Columbia; Waddell, personal diary, 15 August 1976.

149. Laura Bragg to Lyman Bragg, 18 July 1919, 1 October 1919, Laura Bragg Papers, SCHS.

150. *Bulletin* 16, no. 1 (January 1920): 13–14.

151. Cox, "Charleston Poetic Renascence," 17.

152. Sears and Allen, "Museums, Friends, and Lovers," 122.

153. Ibid.

154. Frank Durham, "The Rise of DuBose Heyward and Fall of the Poetry Society of South Carolina," *Mississippi Quarterly* 19, no. 2 (1966): 66–78.

155. Frank Durham, *DuBose Heyward: The Man Who Wrote "Porgy"* (Port Washington, N.Y.: Kennikat Press, 1965), 22; John Bennett to Laura Bragg, 6 December 1921, Laura Bragg Papers, SCHS; Dubose Heyward to Laura Bragg, 14 June 1921, Laura Bragg Papers, SCHS.

156. Sears and Allen, "Museums, Friends, and Lovers," 123.

157. Hart, "Weighing Her Merits."

158. Sears and Allen, "Museums, Friends, and Lovers," 123.

159. Ibid.

160. Cox, "Charleston Poetic Renascence," 19.

161. Sarah Bragg to Belle Heyward, 28 August 1920, Laura Bragg Papers, SCHS; Belle Heyward to Laura Bragg, 20 July 1920, Laura Bragg Papers, SCHS.

162. Laura Bragg to Lyman Bragg, 20 February 1920, Laura Bragg Papers, SCHS.

163. Minutes of the Charleston Museum, 8 March 1920, CMLA; Minutes of the Charleston Museum, 21 March 1919, CMLA.

164. Paul Rea to Laura Bragg, 28 July 1920, Bragg, Laura 1919–1921 File, Laura Bragg Papers, CMLA.

165. Paul Rea to Laura Bragg, 28 July 1920; Minutes of the Charleston Museum, 8 March 1920, CMLA.

166. Paul Rea to Laura Bragg, 27 August 1920, Bragg, Laura M. 1919–1921 File, Laura Bragg Papers, CMLA.

Chapter 3

1. Fraser, *Charleston! Charleston!*, 361; Tobias, "Laura M. Bragg, Rejuvenator of Museums."

2. Fraser, *Charleston! Charleston!*, 348, 366; Boggs, "John Patrick Grace," 151–52.

3. Fraser, *Charleston! Charleston!*, 368; Boggs, "John Patrick Grace," 245.

4. Fraser, *Charleston! Charleston!*, 348; Duffy, "Charleston Politics," 28.

5. Fraser, *Charleston! Charleston!*, 348; Boggs, "John Patrick Grace," 165; Minutes of the Charleston Museum, 7 December 1921, CMLA.

6. Muncy, *Creating a Female Dominion,* xiii; Ryan, 232; Virginia Lee Ridgeway McCombs, "Reinventing the Wheel: The Redefinition of Womanhood in the 1920s" (dissertation, University of Oklahoma Graduate College, 1987), 32, 37.

7. Kendall Taylor, "Pioneering Efforts of Early Museum Women," in *Gender Perspectives,* 21; Jean Weber, "Images of Women in Museums," in *Women's Changing Roles in Museums,* ed. E. C. Hicks (Washington, D.C.: Smithsonian Institution Press, 1986), 21; Kendall Taylor, "To Create Credibility," *Museum News* 69 (1990): 42.

8. Weber, "Images," 33; Taylor, *Gender Perspectives,* 13, 17; Mary Gordon, "An Inside View," in *Gender Perspectives,* 110.

9. McCombs, 36; Muncy, *Creating a Female Dominion,* xiii.

10. *Simmons College Review* 3, no. 2 (December 1920): 88, SCA; *Bulletin* 18, no. 1–2 (January–February 1921): 1.

11. Laura Bragg to Alice Kendall, 16 April 1921, Directors' Correspondence, Archeology Indian Excavation, CMLA; Laura Bragg to Lyman Bragg, 14 December 1921, Laura Bragg Papers, SCHS.

12. *Bulletin* 18, no. 1–2 (January–February 1921): 1, and Rea, *The Museum and the Community,* 74, 274; Laura Bragg to Harold Madison, 11 April 1921, and Laura Bragg to Harold Madison, 14 April 1921, Directors' Correspondence, AAM 1921, CMLA.

13. *Bulletin* 18, no. 1–2 (January–February 1921): 2.

14. Helen von Kolnitz to Richard F. Bach, 15 April 1921, Directors' Correspondence, Metropolitan Museum, CMLA.

15. "Miss Bragg Highly Praised," 3 December 1921, Museum Clipping Book, CMLA.

16. Helen von Klonitz to Richard F. Bach, 15 April 1921.

17. 1930 *U.S. Census,* State Compendium for South Carolina (Washington, D.C.: Government Printing Office, 1931), 3; Helen von Kolnitz to Richard F. Bach, 15 April 1921.

18. Caroline Sinkler to Laura Bragg, 17 November 1920, Directors' Correspondence, Caroline Sinkler, CMLA.

19. Laura Bragg to Caroline Sinkler, 29 November 1920, Directors' Correspondence, Caroline Sinkler, CMLA; Laura Bragg to John Cotton Dana, 4 February 1921, Directors' Correspondence, Newark Museum Association, CMLA; Laura Bragg to John P. Grace, 19 February 1921, Directors' Correspondence, John P. Grace, CMLA.

20. John P. Grace to F. A. Whiting, 12 May 1923, Directors' Correspondence, Cleveland Museum of Art, CMLA; Laura Bragg to John P. Grace, 19 February 1921, Directors' Correspondence, John Grace, CMLA..

21. John P. Grace to F. A. Whiting, 12 May 1923; Laura Bragg to John P. Grace, 19 February 1921, Directors' Correspondence, John P. Grace, CMLA; Laura Bragg to Alice Kendall, 4 May 1921, Directors' Correspondence, Indian Work, CMLA; "Museum Plan for Children," *Charleston Evening Post,* 19 March 1921, Museum Clipping Book, CMLA.

22. Cox, "Charleston Poetic Renascence," 19; Durham, 24; Fraser, *Charleston! Charleston!,* 367.

23. Cox, "Charleston Poetic Renascence," 23; Fraser, *Charleston! Charleston!,* 36; *Poetry Society Yearbook* 1 (1922–23): 108, CLS; *Year Book of the Poetry Society of South Carolina* (October 1921): 12–13, CCPL.

24. Cox, "Charleston Poetic Renascence," 23; Fraser, *Charleston! Charleston!,* 367; Laura Bragg to Caroline Sinkler, 4 February 1921; Waddell interview, 30 October 1971.

25. Laura Bragg to Caroline Sinkler, 4 February 1921; DuBose Heyward to Laura Bragg, undated, Laura Bragg Papers, SCHS; DuBose Heyward to Laura Bragg, 4 September 1921, Laura Bragg Papers, SCHS.

26. John Bennett to family, July 1921, 10 August 1921, 28 August 1921, 1 September 1921, 20 September 1921, and 11 September 1921, John Bennett Papers, SCHS.

27. Yates Snowden to Laura Bragg, 9 September 1921, Directors' Correspondence, Yates Snowden, CMLA; James Henry Rice to Laura Bragg, 5 February 1923, Directors' Correspondence, James Henry Rice, CMLA.

28. "The Children's Room at the Charleston Museum," undated document, Directors' Correspondence, Education Department, CMLA.

29. Waddell interview, 30 October 1971.

30. Boggs, "John Patrick Grace," 167.

31. Laura Bragg to B. F. Cox, 20 December 1921, Directors' Correspondence, Avery Institute, CMLA; "Report of the Director of the Museum for the Year 1921," 1921 *City Year Book,* 371, CMLA.

32. Barbara Belknap, interview by author, tape recording, 29 May 1997, SP; undated document, Bragg-Preston Correspondence, Laura Bragg Papers, CMLA (this information was not published in her 1922 Directors' Report in the *City Year Book*); Laura Bragg to Wallace Rogers, 18 June 1930; Drago, *Initiative, Paternalism, and Race Relations,* 193.

33. Laura Bragg to Lyman Bragg, 14 December 1921, Laura Bragg Papers, SCHS.

34. Laura Bragg to Caroline Sinkler, 25 January 1922, Directors' Correspondence, Caroline Sinkler, CMLA; Durham, 34.

35. *Museum Work,* May-June 1922, 33 Box 15, 87–165, Record Unit 7450, American Association of Museums Records, 1906–1985, Office of Smithsonian Archives, Washington, D.C. (hereafter cited as SIA).

36. Laura Bragg to Frederic Whiting, 5 July 1922, 2, Directors' Correspondence,

Cleveland Museum of Art, CMLA; Laura Bragg to Anna Klotz, 11 July 1922, Bragg, Laura 1922 File, Laura Bragg Papers, CMLA.

37. Robert Whitelaw and Alice Levkoff, *Charleston Come Hell or High Water* (Charleston: R. L. Bryan, 1975), 152; Fraser, *Charleston! Charleston!*, 368, and Laura Bragg to Frederic Whiting, 5 July 1922, Directors' Correspondence, Cleveland Museum of Art, CMLA.

38. Hart, "Weighing Her Merits"; Laura Bragg to T. R. Hoyt, 19 December 1922, Directors' Correspondence, AAM 1922, CMLA.

39. Undated document, Directors' Correspondence, Education 1910–1970, CMLA; Emma Richardson to Laura Bragg, undated, Undated Correspondence, Laura Bragg Papers, CMLA.

40. Laura Bragg to Caroline Sinkler, 3 February 1923, Directors' Correspondence, Caroline Sinkler, CMLA; Laura Bragg to Frederic Whiting, 13 February 1923, and Laura Bragg to Frederic Whiting, 5 February 1923, Directors' Correspondence, Cleveland Museum of Art, CMLA.

41. Laura Bragg to David Doar, 27 March 1923, Directors' Correspondence, David Doar, CMLA; C. N. Hastie to Laura Bragg, 24 February 1923, Laura Bragg to L. V. Coleman, 28 May 1923, H. L. Beck to Laura Bragg, 23 March 1923, Directors' Correspondence, AAM 1923, CMLA.

42. Belle Heyward to Laura Bragg, Easter 1923, Laura Bragg Papers, SCHS; Minutes of the 1923 AAM Annual Meeting, 102, Box 41, 87–165, Record Unit 7450, American Association of Museums Records, 1906–1985, SIA; Minutes of the 1923 AAM Annual Meeting, 103–104, Directors' Correspondence, AAM 1923, CMLA; Samuel G. Stoney, *Plantations of the Carolina Low Country* (Charleston: Carolina Art Association, 1938), 59; Durham, 107.

43. *Museum Work,* May–June 1923, 24–25; Laura Bragg, untitled essay [1930–1931], Laura Bragg Papers, SCHS.

44. *Museum Work,* May–June 1923, 24–25, CMLA; Laura Bragg Papers, SCHS; Waddell interview, 30 October 1971.

45. Minutes of the 1923 AAM Annual Meeting, 142, 32, Directors' Correspondence, AAM 1923, CMLA.

46. L.V. Coleman to Laura Bragg, 13 April 1923, Directors' Correspondence, AAM 1923, CMLA; Rebe Frost to Laura Bragg, 4 March 1923, Laura Bragg Papers, CMLA.

47. Laura Bragg to F. A. Whiting, 19 April 1923, Directors' Correspondence, Cleveland Museum of Art, CMLA; Laura Bragg to L.V. Coleman, 23 April 1923 and 4 May 1923, Directors' Correspondence, AAM 1923, CMLA.

48. Mary Martin Hendricks, interview by author, tape recording, 4 November 1996, SP; Globe Phone Company to Laura Bragg, 14 July 1925, 1925 Correspondence, Laura Bragg Papers, CMLA.

49. Laura Bragg to F. A. Whiting, 19 April 1923; Directors' Correspondence, Cleveland Museum of Art, CMLA.

50. Ibid.; Fraser, *Charleston! Charleston!*, 369–70; Laura Bragg to F. A. Whiting, 2 November 1923, Directors' Correspondence, Cleveland Museum of Art, CMLA.

51. Mary Martin Hendricks, interview by author, tape recording, 4 November 1996,

SP; Herbert interview; F. A. Whiting to Laura Bragg, 14 April 1923, Directors' Correspondence, Cleveland Museum of Art, CMLA; Waddell, personal diary, September 1976.

52. Boyd Saunders and Ann McAden, *Alfred Hutty and the Charleston Renaissance* (Orangeburg, S.C.: Sandlapper Press, 1990).

53. "The Children's Room at The Charleston Museum," undated document; Laura Bragg to F. A. Whiting, 4 May 1923, Directors' Correspondence, Cleveland Museum of Art, CMLA; Laura Bragg to Ned Jennings, 16 February 1923, and Ned Jennings to Carnegie Corporation, 25 November 1926, Directors' Correspondence, E. I. R. Jennings, CMLA.

54. Waddell interview, 30 October 1971; Laura Bragg to F. A. Whiting, 4 May 1923, Directors' Correspondence, Cleveland Museum of Art, CMLA.

55. Laura Bragg to F. A. Whiting, 4 May 1923, Directors' Correspondence, Cleveland Museum of Art, CMLA.

56. L. V. Coleman to Laura Bragg, 4 September 1923, Directors' Correspondence, AAM 1923, CMLA; Laura Bragg to F. A. Whiting, 2 November 1923, Directors' Correspondence, Cleveland Museum of Art, CMLA.

57. Belle Heyward to Laura Bragg, 2 August 1923, Laura Bragg Papers, SCHS; Belle Heyward to Laura Bragg, 23 September 1923, Laura Bragg Papers, SCHS; Belle Heyward to Laura Bragg, 9 October 1923, Laura Bragg Papers, SCHS.

58. Meigs Russell to Laura Bragg, 3 August 1923, Directors' Correspondence, Charleston Chamber of Commerce, CMLA; Clara Mitchell to Laura Bragg, 2 November 1923, Bragg, Laura 1923 File, Laura Bragg Papers, CMLA; Laura Bragg, to L. V. Coleman, 17 October 1923, Directors' Correspondence, AAM 1923, CMLA; Laura Bragg to F. A. Whiting, 2 November 1923.

59. Belle Heyward to Lyman Bragg, 9 January 1924, Laura Bragg Papers, SCHS.

60. Fraser, *Charleston! Charleston!*, 370.

61. Fraser, *Charleston! Charleston!*, 370, 374; Boggs, "John Patrick Grace," 166.

62. Eugenia W. Day to Laura Bragg, 22 January 1924, Laura Bragg to Eugenia W. Day, 25 January 1924, and Eugenia W. Day to Laura Bragg, 30 January 1924, Bragg, Laura 1923 File, Laura Bragg Papers, CMLA; Florence Junior to Laura Bragg, 30 June 1924, and Laura Bragg to Florence Junior, 7 July 1924, Bragg, Laura 1924 File, Laura Bragg Papers, CMLA.

63. "House Party," *Charleston Evening Post,* 1 January 1924, vertical files, CCPL.

64. Laura Bragg to L. V. Coleman, 2 March 1923 and 17 October 1923, Directors' Correspondence, AAM 1923, CMLA; Waddell, personal diary, 12 November 1975.

65. Assistant treasurer to Willard Hotel, 5 May 1924, Directors' Correspondence, AAM 1924, CMLA; Laura Bragg to Henry Dwight, 10 June 1924, Directors' Correspondence, Henry R. Dwight, CMLA; Minutes of American Association of Museums Nineteenth Annual Meeting, 43–44, 148, Box 15, 87–165, Record Unit 7450, American Association of Museums Records, 1905–1985, SIA.

66. L. V. Coleman to Laura Bragg, 29 May 1924, Directors' Correspondence, AAM 1924, CMLA.

67. Laura Bragg to Calvin Bragg Valentine, 28 February 1923; Laura Bragg to Mary Crinigan, 4 September 1924, Directors' Correspondence, Valentine Museum, CMLA.

68. Laura Bragg to Mary Crinigan, 4 September 1924, Directors' Correspondence, Valentine Museum, CMLA.

69. Laura Bragg to L.V. Coleman, 20 September 1924, Directors' Correspondence, AAM 1924, CMLA.

70. "Mann S. Valentine and His Museum," notes for fiftieth anniversary publicity, Record Group II, Early History and Governance, Box 2–1, Valentine Museum Archives, Richmond (hereafter cited as VMA); L.V. Coleman to Laura Bragg, 23 September 1924, Directors' Correspondence, AAM 1924, CMLA; Laura Bragg to Emma Richardson, 24 November 1924, Bragg, Laura 1924 File, Laura Bragg Papers, CMLA; L. V. Coleman to Laura Bragg, 8 October 1924, Directors' Correspondence, AAM 1924, CMLA.

71. Laura Bragg to Emma Richardson, 24 November 1924, and Bragg to Emma Richardson, 6 December 1924, Bragg, Laura 1924 File, Laura Bragg Papers; Laura Bragg to the Eddys, 18 February 1925, Bragg, Laura 1925 File, Laura Bragg Papers, CMLA.

72. Laura Bragg to C. R. Richards, 27 December 1924, Directors' Correspondence, AAM 1924, CMLA; Jouett Cannon to Laura Bragg, 16 January 1925, Directors' Correspondence, Directors' Correspondence, AAM 1925, CMLA. Laura Bragg to Marietta Jackson, 27 January 1925, Bragg, Laura 1925 File, Laura Bragg Papers, CMLA.

73. Laura Bragg to C. R. Richards, 27 December 1924, Directors' Correspondence, AAM 1924, CMLA.

74. Nordlund interview, ca. 1971.

75. Karen Greene, *Porter-Gaud School: The Next Step* (Easley, S.C.: Southern Historical Press, 1982), 51; Waddell, personal diary, 9 May 1976.

76. Waddell, personal diary, 15 August 1976.

77. Anita Pollitzer to Laura Bragg, 26 November 1924, Laura Bragg Papers, SCHS; Alfred Hutty to Laura Bragg, 7 November 1924, Directors' Correspondence, Alfred Hutty, CMLA; Belle Heyward to Laura Bragg, 25 December 1925, Laura Bragg Papers, SCHS.

78. Nordlund interview, ca. 1971; Durham, 27; John Bennett to family, 16 April 1925, John Bennett Papers, SCHS.

79. L.V. Coleman to Laura Bragg, 17 January 1925, Laura Bragg to L.V. Coleman, 24 January 1925, and L.V. Coleman to Laura Bragg, 31 March 1925, Directors' Correspondence, AAM 1925, CMLA.

80. Laura Bragg to L.V. Coleman, 18 April 1925, and L.V. Coleman to Laura Bragg, 21 April 1925, Directors' Correspondence, AAM 1925, CMLA.

81. Laura Bragg to L.V. Coleman, 18 April 1925, and L.V. Coleman to Laura Bragg, 21 April 1925, Directors' Correspondence, AAM 1925, CMLA.

82. L.V. Coleman to Laura Bragg, 21 April 1925, Laura Bragg to Frederic V. Whiting, 5 February 1923, and Laura Bragg to L. V. Coleman, 18 April 1925, Directors' Correspondence, AAM 1925, CMLA.

83. Laura Bragg to L.V. Coleman, 30 April 1925, and L.V. Coleman to Laura Bragg, 4 May 1925, Directors' Correspondence, AAM 1925, CMLA; L. V. Coleman, *The Museum in America: A Critical Study* (Washington, D.C.: American Association of

Museums, 1939), 116–117; L. V. Coleman to Laura Bragg, 4 May 1925, Directors' Correspondence, AAM 1925, CMLA.

84. A. Lawrence to Laura Bragg, 30 April 1925, Bragg, Laura 1925 File, Laura Bragg Papers, CMLA; *Year Book of the Poetry Society of South Carolina,* no. 5, October 1925, 55, Charleston, S.C., CCPL; Howard A. Kelly to Laura Bragg, 23 February 1925, Directors' Correspondence, Howard Kelly, CMLA.

85. Laura Bragg to Marietta Jackson, 27 January 1925, and Laura Bragg to Eddys, 18 February 1925, Bragg, Laura 1925 File, Laura Bragg Papers, CMLA.

86. Laura Bragg to L. V. Coleman, 20 April 1923; Laura Bragg to L. V. Coleman, 4 May 1923; Laura Bragg to Eddys, 18 February 1925.

87. Laura Bragg to L. V. Coleman, 30 August 1923.

88. Laura Bragg to Louise Smith, 6 March 1925, Directors' Correspondence, Louise Barrington, CMLA; Howard Kelly to Laura Bragg, 23 February 1925, Directors' Correspondence, Howard Kelly, CMLA.

89. Laura Bragg to S. A. Barrett, 15 December 1925, Directors' Correspondence, AAM 1925, CMLA; Edward K. Putnam to Laura Bragg, 8 June 1925, Directors' Correspondence, AAM 1925, CMLA.

90. Edmere Cabana to L. V. Coleman, 9 June 1925, and Emma Richardson to L. V. Coleman, 13 June 1925, Directors' Correspondence, AAM 1925, CMLA; Edward K. Putnam to Laura Bragg, 8 June 1925, Directors' Correspondence, AAM 1925, CMLA.

91. Minutes of Regional Council Meeting, Yale Club, New York City, 12 November 1925, and Laura Bragg to the President and Executive Secretary, 6 November 1925, Directors' Correspondence, AAM 1925, CMLA; John Cotton Dana to Laura Bragg, 19 October 1925, Directors' Correspondence, New Jersey State Museum, CMLA.

92. Laura Bragg to Anne King Gregorie, undated, Anne King Gregorie Papers, SCHS; Laura Bragg to Anne King Gregorie, 12 June 1925, Anne King Gregorie Papers, SCHS.

93. Laura Bragg to Anne King Gregorie, 12 June 1925.

94. Anne King Gregorie to Laura Bragg, 15 June 1925, Anne King Gregorie Papers, SCHS.

95. Laura Bragg to Anne King Gregorie, 16 June 1925, Anne King Gregorie Papers, SCHS; Laura Bragg to Anne King Gregorie, 28 November 1925, Anne King Gregorie Papers, SCHS; Laura Bragg to S. A. Barrett, 15 December 1925.

96. "Gregorie Book Aids Library," *The State,* 29 December 1968, vertical files, CCPL; Anne King Gregorie, 22 January 1919, 1918–1936 Diary, 6, Anne King Gregorie Papers, SCHS.

97. Laura Bragg letter to E. C. L. Adams, 3 June 1925, Directors' Correspondence, E. C. L. Adams, CMLA; 1925 *City Year Book,* 246.

98. John Bennett to family, 7 April 1925, John Bennett Papers, SCHS; Laura Bragg to E. C. L. Adams, 28 February 1925, Directors' Correspondence, E. C. L. Adams, CMLA. Also see *Charleston Museum Quarterly* 1, no. 2 (1925), CMLA. For further information on Adams, see *Tales of the Congaree,* ed. Robert O'Meally (Chapel Hill: University of North Carolina Press, 1987).

99. Laura Bragg to E. C. L. Adams, 3 June 1925, Directors' Correspondence, E. C. L. Adams, CMLA.

100. Laura Bragg to Harriet Monroe, 8 June 1925, Directors' Correspondence, E. C. L. Adams, CMLA.

101. Laura Bragg to David Doar, 16 June 1925, Directors' Correspondence, David Doar, CMLA; Minutes of the Charleston Museum, 8 December 1926, CMLA; Minutes of the Charleston Museum, 8 December 1926, CMLA; A. S. Salley to Laura Bragg, 16 May 1929, Laura Bragg Papers, SCHS; David Doar, *Rice and Rice Planting in the South Carolina Low Country* (Charleston: The Charleston Museum, 1936), 5.

102. Laura Bragg to David Doar, 16 June 1925, Directors' Correspondence, David Doar, CMLA; Laura Bragg to Calvin Valentine, 14 December 1925, Valentine Reorganization, VMA.

103. William O'Neill, *Everyone Was Brave: A History of Feminism in America* (Chicago: Quadrangle, 1971), 300; Lasch, 57; Smith-Rosenberg, *Disorderly Conduct,* 267; Faderman, *Romantic Friendships,* 298.

104. Faderman, *Romantic Friendships,* 309; Helen Lefkowitz Horowitz, *The Power and Passion of M. Carey Thomas* (New York: Knopf, 1994), 450.

105. Faderman, *Odd Girls,* 39–40, 47; Ryan, 267; Vicinus, "They Wonder," 484; and Smith-Rosenberg, *Disorderly Conduct,* 277.

106. Faderman, *Romantic Friendships,* 314.

107. Susan George [pseudonym], interview by author, tape recording, 3 June 1997, SP; Waddell, personal diary, 14 January 1977.

108. Waddell, personal diary, 14 January 1977. Barbara Belknap, interview by author, tape recording, 29 May 1997, SP; Nancy Smith, interview by author, tape recording, 9 June 1997, SP.

109. "Former Gibbes Director, Miss Helen McCormack, Dies," *News and Courier,* 23 January 1974, Hinson Clippings, Biography, CLS; 1925 *City Year Book* of Charleston, 245, CCPL; poem, "Remembering Snug Harbor August 1925," written by Helen McCormack, 11 August 1940, Laura Bragg Papers, SCHS; Helen McCormack to Laura Bragg, 25 April 1927, Laura Bragg Papers, SCHS; Laura Bragg to Alexander Ford, 29 January 1926, Directors' Correspondence, Alexander Ford, CMLA.

Chapter 4

1. Belle Heyward to Laura Bragg, undated, Laura Bragg Papers, SCHS; Sarah Bragg to Laura Bragg, 29 January 1926, Laura Bragg Papers, SCHS; Belle Heyward to Laura Bragg, 1 January 1926, Laura Bragg Papers, SCHS.

2. Belle Heyward to Laura Bragg, 1 January 1926; Minutes of the Charleston Museum, 29 April 1925, CMLA.

3. Laura Bragg to Lyman Bragg, 20 February 1926, Laura Bragg Papers, SCHS.

4. Belle Heyward to Laura Bragg, 20 July 1926, Laura Bragg Papers, SCHS.

5. Laura Bragg to Lyman Bragg, 22 September 1926, Laura Bragg Papers, SCHS.

6. Ibid.

7. Belle Heyward to Laura Bragg, 9 October 1926, Laura Bragg Papers, SCHS; DuBose Heyward to Laura Bragg, 2 January 1927, Laura Bragg Papers, SCHS; death

card for Isabel Heyward, 10 October 1926, CCPL; see Waddell's diary, 8 May 1977. Bragg claimed to have never told anyone besides Waddell the story about Faber murdering Belle. Yet she must have (or it must have been common knowledge) because Josephine Pinckney scripted the beginning of a play about Faber's murder of Belle. See Josephine Pinckney's papers at SCHS.

8. Josephine Pinckney to Hervey Allen, Christmas card, n.d., Hervey Allen Papers, University of Pittsburgh Library, Pittsburgh; John Bennett to family, 24 October 1926, and 14 November 1926, John Bennett Papers, SCHS.

9. Sarah Bragg to Laura Bragg, 4 November 1926, Laura Bragg Papers, SCHS; Anna Klotz to Laura Bragg, 8 November 1926, and Barbara Bragg to Laura Bragg, 13 November 1926, SCHS; Yates Snowden to Laura Bragg, 6 November 1926, Directors' Correspondence, Yates Snowden, CMLA.

10. Anita Pollitzer to Laura Bragg, 26 November 1926, Laura Bragg Papers, SCHS.

11. Anita Pollitzer to Laura Bragg, 21 January 1954, Laura Bragg Papers, SCHS; inscription on reverse of Doris Ulmann photograph given to Gene Waddell, 10 October 1977; Gene Waddell, personal communication, March 1999. For further discussion of Aphrodite and same-sex love, see K. J. Dover, *Greek Homosexuality* (Cambridge: Harvard University Press, 1978), 63; Mary R. Lefkowitz, *Women in Greek Myth* (Baltimore: Johns Hopkins University Press, 1986), 58, 115–17, 172.

12. Faderman, *Romantic Friendships,* 317–18, 323; Newton, 562.

13. Ryan, 277; Rayna Rapp and Ellen Ross, "The 1920s: Feminism, Consumerism, and Political Backlash in the United States," in *Women in Culture and Politics: A Century of Change,* ed. Judith Friedlander, Blanche Wiesen Cook, Alice Kessler-Harris, and Carroll Smith-Rosenberg (Bloomington: Indiana University Press, 1986), 56; Faderman, *Odd Girls,* 46, 49.

14. Nancy Sahli, "Smashing: Women's Relationships before the Fall," *Chrysalis* 8 (1979): 27; Rapp and Ross, "The 1920s," 57; Faderman, *Odd Girls,* 57.

15. Vicinus, "They Wonder," 489.

16. Laura Bragg to Lyman Bragg, 22 November 1926, Laura Bragg Papers, SCHS.

17. Lyman Bragg to Laura Bragg, 30 November 1926, Laura Bragg Papers, SCHS.

18. Laura Bragg to Granville Valentine, 17 March 1927, Directors' Correspondence, Valentine Museum, CMLA; Laura Bragg to Lyman Bragg, from 11 April 1927, Laura Bragg Papers, SCHS; Laura Bragg to L.V. Coleman, Directors' Correspondence, AAM 1927, CMLA; Francis Brenner, interview by author, tape recording, 1 March 1999.

19. Laura Bragg to Mildred Babcock, 17 November 1927, Bragg, Laura 1927 File, Laura Bragg Papers, CMLA.

20. Laura Bragg to John Maybank, 10 November 1926, Directors' Correspondence, John Maybank, CMLA; Laura Bragg to Theodora Rhoades, 26 March 1927, Bragg, Laura 1927 File, Laura Bragg Papers, CMLA.

21. Laura Bragg to Lyman Bragg, after Christmas 1926, Laura Bragg Papers, SCHS.

22. Ibid.

23. Howard Kelly to Laura Bragg, 14 May 1926 and 29 March 1927, Directors' Correspondence, Howard Kelly, CMLA; Laura Bragg to Lyman Bragg, after Christmas 1926.

24. Chia Mei Hu to Laura Bragg, 4 January 1927, Laura Bragg Collection, Citadel Archives and Museum, Charleston, S.C. (hereafter cited as CAM); Chia Mei Hu to Laura Bragg, 10 July 1927, Laura Bragg Collection, CAM.

25. John Bennett to family, 17 April 1927, John Bennett Papers, SCHS; Laura Bragg to Mrs. George Holmes, 29 June 1927, Directors' Correspondence, George Holmes, CMLA; Laura Bragg to Lyman Bragg, 11 April 1927.

26. Helen McCormack to Laura Bragg, 18 April 1927, Laura Bragg Papers, SCHS; Helen McCormack to Laura Bragg, 30 April 1927, Laura Bragg Papers, SCHS; Chia Mei Hu to Laura Bragg, 19 April 1927, Laura Bragg Collection, CAM.

27. Helen McCormack to Laura Bragg, from 22 May 1927, Laura Bragg Papers, SCHS.

28. Sears and Allen, "Museums, Friends, and Lovers,": 130.

29. John Bennett to family, 12 May 1929, John Bennett Papers, SCHS.

30. "Six Students from China Enter Here to Enter The Citadel," *News and Courier,* 21 September 1927, Laura Bragg Collection, CAM; Laura Bragg to Theodora Rhoades, 26 March 1927; Harriett Wilson, interview by author, tape recording, 30 May 1997, SP.

31. Shu Chun Liu to Laura Bragg, 6 May 1928, Laura Bragg Collection, CAM.

32. Helen McCormack to Laura Bragg, 18 April and 25 April 1927, Laura Bragg Papers, SCHS; see "Early Childhood," J. Arthur Brown Papers, Avery Research Center for African-American History and Culture, College of Charleston (hereafter cited as ARC). While Brown identifies the students as Japanese in his narrative, there were none at The Citadel at the time. However, "Laura's babies," the Chinese cadets, were then attending The Citadel.

33. John Bennett to family, 16 October 1927 and 20 November 1927, John Bennett Papers, SCHS; Mary Martin Hendricks, interview by author, tape recording, November 4, 1996, SP; John Bennett to family, 25 March 1928, John Bennett Papers, SCHS.

34. Margaretta Childs, interview by author, tape recording, 10 July 1996, SP; Li Sui An to Laura Bragg, 22 December 1929, Laura Bragg Collection, CAM.

35. Shu Chun Liu to Laura Bragg, 6 May 1928, Laura Bragg Collection, CAM.

36. Shu Chun Liu to Laura Bragg, 24 August 1928, Laura Bragg Collection, CAM.

37. Chia Mei Hu, letters to Laura Bragg, 13 May 1927 and 18 May 1927, and Tun Yuan Hu to Laura Bragg, 28 February 1928, Laura Bragg Collection, CAM.

38. Laura Bragg to Robert Marks, 30 July 1930, Laura Bragg Papers, SCHS.

39. Laura Bragg to Henry Canby, 21 February 1928, Robert Marks Papers, COC; "Dr. Marks, Inventor of Money-Making Brainchild, Author, Visiting Here," *News and Courier,* 10 September 1953, vertical files, CCPL.

40. Waddell interview, 30 October 1971, SP.

41. L.V. Coleman to Henry Allen Moe, 27 August 1930, and Allen Moe to L.V. Coleman, 28 August 1930, Bragg, Laura 1930 File, Laura Bragg Papers, CMLA.

42. Henry Allen Moe, 28 August 1930, handwritten note at bottom of page, 1931–1932 John Simon Guggenheim Memorial Foundation Fellowship application form, and acknowledgment receipt from John Simon Guggenheim Foundation, 14 November 1930, Bragg, Laura 1930 File, Laura Bragg Papers, CMLA.

43. Laura Bragg to John Maybank, 16 November 1925, Directors' Correspondence, John Maybank, CMLA; Laura Bragg to E. R. Hardy, 21 April 1926, Directors' Correspondence, AAM 1926, CMLA; Laura Bragg to Southern Bell, 7 January 1926, Bragg, Laura 1926 File, Laura Bragg Papers, CMLA; Laura Bragg to Harry Oberholser, 23 April 1926, Directors' Correspondence, Harry Oberholser, CMLA.

44. "Report of the Director of the Charleston Museum for the Year 1926," *City Year Book,* 214–15, CCPL.

45. "Report of the Director of the Charleston Museum for the Year 1925," *City Year Book,* 241–42, CCPL; Laura Bragg to John Cotton Dana, 9 November 1925, Directors' Correspondence, New Jersey State Museum, CMLA; "Report of the Director of The Charleston Museum for the Year 1926," *City Year Book,* 215, CCPL.

46. Laura Bragg to John Cotton Dana, 9 November 1925.

47. Ibid.; Laura Bragg to Mrs. Pope F. Rodgers, 7 February 1928, Directors' Correspondence, Education Department, CMLA.

48. Laura Bragg to John Cotton Dana, 9 November 1925; 1926 *City Year Book,* 217–19.

49. 1926 *City Year Book,* 217–19; Minutes of the Charleston Museum, 9 February 1927, CMLA; Laura Bragg to J. W. Ott, 16 March 1927, Directors' Correspondence, J. W. Ott, CMLA.

50. Laura Bragg to J. W. Ott, 16 March 1927, Directors' Correspondence, J. W. Ott, CMLA.

51. Laura Bragg to E. R. Hardy, 21 April 1926, Directors' Correspondence, AAM 1926, CMLA; Laura Bragg to D. B. Johnson, 19 January 1929, Winthrop University Archives, Rock Hill, S.C.

52. Laura Bragg to S. H. Edmunds, 11 November 1926, and Laura Bragg to J. H. Hope, 29 November 1926, Directors' Correspondence, South Carolina Department of Education, CMLA.

53. Herbert Ravenel Sass, "The Lowcountry," in *The Carolina Low-country,* ed. Augustus Smythe (New York: MacMillan, 1932), 3–4.

54. Laura Bragg to Richard Halsey, 26 October 1926, Directors' Correspondence, Metropolitan Museum, CMLA; F. A. Keppel to Laura Bragg, 15 September 1926, Correspondence, Carnegie Foundation, CMLA.

55. Laura Bragg to L. V. Coleman, 20 January 1927, Directors' Correspondence, AAM 1927, CMLA.

56. Laura Bragg to S. H. Edmunds, 21 January 1927, Directors' Correspondence, South Carolina Department of Education, CMLA.

57. Laura Bragg to J. H. Hope, 21 January 1927, Directors' Correspondence, South Carolina Department of Education, CMLA.

58. J. H. Hope to Laura Bragg, 24 January 1927, Laura Bragg to J. H. Hope, 27 January 1927; S. H. Edmunds to Laura Bragg, 16 March 1927, Directors' Correspondence, South Carolina Department of Education, CMLA.

59. See "Report of the Director of the Charleston Museum" in 1926 and 1927 *City Year Books,* CCPL; "Ana T. Jeanes Fund," in *African American Encyclopedia,* ed. Michael W. Williams (New York: Marshall Cavendish Corp., 1993), 78–79.

60. Marius B. Péladeau, *Chansonetta: The Life and Photographs of Chansonetta Stanley*

Emmons, 1858–1937 (Waldoboro, Me.: Maine Antique Digest, 1977), n.p.; Laura Bragg to General Education Board, 5 May 1927, Directors' Correspondence, General Education Board, CMLA; 1930 *U.S. Census,* 3.

61. Fraser, *Charleston! Charleston!,* 360; Thomas Stoney to Laura Bragg, 31 March 1926, Directors' Correspondence, Edwin Harleston, CMLA.

62. Laura Bragg to Thomas Stoney, 3 April 1926, Directors' Correspondence, Edwin Harleston, CMLA; Laura Bragg to T. R. Waring, 10 April 1926, Directors' Correspondence, Gibbes Art Gallery, CMLA.

63. Laura Bragg to Edwin Harleston, 22 April 1926, Directors' Correspondence, Edwin Harleston, CMLA; Maurine McDaniel, "Edwin Augustus Harleston, Portrait Painter, 1882–1931," (dissertation, Emory University, 1994), 220; *Edwin A. Harleston, Painter of an Era 1882–1931* (Detroit: Your Heritage House, 1983), 23; Laura Bragg to Edwin Harleston, 29 April 1926, Directors' Correspondence, Edwin Harleston, CMLA.

64. Board Minutes, Charleston County Board of Education, Roll 94, CCSD.

65. Laura Bragg to C. G. Rathmann, 10 June 1927, Directors' Correspondence, AAM 1927, CMLA; Laura Bragg to General Education Board, 19 May 1927, Directors' Correspondence, General Education Board, CMLA.

66. Laura Bragg to J. L. Coker, 19 January 1928, Directors' Correspondence, J. L. Coker, CMLA.

67. Laura Bragg to Sam Rittenberg, 22 March 1928; Laura Bragg to J. H. Hope, 21 May 1928, Directors' Correspondence, South Carolina Department of Education, CMLA.

68. Louise Barrington to Ralph Smith, 13 December 1928, Directors' Correspondence, AAM 1928, CMLA; Laura Bragg to Mrs. Pope F. Rodgers, 7 February 1928, Directors' Correspondence, Education Department, CMLA; "Report of the Director of the Charleston Museum for the Year 1928," *City Year Book,* 248, CCPL.

69. Laura Bragg to Mrs. Pope F. Rodgers, 7 February 1928, Directors' Correspondence, South Carolina Department of Education, CMLA.; Waddell interview, 30 October 1971; Laura Bragg to Educational Department, 19 December 1928, Directors' Correspondence, Newark Museum, CMLA.

70. Laura Bragg to Mrs. J. S. Matthews, 14 December 1928, Directors' Correspondence, South Carolina Department of Education, CMLA.

71. Laura Bragg to Sam Rittenberg, 2 January 1929, Directors' Correspondence, South Carolina Department of Education, CMLA.

72. Laura Bragg to Newark Museum Association, 9 October 1928, and Laura Bragg to Sam Rittenberg, 2 January 1929, Directors' Correspondence, South Carolina Department of Education, CMLA.

73. Laura Bragg to J. H. Hope, 4 January 1929, Directors' Correspondence, South Carolina Department of Education, CMLA.

74. Clark Foreman to Laura Bragg, 8 February 1929, Directors' Correspondence, Rosenwald Fund, CMLA.

75. Susan Dart Butler, "Making a Way to Start a Library," unpublished paper, Dart Hall, CCPL; letter from E. R. Embree (copy), 28 February 1929, Laura Bragg to Clark

Foreman, 14 May 1929; Clark Foreman to Laura Bragg, 8 February 1929, Directors' Correspondence, Rosenwald Fund, CMLA.

76. Clark Foreman to Laura Bragg, 8 February, 1929, and Laura Bragg to Clark Foreman, 14 May 1929, Directors' Correspondence, Rosenwald Fund, CMLA.

77. Laura Bragg to Wallace Rogers, 18 June 1930; Waddell interview, October 1971; James Logan Scrapbook, ARC; Shu Chun Liu to Laura Bragg, Laura Bragg Collection, CAM.

78. Drago, *Initiative, Paternalism, and Race Relations,* 193; "Report of the Director of the Museum for the Year 1926," 1926 *City Year Book,* 246, CMLA.

79. Laura Bragg to Clark Foreman, 14 May 1929; Laura Bragg to E. R. Embree, 25 September 1929 and 17 September 1930; E. R. Embree to Laura Bragg, 28 September 1929, Directors' Correspondence, Rosenwald Fund, CMLA.

80. Fraser, *Charleston! Charleston!,* 376.

81. W. E. Duncan to W. G. Pringle, 15 December 1929, Directors' Correspondence, Rosenwald Fund, CMLA; Sam Rittenberg to Laura Bragg, 22 January 1930, Directors' Correspondence, South Carolina Department of Education, CMLA.

82. Sam Rittenberg to Laura Bragg, 22 January 1930.

83. Laura Bragg to R. D. Schroder, from 8 February 1930, Directors' Correspondence, Education 1920–1970, CMLA.

84. Laura Bragg to E. R. Embree, 25 September 1929; Laura Bragg to L. C. Everard, 8 February 1930, Directors' Correspondence, Education 1910–1970, CMLA.

85. Laura Bragg to H. E. Wheeler, 5 March 1929, Directors' Correspondence, Library, CMLA; Clark Foreman to Laura Bragg, 30 March 1929, Directors' Correspondence, Rosenwald Fund, CMLA; Minutes of the Charleston Museum, 28 December 1923, CMLA; Minutes of the Charleston Museum, 14 March 1928, CMLA; John Bennett to family, 2 March 1924, John Bennett Papers, SCHS; Laura Bragg to Helen McCormack, 26 December 1929, unsigned fragment, Directors' Correspondence, AAM 1929, CMLA.

86. "Free Library is Discussed," *News and Courier,* 19 February 1929; "Clubs Plan Free Public Library," *News and Courier,* 4 March 1929, vertical files, CCPL; "Women Support Public Library," *News and Courier,* 16 March 1929; "Public Library is Endorsed," *Charleston Evening Post,* 28 March 1929, Museum Clipping Book, CMLA.

87. Sidney Rittenberg to Clark Foreman, 14 May 1930, Bragg, Laura 1930 File, Laura Bragg Papers, CMLA; *The History of the Charleston County Public Library* (Charleston: Charleston County Public Library, 1981), 4, CCPL; Laura Bragg to Paul Rea, 31 October 1930, Directors' Correspondence, Paul Rea–Carnegie, CMLA.

88. S. H. Church to C. B. Foelsch, 14 June 1930, Bragg, Laura M./Sculpture of Willard Hirsch File, Laura Bragg Papers, CMLA; Sidney Rittenberg to Clark Foreman, 14 May 1930, Bragg, Laura 1930 File, Laura Bragg Papers, CMLA.

89. Minutes of the Charleston Museum, 31 December 1920, CMLA.

90. Laura Bragg to Margaret Hightower, 12 May 1928, Bragg, Laura 1928 File, Laura Bragg Papers, CMLA; Laura Bragg to Alice Kendall, 3 July 1929, Directors' Correspondence, Newark Museum Association, CMLA; Caroline Triest, interview by author, tape recording, 8 May 1999.

91. Laura Bragg to Alice Kendall, 3 July 1929, Directors' Correspondence, Newark Museum Association, CMLA; Laura Bragg to Mr. Hightower, 13 August 1929, Directors' Correspondence, Valentine Museum, CMLA.

92. Laura Bragg to Alice Kendall, 20 June 1930, Directors' Correspondence, Newark Museum Association, CMLA.

93. Laura Bragg to Clark Foreman, 8 March 1930, Directors' Correspondence, Rosenwald Fund, CMLA.

94. Ibid.; Laura Bragg to L.V. Coleman, 13 May 1930, Directors' Correspondence, AAM 1930, CMLA.

95. Laura Bragg to E. R. Embree, 17 September 1930, Directors' Correspondence, Rosenwald Fund, CMLA.

96. Laura Bragg to J. H. Hope, 5 November 1930, Directors' Correspondence, South Carolina Department of Education, CMLA.

97. "Report of the Director of the Charleston Museum for the Year 1927," *City Year Book,* 231–34, CCPL; Jane Webb Smith, "Creating History: The Valentine Family and Museum," Curator's Essay, VMA.

98. 1927 *City Year Book,* 231–34.

99. "Report of the Director of the Charleston Museum for the Year 1920," 1920 *City Year Book,* 413–14, CCPL; 1924 *City Year Book,* 250–52.

100. Bland, *Preserving Charleston's Past,* 74. In a review of the SPOD files and membership lists, Bragg's name never appears nor is her membership ever cited in any interview, though much is made of Bragg's preservation efforts on behalf of the Museum. When Hart wrote the Bragg article for *Preservation Progress,* the organization's newsletter, she did not cite Bragg as having been a SPOD founder or member.

101. Waddell interview, 30 October 1971; Josephine Pinckney, *Splendid in Ashes* (New York: Viking, 1958) 247–48.

102. Josephine Pinckney to Laura Bragg, 12 August 1922, Laura Bragg Papers, SCHS.

103. 1927 *City Year Book,* 232–33; Laura Bragg to Frederick Keppel, 15 November 1927, Directors' Correspondence, Carnegie Foundation, CMLA.

104. Laura Bragg to William Coffin, 13 October 1927, Directors' Correspondence, William S. Coffin, CMLA.

105. Waddell interview; Bland, *Preserving Charleston's Past,* 72; Laura Bragg to Frederick Keppel, 15 November 1927, Directors' Correspondence, Carnegie Foundation, CMLA; 1927 *City Year Book,* 232–33; Minutes of the Charleston Museum, 19 October 1927, CMLA; Laura Bragg to Albert Simmons, 3 January 1928, Directors' Correspondence, Carnegie Foundation, CMLA; Hosmer-Burton interview transcript, 12, Archives of American Art, Washington, D.C. (hereafter cited as AAA). The Mansion House was once owned by Jehu Jones, a free person of color, who purchased the property on St. Michael's Alley and Broad Street between 1809 and 1815. Jones operated an inn at 33 Broad that was patronized by the white elite, who praised both its comfort and food. See "Jehu Jones: Free Black Entrepreneur," South Carolina Department of Archives and History, Public Programs Document Packet No. 1, Columbia.

106. Al Hester, "From Sustained Yield to Sustaining Communities: The Establish-

ment of Francis Marion National Forest in South Carolina, 1901–1936," 3 December 1997, unpublished paper. I am indebted to Robert Morgan, archeologist for the Francis Marion National Forest, for providing me with a copy of this paper.

107. Laura Bragg to H. C. Bumpus, 15 November 1927, Directors' Correspondence, AAM 1927, CMLA; W. P. Baldwin, *Plantations of the Low Country, South Carolina 1697–1865* (Greensboro, N.C.: Legacy Publications, 1989), 71–82.

108. Undated document attached to letter to Albert Simons from Laura Bragg, 16 June 1927, Directors' Correspondence, Albert Simons, CMLA; Laura Bragg to William H. Kilpatrick, 28 March 1928, Directors' Correspondence, Carnegie Foundation, CMLA.

109. Laura Bragg to Caroline Sinkler, 5 April 1928, Directors' Correspondence, Caroline Sinkler, CMLA; Laura Bragg to C. R. Richards, 19 May 1928, Directors' Correspondence, General Education Board, CMLA; Laura Bragg to Linden Harris, 29 October 1928, Directors' Correspondence, Firemarks, CMLA.

110. Laura Bragg to William Coffin, 11 June 1928, Directors' Correspondence, Carnegie Foundation, CMLA.

111. F. P. Keppel to William S. Coffin, 24 May 1928, Directors' Correspondence, William Coffin, CMLA; William Coffin to Laura Bragg, 26 May 1928, Directors' Correspondence, Carnegie Foundation, CMLA.

112. Frederic P. Keppel to H. W. Kent, 3 January 1928, Carnegie Corporation of New York Archive, Columbia University Rare Book and Manuscript Library, New York (hereafter cited as CRB-M); "FPK and Miss Bragg," memorandum of interview, 27 May 1929, CRB-M; C. R. Richards to Frederic P. Keppel, 29 November 1927, CRB-M.

113. "Report of the Director of the Charleston Museum for the Year 1928," 1928 *City Year Book,* 245–47, CCPL; 1929 *City Year Book,* 260–61.

114. Laura Bragg to William H. Kilpatrick, 28 March 1928, Directors' Correspondence, Carnegie Foundation, CMLA.

115. Laura Bragg to F. P. Keppel, 7 February 1928, and F. P. Keppel to Laura Bragg, 9 February 1928, Directors' Correspondence, Carnegie Foundation, CMLA.

116. William Kilpatrick to Mrs. Thomas Pinckney, 17 February 1928, and F. P. Keppel to Laura Bragg, 25 February 1928, Directors' Correspondence, Carnegie Foundation, CMLA.

117. Laura Bragg to Frederic Whiting, 28 March 1929, Directors' Correspondence, Cleveland Museum of Art, CMLA.

118. Laura Bragg to Horatio Shonnard, 23 April 1929, Directors' Correspondence, Harrietta Plantation, CMLA.

119. Horatio Shonnard to Laura Bragg, 29 April 1929, Directors' Correspondence, Harrietta Plantation, CMLA.

120. "Proceedings of Council," *Journal of City Council* (13 August 1929): 285; Robert P. Stockton, "Preservation in Charleston 1931–1956," *Preservation Progress* 38, no. 2 (Summer 1995): 12.

121. Minutes of the Charleston Museum, 16 May 1928, CMLA; Laura Bragg to William Sloane Coffin, 19 May 1928, CMLA; Minutes of the Charleston Museum, 13 June 1928, CMLA; Laura Bragg to Albert Simons, 16 June 1928, CMLA; Laura

Bragg to J. L. Coker, 4 December 1930, Directors' Correspondence, J. L. Coker, CMLA; Bland, *Preserving Charleston's Past,* 73; C. B. Hosmer, *Preservation Comes of Age* (Charlottesville: University of Virginia Press, 1981), 1:243.

122. Mary Ralls Dockstader, "The Heyward-Washington House, Charleston, South Carolina," undated essay, Heyward-Washington House File, SCHS; Robert P. Stockton, "Dean of Charleston Architects," *Preservation Progress* 20, no. 4 (November 1975): 6.

123. Laura Bragg to J. L. Coker, 4 December 1930, Directors' Correspondence, J. L. Coker, CMLA; Laura Bragg to Frederic Whiting, 28 March 1929, Directors' Correspondence, Cleveland Museum of Art, CMLA; Laura Bragg to Caroline Sinkler, 27 November 1929, Directors' Correspondence, Caroline Sinkler, CMLA; Hosmer, 245; "Heyward House Fund Growing," News and Courier, 15 March 1929, and "See Plantations on Benefit Tour," *News and Courier,* 4 April 1930, Directors' Correspondence, Heyward-Washington House Publicity 1928–1934, CMLA.

124. Stockton, "Dean of Charleston Architects," 6; Minutes of the Charletson Museum, 6 February 1931, PSC; Emma Richardson to Caroline Sinkler, 27 January 1931, Directors' Correspondence, Caroline Sinkler, CMLA.

125. Ward Reynolds, "A Chronology Charleston's Preservation Movement: Part I, 1912–1930," *Preservation Progress* 38, no. 1 (Spring 1995): 10–11; Bland, *Preserving Charleston's Past,* 73–74; Laura Bragg, untitled essay, ca. 1930–1931, Laura Bragg Papers, SCHS.

126. 1924 *City Year Book,* 250–52; 1925 *City Year Book,* 248; see Laura Bragg Papers, SCHS.

127. Paul Rea to Mrs. J. W. Steimons, 28 April 1919, Directors' Correspondence, Laura Bragg–Edgefield Pottery, CMLA; Acquisition record, 29 June 1920, Mrs. C. A. Carwile, Bursar's Office File, CMLA; Notes on collecting trip of Paul Rea to Edgefield County, 24 April [1919], Directors' Correspondence, Laura Bragg-Edgefield Pottery, CMLA.

128. John Bennett to family, 14 December 1924, John Bennett Papers, SCHS; John Bennett to family, 17 November 1929, John Bennett Papers, SCHS.

129. Jill Beute Koverman, "Searching for Messages in Clay," unpublished paper, personal copy; Mrs. Edward K. Webb to Robert T. Thompson, 30 July 1968, Directors' Correspondence, Laura Bragg–Edgefield Pottery, CMLA. I am indebted to Ms. Koverman for providing me with a copy of her paper.

130. Notes collected on trip to various potteries, Miss L. M. B. and E. B. C., June 24–26, 1930, Directors' Correspondence, Laura Bragg–Edgefield Pottery, CMLA; "State Pottery Interesting," *Charleston Evening Post,* 22 July 1930, Directors' Correspondence, Laura Bragg–Edgefield Pottery, CMLA.

131. See Cinda K. Baldwin, *Great and Noble Jar: Traditional Stoneware of South Carolina* (Athens: University of Georgia Press, 1993); Laura Bragg to Helen Comstock, 13 October 1930, Laura Bragg Papers, CMLA.

132 Paul Rea to Laura Bragg, 29 October 1930, Directors' Correspondence, Paul Rea–Carnegie, CMLA.

133. Ibid; Laura Bragg to Paul Rea, 31 October 1930 and 3 November 1930, Directors' Correspondence, Paul Rea–Carnegie, CMLA; Minutes of the Charleston Museum, 31 March 1931, CMLA.

134. Lynne Teather, "Museum Education," in *The Museum: A Reference Guide,* ed. Michael Shapiro (Westport, Conn.: Greenwood Press, 1990), 308.

135. Edward Alexander, *Museums in Motion,* 239–40; Teather, "Museum Education," 304; Linda Downs, "A Recent History of Women Educators in Art Museums," in *Gender Perspectives,* 93.

136. Laura Bragg to Clifton Gray Norman, 25 January 1926, Bragg, Laura 1926 File, Laura Bragg Papers, CMLA; John Coss to Laura Bragg, 19 November 1925, Bragg, Laura 1925 File, Laura Bragg Papers, CMLA.

137. John Coss to Laura Bragg, 19 November 1925, and Laura Bragg to John Coss, 15 December 1925, Bragg, Laura 1925 File, Laura Bragg Papers, CMLA.

138. John Coss to Laura Bragg, 19 November 1925; Laura Bragg to Calvin Valentine, 14 December 1925, Valentine Reorganization, VMA.

139. Laura Bragg to Lyman Bragg, 30 November 1925, Laura Bragg Papers, SCHS; Lyman Bragg to Laura Bragg, 20 December 1925, Laura Bragg Papers, SCHS; Laura Bragg to L. V. Coleman, 25 May 1926, Directors' Correspondence, AAM 1926, CMLA; John Bennett to family, 12 May 1926, John Bennett Papers, SCHS.

140. Laura Bragg to L.V. Coleman, 25 May 1926, Directors' Correspondence, AAM 1926, CMLA; "Columbia Gives Course: Museum Administration," *Museum News* 4, no. 3 (1 June 1926): 1, 33, Box 19, 87–165, Record Unit 7450, American Association of Museums Records, 1906–1985, SIA; Laura Bragg to John Coss, 25 May 1926, Bragg, Laura 1926 File, Laura Bragg Papers, CMLA.

141 "Notes for Announcement for Course in Museum Administration, Columbia University," and Columbia University summer session course announcement, July 6 to August 13, 1926, Bragg, Laura 1926 File, Laura Bragg Papers, CMLA; Laura Bragg to H. C. Bumpus, 17 September 1926, Directors' Correspondence, AAM 1926, CMLA.

142. Laura Bragg to L.V. Coleman, 17 September 1926, Directors' Correspondence, AAM 1926, CMLA; Laura Bragg to Richard Halsey, 26 October 1926, Directors' Correspondence, Richard Halsey, CMLA; Louise Connolly to Laura Bragg, 30 August 1926, Directors' Correspondence, Louise Connolly, CMLA.

143. Louise Connolly to Laura Bragg, undated document, Undated Correspondence, Laura Bragg Papers, CMLA; Louise Connolly to Laura Bragg, 30 August 1926, CMLA.

144. Laura Bragg to L.V. Coleman, 17 September 1926, Directors' Correspondence, AAM 1926, CMLA; Theodora Rhoades to Laura Bragg, 7 September 1926, Bragg, Laura 1926 File, Laura Bragg Papers, CMLA.

145. Laura Bragg to Langdon Warner, 4 October 1926, Bragg, Laura 1926 File, Laura Bragg Papers, CMLA.

146. American Association of Museums, *Excellence and Equity: Education and the Public Dimension of Museums* (Washington, D.C.: American Association of Museums, 1992), 3.

147. Laura Bragg to L.V. Coleman, 17 September 1926, and L.V. Coleman to Laura Bragg, 24 September 1926, Directors' Correspondence, AAM 1926, CMLA.

148. Laura Bragg to John Coss, 30 October 1926, and Emma Richardson to Sallie McAlpin, 30 June 1927, Bragg, Laura 1926 File, Laura Bragg Papers, CMLA; Helen

McCormack to Emma Richardson, 9 July 1927, Directors' Correspondence, Emma Richardson, CMLA; Laura Bragg to Clara Eby, 17 October 1927, to Sallie McAlpin, 20 May 1927, to Libbie George, 23 June 1927, Bragg, Laura 1926 File, Laura Bragg Papers, CMLA; Laura Bragg to Mary Crinigan, 22 June 1927, Directors' Correspondence, Valentine Museum, CMLA; Laura Bragg to S. A. Barrett, 8 March 1928, Directors' Correspondence, Milwaukee Public Museum, CMLA.

149. Laura Bragg to John Coss, 21 February 1928, Bragg, Laura 1928 File, Laura Bragg Papers, CMLA.

150. Clive Giborie, ed., *Lovingly, Georgia* (New York: Simon and Schuster, 1990), xvi.; Anita Pollitzer to Georgia O'Keeffe, 31 July 1927, in *Lovingly, Georgia,* 271; Anita Pollitzer to Georgia O'Keeffe, August, 1927, in *Lovingly, Georgia,* 272–73.

151. Laura Bragg to John Coss, 14 November 1927, Bragg, Laura 1927 File, Laura Bragg Papers, CMLA; Laura Bragg, letters to John Coss and George Cox, 3 November 1927, Bragg, Laura 1927 File, Laura Bragg Papers, CMLA; Columbia University summer session course announcement, 9 July to 17 August 1928, Columbia University Archives and Columbiana Library, New York (hereafter cited as CUA–C); and "Museum Training," undated document, Undated Correspondence, Laura Bragg Papers, CMLA.

152. *Museum News* 5, no. 18 (1 March 1928): 1, and *Museum News,* 5, no. 21 (15 April 1928): 1, Box 19, 87–165, Record Unit 7450, American Association of Museums Records, 1906–1985, SIA; Laura Bragg to John Coss, 16 May 1928, Bragg, Laura 1927 File, Laura Bragg Papers, CMLA; Laura Bragg to S. A. Barrett, 8 March 1928, and S. A. Barrett to Laura Bragg, 13 March 1928, Directors' Correspondence, Milwaukee Museum, CMLA; Katherine Coffey to Laura Bragg, 2 August 1928, Directors' Correspondence, Newark Museum Association, CMLA.

153. Laura Bragg to Alexander Wall, Edward Foyles, and Harriett Howe, 16 May 1928, Bragg, Laura 1928 File, Laura Bragg Papers, CMLA; Laura Bragg to Margaret Hightower, 12 May 1928, Directors' Correspondence, Margaret Hightower, CMLA; Laura Bragg to Carol Andrews, Nancy Parker, and Mrs. J. M. S. Clark, 16 May 1928, and Laura Bragg to Eunice Avery, 12 June 1928, to Lenore Lloyd, 13 June 1928, and to Mrs. H. N. Massey, 16 June 1923, Bragg, Laura 1928 File, Laura Bragg Papers, CMLA.

154. Helen McCormack to Laura Bragg, 19 July 1928, Laura Bragg Papers, SCHS; Helen McCormack to Emma Richardson, 28 July 1928, Directors' Correspondence, Helen McCormack, CMLA; Helen McCormack to Laura Bragg, 6 July 1928 and 1 August 1928, Laura Bragg Papers, SCHS; Helen McCormack to Emma Richardson, 28 July 1928, Directors' Correspondence, Helen McCormack, CMLA.

155. John Coss to Laura Bragg, 9 October 1928, Bragg, Laura 1928 File, Laura Bragg Papers, CMLA; John Coss to Laura Bragg, 29 May 1929, Bragg, Laura 1929 File, Laura Bragg Papers, CMLA.

156. Laura Bragg to John Coss, 8 June 1929, Bragg, Laura 1929 File, Laura Bragg Papers, CMLA.

157. Laura Bragg to John Coss, 11 January 1929, Bragg, Laura 1929 File, Laura Bragg Papers, CMLA; John Coss to Laura Bragg, 29 April 1929, Bragg, Laura 1929

File, Laura Bragg Papers, CMLA; John Cotton Dana to John Coss, 1 June 1929, Directors' Correspondence, New Jersey State Museum, CMLA.

158. Alice Kendall to Laura Bragg, 4 June 1929, Directors' Correspondence, New Jersey Museum Association, CMLA; Laura Bragg to Alice Kendall, 5 July 1929, Directors' Correspondence, AAM 1929, CMLA; and Alice Kendall to Laura Bragg, 11 July 1929, Directors' Correspondence, New Jersey Museum Association, CMLA.

159. Laura Bragg to L. V. Coleman, 20 January 1927, Directors' Correspondence, 1927 AAM, CMLA; Laura Bragg to Granville Valentine, 23 February 1927, Valentine Reorganization, VMA.

160. Laura Bragg to Theodora Rhoades, 26 March 1927, Bragg, Laura 1927 File, Laura Bragg Papers, CMLA; Theodora Rhoades to Laura Bragg, Undated Correspondence, Laura Bragg Papers, CMLA; "Minutes of the 1927 AAM Meeting," 170, Box 41, 87–165, Record Unit 7450, American Association of Museums Records, 1906–1985, SIA; Theodora Rhoades to Laura Bragg, 30 May 1927, Bragg, Laura 1927 File, Laura Bragg Papers, CMLA.

161. H. E. Wheeler to Laura Bragg, 27 April 1927, Bragg, Laura 1927 File, Laura Bragg Papers, CMLA; Laura Bragg to L. V. Coleman, 4 June 1927, Directors' Correspondence, AAM 1927, CMLA; Byron Marshall to Laura Bragg, 5 March 1927, Directors' Correspondence, Ozark Natural Research Society, CMLA; Laura Bragg to Frederic Whiting, 5 February 1923, Directors' Correspondence, Cleveland Museum of Art, CMLA.

162. Clark Foreman to Laura Bragg, 31 January 1928, Laura Bragg to Clark Foreman, 4 February 1928, and Laura Bragg to Clark Foreman, 25 February 1928, Directors' Correspondence, Highlands, CMLA.

163. Helen McCormack to Emma Richardson, 9 August 1928, Directors' Correspondence, Highlands, CMLA; Helen McCormack to Laura Bragg, 20 August 1927, Laura Bragg Papers, SCHS; Clark Foreman to Laura Bragg, 23 May 1929, Directors' Correspondence, Highlands, CMLA.

164. Donald Blake to Laura Bragg, 16 June 1928, Laura Bragg to Donald Blake, 28 June 1928, and Laura Bragg to Donald Blake, 17 September 1928, Directors' Correspondence, Florida Federation of Arts, CMLA.

165. Laura Bragg to L. V. Coleman, 27 February 1929, Directors' Correspondence, AAM 1929, CMLA; Donald Blake to Laura Bragg, 20 March 1929, and Laura Bragg to Donald Blake, 28 March 1929, Directors' Correspondence, Florida Federation of Arts, CMLA.

166. Laura Bragg to Caroline Sinkler, 14 December 1930, Directors' Correspondence, Caroline Sinkler, CMLA; Laura Bragg to Clark Foreman, 8 March 1930, Directors' Correspondence, Rosenwald Fund, CMLA; and 1930 *City Year Book,* 252, CCPL; Laura Bragg to L. V. Coleman, 13 May 1930, Directors' Correspondence, AAM 1930, CMLA.

167. Laura Bragg to Caroline Sinkler, 14 December 1930, Directors' Correspondence, Caroline Sinkler, CMLA.

168. Granville Valentine to Laura Bragg, 20 March 1930, 1929–1930 Bragg Correspondence, Valentine Papers, VMA; Emma Richardson to Helen McCormack, 31

March 1930, Directors' Correspondence, Valentine Museum, CMLA; Laura Bragg to Alice Kendall, 20 June 1930, Directors' Correspondence, Newark Museum Association, CMLA.

169. Laura Bragg to Emma Richardson, 24 October 1924, Undated Correspondence, Laura Bragg Papers, CMLA; Granville Valentine to Laura Bragg, 6 April 1925, Directors' Correspondence, Valentine Museum, CMLA.

170. Granville Valentine to Laura Bragg, 6 April 1925, Directors' Correspondence, Valentine Museum, CMLA.

171. Granville Valentine to Laura Bragg, 22 March 1926, and Calvin Valentine to Laura Bragg, 19 April 1926, Directors' Correspondence, Valentine Museum, CMLA; John Bennett to family, 11 April 1926, John Bennett Papers, SCHS.

172. Calvin Valentine to Laura Bragg, 19 April 1926, Directors' Correspondence, Valentine Museum, CMLA.

173. Granville Valentine to Laura Bragg, 15 March 1927, Valentine Reorganization File, VMA; Granville Valentine to Laura Bragg, 8 June 1927, Valentine Reorganization File, VMA; Laura Bragg to Granville Valentine, 11 June 1927, Directors' Correspondence, Valentine Museum, CMLA.

174. Laura Bragg to Granville Valentine, 11 June 1927, Directors' Correspondence, Valentine Museum, CMLA.

175. Granville Valentine to Laura Bragg, 20 June 1928, Valentine Reorganization File, VMA.

176. Laura Bragg to Granville Valentine, undated, Valentine Reorganization File, VMA; Granville Valentine to Laura Bragg, 5 September 1928, 1929–1930 Bragg Correspondence, Valentine Papers, VMA.

177. Helen McCormack to Laura Bragg, 7 September 1928, Directors' Correspondence, Helen McCormack, CMLA.

178. The Valentine Museum accession slip, 22 October 1928, Laura Bragg Papers, SCHS.

179. Granville Valentine to Laura Bragg, 26 December 1938, 1929–1930 Bragg Correspondence, Valentine Papers, VMA.

180. Helen McCormack to Laura Bragg, 6 March 1929, Laura Bragg Papers, SCHS.

181. LMB [Laura Bragg], note to Helen McCormack, 13 March 1929, Directors' Correspondence, Helen McCormack, CMLA; Helen McCormack to Laura Bragg, 6 March 1929, Laura Bragg Papers, SCHS.

182. Laura Bragg to Granville Valentine, March 1929, Valentine Reorganization, VMA.

183. "Report of the Director of the Charleston Museum for the Year 1929," 1929 *City Year Book,* 260, CCPL; Waddell diary, 16 June 1976.

184. Helen McCormack to Laura Bragg, 10 May 1929, Laura Bragg Papers, SCHS.

185. Howard Kelly to Laura Bragg, 10 May 1929, Directors' Correspondence, Howard Kelly, CMLA.

186. Helen McCormack to Emma Richardson, 30 June 1929, Directors' Correspondence, Helen McCormack, CMLA.

187. Helen McCormack to Emma Richardson, 6 August 1929, Directors' Correspondence, Helen McCormack, CMLA; Laura Bragg to Emma Richardson, 13 August 1929, Bragg, Laura 1929 File, Laura Bragg Papers, CMLA.

188. Laura Bragg to Granville Valentine, 19 September 1929, Valentine Reorganization, VMA; Y. L. Lui to Laura Bragg, 20 September 1929, Laura Bragg Collection, CAM.

189. Laura Bragg to Granville Valentine, March 1929, Valentine Reorganization, VMA; Ledger Sheet for Year 1929, 1 January 1930, Valentine-Wickham File, Drawer 36, Valentine Museum, 1928–1930, VMA; DuBose Heyward to Laura Bragg, June 1929, Laura Bragg Papers, SCHS; Granville Valentine to Laura Bragg, 12 September 1930, 1929–1930 Bragg Correspondence, Valentine Papers, VMA; Laura Bragg to Granville Valentine, 18 September 1930, Valentine Reorganization, VMA.

190. Laura Bragg to Granville Valentine, 18 September 1930, Valentine Reorganization, VMA.

191. Granville Valentine to Laura Bragg, 12 September 1930, 1929–1930 Bragg Correspondence, Valentine Papers, VMA.

192. Laura Bragg to Granville Valentine, 18 September 1930, Valentine Reorganization, VMA; Granville Valentine to Laura Bragg, 22 September 1930, Valentine Reorganization File, VMA; Granville Valentine to Laura Bragg, 8 October 1930, 1929–1930 Bragg Correspondence, Valentine Papers, VMA.

193. Helen McCormack to Laura Bragg, 9 November 1930, Laura Bragg Papers, SCHS; Helen McCormack to Emma Richardson, 13 November 1930, Directors' Correspondence, Valentine Museum, CMLA; Helen McCormack to Granville Valentine, 11 November 1930, Valentine Reorganization File, VMA.

194. Thomas Lesesne, *History of Charleston County, South Carolina* (Charleston: A. W. Cawston, 1931), 202.

195. James Hagood to Laura Bragg, 23 June 1930, Directors' Correspondence, James Hagood, CMLA; Fraser, *Charleston! Charleston!,* 378; Alice Kendall to Laura Bragg, 7 July 1930, Directors' Correspondence, New Jersey State Museum, CMLA.

196. Fraser, *Charleston! Charleston!,* 378; Laura Bragg to Caroline Sinkler, 13 January 1931, Directors' Correspondence, Caroline Sinkler, CMLA; Laura Bragg to Paul Rea, 29 January 1930, Directors' Correspondence, Paul Rea–Carnegie Foundation, CMLA.

197. Laura Bragg to Paul Rea, 29 January 1930 and Paul Rea to Laura Bragg, 10 February 1931, Directors' Correspondence, Paul Rea–Carnegie Foundation, CMLA.

198. Paul Rea to Laura Bragg, 10 February 1931, and Paul Rea to Laura Bragg, 23 February 1931, Directors' Correspondence, Paul Rea–Carnegie Foundation, CMLA.

199. Laura Bragg to Z. Marshall Crane, 29 May 1931, Directors' Correspondence, Berkshire Museum, CMLA; Laura Bragg to L. V. Coleman, 29 May 1931, Directors' Correspondence, AAM 1931, CMLA.

200. Helen McCormack to Laura Bragg, 13 March 1931, Laura Bragg Papers, SCHS.

201. Laura Bragg to A. J. Buist, undated, Undated Correspondence, Laura Bragg Papers, CMLA.

202. Ibid.; A. J. Buist to James Hagood, 3 February 1931, Directors' Correspondence, A. J. Buist, CMLA; George Buist to Emma Richardson, 28 February 1931, Directors' Correspondence, Heyward-Washington House, CMLA.

203. Helen McCormack to Laura Bragg, 23 March 1931, Laura Bragg Papers, SCHS.

204. Laura Bragg to J. L. Coker, 24 March 1931, Directors' Correspondence, J. L. Coker, CMLA.

205. Ibid.

206. Minutes of the Charleston Museum, 30 March 1931, CMLA.

207. Helen McCormack to Laura Bragg, 1 April 1931, Laura Bragg Papers, SCHS.

208. Laura Bragg to L.V. Coleman, 29 May 1931, Directors' Correspondence, AAM 1931, CMLA; Laura Bragg to Paul Rea, 22 April 1931, Directors' Correspondence, Paul Rea–Carnegie Foundation, CMLA; Laura Bragg to L.V. Coleman, 29 May 1931.

209. Waddell interview, 30 October 1971; Laura Bragg to Z. Marshall Crane, 29 May 1931, Directors' Correspondence, Berkshire Museum, CMLA.

Chapter 5

1. Sally Ridgeway, "Art and Education: Tracking in a Museum to Maintain Elitism: A Look at the Berkshire Museum, 1931–1939," unpublished manuscript, 1990, 4; (I am grateful to the author for providing me with a copy of her paper); George F. Willison, *The History of Pittsfield, Massachusetts, 1916–1955* (Pittsfield, Mass.: The City of Pittsfield, 1957), 149.

2. Fraser, *Charleston! Charleston!,* 374; Willison, *History of Pittsfield,* 154.

3. Fraser, *Charleston! Charleston!,* 379; Willison, *History of Pittsfield,* 156, 161.

4. 1927 *City Year Book,* 232; "July 1, 1931 Report of the Treasurer," Directors' Correspondence, G. M. Buist, CMLA.

5. "Zenas Crane (1840–1917)," undated document, BM; Henry Seaver to Mr. Hayward, 19 June 1937, Seaver material, BM.

6. Willison, *History of Pittsfield,* 384; Laura Bragg to Margaret Sizer, 26 May 1931, Bragg, Laura 1931–1937 File, Laura Bragg Papers, CMLA; "The Berkshire Museum," undated document, Laura Bragg Correspondence, BM.

7. Clothilde R. Martin, "Crane House Reflects Old South," *News and Courier,* 1 March 1931, vertical files, CCPL; Laura Bragg to Z. Marshall Crane, 29 May 1931, Directors' Correspondence, Berkshire Museum, CMLA.

8. Ridgeway, "Art and Education," 5; Semel, *The Dalton School,* 12.

9. "Crane Family Makes New Benefaction to Art Museum to Enlarge its Usefulness," *Berkshire Eagle,* 17 June 1931, Museum Clipping Book, BM.

10. Laura Bragg to Z. Marshall Crane, 29 May 1931, Directors' Correspondence, Berkshire Museum, CMLA; Willison, *History of Pittsfield,* 384; "Miss Margaret Hightower, Curator of Science Department," and "Miss Mary Martin New Art Assistant at Museum Arrives," *Berkshire Eagle,* 1 August 1931, Museum Clipping Book, BM.

11. Laura Bragg to Z. Marshall Crane, 29 May 1931; "Museum Charter, 1932," Labels for Zenas Crane Exhibit, BM.

12. "New Curator of Museum Happy at Local Prospects," *Berkshire Eagle,* 6 July 1931, Museum Clipping Book, BM.

13. Laura Bragg to Z. Marshall Crane, 29 May 1931.

14. Ibid; Laura Bragg to Margaret Sizer, 26 May 1931, Bragg, Laura 1931–1937 File, Laura Bragg Papers, CMLA.

15. Bartlett Hendricks, interview by author, tape recording, 4 November 1996, SP; Mumford, "The Art Galleries," and Elizabeth McCausland, "The Reopening of the Berkshire Museum."

16. Laura Bragg to Z. Marshall Crane, 29 May 1931.

17. "Many View Loan Exhibition at Reception Given for New Director of Berkshire Museum," *Berkshire Eagle,* 1 September 1931, Museum Clipping Book, BM; Margaret Hightower to Emma Richardson, 24 September 1931, Bragg, Laura 1931–1937 File, Laura Bragg Papers, CMLA; Mary Martin Hendricks, interview by author, tape recording, 4 November 1997, SP; Ridgeway, "Art and Education," 9.

18. "Art Show in Pittsfield," *New York Times,* 31 August 1931, and "Exhibition of Contemporary Art," *Springfield Sunday Union and Republican,* 27 August 1931; "W. Wesley Wiseman's Talks on Art Attract People to Museum," *Berkshire Eagle,* 3 September 1931; "Evening Talk to be Given at Museum," *Berkshire Eagle,* 4 September 1931, all in Museum Clipping Book, BM.

19. "W. Wesley Wiseman of New York Gives Final Gallery Talk Here," *Berkshire Eagle,* 5 September 1931, Museum Clipping Book, BM.

20. "To the Berkshire Courier," 11 November 1931, 1931 Exhibit Files, BM.

21. "Reception Given for Anna Heyward Taylor," *Berkshire Eagle,* 18 November 1931, Museum Clipping Book, BM; Ridgeway, "Art and Education," 9; Laura Bragg to Anna Heyward Taylor, 12 December 1931, Anna Heyward Taylor File, BM.

22. Laura Bragg to Maud Knowlton, 23 March 1932, Ned Jennings File, BM; Laura Bragg to Herbert Tschudy, 26 October 1932, Ned Jennings File, BM.

23. Waddell interview, 30 October 1971; Margaret Hightower to Emma Richardson, 24 September 1931, Bragg, Laura 1931–1937 File, Laura Bragg Papers, CMLA; Helen McCormack to Laura Bragg, 9 January 1932, Laura Bragg Papers, SCHS.

24. "Berkshire Museum Will Be Open on Christmas Day," *Berkshire Eagle,* 21 December 1931, Museum Clipping Book, BM.

25. Minutes of the Charleston Museum, 9 December 1931, CMLA; Milby Burton to Paul Rea, 2 December 1931, Directors' Correspondence, Paul Rea–Carnegie, CMLA.

26. George Buist to Milby Burton, 17 December 1931, Directors' Correspondence, George Buist, CMLA; Mabel Pollitzer to Laura Bragg (1), 30 January 1932, Laura Bragg Papers, SCHS.

27. Mabel Pollitzer to Laura Bragg (2), 30 January 1932, Laura Bragg Papers, SCHS.

28. Ridgeway, "Art and Education," 2.

29. "Schools Have Exhibits of Museum," *Berkshire Evening Eagle,* 18 February 1932; "Traveling School Exhibits To Be on View at Reception for Teachers and Parents," *Berkshire Evening Eagle,* 18 October 1932, both in Museum Clipping Book, BM.

30. "Traveling School Exhibit and Laura Bragg," Labels for Zenas Crane Exhibit, BM; Notes on the letter "Museum Protest," 1937, Laura Bragg's Response, BM;

"Traveling School Exhibit, Growth of the U.S. due to Industry-Oil," Labels for Zenas
Crane Exhibit, BM; "Carrying Art to the Schools," *New York Times,* 22 March 1936,
Museum Clipping Book, BM.

31. "Report of the Director for the Year 1934," 1 January 1935; "Museum Truly
Berkshire Institution, Director Says," *Berkshire Evening Eagle,* 28 January 1933;
"Report of the Director for the Year 1933," 1 January 1934; "Schools Have Exhibits
of Museum," *Berkshire Evening Eagle,* 18 February 1932, all in Museum Clipping
Book, BM.

32. "Schools Have Exhibits of Museum"; Laura Bragg to Francis Barrington, 11
February 1932, Bragg, Laura 1931–1937 File, Laura Bragg Papers, CMLA; "Summary
of Types of Educational Work in the Museums of the Country," February 1932,
Directors' Correspondence, Metropolitan Museum, CMLA.

33. Lawrence A. Cremin, *The Transformation of the School: Progressivism in American
Education* (New York: A. A. Knopf, 1969), viii.

34. Herbert Kliebard, *The Struggle for The American Curriculum* (New York: Routledge, 1995), 158–59, 166–68.

35. Carl F. Kaestle, "The Public Schools and The Public Mood," *American Heritage*
11 (February 1990): 74; Laura Bragg, "Culture Museums and the Use of Culture
Material," *Museum Work* 8 (1925): 76.

36. "Schools in Berkshire Hills Benefit by Art Exhibitions Arranged under Federal
Aid," *Christian Science Monitor,* 13 April 1934; "Work of Berkshire PWA Artists Goes
on Display at Local Museum Today," *Berkshire Evening Eagle,* 18 May 1934, both in
Museum Clipping Book, BM.

37. "Report of the Director for the Year 1934," 1 January 1935, BM.

38. "Carrying Art to the Schools," *New York Times,* 22 March 1936, Museum Clipping Book, BM.

39. "Time-of-Washington Loan Exhibit to Feature Local Bicentenary Obser-
vance," *Berkshire Evening Eagle,* 23 January 1932; "County Scoured by Museum for
Olden Time Exhibition," *Berkshire Eagle,* 8 February 1932; "Reception Opening
Washington Exhibition Event of Holiday," *Berkshire Eagle,* 23 February 1932;
"Museum Truly Berkshire Institution, Director Says," *Berkshire Evening Eagle,* 28 Jan-
uary 1933, all in Museum Clipping Book, BM.

40. "Museum Exhibition of Chinese Paintings Will Open Monday," *Berkshire
Eagle,* 8 July 1932; "Loan Exhibition Opens With Reception," *Berkshire Eagle,* 12 July
1932, both in Museum Clipping Book, BM.

41. "Exhibition of Modern Art Opens at Museum with Reception," *Berkshire
Eagle,* 2 August 1932, Museum Clipping Book, BM.

42. "Shaker Exhibition at Museum Opens with Large Reception," *Berkshire Eagle,*
11 October 1932; "Shakers to Give Talks on Phases of Life," *Berkshire Eagle,* 13 October 1932; "Society to Preserve Shaker Antiquities May Be Formed," *Berkshire Eagle,*
28 October 1932; "Museum Truly Berkshire Institution," *Berkshire Eagle,* 28 January
1933; "Museum Truly Berkshire Institution"; all in Museum Clipping Book, BM;
Helen McCormack to Laura Bragg, 25 October 1932, Laura Bragg Papers, SCHS.

43. "Attendance at the Museum Doubles," *Berkshire Eagle,* 27 January 1933,

Museum Clipping Book, BM; Bartlett Hendricks, interview by author, tape recording, 4 November 1996, SP.

44. "Retiring Museum Director Leaves," *Springfield Sunday Union and Republican,* 24 September 1939, Museum Clipping Book, BM.

45. Mary Martin Hendricks, interview by author, tape recording, 4 November 1996, SP.

46. "Report of the Director for the Year 1933," 1 January 1934, BM; "600 Attend Negro Sunday Program at Berkshire Museum," *Berkshire Eagle,* 6 February 1933, Museum Clipping Book, BM.

47. "Report of the Director for the Year 1933."

48. Ibid.

49. Ibid.

50. Ibid.

51. "Special to *The New York Times,*" 6 April 1933, 1933 Exhibit Files, BM.

52. "Report of the Director for the Year 1933," 1 January 1934, BM; "New Painting on Museum Walls," *Berkshire Eagle,* 20 May 1933, Museum Clipping Book, BM.

53. Laura Bragg to Mrs. Eliot Watrous, 6 May 1932, Watrous File, BM.

54. "Modernity Rules in Exhibition at Museum," *Berkshire Eagle,* 10 August 1933, Museum Clipping Book, BM; *Dictionary of American Biography,* s.v. "Calder, Alexander"; "Museum Acquires Calder's Art in Motion," *Art Digest,* November 1934; Marion Grant, "Alexander Calder at the Berkshire Museum," 17 May 1990, unpublished paper, BM. I am grateful to the author for providing me with a copy of her paper.

55. "Many Fine Paintings in Loan Exhibition at Berkshire Museum," *Berkshire Eagle,* 31 August 1933, Museum Clipping Book, BM.

56. Ibid.

57. Mary Martin to Emma Richardson, 2 April 1932, 1931–1937 Correspondence, Laura Bragg Papers, CMLA; Josephine Pinckney to Laura Bragg, 30 January 1933, Laura Bragg Papers, SCHS.

58. "Miss Laura Bragg Speaks at Club Meeting," *Berkshire Eagle,* 31 January 1933; "Hervey Allen To Be Subject for Miss Bragg's Talk," *Berkshire Eagle,* 17 November 1933; "Museum Director is Guest Here at Art Body Meeting," *Birmingham News,* 27 April 1933, all in Museum Clipping Book, BM.

59. "Museum Director is Guest Here at Art Body Meeting," *Birmingham News,* 27 April 1933, Museum Clipping Book, BM.

60. Laura Bragg to H. E. Wheeler, 26 February 1934, Laura Bragg Papers, SCHS; James Chillman to Laura Bragg, 9 April 1935, Laura Bragg Papers, SCHS.

61. "Bragg Speaks of Homecoming," *News and Courier,* 15 April 1933, vertical files, CCPL.

62. Helen McCormack to Laura Bragg, 22 May 1933, Laura Bragg Papers, SCHS.

63. "CWA Art Projects for County Under Way," *Berkshire Eagle,* 9 January 1934, Museum Clipping Book, BM; Oath of Office, Standard Form No. 8, Works Project Administration File, BM; "Few Local Artists To Get Work," *Berkshire Eagle,* 22 December 1933, Museum Clipping Book, BM.

64. Francis Henry Taylor, telegram to Laura Bragg, 12 December 1933, Works Pro-

ject Administration, BM; Laura Bragg to Francis Henry Taylor, 19 December 1933, Works Project Administration File, BM; "Projects for Berkshire County Developing as Part of the Work of the Committee on Public Works," Works Project Administration File, BM.

65. Margaret Hightower to Laura Bragg, 23 December 1933, Works Project Administration File, BM.

66. Laura Bragg to W. S. Darrell, 26 January 1934, Works Project Administration File, BM; Laura Bragg to Francis Henry Taylor, 8 January 1934, Works Project Administration File, BM; A. W. Kannaghan, Publicity, 17 January 1934, Works Project Administration File, BM.

67. "Report of the Director for the Year 1934," 1 January 1935, BM; *North Adams Transcript,* 17 May 1934, Works Project Administration File, BM; "Final Report on Work Done in Berkshire County," 9 June 1934, Works Project Administration File, BM.

68. Minutes of the Trustees Meeting, 28 December 1933, BM; "Report of the Director for the Year 1934," 1 January 1935, BM.

69. "Report of the Director for the Year 1934"; Frances Palmer, "History of the Museum's Mineral Collection," 5 April 1968, address, Greylock Mineral Club File, BM.

70. Palmer; "Report of the Director for the Year 1934," 1 January 1935, BM.

71. Laura Bragg to Richard Lull, 13 February 1934, Lull File, BM.

72. "Doctor Lull Speaks on Evolution," *Berkshire Eagle,* 16 March 1934, Museum Clipping Book, BM.

73. Mary Martin Hendricks, interview by author, tape recording, 4 November 1996, SP.

74. "Miss Hightower to Marry MacCarthy," *Berkshire Eagle,* 17 April 1934, Museum Clipping Book, BM; Helen McCormack to Laura Bragg, 30 May 1934, Laura Bragg Papers, SCHS.

75. Chia Mei Hu to Laura Bragg, 26 August 1932, Laura Bragg Collection, CAM; Chialu Chen to Laura Bragg, 16 June 1934, Laura Bragg Collection, CAM; Wen Jo Tu to Laura Bragg, 18 August 1934, Laura Bragg Collection, CAM, Charleston; John Jouett to Laura Bragg, 25 July 1934, Laura Bragg Collection, CAM.

76. Death notice for Sarah Bragg, *Exeter Newsletter,* 21 September 1934, Exeter Historical Society, Exeter, N.H.; Sarah Bragg to Laura Bragg, 27 January 1928, Laura Bragg Papers, SCHS.

77. Helen McCormack to Laura Bragg, 17 January 1935, Laura Bragg Papers, SCHS.

78. Laura Bragg to Robert Marks, 14 June 1934, Robert Marks Papers, COC; "Gertrude Stein, Question Mark of Literature, Will Speak Here," *Berkshire Eagle,* 16 October 1934, Museum Clipping Book, BM; Joye Uzzell Pregnall, interview by author, tape recording, 10 September 1997, SP.

79. "Gertrude Stein Comes, Talks, Conquers Audience at Museum," *Berkshire Eagle,* 12 January 1935, Museum Clipping Book, BM.

80. Ibid.; "Is She Facetious or Sick?" *Berkshire Eagle,* 11 January 1935, and "Dr. Ludwig Lewisohn Calls Miss Stein Borderline Case," *Berkshire Eagle,* 15 January 1935, both in Museum Clipping Book, BM.

81. "Miss Laura Bragg Reviews Current Art Events," *Berkshire Eagle,* 26 March 1935; Henry Francis to Contessa Frances du Beast, 28 May 1935; Henry Francis to Contessa Frances du Beast, 30 April 1934; Minutes of the Trustees Meeting, 23 November 1934, BM; "Sale of Bingham Painting by Berkshire Museum Is Criticized and Defended," *Berkshire Eagle,* 1 March 1935, Museum Clipping Book, BM.

82. Charles Kitteredge to Laura Bragg, 21 February 1935, Laura Bragg File, BM.

83. "Sale of Bingham Painting by Berkshire Museum Is Criticized and Defended," 1 March 1935, Museum Clipping Book, BM.

84. "To the President and Board of Trustees of the Charleston Museum," 1935, A. J. Buist File, CMLA; "History of Charleston County Public Library" (Charleston: Charleston County Public Library, 1981), 5.

85. A. Johnston Buist to Laura Bragg, 10 May 1935, James Hagood to A. Johnston Buist, 25 June 1935, A. Johnston Buist to James Hagood, 26 June 1935, all in Directors' Correspondence, A. J. Buist, CMLA.

86. Helen McCormack to Emma Richardson, 25 May 1935, Directors' Correspondence, Valentine Museum, CMLA; Helen McCormack to Emma Richardson, 5 June 1935, Directors' Correspondence, Valentine Museum, CMLA; Helen McCormack to Laura Bragg, 3 June 1935, Laura Bragg Papers, SCHS.

87. Untitled document, 28 December 1935, Laura Bragg File, BM.

88. "Art of Louis Eilshemius at the Berkshire Museum," *Springfield Sunday Union and Republican,* 13 January 1935, Museum Clipping Book, BM; Catalog of Eilshemius Paintings, 1935 Exhibit File, BM; Laura Bragg to Louis Eilshemius, 15 May 1935, 1935 Correspondence, BM.

89. "Abstract Alfred Maurer," Labels for Zenas Crane Exhibit, BM.

90. Elizabeth McCausland, *Alfred Maurer* (New York: Winn, 1951), 256; Waddell interview, 30 October 1971; Elizabeth McCausland, "Four Recent Accessions of the Berkshire Museum," *Springfield Sunday Union and Republican,* 14 April 1935, Museum Clipping Book, BM; Minutes of the Trustees Meeting, 1 April 1935, BM.

91. Laura Bragg to G. Adolph Glasegold, 29 April 1935, Whitney Exhibit File, BM.

92. "Whitney Collection to be Shown at Berkshire Museum Starting August 1," *Berkshire Eagle,* 9 July 1935, and Stuart Henry, "Whitney Exhibit at Museum is Sweeping Cross-Section of Modern Art in America," *Berkshire Eagle,* 2 August 1935, both in Museum Clipping Book, BM.

93. Carolyn Ahearn, interview by author, tape recording, 21 June 1997, SP.

94. Ibid.

95. "Zenas Crane (1840–1917)," undated document, BM; "Total of $244,500 Left to Public Institutions by Will of Mrs. Crane," *Berkshire Eagle,* 12 September 1934, Museum Clipping Book, BM.

96. Charles Kitteredge to Laura Bragg, 22 January 1935, Laura Bragg Correspondence, BM; Minutes of the Trustees Meeting, 25 June 1935, BM.

97. "The Berkshire Museum," undated document, Laura Bragg Correspondence, BM; Henry Seaver to Miss Thomson, 12 November 1936, Seaver material, BM.

98. Henry Seaver to Joseph Hollister, 11 June 1937, Seaver Material, BM; "Neighbor Museum Expanding Berkshire Museum To Have Addition," *Springfield Union and*

Republican, 25 August 1935, Museum Clipping Book, BM; Minutes of the Trustees Meetings, 25 June 1935, 8 July 1935, 4 November 1935, BM.

99. "Addition to Berkshire Museum in Memory of Mrs. Crane To Be Built," *Berkshire Eagle,* 10 July 1935, Museum Clipping Book, BM.

100. "My comments on the work at the Museum," November 1936, Seaver material, BM: Henry Seaver to Mrs. E. R. Frazier, 10 March 1937, Seaver material, BM; Henry Seaver to Joseph Hollister, 11 June 1937, Seaver material, BM.

101. "Former Gibbes Director, Miss Helen McCormack, Dies," *News and Courier,* 23 January 1974, CLS; Helen McCormack to Laura Bragg, 1936, Laura Bragg Papers, SCHS.

102. Helen McCormack to Dearest Family, 10 October 1936, Helen McCormack Papers, SCHS; Helen McCormack to Dearest Family, 14 October 1936, Helen McCormack Papers, SCHS; Helen McCormack, card to Laura Bragg, October 1936, Laura Bragg Papers, SCHS.

103. "The Museum, c. 1937," Labels for Zenas Crane Exhibit, BM.

104. Grant Howard Devree, "The Berkshire Museum Takes a Forward Step," *New York Times,* 4 July 1937; "Berkshire, the Ideal Small City Museum, Reopens in Modern Dress," *Art Digest* 11, no. 19 (1 July 1937): 5–7; Elizabeth McCausland, "Reopening of the Berkshire Museum," *Art News* (12 June 1937): 8–15; and "Field Notes: Berkshire Reopening," *Magazine of Art,* 1937, Museum Clipping Book, BM. (Information on these items is incomplete in clipping book.)

105. A. E. Gallatin to Laura Bragg, 19 April 1937 and E. Gallatin to Laura Bragg, 27 May 1937, Gallatin File, BM; McCausland, "The Reopening of the Berkshire Museum"; "Master Painters Call Pittsfield to Remade Gallery," *Christian Science Monitor,* 25 June 1937, Museum Clipping Book, BM.

106. "Ellen Crane Memorial Gallery," Labels for Zenas Crane Exhibit, BM; Elizabeth McCausland, "Reopening of the Berkshire Museum."

107. "Frank Crowinshield To Speak at Museum Opening Saturday," *Berkshire Eagle,* 22 June 1937, Museum Clipping Book, BM; "Master Painters Call Pittsfield to Remade Gallery."

108. Minutes of the Trustees Meeting, 19 September 1938, BM; Henry Seaver to Joseph Hollister, 11 June 1937, Seaver material, BM; "Zenas Crane (1840–1917)," undated document, BM.

109. Minutes of the Trustees Meeting, 21 September 1937, BM; "Report of the Director for the Year 1937," 1 January 1938, BM.

110. Minutes of the Trustees Meeting, 15 January 1938, BM; "Museum Seeks Support of Public," *Berkshire Eagle,* 1 April 1939, Museum Clipping Book, BM; "Story of Life," *Berkshire Eagle,* 14 May 1938, Museum Clipping Book, BM; Laura Bragg to Helen Tee-Van, 21 October 1938, Tee-Van File, BM.

111. "Modern Art Is Being Exhibited," *North Adams Transcript,* 6 August 1935, Museum Clipping Book, BM.

112. Helen Tee-Van to Laura Bragg, 28 November 1937, Tee-Van to Laura Bragg, 11 February 1937, Tee-Van to Laura Bragg, 24 October 1938, and Laura Bragg to Tee-Van, 21 October 1938, Tee-Van File, BM.

113. Laura Bragg to Helen Tee-Van, 29 November 1938, Laura Bragg to Tee-Van,

4 January 1939, and Laura Bragg to Tee-Van, 4 January 1939, Tee-Van File, BM; William Halsey, interview by author, 16 September 1996, SP.

114. Ridgeway, "Art and Education," 10–11; "Lecture Open to Public," *Berkshire Eagle,* 5 July 1938, Museum Clipping Book, BM.

115. "Miss Bragg Resigns as Director of the Berkshire Museum," *Berkshire Eagle,* 3 May 1939, Museum Clipping Book, BM; Laura Bragg to Elizabeth McCausland, 15 February 1939, Elizabeth McCausland Papers, Roll D373, AAA.

116. "Plan for Proposed Exhibition," Elizabeth McCausland Papers, Roll D373, AAA; Elizabeth McCausland to Laura Bragg, 8 June 1939, Elizabeth McCausland Papers, Roll D373, AAA; Laura Bragg to Elizabeth McCausland, 9 June 1939, Elizabeth McCausland Papers, Roll D373, AAA.

117. Laura Bragg to Elizabeth McCausland, 9 June 1939, Elizabeth McCausland Papers, Roll D373, AAA; Elizabeth McCausland to Laura Bragg, 8 July 1939, Elizabeth McCausland Papers, Roll D373, AAA.

118. Ruth Green Harris, "Far From the City Heat," *New York Times,* 13 August 1939, Museum Clipping Book, BM.

119. Henry Seaver "Some more notes," 1937 Museum Controversy File, BM; Stuart Henry to Elizabeth McCausland, 9 September 1939, Elizabeth McCausland Papers, Roll D373, AAA, Washington; Laura Bragg to Elizabeth McCausland, 12 September 1939, Elizabeth McCausland Papers, Roll D373, AAA; Patricia Allen to Elizabeth McCausland, 30 October 1939, Elizabeth McCausland Papers, Roll D373, AAA.

120. "Retiring Director of the Berkshire Museum Honored," *Berkshire Eagle,* 29 September 1939; "Retiring Museum Director Leaves," *Springfield Sunday Union and Republican,* 24 September 1939, both in Museum Clipping Book, BM.

121. Laura Bragg to Dr. Chao-Chun Hu, 23 May 1939, Laura Bragg Collection, CAM; "Japanese Boycott Group Will Seek Cooperation of Local Store Owners," *Berkshire Eagle,* 4 February 1938, and "Miss Bragg Heads China Relief Group," *Berkshire Eagle,* 11 May 1938, both in Museum Clipping Book, BM.

Chapter 6

1. Fraser, *Charleston! Charleston!,* 386.

2. Fraser, *Charleston! Charleston!,* 387.

3. Tobias, "Laura M. Bragg, Rejuvenator of Museums"; Nordlund interview, Joye Uzzell Pregnall, interview by author, tape recording, 10 September 1997, SP; "Reports Here in January," *Charleston Evening Post,* 9 November 1940, Directors' Correspondence, Helen McCormack, CMLA.

4. Gene Waddell, interview with Sears and Allen, tape recording, 3 October 1996, SP.

5. Chao-Chun Hu to Laura Bragg , 23 May 1939, Laura Bragg Collection, CAM; Mary Martin Hendricks, interview by author, tape recording, 4 November 1996, SP; Gene Waddell, interview by author, tape recording, 9 August 1996, SP; "Laura M. Bragg," *News and Courier,* 9 October 1981, vertical files, CCPL.

6. Gene Waddell, interview by author, tape recording, 9 August 1996, SP.

7. Minutes of the Trustees Meeting, 20 November 1939, BM; Laura Bragg to Ching-Chi Tseng, 15 December 1947, Laura Bragg Collection, CAM.

8. Norman Lunsignan to Laura Bragg, 10 September 1941, Laura Bragg Papers, SCHS; Norman Lunsignan to Laura Bragg, 18 September 1941, Laura Bragg Papers, SCHS; "Miss Bragg Directs Museum at Highlands," *News and Courier,* 17 June 1941, vertical files, CCPL.

9. Jack Leland, "Laura Bragg, Cultural Lady Bountiful," 10 October 1976, vertical files, CCPL; Laura Bragg to Donald Herold, 23 May 1973, Bragg, Laura 1973–1976 File, Laura Bragg Papers, CMLA; Gregg Privette, interview by author, tape recording, 9 July 1997, SP; Nancy Smith, interview by author, tape recording, 9 June 1997, SP; Lucile MacLennan, interview by author, tape recording, 1 July 1997, SP, and Kenney interview, 7 April 1974, Laura Bragg Papers, SCHS.

10. Joye Uzzell Pregnall, interview by author, tape recording, 10 September 1997, SP; Elizabeth McCausland to Laura Bragg, 19 February 1948 and 22 September 1949, Laura Bragg Papers, SCHS; L. V. Coleman to Laura Bragg, 9 May 1959, Laura Bragg Papers, SCHS.

11. Lucile MacLennan, interview by author, tape recording, 1 July 1997, SP; Mardelle Musk, "Keeping Posted," *Charleston Evening Post,* 28 November 1952, vertical files, CCPL, and Laura Bragg to Bernice Poutas, 15 November 1961, SCA; Nancy Smith, interview by author, tape recording, 9 June 1997, SP; Hal Norvell, interview by author, tape recording, 16 June 1997, SP.

12. Nancy Smith, interview by author, tape recording, 9 June 1997, SP; Gregg Privette, interview by author, tape recording, 9 July 1997, SP.

13. Gene Waddell, interview by author, tape recording, 9 August 1996, SP; Barbara Belknap, interview by author, tape recording, 29 May 1997, SP.

14. Barbara Belknap, interview by author, tape recording, 29 May 1997, SP; Harlan Greene, unpublished manuscript, SCHS.

15. Gregg Privette, interview by author, tape recording, 9 July 1997, SP; Gene Waddell, personal communication, 2 June 1997; Lucile MacLennan, interview by author, tape recording, 1 July 1997, SP; Gene Waddell, interview by author, tape recording, 9 August 1996, SP; Susan George [pseudonym], interview by author, tape recording, 3 June, SP.

16. Gregg Privette, interview by author, tape recording, 9 July 1997, SP; Susan George [pseudonym], interview by author, tape recording, 3 June 1997, SP.

17. "Miss Bragg To Have Class on Art Again," *News and Courier,* 26 October 1947, vertical files, CCPL; Susan George [pseudonym], interview by author, tape recording, 3 June 1997, SP; Barbara Belknap, interview by author, tape recording, 29 May 1997, SP.

18. Lucile MacLennan, interview by author, tape recording, 1 July 1997, SP; Joye Uzzell Pregnall, personal communication, 16 October 1997; Harriet Wilson, interview by author, tape recording, 30 May 1997, SP.

19. Laura Bragg to Lyman Bragg, September 1904, Laura Bragg Papers, SCHS; see DuBose Heyward, Josephine Pinckney, Anita Pollitizer, and Helen McCormack Collections at the SCHS.

20. Gene Waddell, interview by author, tape recording, 9 August 1996, SP; "K. K. Paluev Dies at 64; Services To Be Wednesday," *Berkshire Eagle,* 9 June 1958, Berkshire

Athenaeum, Pittsfield; Mary Martin Hendricks, interview by author, tape recording, 4 November 1996, SP.

21. Rapp and Ross, "The 1920s," 56, and Faderman, *Odd Girls,* 46.

22. Nancy Lynah-Gwynette, interview by author, tape recording, 3 June 1997, SP.

23. Waddell interview, 30 October 1971, SP; Minutes of the Charleston Museum, 19 May 1935, CMLA.

24. Lucile MacLennan, interview by author, tape recording, 1 July 1997, SP; Susan George [pseudonym], interview by author, tape recording, 3 June 1997, SP.

25. Gene Waddell, interview by author, tape recording, 9 August 1996, SP; Barbara Belknap, interview by author, tape recording, 29 May 1997, SP, and Lucile MacLennan, interview by author, tape recording, 1 July 1997, SP.

26. Lucile MacLennan, interview by author, tape recording, 1 July 1997, SP.

27. Barbara Belknap, interview by author, tape recording, 29 May 1997, SP; Hal Norvell, interview by author, tape recording, 16 June 1997, SP; Lucile MacLennan, interview by author, tape recording, 1 July 1997, SP; Gene Waddell, personal communication, 2 June 1997.

28. Barbara Belknap, interview by author, tape recording, 29 May 1997, SP; Nancy Smith, interview by author, tape recording, 9 June 1997, SP.

29. Nancy Lynah-Gwynette, interview by author, tape recording, 3 June 1997, SP; Lucile MacLennan, interview by author, tape recording, 1 July 1997, SP.

30. Susan George [pseudonym], class notes, 22 February 1974, May 1962, July 1963, July 1961, 19 February 1969, SP.

31. Lucile MacLennan, interview by author, tape recording, 1 July 1997, SP; Nancy Lynah-Gwynette, interview by author, tape recording, 3 June 1997, SP; Gene Waddell, personal communication, 2 June 1997.

32. Ching-Chi Tseng to Laura Bragg, 15 December 1947, Laura Bragg Collection, CAM; Nancy Lynah-Gwynette, interview by author, tape recording, 3 June 1997, SP; Musk, "Keeping Posted."

33. Will Durant, "The Renaissance: A History of Civilization in Italy from 1304–1576 A.D.," pt. 5 of *The Story of Civilization* (New York: Simon and Schuster, 1953); "Castiglione, Baldassare, Conte," *Microsoft Encarta 98 Encyclopedia* (Microsoft Corporation, 1993–1997); Gene Waddell, personal communication, 13 March 1997; Lucile MacLennan, interview by author, tape recording, 1 July 1997, SP.

34. Gregg Privette, interview by author, tape recording, 9 July 1997, SP; Gene Waddell, interview by author, tape recording, 9 August 1996, SP.

35. Gene Waddell, interview by author, tape recording, 9 August 1996, SP; Lucile MacLennan, interview by author, tape recording, 1 July 1997, SP; Hal Norvell, interview by author, tape recording, 16 June 1997, SP; Gregg Privette, interview by author, tape recording, 9 July 1997, SP.

36. Joye Uzzell Pregnall, interview by author, tape recording, 10 September 1997, SP; Deborah Uzzell Wooten, interview by author, tape recording, 5 May 1997, SP.

37. Gene Waddell, interview by author, tape recording, 9 August 1996, SP.

38. Gene Waddell, interview by author, tape recording, 9 August 1996, SP; Gene Waddell, personal communication, 2 June 1997.

39. Gregg Privette, interview by author, tape recording, 9 July 1997, SP.

40. Gregg Privette, interview by author, tape recording, 9 July 1997, SP.

41. Gregg Privette, interview by author, tape recording, 9 July 1997, SP; Gene Waddell, personal communication, 2 June 1997, SP; Hal Norvell, interview by author, tape recording, 16 June 1997, SP; Leland, "Laura Bragg, Cultural Lady Bountiful."

42. Gregg Privette, interview by author, tape recording, 9 July 1997, SP; Hal Norvell, interview by author, tape recording, 16 June 1997, SP.

43. Gregg Privette, interview by author, tape recording, 9 July 1997, SP; Gene Waddell, interview by author, tape recording, 9 August 1996, SP; Lucile MacLennan, interview by author, tape recording, 1 July 1997, SP; Fred Herbert, personal communication, 27 April 1999.

44. Hal Norvell, interview by author, tape recording, 16 June 1997, SP.

45. Hal Norvell, interview by author, tape recording, 16 June 1997, SP; Laura Bragg to Elizabeth McCausland, 15 February 1939, Laura Bragg Papers, SCHS; Nancy Lynah-Gwynette, interview by author, tape recording, 3 June 1997, SP.

46. Hal Norvell, interview by author, tape recording, 16 June 1997, SP.

47. Ralph Nordlund, interview by author, 29 May 1997, SP.

48. Ibid.

49. Ibid.

50. Ibid; Gregg Privette, interview by author, tape recording, 9 July 1997, SP.

51. Gregg Privette, interview by author, tape recording, 9 July 1997, SP; Lucile MacLennan, interview by author, tape recording, 1 July 1997, SP.

52. Gene Waddell, personal communication, 24 September 1997.

53. Gene Waddell, personal communication, 26 May 1998.

54. Gregg Privette, interview by author, tape recording, 9 July 1997, SP; Hal Norvell, interview by author, tape recording, 16 June 1997, SP; Deborah Uzzell Wooten, interview by author, tape recording, 21 May 1997, SP.

55. Laura Bragg to Donald Herold, 3 April 1976, Bragg, Laura 1973–1976 File, Laura Bragg Papers, CMLA.

56. Laura Bragg to Gene Waddell, 14 March 1971, personal copy; Lucile MacLennan, interview by author, tape recording, 1 July 1997, SP.

57. Gene Waddell, interview by author, tape recording, 9 August 1996, SP; Gene Waddell, personal communication, 24 September 1997.

58. "A Fitting Tribute To Laura Bragg," *News and Courier,* 26 November 1978, vertical file, CCPL.

Epilogue

1. Ellen Fitzpatrick, *Endless Crusade: Women Social Scientists and Progressive Reform* (New York: Oxford University Press, 1990), xiii.

2. Banks, *Social Origins,* 165; Muncy, *Creating a Female Dominion,* 30.

3. Link, *Paradox,* xi.

4. Yellis, "Museum Education," 168–69; and Hooper-Greenhill, "Gallery Education," 9; Alexander, *Museums in Motion,* 12; Hooper-Greenhill (1994) 230; Burget, "A Study of the Administrative Role," 18.

5. Muncy, *Creating a Female Dominion,* xiv; James Stanley Lemons, *The Women Citizen: Social Feminism in the 1920s* (Urbana: University of Illinois Press, 1975), 156.

6. Alexander, *Museums in Motion,* 239–40, and Teather, "Museum Education," 304.

7. Fraser, *Charleston! Charleston!,* 311; Grantham, *Southern Progressivism,* 54–57.

8. Rosalind Rosenberg, *Beyond Separate Spheres: Intellectual Roots of Modern Feminism* (New Haven: Yale University Press, 1982), 245; Drago, *Initiative, Paternalism, and Race Relations,* 125–26.

9. Carnegie Corporation, "Memorandum on the Report of the Advisory Group on Museum Education" (New York: Carnegie Corporation, 1923), 9.

10. Joyce Antler, *Lucy Sprague Mitchell: The Making of a Modern Woman* (New Haven: Yale University Press, 1987), xiv; Joyce Antler, "Feminism as Life Process: The Life and Career of Lucy Sprague Mitchell," *Feminist Studies* 7 (1981), 134, 154.

11. Joye Uzzell Pregnall, personal communication, 16 October 1997.

12. Hall, "Partial Trtuths," 15; Scott, *Southern Lady,* 225–26, 229.

13. Link, "Privies," 641; Anderson, 60, and Grantham, *Southern Progressivism,* 59.

14. Dee Garrison, *Apostles of Culture: The Librarian and American Society, 1876–1920* (New York: Free Press, 1979), xiv.

15. Mary Martin Hendricks, interview by author, tape recording, 4 November 1996, SP.

16. Elizabeth McCausland, "Reopening of the Berkshire Museum," *Art News* (12 June 1937); "Show at Museum Closes," *New York Times,* 19 August 1936, Museum Clipping Book, BM.

17. Faderman, *Odd Girls,* 11; Susan Ware, "Unlocking the Porter-Dewson Partnership: A Challenge for the Feminist Biographer," in *Challenge of Feminist Biography,* 59.

18. Belle Heyward, card to Laura Bragg, July 1926, Laura Bragg Papers, SCHS.

19. Waddell, personal communication, 6 June 1997; Waddell, interview with Sears and Allen, 3 October 1996, SP.

Bibliography

Primary Sources

Manuscripts

American Association of Museums, National Office, Washington, D.C.
  Association History General Files

Archives of American Art, Washington, D.C.
  Hosmer Collection: Interviews of Charles Hosmer with Milby Burton, Alston Deas, Helen McCormack, Albert Simons, and Robert N. S. Whitelaw
  Elizabeth McCausland Papers

Avery Research Center for African American History and Culture, College of Charleston, Charleston, S.C.
  James Logan Scrapbook
  J. Arthur Brown Papers

Berkshire Museum, Pittsfield, Mass.
  Laura Bragg Papers
  Museum Clipping Book

Beinecke Rare Book and Manuscript Library, Yale University, New Haven, Conn.
  Josephine Boardman Crane Collection

Boston University School of Theology, Boston, Mass.
  New England Conference Records of the Methodist Episcopal Church
  New Hampshire Conference Records of the Methodist Episcopal Church

Cathedral of St. Luke's and St. Paul's Episcopal Church, Parish Office, Charleston, S.C.
  St. Luke's Canonical Register

Charleston Library Society, Charleston, S.C.
  Hinson Clippings
  Poetry Society of South Carolina Files

Charleston Museum Library/Archive, Charleston, S.C.
  Laura Bragg Papers

Directors' Correspondence
Laura Bragg/Edgefield Pottery Collection
Museum Clipping Book

Citadel Archives and Museum, Charleston, S.C.
Laura Bragg Collection

College Archives, Simmons College, Boston, Mass.
Class of 1906 Archival Collection

Columbia University Archives and Columbiana Library, Columbia University,
New York
Columbia University Summer Session Bulletins

Columbia University Rare Book and Manuscript Library, Columbia University,
New York
Carnegie Foundation Archives

Commonwealth of Massachusetts Archives, Boston
Birth Registry

Orr's Island Library, Orr's Island, Me.
1906 Library Register

Records and Archives, Charleston County School District, Charleston, S.C.
A. J. Buist Letterpress Book, 1911–1919

Special Collections Library, Duke University, Durham, N.C.
Sears Papers

Smithsonian Institution Archives, Washington, D.C.
American Association of Museums Records, 1906–1985
Museum News

South Carolina Historical Society, Charleston, S.C.
John Bennett Papers
Laura Bragg Papers
Anne King Gregorie Papers
DuBose Heyward Papers
Helen Gardiner McCormack Papers
Josephine Pinckney Papers
Anita Pollitzer Papers

Albert Simons Papers
Heyward–Washington House File
Society for the Preservation of Old Dwellings Files

South Carolina Room, Charleston County Public Library, Charleston, S.C.
Vertical Files

South Caroliniana Library, University of South Carolina, Columbia, S.C.
Equal Suffrage League of South Carolina Minutes
Josephine Pinckney Papers
Anita Pollitzer Papers
Yates Snowden Papers

Special Collections, College of Charleston Library, Charleston, S.C.
College of Charleston Academic Affairs–Museum Resolutions
Robert Marks Papers
The Charleston Museum Files

United Methodist Church Archives, Madison, N.J.
Mission Biographical Reference Files

University of Pennsylvania Library, Philadelphia, Pa.
Hervey Allen Papers

Valentine Museum Archives, Valentine Museum, Richmond, Va.
Valentine Museum Reorganization Files
Valentine Museum History

Waddell, Gene. Personal diary (in possession of writer; author has copy).

Winthrop University Archives, Rock Hill, S.C.
Winthrop Museum Files
Constance Myers–Laura Bragg interview. 27 March 1974

Interviews

Ahearn, Carolyn. Interview by author. Tape recording. Lenox, Mass., 21 June 1997. SP.
Belknap, Barbara. Interview by author. Tape recording. Charleston, S.C., 29 May 1997. SP.
Brenner, Francis. Interview by author. Tape recording. Charleston, S.C., 1 March 1999.

Childs, Margaretta Pringle. Interview by author. Tape recording. Charleston, S.C., 10 July 1996. SP.

Dobbins, Grace. Interview by author. Charleston, S.C., 10 February 1998.

George, Susan [pseudonym]. Interview by author. Tape recording. Charleston, S.C., 3 June 1997. SP.

Halsey, Corrie McCallum. Interview by author. Tape recording. Charleston, S.C., 16 September 1996. SP.

Halsey, William. Interview by author. Tape recording. Charleston, S.C., 16 September 1996. SP.

Hendricks, Bartlett. Interview by author. Tape recording. Lanesboro, Mass., 4 November 1996. SP.

Hendricks, Mary Martin. Interview by author. Tape recording. Lanesboro, Mass., 4 November 1996. SP.

MacLennan, Lucile. Interview by author. Tape recording. Charleston, S.C., 1 July 1997. SP.

Nordlund, Ralph. Interview by author. Tape recording. Charleston, S.C., 29 May 1997. SP.

Norvell, Hal. Interview by author. Tape recording. Washington, D.C., 16 June 1997. SP.

Lynah-Gwynette, Nancy. Interview by author. Tape recording. Charleston, S.C., 3 June 1997. SP

Pregnall, Joye Uzzell. Interview by author. Telephone conversation. Tape recording. 10 September 1997. SP.

Privette, Gregg. Interview by author. Tape recording. Florence, S.C., 9 July 1997. SP.

Sanders, Albert. Interview by author. Tape recording. Charleston, S.C., 13 May 1997. SP.

Smith, Nancy. Interview by author. Tape recording. Charleston, S.C., 9 June 1997. SP.

Triest, Caroline. Interview by author. Tape recording. Charleston, S.C., 8 May 1999.

Waddell, Gene. Interview by author. Tape recording. Charleston, S.C., 9 August 1996. SP.

Wilson, Harriett. Interview by author. Tape recording. Charleston, S.C., 30 May 1997. SP

Wooten, Deborah Uzzell. Interview by author. Tape recording. Charleston, S.C., 21 May 1997. SP.

Zeigler, John. Interview by author. Charleston, S.C., 26 March 1998.

Other Interviews

Bragg, Laura. Interview by Miriam Herbert, 2 June 1972. Tape recording. Laura Bragg Papers, SCHS.

Bragg, Laura. Interview by Jessica Kinney, 7 April 1974. Tape recording. Laura Bragg Papers, SCHS.

Bragg, Laura. Interview by Constance Myers, 24 March 1974, Dacus Library, Winthrop University Archives.

Bragg, Laura. Interview by Ralph Nordlund. Charleston, S.C., ca. 1971. SP.

Bragg, Laura. Interview by Gene Waddell. Tape recording. Charleston, S.C., 30 October 1971. SP.

Waddell, Gene. Interview by James Sears and Louise Allen. Tape recording. Charleston, S.C., 3 October 1996. SP.

Printed Primary Sources

Reports, Yearbooks, and Directories

Annual Catalogue of Simmons College, 1902–1903, 1903–1904, 1904–1905, 1905–1906.

Bulletin of the Charleston Museum, 1909–1921.

Charleston City Directory. Various publishers, 1910, 1911, 1914.

Charleston Museum Quarterly, 1923–1925.

Exeter Newsletter, 1914, 1918, 1927, 1934 (Copies in Exeter Historical Society and Exeter Library, Exeter, N.H.).

Preservation Progress 20, no. 4., 38, no. 2., 38, no. 10.

Simmons College Yearbook, 1902–1906.

Year Book of the Poetry Society of South Carolina, 1921 (Copy in Charleston Museum Library/Archive), 1922–1923 (Copy in Charleston Library Society), 1925 (Copy in Charleston County Public Library).

Yearbook, City of Charleston. Various publishers, 1907, 1916, 1925–1930.

Secondary Sources

Articles, Books, and Reports

Alexander, Edward. *Museums in Motion: An Introduction to the History and Functions of Museums.* Nashville: American Association for State and Local History, 1979.

Allen, Louise. "Bragg Boxes, Progressive Social Reform: Windows on the World." Paper presented at the annual meeting of the American Educational Research Association, San Diego, Calif., 1998.

———. "Laura Bragg's Intellectual Revolution: Bridging the Color Line at the Charleston Museum." Paper presented at the annual meeting of the South Carolina Historical Association, Columbia, S.C., 1999.

American Association of Museums. *Excellence and Equity: Education and the Public Dimension of Museums.* Washington, D.C.: American Association of Museums, 1992.

Anderson, James D. *The Education of Blacks in the South, 1860–1935.* Chapel Hill: University of North Carolina Press, 1988.

Anderson, Mary Crow. *Two Scholarly Friends*. Columbia: University of South Carolina Press, 1993.

Antler, Joyce. *Lucy Sprague Mitchell: The Making of a Modern Woman*. New Haven: Yale University Press, 1987.

———. "Feminism as Life Process: The Life and Career of Lucy Sprague Mitchell." *Feminist Studies* 7 (1981) 134–57.

Baldwin, Cinda. *Great and Noble Jar: Traditional Stoneware of South Carolina*. Athens: University of Georgia Press, 1993.

Baldwin, William P., and Agnes L. Baldwin. *Plantations of the Low Country: South Carolina 1697–1865*. Greensboro, N.C.: Legacy Publications, 1989.

Banks, Olive. *The Social Origins of First Wave Feminism*. Athens: University of Georgia Press, 1986.

Bergen, Philip. *Old Boston in Early Photographs, 1850–1918*. New York: Dover Publications, 1990.

Bernhard, Virginia, Betty Brandon, Elizabeth Fox-Genovese, and Theda Perdue. *Introduction to Southern Women: Histories and Identities*. Columbia, Mo.: University of Missouri Press, 1992.

Bland, Sidney. *Preserving Charleston's Past, Shaping its Future: The Life and Times of Susan Pringle Frost*. Columbia: University of South Carolina Press, 1999.

Blumer, Herbert. "The Future of the Color Line." In *The South in Continuity and Change*, edited by John C. McKinney and Edgar T. Thompson. Durham: Duke University Press, 1965.

Bragg, Laura Mary. "Culture Museums and the Use of Culture Material." *Museum Work* 8 (1925): 75–83.

Brasher, J. Lawrence. *The Sanctified South: John Lakin Brasher and the Holiness Movement*. Urbana: University of Illinois Press, 1994.

Brownlee, Fred L. *New Day Ascending*. Boston: Pilgrim Press, 1946.

Buhle, Mari Jo. *Women and American Socialism, 1870–1920*. Urbana: University of Illinois Press, 1981.

"Class of 1906." *Simmons College Review* 1, no. 1 (November 1918).

Coleman, L. V. *The Museum in America: A Critical Study*. Washington, D.C.: American Association of Museums, 1939.

"Columbia Gives Course: Museum Administration." *Museum News* 4, no. 3 (1 June 1926).

Cook, Blanche Wiesen. "Female Support Networks and Political Activism: Lillian Wald, Crystal Eastman, Emma Goldman, Jane Addams." *Chrysalis* 3 (1977): 43–61.

Cott, Nancy. *The Grounding of Modern Feminism*. New Haven: Yale University Press, 1987.

Cremin, Lawrence A. *The Transformation of the School: Progressivism in American Education*. New York: A. A. Knopf, 1969.

Crow, Duncan. *The Victorian Woman*. London: George Allen and Unwin, 1971.

Crum, Mildred. *Old Seaport Towns of the South*. New York: Dodd, Mead and Company, 1917.

Doar, David. *Rice and Rice Planting in the South Carolina Low Country*. Charleston, S.C.: The Charleston Museum, 1936.

Dover, K. J. *Greek Homosexuality*. Cambridge: Harvard University Press, 1978.

Downs, Linda. "A Recent History of Women Educators in Art Museums." In *Gender Perspectives: Essays on Women in Museums*, edited by Jane Glaser and Artemis Zenetou, 92–96. Washington D.C.: Smithsonian Institution Press, 1994.

Drabble, Margaret. *A Natural Curiosity*. New York: Viking, 1989.

Drago, Edmund. *Initiative, Paternalism, and Race Relations: Charleston's Avery Normal Institute*. Athens: University of Georgia Press, 1990.

Durant, Will and Ariel Durant." The Renaissance: A History of Civilization in Italy from 1304–1576 A.D." Pt. 5 of *The Story of Civilization*. New York: Simon and Schuster, 1953).

Durham, Frank. *DuBose Heyward: The Man Who Wrote "Porgy."* Port Washington, N.Y.: Kennikat Press, 1965.

Dworkin, Martin S., ed. *Dewey on Education*. New York: Teachers' College, 1959.

Edgar, Walter. *South Carolina: A History*. Columbia: University of South Carolina Press, 1998.

Edwin A. Harleston: Painter of an Era, 1882–1931. Exhibition Catalog. Detroit: Your Heritage House, 1983.

Faderman, Lillian. *Surpassing the Love of Men: Romantic Friendships and Love Between Women from the Renaissance to the Present*. New York: Morrow, 1981.

———. *Odd Girls and Twilight Lovers: A History of Lesbian Life in Twentieth-Century America*. New York: Columbia University Press, 1991.

———. "Nineteenth-Century Boston Marriages As a Possible Lesson for Today." In *Boston Marriages: Romantic but Asexual Relationships among Contemporary Lesbians*, edited by Esther Rothblum and Kathleen Brehony, 29–42. Amherst: University of Massachusetts Press, 1993.

Fields, Suzanne. *Like Father, Like Daughter: How Father Shapes the Woman His Daughter Becomes*. Boston: Little, Brown, 1974.

Fitzpatrick, Ellen. *Women Social Scientists and Progressive Reform*. New York: Oxford University Press, 1990.

Fraser, Walter J. *Charleston! Charleston! The History of a Southern City*. Columbia: University of South Carolina Press, 1989.

Freedman, Estelle. "The New Woman: Changing Views of Women in the 1920s." *Journal of American History* 61 (1974): 374–95.

———. "Separatism as Strategy: Female Institution Building and American Feminism." *Feminist Studies* 5 (1979): 512–29.

Garrison, Dee. *Apostles of Culture: The Public Libraries and American Society, 1876–1920*. New York: Free Press, 1979.

Giborie, Clive, ed. *Lovingly, Georgia*. New York: Simon and Schuster, 1990.

Giele, Janet Zollinger. *Two Paths to Women's Equality: Temperance, Suffrage, and the Origins of Modern Feminism.* New York: Twayne, 1995.

Gordon, Asa. *Sketches of Negro Life and History in South Carolina.* Columbia: University of South Carolina Press, 1971.

Gordon, Mary. "An Inside View." In *Gender Perspectives: Essays on Women in Museums*, edited by Jane Glaser and Artemis Zenetou, 108–112. Washington D.C.: Smithsonian Institution Press, 1994.

Grantham, Dewey G. *Southern Progressivism: The Reconciliation of Progress and Tradition.* Knoxville: University of Tennessee Press, 1983.

Greene, Karen. *Porter-Gaud School: The Next Step.* Easley, S.C.: Southern Historical Press, 1982.

Hall, Jacqueline Dowd. "Lives Through Time: Second Thoughts on Jessie Daniel Ames." In *The Challenge of Feminist Biography: Writing the Lives of Modern American Women*, edited by Sara Alpern, Joyce Antler, Elisabeth Israles Perry, and Ingrid Weinther Scobie, 139–58. Urbana: University of Illinois Press, 1993.

————. "Partial Truths: Writing Southern Women's History." In *Southern Women: Histories and Identities*, edited by Virginia Bernhard, Betty Brandon. Elizabeth Fox-Genovese, and Theda Perdue, 11–29. Columbia, Mo.: University of Missouri Press, 1992.

Harrison, James G. "South Carolina's Poetry Society After Thirty Years." *Georgia Review* 7 (Summer 1953), 204–9.

Heilbrun, Carolyn. *Writing a Woman's Life.* New York: Norton, 1988.

Hill, Levirn, ed., *Black American Colleges and Universities.* Detroit: Gale Research, 1994.

History and Development of Negro Education in South Carolina. Columbia: South Carolina Department of Education, 1949.

History of Charleston County Public Library. Charleston, S.C.: Charleston County Public Library, 1981.

Hooper-Greenhill, Eilean. *The Educational Role of the Museum.* London: Routledge, 1994.

————. *Museum and Gallery Education.* London: Leicester University Press, 1994.

Horowitz, Helen Lefkowitz. *The Power and Passion of M. Carey Thomas.* New York: Knopf, 1994.

Hosmer, Charles B. *Preservation Comes of Age.* Charlottesville, Va.: University of Virginia Press, 1981.

Information for Guides of Historic Charleston. Charleston, S.C.: Tourism Commission, 1985.

Interpreting Women's Lives: Feminist Theory and Personal Narratives. Bloomington: Indiana University Press, 1989.

James, Henry. *The American Scene.* New York: Harper Brothers, 1907.

Kaestle, Carl F. "The Public Schools and The Public Mood." *American Heritage* 11 (February 1990), 66–74.

Kett, Joseph F. "Women and the Progressive Impulse in Southern Education." In *The Web of Southern Social Relations*, edited by Walter J. Fraser, R. Frank Saunders, and Jon L. Wakelyn. Athens: University of Georgia Press, 1985.

Kirby, Jack Temple. *Darkness at the Dawning: Race and Reform in the Progressive South*. Philadelphia: J. B. Lippincott, 1972.

Kliebard, Herbert M. *The Struggle for the American Curriculum*. London: Routledge, 1995.

Kraditor, Aileen. *Up from the Pedestal: Selected Writings in the History of American Feminism*. Chicago: Quadrangle, 1969.

Kurian, George Thomas. *Datepedia of the United States, 1790–2000: America Year by Year*. Lanham, Md.: Bernam, 1994.

Lander, Ernest McPherson. *Perspectives in South Carolina History: The First 300 Years*. Columbia: University of South Carolina Press, 1973.

Lasch, Christopher. *The New Radicalism in America (1889–1963): The Intellectual as a Social Type*. New York: Knopf, 1965.

Lefkowitz, Mary R. *Women in Greek Myth*. Baltimore: Johns Hopkins University Press, 1986.

Lemons, James Stanley. *The Women Citizen: Social Feminism in the 1920s*. Urbana: University of Illinois Press, 1975.

Lesesne, Thomas. *History of Charleston County, South Carolina*. Charleston, S.C.: A. W. Cawston, 1931.

Link, William A. *The Paradox of Southern Progressivism, 1830–1930*. Chapel Hill: University of North Carolina Press, 1992.

———. "Privies, Progressivism, and Public Schools: Health Reform and Education in the Rural South, 1909–1920." *Journal of Southern History* 54, no. 4 (November 1988), 623–42.

Litwack, Leon. *Trouble in Mind: Black Southerners in the Age of Jim Crow*. New York: Knopf, 1998.

Luker, Ralph. *The Social Gospel in Black and White: American Racial Reform, 1885–1912*. Chapel Hill: University of North Carolina Press, 1991.

McCausland, Elizabeth. *Alfred Maurer*. New York: Winn, 1951.

McMillen, Neil C. *Dark Journey: Black Mississippians in the Age of Jim Crow*. Urbana: University of Illinois Press, 1989.

Mark, Kenneth L. *Delayed by Fire: Being the Early History of Simmons College*. Concord, N.H.: Rumford Press, 1945.

"Memorandum on the Report of the Advisory Group on Museum Education." New York: Carnegie Corporation, 1932.

Miller, Lillian. Introduction to *Gender Perspectives: Essays on Women in Museums*, edited by Jane Glaser and Artemis Zenetou. Washington, D.C.: Smithsonian Institution Press, 1984.

Molloy, Robert. *Charleston: A Gracious Heritage.* New York: D. Appleton–Century Company, 1947.

Mumford, Lewis. "The Art Galleries." *New Yorker,* 14 September 1937.

Muncy, Robin. *Creating a Female Dominion in American Reform, 1890–1935.* New York: Oxford University Press, 1991.

Newby, Idus A. *Black Carolinians: A History of Blacks in South Carolina from 1895 to 1968.* Columbia: University of South Carolina Press, 1973.

Newton, Esther. "The Mythic Mannish Lesbian: Radclyffe Hall and the New Woman." *Signs* 9 (1984): 557–75.

O'Meally, Robert, ed. *Tales of the Congaree.* Chapel Hill: University of North Carolina Press, 1987.

O'Neill, William. *Everyone Was Brave: A History of Feminism in America.* Chicago: Quadrangle, 1971.

Paul, Heather. "In Preparation for the Future." In *Gender Perspectives: Essays on Women in Museums,* edited by Jane Glaser and Artemis Zenetou, 115–24. Washington, D.C.: Smithsonian Institution Press, 1994.

Peladeau, Marius B. *Chansonetta: The Life and Photographs of Chansonetta Stanley Emmons, 1887–1937.* Waldoboro, Me.: Maine Antique Digest, 1977.

Pinckney, Josephine. *Splendid in Ashes.* New York: Viking, 1959.

Rapp, Rayna and Ellen Ross. "The 1920s: Feminism. Consumerism. and Political Backlash in the United States." In *Women in Culture and Politics: A Century of Change,* edited by Judith Friedlander, Blanche Wiesen Cook, Alice Kessler-Harris, and Carroll Smith-Rosenberg, 52–61. Bloomington: Indiana University Press, 1986.

Rea, Paul Marshall. *The Museum and the Community.* Lancaster, Pa.: Science Press, 1932.

Rheims, Maurice. *The Strange Life of Objects: Thirty-Five Centuries of Art Collecting and Collections.* New York: Athenaeum, 1961.

Robinson, Duane L. *General Catalogue of Middlebury College.* Middlebury, Vt.: Middlebury College Publications, 1950.

Rosenberg, Rosalind. *Beyond Separate Spheres: Intellectual Roots of Modern Feminism.* New Haven: Yale University Press, 1982.

Rupp, Lelia J. "Imagine My Surprise: Women's Relationships in Historical Perspective." *Frontiers* 5, no. 3 (1981), 61–70.

Ryan, Mary. *Womanhood in America: From Colonial Times to the Present.* New York: New Viewpoints, 1975.

Sahli, Nancy. "Smashing: Women's Relationships before the Fall." *Chrysalis* 8 (1979): 17–27.

Sass, Herbert Ravenel. "The Lowcountry." In *The Carolina Lowcountry,* edited by Augustus Smythe. New York: MacMillan, 1932.

Saunders, Boyd and Ann McAden. *Alfred Hutty and the Charleston Renaissance.* Orangeburg, S.C.: Sandlapper Press, 1990.

Schneider, Dorothy and Carl Schneider. *American Women in the Progressive Era, 1900–1920.* New York: Facts on File, 1993.

Scott, Anne Firor. *Making the Invisible Woman Visible.* Urbana: University of Illinois Press, 1984.

———. *The Southern Lady: From Pedestal to Politics, 1830–1920.* 25th anniversary ed. Charlottesville: University Press of Virginia, 1995.

Sears, James T., and Louise A. Allen. "Museums, Friends, and Lovers in the New South: Laura's Web, 1909–1931." *Journal of Homosexuality* 40, no.1 (Summer 2000) 105–44.

Semel, Susan. *The Dalton School: The Transformation of a Progressive School.* New York: Peter Lang, 1993.

Smith-Rosenberg, Carroll. *Disorderly Conduct: Visions of Gender in Victorian America.* New York: Knopf, 1985.

Sochen, June. *The New Woman: Feminism in Greenwich Village, 1910–1920.* New York: Quadrangle, 1972.

Stoney, Samuel G. *Plantations of the Carolina Low Country.* Charleston, S.C.: Carolina Art Association, 1938.

Strohecker, Henry O. *Present Day Public Education in the County and City of Charleston, 1929.* Charleston, S.C.: Charleston County Board of Education, 1929.

Taeuber, Karl, and Alma F. Taeuber. *Negroes in Cities: Residential Segregation and Neighborhood Change.* Chicago: Aldine, 1965.

Taylor, Kendall. "To Create Credibility." *Museum News* 69 (1990): 41–42.

———. "Pioneering Efforts of Early Museum Women." In *Gender Perspectives: Essays on Women in Museums,* edited by Jane Glaser and Artemis Zenetou, 11–27. Washington, D.C.: Smithsonian Institution Press, 1994.

Teather, Lynne. "Museum Education." In *The Museum: A Reference Guide,* edited by Michael Shapiro, 299–327. Westport, Conn.: Greenwood, 1990.

Thirty-Second Annual Report, 1900. Columbia: South Carolina State Department of Education, 1901.

Thomas, Albert Sidney. *A Historical Account of the Protestant Episcopal Church in South Carolina, 1820–1957.* Columbia: R. L. Bryan, 1957.

Thomas, Mary Martha. *The New Woman in Alabama.* Tuscaloosa: University of Alabama Press, 1992.

U.S. Bureau of the Census. *Fifteenth Census of the United States Taken in the Year 1930.* State Compendium for South Carolina. Washington, D.C.: Government Printing Office, 1931.

———. *Thirteenth Census of the United States Taken in the Year 1910.* Prepared under the Supervision of William C. Hunt, Chief Statistician. Washington, D.C.: Government Printing Office, 1916.

Vanderwarker, Peter. *Boston Then and Now.* New York: Dover Publications, 1982.

Vicinus, Martha. "They Wonder to Which Sex I Belong: The Historical Roots of the Modern Lesbian Identity." *Feminist Studies* 18 (1992): 467–97.

Ware, Susan. "Unlocking the Porter-Dewson Partnership: A Challenge for the Feminist Biographer." In *The Challenge of Feminist Biography: Writing the Lives of Modern American Women*, edited by Sara Alpern, Joyce Antler, Elisabeth Israles Perry, and Ingrid Weinther Scobie, 139–58. Urbana: University of Illinois Press, 1993.

Washington, Booker T. "A Cheerful Journey Through Mississippi." *World's Work*, February 1908.

Watkins, Jessie M. "The First Twenty-Fifth Reunion." Reprinted from *Boston Evening Transcript*, 10 June 1931.

Weber, Jean. "Images of Women in Museums." In *Women's Changing Roles in Museums*, edited by E. C. Hicks, 21–22. Washington, D.C.: Smithsonian Institution Press, 1986.

———. "Changing Roles and Attitudes." In *Gender Perspectives: Essays on Women in Museums*, edited by Jane Glaser and Artemis Zenetou, 32–36. Washington, D.C.: Smithsonian Institution Press, 1994.

Wheeler, Marjorie Spruill. *New Women of the New South: The Leaders of the Woman Suffrage Movement in the Southern States*. New York: Oxford University Press, 1993.

Whitelaw, Robert, and Alice Levkoff. *Charleston Come Hell or High Water*. Charleston, S.C.: R. L. Bryan, 1975.

Willison, George F. *The History of Pittsfield, Massachusetts, 1916–1955*. Pittsfield: City of Pittsfield, 1957.

Yellis, Kenneth. "Museum Education." In *The Museum: A Reference Guide*, edited by Michael Shapiro, 167–97. Westport. Conn.: Greenwood, 1990.

Theses, Dissertations, and Unpublished Papers

Allen, Louise Anderson. "Laura Bragg: A New Woman Practicing Progressive Social Reform as a Museum Administrator and Educator." Dissertation, University of South Carolina, 1997.

Boggs, Doyle Willard. "John Patrick Grace and the Politics of Reform in South Carolina, 1900–1931." Dissertation, University of South Carolina, 1977.

Burget, Albertine. "A Study of the Administrative Role of Directors of Education Departments in Non-School Cultural Organizations." Dissertation, Loyola University (Chicago), 1986.

Butler, Susan Dart. "Making a Way to Start a Library." Unpublished paper. Dart Hall, Charleston County Public Library, Charleston.

Cox, Headley Morris. "The Charleston Poetic Renascence, 1920–1930." Dissertation, University of Pennsylvania, 1958.

Dockstader, Mary Ralls. "The Heyward-Washington House, Charleston, South Carolina." Unpublished essay. South Carolina Historical Society, Charleston.

Duffy, John Joseph. "Charleston Politics in the Progressive Era." Dissertation, University of South Carolina, 1963.

Grant, Marion. "Alexander Calder at The Berkshire Museum." Unpublished paper, 17 May 1990. Copy in author's files.

Hester, Al. "From Sustained Yield to Sustaining Communities: The Establishment of Francis Marion National Forest in South Carolina, 1901–1936." Unpublished paper, 3 December 1997. Copy in author's files.

Koverman, Jill Beute. "Searching for Messages in Clay." Unpublished paper. Copy in author's files.

McCombs, Virginia Lee Ridgeway. "Reinventing the Wheel: The Redefinition of Womanhood in the 1920s." Dissertation, University of Oklahoma Graduate College, 1987.

McDaniel, Maurine Akua. "Edwin Augustus Harleston, Portrait Painter, 1882–1931," Dissertation, Emory University Graduate Institute of Liberal Arts, 1994.

Moore, Burchill R. "A History of the Negro Public Schools of Charleston, South Carolina, 1867–1942." Thesis, University of South Carolina, 1942.

O'Neill, Stephen. "From the Shadow of Slavery: The Civil Rights Years in Charleston." Dissertation, University of Virginia, 1994.

Ridgeway, Sally. "Art and Education: Tracking in a Museum to Maintain Elitism: A Look at the Berkshire Museum, 1931–1939." Unpublished manuscript, 1990. Copy in author's files.

Tetzlaff, Monica M. "Cultivating A New South: Abbie Holmes Christensen and the Reconstruction of Race and Gender in a Southern Region, 1852–1938." Dissertation, University of Pennsylvania. 1995.

Index

Clark, Daniel, 181
Cleveland Museum of Art, 34, 70, 85, 136
Coffin, William Sloan, 134–35, 218
Coggeshall, Calvert, 177
Coker, J. L., 122–23, 161
Coleman, Laurence Vail: and American Association of Museums 1923 annual meeting in Charleston, 85; and Bragg as director of Berkshire Museum, 3, 165; on Bragg's contributions, 200; and Bragg's illness, 87–88; and Bragg's leave of absence from Charleston Museum, 162; and Bragg's museum course at Columbia University, 142, 145, 146–47; Bragg's relationship with, 97, 119; and culture museums concept, 94–95; and expansion of southern museum work, 149; and fireproof wing for Charleston Museum, 135; and funding for Charleston Museum, 119; and Guggenheim fellowship for Bragg, 115–16; *Manual for Small Museums* by, 95, 141; recommendations for Charleston Museum staff by, 96; and Rhoades's knowledge of Chinese culture, 144; and survey of southern museums by Bragg, 91
Coleman, Richard, 209
College of Charleston, 2, 32, 61, 70, 72, 102, 115, 201, 208, 212
Colonna, Vittoria, 107
Colonial Room, *following p. 71*
Colt, Frances Crane (Mrs. Samuel), 166, 189, 190, 193, 195
Columbia, S.C., 100
Columbia University, 2, 87, 93, 104, 105, 109, 113, 129, 133, 136, 141–48, 149, 215
Confederate veterans, 62

Congregational Church, 11
Connolly, Louise, 143–44, 154
Contemporary Verse, 77, 81
Contributions from The Charleston Museum, 99
Cook, Mrs., 22–23
cooking. *See* housework and cooking
Coolidge, Calvin, 90
Copley, John Singleton, 176
Coss, John, 141–42, 145–48
cotton industry, 72, 89
Council of the Museum Association, 96
Counts, George, 172, 175
Cox, Benjamin F., 63, 80
Cox, George, 146
Coxe, Eckley, 81
Crane, Charles, 189
Crane, Ellen (Mrs. Zenas), 175–76, 189–91
Crane, Mrs. W. Murray, 165, 166, 172
Crane, Z. Marshall, 165, 175, 185, 189, 190
Crane, Zenas Marshall, 3, 159, 160, 163–67, 176, 189, 191, 219–20
Cremin, Lawrence, 51
Crowninshield, Frank, 193
culture museums, 94–95, 101, 162
Cunningham, Miss, 15, 17
Currier Gallery of Art (Manchester, N.H.), 168–69

Dallas, Tex., 151
Dalton School, 165, 172
Damrosch, Frank, 194
Dana, John Cotton, 20, 36, 76, 97, 144, 147, 148
Dancing Torpedo Shape (Calder), 177
Daniel Cannon Room, *following p. 71*
Dart, Rev. J. L., 125
Daughters of the Confederacy, 62
Dave (slave), 139–40